WOMEN OF
NO ACCOUNT

D1436024

By the same author

Women are Bloody Marvellous!
Jude
Jaen

WOMEN OF NO ACCOUNT

Betty Burton

BCA

LONDON · NEW YORK · SYDNEY · TORONTO

This edition published 1989 by
BCA
by arrangement with Grafton Books

CN 1692

2nd reprint 1992

Printed and bound in West Germany
by Mohndruck, Gütersloh

For
JOSHUA BENEDICT, ZOË and CHRISTINE

CONTENTS

THANKS
To Bob Bushaway for his help
and encouragement in the early days of my
research into the 'SWING' UPRISINGS

THE FOODBOWL OF ENGLAND

In the nineteenth century, Hampshire is the foodbowl of England.

Each day, from hundreds of hamlets and villages, a steady stream of men and women carrying baskets and panniers, drovers and flockmasters with herds and flocks, leave those villages along the tracks and lanes. Laden carts, wagons and pack-animals carry the choicest products of the countryside into London and the big cities of the South.

The good fertile fields of the foodbowl yield up cereals, vegetables and meat; lush clover leys and meadows produce cream, butter and fine cheeses; fat mutton and tender lamb thrive on the good Hampshire downlands, and there are rich pickings of apples, pears, plums, medlars, strawberries, cobs and walnuts. In its glassy streams, purified by the chalkhills, trout, salmon and pike grow fat until they are ready for the taking.

In the kitchens of London's solid houses, clubs and hotels, the cooks, chefs and scullions bake and steam and roll and pound.

In the dining rooms of London, the hosts carve, the butlers and footmen offer and serving-maids wait.

At the dining table a plump hand reluctantly waves aside the sixth course, or perhaps a chomping jaw moves quicker at the prospect of the golden crumble and salty tang of a mature cheese.

Breeches' buttons strain.

Fine seams stretch.

Boning creaks.

Gall floods.

Gut contracts.

Replete families relax and wait for the certain next ching of the dinner bell and the distant clatter of plates, when they will again dip into the foodbowl.

So, if this is what it is like to live outside the foodbowl . . . then what a delight it must have been to live within it, to be the planter, sower, reaper and producer of such nourishment and delight to the palate!

A visiting American, Henry Coleman, saw what it was like and reported at the time . . .

'They seem to me to grow old quite early . . .

In a very low condition, ignorant and servile. I cannot help thinking that the condition is a hard one in which incessant and faithful labour for so many years, will not enable the frugal and industrious to make some small provision for the period of helplessness and decay, in a country where the accumulations of wealth in some hands, growing out of this same labour, are enormous.'

PART ONE

Cantle 1817 – Florence 1822

MAIDS AWAKENING

LIDI TOOSE AT fifteen years old was going to her first Harvest Home as a woman, at least, that is how she felt. She looked furtively down at her bodice which last harvest had been flat uninteresting but was now becoming rounded, tingling and alive. Her new figure caused her to hold her head up and walk with a womanly swing which made her bunch of dark-red hair bounce.

When there was partnering for a chain-dance, she had made up her mind that it would be Alec James who would swing her around and dip under the arches. The thought of his long dark lashes that made his wide eyes seem full of secrets made her fairly hold her breath for a moment.

For a month now, ever since they had all been helping with the Estate harvest, the images of Alec's hand sliding down the back of Molly Brown's skirt when he thought no one was looking, kept coming back to her. Lidi wanted him to do that to her, to be secret and knowing. Alec James, son of Tazey James the innkeeper, was nineteen and the idol of the village girls.

The harvest moon was rising on that warm night when Lidi, with her step-mother, walked link-armed up the lane towards Mill Farm. Her father and twin-sister Sarah walked ahead in a straggling line of other villagers on their way to the supper and dancing. Sarah had always thought herself to be their Pa's girl, walking and sitting close by him, yet it was Lidi who was emotionally close to him.

In looks, both girls resembled their small, red-haired mother whom they scarcely remembered. Although they were twins, they were not identical, nor much alike except in looks. More than ever, now that they had grown womanly, did people say, 'They'm Hanna Toose all over again.' So far as their nature and character went, this was true only of Sarah – Lidi was John Toose in every way.

'You all right, Auntie Tan?'

Tansy, John Toose's second wife, to whom he had been married for only a few months, was in the last weeks of pregnancy but, being young (less than eight years older than her step-daughters) and naturally light-hearted and always set on enjoying as much of life as she could, she was quite willing to haul her heavy body up the slope to where there would be people, music and laughter.

'Lidi my dear girl, I think 'tis about time you stopped calling me "Auntie" Tan.'

'Well, I couldn't hardly ever call you "Mother"!'

'Lor dumble us, if you ever did I should think I was getting wrinkles and turning grey – anyhow, I an't your mother and won't ever try to be. I told John when he ast me to wed him that I thought I would be getting an husband and two sisters.'

Lidi didn't respond for she knew how Sarah felt about that. As much as Lidi had welcomed Tansy, Sarah had resented her.

Sarah had been sullen: 'I can look after the house just as well as Tansy Jepp.' Which was true. Sarah had been the one to gradually take over the wifely household duties from Nana-Bess, who had trudged back and forth, between her home at Croud Cantle Farm at the edge of the village, and Shaft's Cottage, the rented house in the centre, to look after John Toose and his children.

'I an't saying you can't, Sarah; you're going to make some young man a wife as good as your mother ever was,' their Pa had said, 'but I been a widower for too long – and there's more to it than baking bread and scrubbing clouts.'

And so it was proved, for Tansy had become Mistress Toose with her skirtbands already loosened.

'I could call you Tansy.'

'It's me name.' She pressed Lidi's arm. 'I think dear old John had the idea that "Auntie" Tan'd make me seem . . . older like, but I asts you with a face like mine and then changing me name to Tansy Toose . . .' She laughed, as she laughed at everything, with more gusto than perhaps was warranted. But nobody ever objected, Tansy could lighten most moods. It seemed lately that her pleasant nature was even winning over Sarah.

The baby was due in less than a month, and Tansy had promised her step-daughter that she could help at the birthing. Lidi was excited at the prospect. She had been helping birth lambs and even calves and foals at her Aunt Jude's place, since she was a child, but this was the first time with a baby.

As Tansy laughed she cupped her belly.

Lidi halted their walk. 'You sure you're all right? It's a long drag. You should sit down a minute.'

'I'm well enough, Lidi. I shan't be calling you from Barney's

Reel to attend me. Anyway,' she added, 'I doubt if you'd hear once young Alec's got his hands round yer waist.'

Lidi blushed to hear her secret said so loud, but Tansy was like that. 'Shh, Auntie Tan.'

'It's all right, girl, nothing to be coyish about liking the touch of a man's hand upon you. Just only don't get carried too far too quick. Not at your age anyway. It's all right for an old woman like me, but you should find out what else there is to choose before you settle for a belly like this. I reckon women should take a man because *they* wants to, make babies because they *wants* them. I know that's easier said than done. But you'm happier for it in the long run.'

It was when Tan was like this that Lidi felt so much younger than her step-mother, when she became serious and understanding. When Tansy was like this, Lidi did feel that it must be something like having a mother. Tansy never said 'do this' or 'do that'. Lidi wished that Sarah could see how lucky they were that their father had married Tansy. There were plenty of others who wouldn't have minded being Mistress Toose, sharing in that nice little horticulture and seed business of John Toose. And there were plenty who rolled their eyes that John Toose, of all men, should have taken on one of the Jepp girls – and Tansy at that.

John Toose and Tansy Jepp, like many a village couple, had first held hands in a weaving chain of dancers.

Tansy at twenty-three was fair and freckled with high colour on her cheeks and lips. She had round hips and breasts of which only she seemed unaware. Tansy Jepp at twenty-three last winter when John Toose joined hands with her in a dance, was beautiful and the most desired girl in the four parishes.

Until that evening, the hardworking widower had never been seriously interested in any woman since his Hanny had died from a fevered labour with a still-born son.

Bess Smith had bemoaned his unmarried state for years. At this, John had always smiled his kindly smile at the old lady, took one or two village girls to fairs openly to give her something to think about, and occasionally visited a few clean pintle-maids well away from Cantle village.

And so, to the accompaniment of the steady beat of heavy dancing feet and a lax-skinned drum, outside in the icy clear air at the New Year dance, John Toose, with unusual abandonment so close to his home ground, did everything that he could think of to fulfil Bess's wishes, and his own sudden passionate desire for Tansy Jepp.

Tansy was ready for John's dextrous maturity after a summer with her inept lover, Jo Bunce.

'I reckon we a have to get wed now, Tan, whether you likes to or not.'

Tansy had playfully pinned him back against the sharp napped flint wall of the outhouse which had protected them during their quickly taken passion, and laughed close to his ear.

'I likes to all right, Master Toose, and I shall wed thee whether you likes to or not.'

And John Toose, at forty years, ten of them as a widower, with two grown girls, had to admit that he indeed would like to marry Tansy Jepp.

'I don't mind admitting it, Vi,' Tansy told her sister, 'but when the chain got broke and the partners got mixed up and it was John what danced me through the tunnel, I knew there and then that if I didn't marry him, then I shouldn't marry nobody.'

'And what about Jo Bunce?'

'I could never a married Jo Bunce.'

'You pretty nearly did and he thought you would.'

But Jo Bunce was over for Tansy and, looking at the desirable, older John, she wondered how she could have ever thought of taking the barrel-chested youth, Jo.

Nana-Bess span and wove and stitched for Tansy and the baby, and on the wedding day produced a feast even better than the one she had made years ago for John's first marriage.

The Jepps lived in Motte, the next parish, but because Tansy worked for the Reverend and Mrs Gidley-King at the Rectory, it was taken as said that she should like to be wed at the church in Cantle village.

Tansy's father did not take it amiss that Tansy got herself poddy by a man not that much younger than himself. 'Our Tan was always a bit flippy,' he told his new son-in-law, 'not but what she an't a good girl and will make a good wife – but she's like my old hoss I used to have, she do need somebody with the experience holding the reins. Jo Bunce wouldn't a been no good for our Tan, he wouldn't a had the patience, he'd a been the kind to a flick her with the whip, and then I should a have to a flicked he. For I tell you John, I be fiercely proud o' my gels.'

There was already a family connection, for May Jepp had been May Toose, one of John's many cousins. They had five daughters and had decided to name each baby after a flower, which caused some amused speculation as to what they would have named a son. Knapweed? Periwinkle? As it was they were never to find out. The girls were Primrose, Tansy, Violet, Jasmine and Marigold. None of them was plain looking, but Tansy was by far the most lovely.

The Jepp family appeared to get on very well together. Sam was a carter. Violet and Marigold were daily dairy-maids living at home. Jasmine and Primrose helped their father in his carter business, being, as Sam Jepp said, twice as bright and three times as pretty as any carter's lad in the land, and so they never lacked a helping hand to load the heavy stuff.

Sam Jepp was a good businessman and his business was doing very well.

But then so was John Toose.

'Didn't you ever want a man before . . . before Pa?' Lidi asked.

Tansy's advanced condition and the increasing climb of the pathway caused her to slow down now.

'You skip on ahead Lidi and get started on your dancing. Look at my man up there, talk the hind leg off a donkey. See, he's so bent on telling everybody how to put the world to rights that he hardly knows that he's racing ahead.'

'I'd rather walk with you.' Lidi wanted to tell Tansy, and thrill herself by saying his name aloud. 'Alec James came down there, when we were gleaning Raike Bottom Field.'

'Did he now – the pretty lad with his come-to-me eyes.'

'And he asked if I was going to the supper tonight, and I said I might, it all depended, and he asked depended on what, and I said depended on whether I was going or not. I could tell he was hoping I would. So it won't matter if I'm not early. It a make him wonder if I'm going to come at all.'

'Oh Lidi, you'm a sight cockitty for fifteen, I don't know what we're going to do with you.'

They walked quietly and slowly, the gap between them and the rest of the party growing. Lidi could hear the edge of her father's voice in the distance, a familiar comforting sound, a memory of childhood, that rose up through their bedroom floor as their father read aloud pamphlets and newspapers to small groups of neighbours who frequented the Toose hearth.

'I've seen him when there's any young girl about, young Alec; he's a handsome enough youth, but he's a taker.'

'Auntie Tan!'

'Tansy. 'Tis true. You watch young Alec, he's one who's out for what he can get – and that means every virgin maid in this village – and any what isn't too. He's his father all over again – but you got to admit that Taze James have got that way of looking at any woman that comes before his eye and making her feel there an't another one in sight.'

'But he's *old*.'

Folding her hands over her belly, Tansy laughed loudly.

'Like my husband?'

'Father isn't old.'

They walked very slowly; again Lidi thought of Alec James' stealthy, sliding hand.

'Tansy, can I ask you something . . . well? . . .'

'You can ast, don't means that I can tell.'

'Well, before I knew you, I used to see you, and everybody always talked about Tansy Jepp – you know how they do – not really saying anything. And you were always said to be the beauty of the four parishes, and that you could have any man you chose.'

'Ah well, people can say things like that – and 'tis true really, for I got the man I chose, because I got your father.'

'It seems to me that you are the most . . . well, everything about you tells that you are a *woman*.'

Tansy laughed again. ''Tis a fact that no man or boy ever got a belly like this.'

Lidi could never have talked like this in the daylight, and without Tansy's barrier of the child. The child put Tansy apart, placed her in the same category as Lidi's ancient great-grandmother, who had for years sat silent and apparently in a world of her own – special states which made it easy to talk in their presence. Now, in the dark night on this slow, intimate walk and with Lidi aware of her own developing instincts, her hot, desirable, impulses and the quite frightening uprising of passionate thoughts, Lidi could unravel words that had been bundled up in her mind.

'Can't women have . . . do they always have to . . . Well, Tansy, I've heard that there are ways . . . for women . . . powders and draughts, so that if they have that hot kind of nature, then they don't get poddy when they go with a man.'

Tansy laughed.

'To have your cake and eat it? Ha, the Alec Jameses of this world would like that.'

'Perhaps some girls might like that too.'

'Penny-royal and the bitter brew, you heard of?'

'It's what the girls say that can stop babies growing.'

'Which girls? Them that stands in groups at the ford and tells things about the Tansy Jepps of this world and their hundred swains? Girls who end up with breasts like a byre animal from suckling ten babes? A lot they know!'

'And . . .'

'Well, what else do they say?'

Tentatively, it seeming so improbable, 'They say that there are little linen bags . . . which men may wear.'

This time Tansy had to stop to laugh.

'Dear Lord, Lidi, let's rest on this here log.'

She held onto Lidi's hands as she lowered herself.

' 'Tis true, so I believe. And I tell you how I know, and it's not because Tansy Jepp ever saw such things, for I reckon I should a fell about laughing to see a man with one of they. I learnt about them because my mistress, who I used to work for at the Rectory, was a tight-pursed lady who got her pleasure out of mentioning such things to her women servants. She would read such *things* out of books, that any village girl would blush to hear in a harvest field – and there an't much you don't hear in a harvest field, as you well knows. Well, she once showed me a drawing of such a little bag. Well, I tell you my dear, I fair laughed at the thought of it. There is such things. Dear little linen bags that's made fer gentlemen to wear in bed when they lay with pintle-wenches and drabs and fear taking the pox. But I can't say that I would care much to take my love . . . all wrapped up in linen.'

'Well, I could never take the penny-royal.'

'Lidi Toose, this conversation is taking too sour a turn by half. You should be thinking of dancing and feasting. Marry knows we have little enough of either these days of too many poor people, and too many leaving the village. Come, hoist me up.'

She took Lidi's arm and they stepped out a little faster now that they had reached the track up to the barn where the Harvest Home was under way.

'But, it's right that you should ask about such things. A woman's body is a trap for her from the time she first ties the tapes of her own cloths. Look at it this way (if you can, when the moment comes – and it will). Remember that the pleasuring between a man and a woman can be equal in the desire, equal in the satisfaction . . . the unequalness comes with the consequences. When the first man bears a child, then a good many things will change.'

The woman held the young girl's hand to her cheek and kissed her knuckles.

'There are so *many* things that a free woman may do these days, specially one who can read and write and has a head on her shoulders like yours. Don't waste yourself. Your Aunt Jude told me that you was such a demon for learning, she reckoned it was like pouring into a cask with the bung missing. And your father's that proud of the work you're doing with him in breeding that there new strain of strawberries, that he couldn't wish more if you'd been a son.'

Lidi did not experience Alec James' hand sliding secretly into her waistband; he had started on the strong cider early that day, and was asleep among the corner cobwebs before the first tart was sliced.

Also, before that time, Tansy had said, 'Oh Marry! Jist look at that, John,' as she stared down in wonder at the pool that her broken waters had made upon the barn floor.

Good as her promise, Tansy told the midwife to just watch and let Lidi get the baby. With the same skill with which she had delivered lambs and calves at her Aunt Ju's, Lidi, with infinite gentleness, greased Tansy and eased the baby into the world.

'Look, Tan. I got a brother.'

HAMPSHIRE, ENGLAND, JANUARY

Although there is only a nail-paring of a moon, the
Poacher is out. The moon gives enough light on the crest of the
downs to silhouette the billowy shape of a solitary elm and the
harsh angles of a gibbet close by. The road over the hill is narrow
and leads directly to a chalk and flint track so neglected that it is now
too narrow for a horse and rider to pass a hay-cart.

On the west side of the lane is a brick wall twelve feet high
behind which plantations of mature timber grow. The wall and the
trees stretch for several miles in each direction, curving gradually so
that, with the river running north-south, the boundary forms a 'D'.
It encloses farms, stables, woodlands, pasture, three lodges and a
house which is so well built that six caryatids have nothing to do but
to watch peacocks and cedars display on fine lawns.

For forty-eight weeks of the year the house is occupied only by
servants, but for the rest it is filled with jolly, noisy people.

At these times, the house is like a creature awoken from
hibernation.

Smoke from kitchen ranges and log fires drifts over the cedars;
lamps and candles make colours flash from crystal drops on
chandeliers which, in turn, glitter on polished window-panes – the
window-panes reflect young men as they snatch glimpses of their
finery and their mannerly gestures.

The house breathes out odours of spices and roasting meats, of
delicate toilet-waters, yellow soap, metal polish and boot-black.

Its doors release sounds of laughter, of silver clinking on fine
porcelain, of music and dancing.

The little sliver of moon shines upon the house with the
caryatids. Now though, except for small panes close under the
roof, the windows are darkened. It is January; the jolly people have
long since tired of open views and the killing of game-birds and
salmon, their blood-lust is satisfied for now. They have gone to
their bright theatres, assembly rooms and card-tables.

Outside the high walls and on the field side of a hedge a man
moves quickly and quietly over ground whose contours are as

familiar to him as those of his own small plot. Working his way along a low bank, he walks a few paces then, crouching at exactly the right places, examines his snares. He snaps necks and pockets limp, warm carcasses.

As he works he listens.

A dog-fox barks. A vixen answers with a human shriek. The dog barks and barks again.

Small scrabbling creatures, disturbed by the man, crackle dead angelica stems in their flight.

An owl's wings beat powerfully, quietly as it swoops.

At ear-level, small roosting birds rustle among shrivelled haws and twigs.

The man hears all this but listens only for tell-tale human sounds; he listens for a man with a shot-gun; he listens for the hust-hust sound of legs encased in coarse corduroy breeches rubbing, or the crackle of leaves, stealthy, underfoot, which carry far on the still, frosty air.

It is the old game.

Hunter and hunted.

Each listening for the other.

The man with the gun is the hunter, the man who has hunted the birds is the prey.

Down the ages, the Poacher's ancestors have been proud of their skill. They have been the main source of supply of meat for their neighbours, not only those of their own station in life, but the apothecary, the carpenter, the smith and potter, the taverner, the vicar and many a magistrate. It has always been a respected and respectable way of life.

In these days though, it is no longer a game, and, although the man is still respected for his skill, it is a dangerous occupation. The birds in his pockets are evidence of a crime that carries the awful penalty of transportation and even death. The pheasant and hare are no longer in common ownership.

Each time he goes about his work, he risks his neck, but it is the only work he knows, the only work he can get.

This time, he is lucky.

SPRING 1818

Under Nursery-maid

SARAH TOOSE AWOKE with a start. Late! It was broad daylight, then she sank into the pillow and smiled.

A pillow.

A pillow with a white cotton cover, awakening after dawn, with no cattle lowing for her, no walk along Howgaite Path to Aunt Jude's and sit milking in a rising mist or a bitter wind, no churns or presses to scour.

A room of her own. Six feet by five with a narrow bed and a chest, and a door which closed but had no lock. At almost sixteen, Sarah had never known the luxury of privacy. At home she and Lidi had never fallen asleep or awoken alone, or dressed except in shared clothes. On a hook behind this door hung a dark-blue dress, a plain white apron and a frilled cap. In the laundry at the bottom of the house hung another similar. Made to fit. Unshared.

This was her first year as Under Nursery-maid at Stonebridge Manor. She still missed her father, but each day she missed him less. Since the baby Jack came, she had been unable to think of her father in the old way. Suddenly, he became embarrassing to her. Father had always been kind, patient, smiling and full of knowledge – as solid as a roof beam. Then when Tansy Jepp had come, Pa had got like some stupid ploughboy, grinning at her, touching her.

Nana-Bess had always been on to him to get another wife, and Sarah had liked the idea. If he had to marry, Sarah would have preferred a mother who would perhaps sit sometimes and brush Sarah's hair, or they would stand together in the kitchen, chopping suet for Sarah to make Pa his favourite pond-pudding, then him sitting comfortably with his plump, brown-haired wife.

But it was Tansy Jepp who had barged in and changed their father. When the baby came, it was even worse. Sarah couldn't stand the sight of the child and of Father touching him and touching her as she opened her bodice to suckle it. You never saw men in the fields taking notice of a woman suckling.

Sarah could never look upon that scene without being forced to think of what Father and Tansy Jepp had done together – worse, what they still did, muffled sounds coming from the front sleeping chamber, her laughing in the dark of the night, his deep voice low and rumbling.

No matter how much she had tried to imagine that they had just happened to be awake and were lying side by side companionably, the vision of bulls and rams and stallions she had watched mounting their mates in the fields always forced itself into her mind.

That he and her mother had long ago been lovers and had begotten herself and Lidi and the child that had died, had seemed right and proper – young lovers giving their love to one another.

But Father was a man with grey in his beard, and Tansy Jepp, it was said, had been sent by her mother to work at the Rectory where the rector might keep an eye on her and stop her being so flighty and free.

Sarah herself had seen, only months before she and father wed, Jo Bunce holding up bunches of cherries for Tansy Jepp to bite at, teasing her, snatching them away as her teeth bit, she laughing, spitting back the stones at his broad chest. There hadn't seemed anything wrong about that – Jo Bunce, all straining chest and black beard and wet, red lips was Tansy Jepp's sort.

What had really hurt was that there must have been one day, one ordinary morning when, all unsuspecting, Sarah had gone up to Aunt Ju's as usual, thinking that there was nothing different about that day, and there had been.

Pa and Tansy Jepp had done that, together.

Lain like any other couple you might come across by accident under the willows at Chard Lepe Pond; or stood together behind the hedge as you could often glimpse at the harvest fields.

What had hurt more was his response when Sarah said that she would like to take work as a nursemaid.

'All right then, my Little Maid, if that's what you wants, then I shan't stand in your way.'

He hadn't said, 'Don't go, Little Maid, stop here because I shall miss you that much,' nor even tried to persuade her that Aunt Jude couldn't do without her at Croud Cantle, just 'I shan't stand in your way.'

But now, Sarah was getting over all that. The last time she had gone home she had gone in her dark-blue dress feeling pretty and well turned out.

Father had greeted her with many bear-hugs. 'Look Tan, look at what living at Mistletoe Hall have gone and done to my Little Maid.'

Pleased, Sarah had patted him like a naughty child. 'Don't call them Mistletoe, my mistress is a kind and pretty lady.'

'Ah, my sweetheart, they'm all Mistletoe, all That Lot that puts their roots into the rest of us and lives off what we work for. And don't be taken in by prettiness nor kind words by any of That Lot. They a have a use for you just so long as it suits them.'

'John,' Tansy had said. 'Don't be making speeches to the girl just when she got home.'

But Sarah had wanted him to make his speeches – just as he had always done from her earliest memories of him.

That was Pa.

That was Master John Toose, whose neighbours looked to him for guidance.

That day, he had made her turn round so that they could all see the dress, and lifted the hem of her skirt to admire her white stockings and black shoes with large buckles. Then he had kissed her on the top of her head as he had always done and looked very pleased.

Not once on that day visit home had he picked up the baby and told it what a proper little man it was, or fingered Tansy's bodice laces as he watched her suckle it, but had asked Sarah everything about her duties, showed concern as to whether her mistress was a thoughtful employer, and talked to her seriously about any 'prospects' there might be for her.

'If you've chosen to go away from this kind of village life, then I want for you to make what you can of your position, take back from "Them" as much as you can. Remember they've only got what was taken from the likes of the people you grew up amongst.'

Her old, familiar father, his finger wagging, making his point. The deep rumbling voice that used to rise up from below as he read aloud to their neighbours when she and Lidi were small children in their beds. Then in later years, as growing girls, they too would be with the others and listen to the men arguing their agreement about wages and tithes and things being fair and others being unjust; the hiss of their spit into the fire; the transparent red of the hot poker, blackening as it was lowered into the centre of the spiced alepot, and the smell of it as steam rose – a bundle of warm associations with Father in a passionate full flow of words.

'Don't never be satisfied if you know you can better yourself. There's too much difference between us that lives on their own labour, and the

Mistletoe that feeds on the labour of others – we who get our bread honest can't hope to make a fairer society if we don't better ourselves. 'Tis our bounden duty to get to know as much as They do, for if we don't then we shan't ever take back what does rightfully belong to all of us equally.'

Her old, deep love for the father he had been returned.

And when Sarah had sat upright, with her long hair twisted and pinned on top, in the plain dress that fitted to her neat waist and swelling breasts, she knew that Tansy Jepp with her loosely-laced bodice and bouncing bosom and hips was not of the same quality as herself.

Poor Father, she could no longer feel angry with him.

When Sarah had left Cantle that day, she had walked up Bellpitt Lane and over Winchester Hill towards West Meonstoke and Stonebridge Manor; she was returning there feeling pleased to be doing so. The previous walk, to take up her position, had been sour and anguished, a punishment to Pa as well as to herself for not being able to provide him with everything he desired.

Now, suddenly life seemed bright again. Sarah Toose was an Under Nursery-nurse and could become anything she chose. Tansy Jepp had been put in her place.

Sarah knew that she was once more her father's favourite.

The master of Stonebridge Manor was a white-templed military moustachioed gentleman, Mr Osbert Broughlake. His young wife was Mrs Delphine and, so as to distinguish her from The First Mistress and The Last Mistress, the Master's two, childless previous wives, was always referred to as such by the older and longer-established members of the staff.

The difference in the Master's and Mistress's ages was much the same as between Sarah's father and Tansy, and their new babe was the same age as Jack. But the Master's hand – unlike Sarah's poor father – was never, in public, seen closer to his wife than was necessary to finger-tip her into an assembly. And the Mistress's breast was never exposed for the benefit of the child as was Tansy's at the instant demand of Jack. Mrs Delphine's breast – to suit the revealing Empire fashion, thrust up as high as the armpits and held in draped cups of soft silks, gauze or muslin – was a commodity too valuable to Mrs Delphine for it to be dragged down like that of any wet-nurse, when the latter might be had for a few pence. And necessary. For ladies were not so fortunate as the cottage women who sold their full-flowing breasts. Ladies had household accounts, and menus, and guest-lists to attend to.

Sarah was responsible (under the rather lazy eye of the Upper Nurse) only for the elder child.

The Upper Nurse, Margaret Roberts, had some distant connection with the Toose family, which was how Sarah came to be recommended for the position. When the girl had been brought before her, Mrs Delphine was pleased to have found an Under Nursery-maid who fulfilled all her requirements of a good servant. The girl was pleasant, was obviously at ease with her clean appearance, and not merely scrubbed for the occasion, and she could iron and sew. Her hands were red and rough, but that showed that she was used to hard work. A bonus was that she was, for a farm-girl, quite well spoken, and not only that, she could read and write. Mrs Delphine was not a Mistress to be put about by literacy in a servant, just so long as one was careful about reading matter.

Whether she fulfilled the other necessities of any servant, truthfulness, docility and obedience, only time would tell. Mrs Delphine's Mama had given few pieces of advice to her nuptial daughter, except those that would promote the new wife and mistress as being one who knew 'what was what'. 'Never question a servant on matters of honesty, for the lower orders lie as naturally as the well-bred tell the truth, so one may quite as well wait to catch them out, and send them packing without notice or reference.' She advised that the same 'what was what' reputation might be gained as a wife, by locking the bedroom door to a husband in his cups. 'It is better to establish this on the very first occasion, when he will be mortified at the suggestion that he is treating his wife with no more respect than a harlot. You may not stop him over-indulging in port and brandy, but you will stop him breathing his fumes into your face, which any lady of breeding will abhor.'

Of course, Sarah knew nothing of such things, only that she saw in her mistress a kind and gentle, almost virginal, lady who had said only that she had 'a liking to see my servants in plain clothing but of a good suitable colour', and ordered the Housekeeper to set the girl up in 'blue . . . blue not celeste nor zaffre . . . oh no, not with that hair . . . get her something prussic and dark.'

Although she did not have to be at the beck and call of Margaret

Roberts and the baby-preparing ritual for another half an hour, Sarah got out of bed, washed her face, neck and arms then stood in the bowl to wash her feet whilst she dried herself.

Sarah savoured the two ends of the day when she was not 'Toose'.

She opened the window, threw back her bedcovers for airing whilst she brushed and pinned up her thick red hair and dressed in the long deep-blue dress, white cap and voluminous apron, then went to spend five minutes looking out at her good fortune.

'Tooey?' A young voice in a whisper.

'Ninn. You're a bad'n and no mistake. If Margaret finds you running round with bare feet, she'll be after your tail and blame me.'

Although he was no longer a baby, Sarah gathered into her arms the solid little boy she found standing at her door in a long trailing nightshirt.

'Oh Ninn, you got yourself wet.'

'Help me get dressed before Margaret sees.'

'Quick then.'

Sarah whisked across to the night-nursery and brought back the boy's day clothes.

'We won't have time for much of a wash, but it'll have to do.'

'Don't let her see my nightshirt. I couldn't help it.'

'Don't you worry my sweetly, I shall drop it in the wash-bowl by accident.'

'I can't help doing it. I know it's only babies do pee-pee, but I'm asleep and it just comes out.'

'Ach, lots of children do it, and you haven't done it at all lately. I dare say you had a bad dream.'

'It wasn't a bad dream, it was that my Papa died.'

'Goodness lovey, that's a really bad dream.'

'I don't think it's bad. If my Papa died, then I shouldn't have to go out with the guns.'

Sarah held the child close, wishing that she could protect him from the irascible attentions of a father who thought that to make a man of a small boy, one must thrust a shotgun into his hand at a very early age and ridicule him when he flinched at a pulled trigger. She took any excuse to hold him, sensing his need to have arms about him. Poor little soul.

Most of Sarah's duties were to do with Ninn, though Margaret Roberts, experiencing her new-found pleasure of having someone in a lower situation in the nursery, gave over to Sarah quite a few of the more irksome chores. But for most of the time Sarah could not complain unless it should be on the grounds of unfairness, for compared to her work back home, well . . . this was a holiday. Especially those hours when it was her duty to take Ninn into the grounds and exercise him.

Mr Broughlake had given instructions that the boy was to walk for a certain distance, run for a given amount of time, to practise with quoits and balls, hit with bats and take deep breaths. When given as an order, the regime sounded like a discipline, but Sarah soon realised that what she had been instructed to oversee was what every ploughboy and stone-picking girl wants to leave their work to do. To play in the open fields and woods.

When nursery breakfast was finished, Sarah asked if she might not pack some food for Master Ninn and herself, and let him stay out in the park longer than usual. Margaret had no objection, once the chores were done.

Ninn was excited at the prospect of being away from the house for a long time.

'Which way shall we go?' Sarah asked the child when they were out of the house.

'Is it my turn?'

'Turns' had been a new concept for Ninn when Sarah had taken charge of him. At first he had stamped and insisted that he have his own way as Margaret and Miss Truckle the Governess always allowed, but before long, when Sarah had proved, by sticking to the Master's boring rules of exercise, that he was the loser, he soon got the hang of joint decision on a small scale.

'No Master Ninn,' she had said without rancour, 'if you wants to treat me like a servant then there's nothing I can do about it, and I shall behave like one and do exactly as the Master orders. Come on, quick march, quick march, no talking.'

That was the hardest part, being firm with him, but he had been on the way to becoming a little tyrant and she could not bear the prospect of that, for she saw how sweet and good-natured he really was, and had taken to the small, lonely child as soon as she set eyes on him, and wanted him to be more likeable.

Although he was a sturdy-looking little boy, Sarah had at once seen that he was frail – not physically, but because of a kind of sensitivity. The philosophy that boys were fearless and strong, were protectors, defenders, was dear to the heart of her Master.

Sarah thought that if she babied Ninn, it only balanced a bit of the father's harshness. And as for his mother . . . well she had been only about Sarah's present age when Ninn was born.

In the few months since Sarah had been in the nursery, Ninn had learnt a few things. 'I'm a person no different from you, Master Ninn, and won't be treated like a slave, and you're a person no different from me and should get a bit of cuddling when you wants it.' Ninn was beginning to learn respect for the people he had thought (from the example of most of the adults around him) were put on earth only to serve his wants.

'Let's go right on through the woods and see what's the other side.'

'All right. Here, I got the food to carry, so you take the bats and balls.'

He did it without pout or demur. Sarah felt pleased at the progress they were making. These days, she loved being out with the boy and was sorry that the job could not last very long. The boy was already receiving a few lessons from Miss Truckle, and soon a tutor would come and take him over.

They progressed through the woods by skimming quoits. There had been a week of wet weather recently, but now the sun was hot, bringing up the moist green smell of moss and rich compost in the little dell where the boy and his nursemaid sat and ate a few plain arrowroot biscuits.

In this part of the woods the soil was acidic so that laurel bushes grew dark-green and glossy. They reminded her of the rows and rows of lovely rhododendrons that Father now grew for sale.

Underfoot, tormentil blooming brilliant yellow, its flowers and leaves again reminding Sarah of home, of the strawberry plants that Lidi thought were so exciting that she would spend days inspecting rows and rows of plants to see if one grew more free of rust or produced unexpectedly large berries. The last of the bluebells were giving place to the first of the foxgloves. Ninn skimmed a quoit at a plant and brought it down.

'What did you want to go and do that for?'

The boy looked puzzled.

'It isn't anything.'

'Who says it isn't anything?'

'Well, it isn't anything, is it? Just a flower. There are plenty more – everywhere.'

'And how many boys are there – everywhere? Plenty so that we can just knock them down?'

He pondered for a moment.

'Hey?'

'Some.'

'More than there's foxgloves?'

'I don't know. I haven't seen boys very much.'

Now it was Sarah's turn to ponder. That was true, how could a child who seldom went outside the high walls of the Estate, know that the world was full of small boys?

'Well, I reckon that there are as many boys as there are foxgloves, but that don't mean to say if you see a boy you can knock him down with your old quoit.'

The more she saw of Ninn's life, the more she came to realise how lucky she was to have been a child in a family such as her own. With Nana-Bess pounding the dirt from their clouts and hurling vegetables into the stewpot; with Aunt Ju always hauling her and Lidi off up Tradden to look for something growing or running or flying, then sitting them down at the long table at Croud Cantle and making them read and write and do their numbers; and Uncle Drew and Rosie who kept the 'Rest Harrow', even Great-grandma who never did anything except sit and stare at the logs burning - they all belonged together. Often had their dinners together, went to Harvest Suppers and Spring Jigs together.

She and Lidi were part of them.

Not like Ninn who was part of nothing and nobody except as the next in line for Stonebridge Manor.

She suddenly picked him up and hugged him close. The boy did not struggle away, but lay for a minute with his eyes closed, sucking his shameful and forbidden thumb. Then she tossed him and dumped him down.

'Come on you lazy lump, let's get on through and see what's the other side.'

'Tooey?' A frown that had no business on such a baby face. 'I expect Mama will keep you.'

'Keep me for what?'

'When I must have a tutor as Papa says.'

'Well young master Ninn me lad me boy,' Sarah tried to sound jokey, but it came out false, 'that isn't just properly settled yet.'

It was not at all settled. Sarah's appointment was for an unspecified period, probably until next year, nothing mentioned about anything more.

'Tell Mama that you must stay.'

'The Mistress isn't likely to take much notice of Sarah "Tooey".'

'If I tell her that it is because of you that I don't pee-pee like a baby any more, then she will let you stay. Before you came here, she told Roberts that she would give anything to cure me of pee-pee in bed before Papa discovered it.'

Poor little thing. Back home children his age and older were not expected to control themselves like grown people, the most that any cottager would expect of children of five was that they use the outside of the house not too close to the door.

'I'll tell you what, don't let's neither of us think of it until we hear when they've got a tutor for you. Something might have turned up by then. My Nana-Bess always says "don't trouble Trouble, till Trouble troubles you".'

SHAFT'S COTTAGE, CANTLE

JOHN TOOSE AT not much more than forty was, in the terms of the Cantle people from whom he sprang, a successful man.

He had been one of a very large family of children of a poverty-stricken Cantle cottager who, as of necessity rural labourers did, sent his children to earn what pence they could almost as soon as they could walk. As a small child, he had been sent up to the Nugents at Croud Cantle and had attached himself to the place in the way that a stray animal who is given food will do.

He had grown up on the Croud Cantle holding, picking stones from the fields, standing with clappers scaring birds from young crops and sleeping anywhere he could find a warm corner. He had been fed by his mistress, Bella Nugent, and taught to read and write by her daughter Jude, and, even as a boy, had loved their ward, Hanna, who had been rejected by her mother Jaen, the elder of the two Nugent daughters.

Hanna, neat, capable, serious and hardworking, with small pretty features and the same lovely abundant red hair that had been passed on to her daughters, had loved him in return.

When she had died from the childbed fever, John Toose thought that life was scarcely worth living without her, and tried to make the days pass faster by working himself into the ground. His only moments of comfort were those at either end of the day that he spent with his little girls, who, with each year that passed, grew more like his memory of their mother.

His success with plant and shrub growing started years back when the old lady Nugent who was then his mistress had said that he could put a few rod of land to his own use. The plot was too small to grow a crop of vegetables worth the taking, so he had started with savory herbs for cooking and preserving. Very soon his little bunches of herbs were sold on the market along with other Croud Cantle produce.

By the time he had become a man and married his 'Hanny' he had become known locally as a good and reliable horticulturalist whose plants were as clean and well-grown as any. Over the years his own strains of strawberry plants and exotic shrubs had brought him to the notice of some of the big houses in and around the four parishes and more recently further afield.

His Radical beliefs had come about slowly. Jude Nugent, who had taught him literacy, gave him Radical and political tracts to practise his reading, as she later did to Lidi and Sarah, and as she, as a girl, had been given them herself. After Hanna's death, as with his work, he had thrown himself into the cause of making a more egalitarian society as some young men take up a religion. He was not a mere theorist but as well as he could do so, he practised and evangelised. And so had been his life until he met Tansy and felt his body surge like a youth.

'Tansy Jepp?'

'Tansy up at the Rectory? And John?'

'John Toose and Tansy Jepp getting wed?'

Not until neighbours heard it from his own lips did they believe it to be true, but Tansy's belly swelled and people raised their eyebrows and conjured pictures of how and when it happened. Speculated as to whether it was done by John Toose at all, or whether it was one of his neighbourly actions in helping a woman who had got herself poddy and had been left. But then . . .

'*Still waters run deep.*'

And John Toose was still waters.

And '*It's the quiet ones you have to watch.*'

And John Toose was a quiet man.

'*Well! Talk about a jacket made out of tweed and muslin . . .*'

But all in good time, Tansy Jepp, the prettiest young woman in the four parishes, went to St. Peter's with the man who did business with landscape gardeners of large estates, and who was not shy of making a speech in a market square.

He might well have afforded better had he not been such a good neighbour and a fair employer but John Toose lived in a small house, in a simple manner.

A neighbour coming to him for help, got whatever John was able to give. He was a man that might have been envied that he was successful and independent of any master – yet few begrudged him anything, for he was well liked.

'*There ben't a decenter man, ever stepped foot in a pair of boots than John Toose.*'

But his independence was not total. His land was rented. It was

Croud Cantle land, administered by Jude Nugent though belonging to his old mistress, Bella Nugent, who had lived in a silent world of her own for years.

Being one of the Nugents by virtue of his marriage to Hanna, John had been offered the land at a peppercorn rent when he and Hanna married. They had been an independent couple who wanted to make something of themselves without favours, so at first they paid with produce which was sold on the Croud Cantle market stall, and once they were established, paid a cash rent. It was known as the Toose Field and it seldom crossed anyone's mind that the land was not Toose's own.

Shaft's Cottage in which the Tooses lived belonged to the Church. Almost every dwelling in the village of Cantle, belonged either to the Church or to the Estate.

No one ever came to a firm conclusion as to which was the worse landlord.

The Estate cottages were tied to a job – cowman's cottage, labourer's cottage, flockmaster's or shepherd's cottage; and whilst many landowners would not lightly leave ancient workers with no roof over their heads, nevertheless tenancy of a place to live in, to bring up one's children and end one's days in, was very insecure. And in recent times, with the old ways of patronage and duty to the community of the landowners waning, it was becoming ever more so.

Church property in Cantle, with the exception of the Rectory and three almshouses, was not tied, but as a landlord the Church was rackrent and neglectful of its tenants. But, except as an argument of Radical theory, John Toose did not complain – he would not have accepted a privilege that was not given similarly to other Church tenants. So, whilst his means of livelihood was as secure as any may be where nature has a hand in it, his home was only secure from Lady Day to Lady Day.

Shaft's Cottage was old, built of mellow weatherworn brick and napped flint. A low-lying cottage, its small windows and shaggy thatch kept the place cool in summer and warm in winter. Beside it was a barn and yard in which the orders were assembled and loaded, and a stable for the cart-horse. Within the thatch small creatures had nests in which they rustled at night, and a pair of fantails stalked this as their territory.

A wooden porch had shelves on which some plant or other was always displayed.

Inside was a kitchen, of which part was a wash-house with its own brick buk-wash boiler which, about once a month, filled the place with steam and the smell of yellow soap. There were one or two pretty souvenirs over the fireplace, two pictures of dogs which Hanna had painted only weeks before she died and, most exceptionally in so humble a cottage, an ever-growing row of books which were well read. Slim volumes nicely cut – Smart, Goldsmith, Crabbe. *The Lay of the Last Minstrel* and *Sense and Sensibility* rubbed spines with *Soil Structure – a Treatise*, 'Chinese' Wilson – *Lilium Regale* and *Deciduous Trees and Shrubs*, all kept in place by a thick pile of Radical pamphlets. The hearth was the heart of the home, the deep pad of wood-ash was carefully preserved to create a good fire which was seldom let out.

A narrow flight of ladder-like stairs led to the floor above which had been partitioned off into four sleeping-chambers each with its own tiny window. Only two rooms had the benefit of the warmth of the wide chimney breast.

Toose Field adjoining Croud Cantle land was tucked away from the rest of the village, Croud Cantle Farm being the furthermost place on the south side of the village. Cantle was favoured by being in temperate Hampshire, and sheltered by the downs; the Toose Field was well suited to the various branches of horticulture and plant breeding that was John Toose's livelihood.

LIDI'S BIT

I<small>T WAS JUNE</small>. In Toose Field was a small plot, known by the family as Lidi's Bit. Its closeness to Chard Lepe Pond kept the soil moist; small trees and low bushes created dappled light and humid air on which the sweet, heavy perfume of lily of the valley hung. Next to those in bloom were seedlings of the same plant.

Then low-growing spikes of asphodel beginning to show red buds and one or two small yellow flowers.

Tall stems of martagon lily, pink fat buds at the top and opened blooms with curled-back petals showing dark-red spots to lure insects to the pink stamens.

Bare wiry stems of several different varieties of fritillaries, their bell blooms just gone over.

In the deepest shade, violets that all appeared alike until one looked closely at the variety of leaf-shape and colour.

In the most open part common purple and orange-throated wild pansies and some more startling ones with huge flowers where the throat colour was vivid and extended over almost the entire petal.

None of these grew haphazardly. They were in neat rows, identified with white-painted labels. Some plants wore little bags, others were tied with coloured cords. The entire plots declared neatness, care and attention.

Lidi was intent on a row of fritillary plants. Some were just dark-green leaves, some were in green bud, some just showing colour and others with shrivelled, dead heads had coloured cords tied about their stems. Those without coloured ties, Lidi was carefully removing and tossing into a basket. Absorbed in her task, she did not hear her father approaching .

'Do you reckon you've got anything promising this year?'

'Pa!' Lidi showed her delight. 'You haven't been down here for ages.'

'Ah well, you know how it is . . . good intentions. Have you got a winner?'

'I don't know, Pa. There's a dozen that looks promising, but like you always told me . . .'

' "You can't eat your butter with the milk still in the udder," and that's as true a saying as you'll get.'

'And as false a bit of rhyme as anybody'd want.'

He inspected the rejects. 'You'm discarding a decent few.'

'I know. I never like this part. When I've finished, I look into the basket at all the ones I've thrown out, and I always wonder if there's one I overlooked when they were in bloom and I've thrown it away and it might have been the greatest marvel of a lily that anybody's ever seen.'

John Toose grinned and nodded.

'A plantsman don't ever get over that one, but I'll tell you one thing, Lidi, it's what makes a good plant-breeder look twice at every new cross.'

Lidi's gaze became withdrawn, and a faint smile showed John Toose that his daughter was away with her dream. 'It's what I want more than anything, Pa . . . to make a perfect flower . . . to create something new, a new lily.'

'And that's why you have to be choosy if you mean to make a reputation for yourself. You just have to be philosophical and hope that the marvel is here in the ones that's kept.' He examined a plant with a knowledgeable touch.

'It's like people, there's times when I can hardly bear to think of all the marvels that have been wasted over the centuries: some dying before they're hardly born, some drowning, others shoving a breast-plough when they might be writing music or sitting as a judge . . . all wasted. I tell you one thing, if I was in charge of the world, I shouldn't be so wasteful. I don't reckon gods make half as good plantsmen as us.'

Lidi sat back on the little box-stool which she used when she was working along a row plant by plant, and gave him a broad smile. 'Pa, I don't know anybody else who could turn selecting out a row of seedlings round into politics and religion, and still keep to the first subject.'

He ruffled her hair, keeping a strand between his fingers, feeling it as he had done the seedling. Lidi held his hand to her head for a brief moment. She knew it was seeing her hair or Sarah's, uncovered and blowing free, that often made him think of their mother.

'Ah child, there was never daughters looked so much like their mother as you two.' He settled down beside her, his knees drawn up to his chin, watching her slide the curved blade into the moist soil – deftly, down, under and up, taking out a bulb without disturbing its neighbour. 'I don't suppose you can hardly remember your mother.'

He always started his reminiscence with that phrase. Over the years he had related dozens of incidents of the early years of their marriage.

> *The day your Ma bought me that there china bird . . .*
> *The day your Ma and me got wed . . .*
> *Once, when your Ma was about five . . .*

She had been about four when her Ma had died, and could remember some things, a feeling, a presence, the changes when Nana-Bess came to make the food and see to the washing. But it was difficult now to distinguish fact from Pa's stories. Lidi and her father had talked about her mother many times, but he had never found another way of opening up when he wanted to talk about 'Hanny', and it was only Jude or Lidi to whom he ever did so.

'I remember her crackly skirt,' Lidi said.

John Toose inclined his head and slowly nodded. 'Ah, that would be her stiff, white apron. I dearly loved to come into the kitchen when she had put on a fresh cap and tied on a cornstarched apron – she used to tie it tight about her waist. She wasn't very tall, about the same as you and Sarah, but she had that perfect a little figure, neat waist, and her hair . . . ah just like yours. When she lived up the farm, people used to say she looked like Jude, but she didn't really – you know what your Aunt Jude's hair's like.'

Lidi smiled; Aunt Ju's hair was often a topic when she arrived anywhere. Windblown and careless of it as a child. The only time any of it was lopped was when it had become too knotted by high winds or entangled with its cord-tie to brush out. And it was more often than not allowed to escape the only concession Jude made to control it – the bit of cord. Jude's hair had always been like some glorious haystack made by an inexperienced farmhand; once red, now that she was in her fifties it was gradually changing to the colour of clotted cream. Lidi adored her aunt, and the wildness of her hair was something that Lidi tried to capture for herself when they went out 'roaming Tradden' together, but in high winds Lidi's hair would twist and curl itself into ringlets and stay close to her head as Hanna's had done.

'Ah you'd a liked her, Lidi, you'd a been good friends.' His thoughts drained from his eyes and soaked into his mind. For a minute his gaze ceased following the curved blade in Lidi's hand – then he came back. 'But you get on famous with Tan don't you?'

'I like Tan – nobody could help it.'

'Sarah don't . . . not *really* get on.'

'Well, anybody can understand that. It was a bit of a shock to her, she never gave it a thought but what she would stay looking after you for ever.'

'I know. I wasn't very tactful at bringing Tan in. It never occurred to me. I suppose I must have thought that Sarah would be glad for somebody to take over her duties. I thought it'd be that nice for you both to have somebody older.'

'Tansy isn't exactly older.'

John Toose grinned.

'And that's a fact, there's times when I think she'd join in the maypole if I let her.' He said it affectionately and laughed. 'Not that anybody'd stop her if she took a mind to do it. But you like her Lidi, don't you?'

'Pa, you know I love Tan. I don't know what I'd do without her. She's always in a good mood, she never lets anything get her down. You can't ask much more than that from somebody to live with.'

'No, you're right, you're right.' Said with the gladness of a man who had had his wavering beliefs reaffirmed.

Lidi said nothing, but did not forget his tone of voice – it accounted for the tapping fingers, slight frown and over-jolly laugh that Lidi had noticed sometimes when Tan was being boisterous and funny. *Oh Pa, you've got to keep on enjoying her company or it would be bad.*

'I'm glad you married her. It's like having an older sister to talk to. I can talk to Tan about anything, she never judges, never puts you down.'

'That's right, she's really nice. And she's pretty. There's not many men I come across that's got a prettier one – not an old clod-hopper with grey hairs in his beard.'

Lidi plucked an asphodel that had strayed from its own trial-bed into her fritillary plot, and tucked it into his beard, turning away ideas that seemed disloyal to him. 'Pa you're fishing for compliments – you know you're the best catch in the four parishes, to say nothing of the handsomest. I reckon that's all you came down here for.'

Even as she said it, about his being a catch, Lidi felt a pang of an even greater disloyalty – to Tansy.

It was Pa who had got the best of the deal, wasn't it? He had given up nothing for something. And what had Tansy got? She had stopped being Tansy Jepp, that was for certain. Had handed over herself in exchange for what? The only benefit so far as Lidi could tell was whatever secure future her Pa might have. And nothing else. Nothing. When such thoughts intruded, Lidi thrust them away. It was as though she had noticed a hairline crack that threatened to turn stability into crumbling ruin, if she prodded it.

'Now that you and Sarah are women, in no time at all you'll be talking about getting wed. You need a woman about.'

'Oh Pa! I don't intend getting wed for another ten years or more. I've got plans.'

He smiled fondly at his favourite child. 'Oh plans is it. Ha! You'll see my sonny, the giddy-worm a get you and you'll keel over like the rest of us.'

'Aunt Ju didn't.'

'Your Aunt Jude wanted to teach children their letters. She never wanted to be a wife.'

'No more do I!'

'Of course you want to. It's the natural thing.'

'I hate scrubbing the wash just so it can straight away be soiled all over again, and bread-making and it gets eaten, and scouring dishes so that they can be made dirty again and I hate spinning and sewing and mending. I can't stand it. It's boring and tedious, and it makes me sick to think of all the times it has to be done.'

John Toose's laugh rang out. 'My life Lidi, you never did like to curb an excess of words.'

'And who did I inherit that from pray?'

'When you meet the right lad, and you get a place of your own and little ones, you will wonder what you ever saw in all this lily stuff.'

All this? That hurt. It was like a spark flying from the fire, catching a splinter, a grit in the eye, though she only flinched in her mind.

He thinks it's a game. He pretends it's important, and he is quite interested, but he's not serious.

'I'm a good plantsman, Pa. I know chalk soil all right.'

'Of course you are, my Gel. As good as many I've seen on some big estates. You've got an eye for what will cross well, and light fingers with seedlings. And you got enough sense to go with the soil and not fight it. Of course you're good.'

'No Pa. I mean I'm seriously good, and I want to learn as much as you and perhaps have a few acres of my own.'

He frowned very slightly, but did not reply.

Her idea was as yet unformed, scarcely off the ground. It had begun when her father had described some of the reconstruction work he saw taking place on the large estates. The opening up of large open areas of parkland with wide vistas of lakes and rivers and trees; the mixed and beautiful shrubberies and long winding flowering borders. The newly rich were spending vast sums of money on their surroundings.

Lidi's imagination had been fired by the possibilities that the new ideas opened up. When there was no daylight left, or her trial grounds were dormant, she would spend hours with lists of plants, their colours, flowering seasons, habitat, and size, then she would plant them out to scale on paper in pencilled borders. In the last two years she had created on paper a totally silver-leafed border, a white flowering one and another in which there were evergreens, berried shrubs and variegated plants of so many kinds that there was never a winter season of bareness. Now, she was ready to try something out on their own land. Nothing very large, but a small show-garden to which she might bring prospective customers.

Lidi went on, 'Shall I tell you what I'd really like to do? I would like to plan gardens. Make a business of it. You know all those drawings I've been doing lately? Well, they are designs for gardens, big gardens. But I could do small ones – or huge parks and estates. I know what trees I would put and where, the paths, the water-gardens . . . everything. Oh Pa, you can't compare all that "place of your own and little ones" to something like I want to do.'

'That's Jude talking.'

'It's not! Do you think I'm so stupid I can't think for myself?'

'Her influence then.'

'No Pa, yours!'

'Never. I never filled your noddle with such stuff. I want to see you and Sarah settled and happy as your Ma was.'

'Then you should have stopped up my ears when you were spouting on about the way the talents of common people are wasted, and rights and equality and all that. You shouldn't be always saying that people should stretch out just a bit further than they can reach. Reach out for liberty and equality. Fraternity, isn't that what you've been preaching all these years?'

A look of puzzlement crossed his face and was gone.

'You didn't mean me then. You didn't mean me or Sarah or any girls or women.'

Although this might be the first time that her words had had an airing, their substance had swirled about her thoughts for a year or two – ever since Tansy came to live with them. Listening to her Pa and his cronies supping amd smoking and arguing whilst Tansy suckled Jack as she patched and mended, tending the fire, heating the mulling poker, set her thinking. 'When you talk about the common "people", you mean *men*. We don't count. Not even with a Radical like you. Fraternity! That's it. "Brotherhood", isn't that what it means? Not sisterhood. Is there even a word that means the same? In that "fairer kind of a kingdom" you're always on about, you don't reckon we're of much account.'

Neither said anything for minutes. Lidi continued her work on the bulblets, John Toose sat running a bent grass between his teeth, looking into his own mind, the disturbance his fiery daughter had caused spreading out in ever increasing circles.

Not willing to be troubled further, he left her outburst where it was; suddenly he clapped his hands and arose. 'Ah, I nearly forgot what I come for. It was to tell you about the laurel-tulip tree I've been to see up at the Big House. You know about the La Maillardière tree?'

'The yellow, perfumed one?' The mention of the magnolia excited Lidi's interest and soothed the smarting she had received.

'Ah. They've got a beauty in flower up there. Aw Lid . . .' he closed his eyes, 'you never saw such beauties, the form of the blooms . . . perfect, the deep-gold stamens like they was held in a delicate porcelain bowl, and dark leaves – that glossy you could near see your face in.'

'Did he give you one?'

'Ha. Did he? Not young Goodenstone, not he! What he got he keeps. But he did tell me somebody who's propagating from the French one and who might let me have a few.'

'A few! They must cost a fortune.'

'Well, you have to hazard a bit if you want to get into the new plants.'

'Would they take here?'

'I reckon they would. This part next to your plots has always kept in pretty good heart over the years. I'd have to build it up with a good few hundred bushels of leaf-mould and hoss muck, raise the beds up a bit or I thought I might only grow pot stuff and sell on before they got to planting out stage. I think we can do it here all right. Oh Lidi, you knows how much I always wanted to get into something like that, to specialise . . . ah a delight such as anybody ever saw.'

It was seldom that John Toose was in ill-temper with either of his daughters, and Lidi could forgive her Pa almost anything. They were now back on their usual footing.

'Not like my new lilies though.'

'Dear Gel, I forgot, getting carried away with my tulip-laurel. You was going to tell me about your new ones.'

'Well, nothing's sure, but oh there's that row there, that's come up true for three years, a good six inches taller than the species, delicate looking yet stood up to that big storm – and the colour . . . well it's like dog-rose pink.'

'It sounds a good'n. Does it keep the checker pattern?'

'Just like the ordinary snake's-head.'

'I should a like to see it.'

'You should have come and looked.'

'The days seem that short . . .' He looked apologetic.

'I know. It's all right, I was only teasing.'

'I got a lot on my mind.'

'You should give up trying to change the world.'

'I shan't ever do that.'

Lidi's eyes took on a tender and protective look and her voice a playful chiding tone. 'Just you don't go and wear yourself out before little Jack's had his chance at having a Pa like you've been to Sarah and me.'

He did not respond at first, his face froze half-way through an expression.

Then recovering and putting on Nana-Bess's tight clacking voice, 'Lor dumble us, you gets more like your Nana-Bess every day.' He picked up the basket of rejected bulbs and made to go but hung back, fussing over a few weeds, putting odd bits and pieces into the basket, his back to Lidi.

'I was going to ask you about the babe. What do you reckon to him, little Jack?'

A casual-sounding inconsequential question, but Lidi was alert to something behind it. Her Pa seldom asked 'what do you reckon' unless he wanted a serious opinion.

'I absolutely love him. He's a sweet thing.'

'I know, I know, but . . .' he paused, searching for the right words. 'I dare say I forgot what they're like, and I dare say boy babes might be different from girls, and anyway, I've only had you two to judge by . . . I never was much of a one for looking at babes that wasn't mine.'

His throat was restricted.

'Pa. Whatever's wrong?'

He was silent, then, still picking at minute weeds, said, 'I don't know, Gel. Perhaps 'tis nothing . . . it's why I asked you . . . I couldn't say anything to Tan. I haven't even liked to think anything about it . . . but . . .' He was obviously struggling to make his voice normal. 'Well, you know what I reckon?' He rushed on to get it said: 'I think he can't see proper,' then jumped to his feet and stood looking at the sky.

The day suddenly went grey and chill although the near-noon sun cast short shadows and was hot on the earth.

Neither thought nor word moved in Lidi's mind.

The silence between them seemed endless.

At last he lowered the basket and held out his hand to her, still not looking at her. Lidi went to him, grasped him about his thick waist, her head only coming up to his chest, and held him for a moment. She could feel the short convulsions of the silent dry sobs that he was controlling.

'Oh Pa.'

He held on to her for a moment, then released her and sat down upon the little working-stool.

'I haven't ever noticed anything, he seems just normal to me. Perhaps it's not that, perhaps . . .'

But she knew her father.

If he hadn't been sure, he would never have mentioned it.

His was not an excitable nature, he was cautious, he pondered things, thought twice before speaking once, only in his open-air speaking at meetings was he given to passion and vivid phrases. If he thought that Jack could not see, then he had probably been observing him for a long time, and was convinced that he was not mistaken.

'What are we going to do?'

'Leave things be for now. It's no good worrying Tan. I wouldn't have said anything now, except that I must go on this journey north to buy the new stock. I thought . . . I was going to ask you to . . . well just keep an eye. Don't fuss around or anything, just watch him – casual like.'

'Of course, but nothing's going to happen to him is it?'

'I don't mean like that. I mean observe. Just you watch when you jiggle something at him without making a sound, then see him when it's a bell, or when you speak to him. He hears everything all right, he turns his head but he don't follow anything with his eyes unless it's right close up to his face.'

She suddenly saw in her mind's eye what she had seen many times; she saw her father whilst eating his meals, or taking his ease beside the hearth – bending sideways over the wooden swinging-crib, waving his fingers, dangling the stuffed bit of cloth tied to resemble a mouse that Nana-Bess had made for him, or watching as Tan put him to the breast, he dangling her cap-ribbons or bodice cords at the suckling babe. It had appeared to Lidi that her Pa watched because he was delighted at the sight of his son at Tansy's heavy white breast.

'I hope you're wrong, Pa. Oh, don't that sound weak. But I hope it more than anything.'

THE HAMPSHIRE REPORTER

JANUARY 1819

On Wednesday last, a numerous Meeting was held in the
Town Hall at Alresford
CHARLES ARCHER Esq
In the Chair

The purpose of this Meeting was to consider the
consequence of the Dangers to which Life and Property are
exposed in regard to the recent local Firing of Ricks.
It was resolved that it be Considered that a Subscription
be entered into to defray the expense of a
CONSTABULARY FORCE

The Chairman asked that a Liberal Subscription be made and
this was Agreed to.

AN ADDRESS
TO THE INHABITANTS OF ALRESFORD,
ALTON, BLACKBROOK AND THE MEON VALLEY.

FELLOW COUNTRYMEN,
You have heard that there are persons going about this
countryside setting fire to ricks and breaking machinery.
It is your DUTY to come forward.

HONEST LABOURERS,
It is upon you that the results of such destruction will
most severely fall.

DESTROYING CORN
Must raise the price of bread.

BREAKING MACHINERY
Will give OUR markets to FOREIGNERS.

INDUSTRIOUS LABOURERS,
Be faithful to your EMPLOYERS. Give every assistance.
Inform MAGISTRATES whose most anxious wish is to
protect you.

(Published by Arden Press, July 1819)

BUYING MAGNOLIAS

LIDI WATCHED, A little envious, as in late July 1819, her father left to go on his journey to the north.

It had taken the best part of a year after his first expedition in search of the plants he wanted, for him to arrange to purchase the stock.

Quite apart from not wanting to leave Tansy after the Black-brook doctor had confirmed that Jack did have some serious sight defect ('Perhaps not total blindness, but very poor vision') there were the usual spring orders to fill.

He set off by horse and light cart promising that he should be back quickly.

''Tis all down the country coming back, so I shall come at a fair lick.' He seemed to be getting back to his old self after a long period of hollow eyes from keeping Tansy from getting too broken after the blow the doctor had given them.

At first she had refused to believe it, dragging anybody to 'Come, come quick, he's looking straight at me', and often he was – but he was not seeing her. They all shed tears over him, petted him, treated him as though he might break, then as soon as he began moving around, began to concentrate on the practicalities of making him safe. Now, almost a year later, the family had accepted his blindness.

Sarah had been home for a visit and in her turn had shed tears, picking him up and telling him there there everything would be all right, but knowing that it would never be. To know that those were almost unseeing eyes in the baby's pretty face frightened and depressed her.

When she returned to Stonebridge she became light-hearted again. Ninn had no imperfections. She couldn't have borne to have charge of a child like Jack, or one that was ailing or crippled. She had begun to become attached to Ninn in the same way that she was becoming attached to Madam for her flawless appearance, to the house where no cracks appeared unless they were at once mended, to the unspoiled privacy of her little room, working-dresses and feet that were not bespattered with cow-dung and mud, and the whole order and perfection of Stonebridge Manor.

John had become firm. 'I won't have nobody showing pity nor treating him no different except where it has to be so.'

'But he is different,' Sarah had said.

'Only if you teach him so. He must learn to be like the rest of us. All right, perhaps he won't go riding round the country on fast horses, and maybe we shall have to teach him things so that he can get about safe, but I won't have him grow up thinking that it's an affliction he's got. He's not the first babe that can't see proper, and he won't be the last.'

Brave sentiments. High ideals. Only in the night did John Toose lie awake wondering about his son.

However, when he set off for Manchester, he seemed much like his old self. He patted his pocket and assured Lidi that he had got her drawing of the plant she had heard grew there, and the name and yes, he would ask about the pink sedum she so much wanted and which did not grow in their area and promised if there was any to be had that he would bring some back.

'It'd be a new line, a novelty, and it'd sell like hot cake in Blackbook and Waltham.'

Lidi was always looking for a new line, a pretty plant that would divide easily and would not give up the ghost in the neglected little town gardens. Many of her best sales were of such plants.

She argued that flowers that were either extremely hardy or derived from plants native to the area would always be popular because town people *would* neglect their gardens. The argument that if the plants died then she would sell more did not appeal to her. 'No, they'd blame us for selling poor quality and wouldn't come back. But if they have an easy, perky little plant that grows in spite of them, then they will buy from us again.'

And so far she had proved right, for Lidi's garden plants made a contribution to the family income.

John's business in Manchester was transacted more quickly than he had anticipated. The Head Gardener soon saw that his precious plants would be safe in the hands of this careful and knowledgeable plantsman. The estate owner, at whose behest the plants had been brought into the country, had ordered that only a few of the very best horticulturalists should be allowed to take plants to increase the stock of them. He was a knowledgeable old man who fired questions at John as though he were in the field letting off at game-birds.

As it would take a few days to have travelling cradles made to secure the plants in their large earthenware basins in the cart, John took the opportunity to ride out to see what he could find for Lidi.

He thought the country around there was quite grand, and had to admit that, although it didn't come up to Hampshire, it was certainly a decent enough place to be in.

On the higher ground, the soil was in no way as chalky as it was around the four parishes. He found several wild plants that he thought might please Lidi. He dug them out with good root-balls which he enclosed in damp moss and squares of sacking.

Early on the morning of his second day, he was riding out when the sound of drumming and shouting reached him. Thinking that soldiers or Yeomanry were out training, he rode in that direction and came upon an amazing sight. Hundred upon hundred of people, men and women, were forming columns marching up and down, raising and lowering flags and banners to the order of various commanders – and not all those commanders were men.

When he got close, he dismounted, and stood on a rise looking down. He watched a column of women, four or five abreast and flanked on each side by a single column of men, walk in orderly formation, and upon an order a number of the women lifted banners.

Blue and white belling and flapping in the brisk breeze. Even from where he stood, he could clearly read the message.

UNITY AND STRENGTH

LIBERTY AND FRATERNITY

PARLIAMENTS ANNUAL – SUFFRAGE UNIVERSAL

His heart rose at the sight. And what was it? A veritable army of radicals? Combinationists? Suffragists?

He led his horse down to a group of the people and asked.

'Why man, weer hast tha' been hiding these last weeks?'

'I'm up from the south.'

'Why, 'tis the hoostins t'morrow. Henry Hunt's been granted leave to address a meeting. Eh, but it'll be a grand sight.'

'Henry Hunt? To speak at the hustings? I should like to hear that.'

'Aye, tha's heered of our old Henry in your part then?'

John grinned widely. 'Ah, a course I've heard of Henry Hunt. But hast *thee* heard of *our* William Cobbett?'

The man grinned back at the challenge. 'Bie, but he's got a sharp pen to pike at t'Gree-at Wen, isn't that what he calls it – Loondun, t'Gree-at Wen?'

John spent the entire day with the people there, hundreds of them, from Manchester and surrounding districts.

'Eh lad, this is nowt to what it'll be, why theer's thousands more out on t' moors around Salford, Rochdale and places.'

John's blood surged at the thought of so many people who were followers of the Radical, Henry Hunt.

'Henry's said that we sh'll be sober and decorous – and so we shall be. Look on us, drilled like soldiers these last weeks, we sh'll march into Manchester wi' our banners flying, dressed in our Sunday best. Aye, we sh'll make folk right proud.'

John determined to make a detour through Manchester on his journey home on the day of the meeting. If he did not see the parades and listen to the speeches and be in the crowds of working people who were unafraid to openly carry banners and support a Radical, then he would regret it for the rest of his life. This was what he needed to rekindle his spirits, for rural workers were becoming more and more cowed and frightened. Already fragmented because they worked in small groups or as single hands, and further disunited by the growing competition for work, he had recently found it hard to get any of them to agree that they should think of combining and uniting as industrial workers such as those on the moors were doing.

'UNITY AND STRENGTH' – with the degradation and growing poverty of rural workers in the south of England, the day when they might openly carry such a banner seemed a very long way off. But then, not so many years ago, it must have seemed unlikely for the people on the moors to be so open.

8

'CUT 'M DOWN. CUT 'M DOWN.'

Lancashire, England – August 1819

A TROOP OF cavalry and a corps of the Yeomanry appeared as shades in the white mists of first dawn on a day that promised to be very fine. Even the horses seemed without substance, their gentle snorts and uneasy movements of hooves leaching into the fast disappearing moisture of the August morning.

The sounds from the stables had gone on all night, then, just before dawn, some birds began their twittering, and now with the first grey light the crunch of boots and chink of metal was to be heard.

From various sounds made by buglers and cooks and others who must rise early, a young groom/servant curled up in a blanket on some hay reckoned he had ten minutes before he would need to be up and dipping buckets and spitting and polishing his master's boots. Ten minutes in which to dissolve into his usual morning daydream.

He imagined himself. The tip of the nodding plume of his stiff braided cap; his stiff-collared, gilt-buttoned and frogged jacket; his white gauntlets, one clutching the reins of his horse, the other brandishing his sabre; his boots shone in the stirrups, breeches clung to his calves and thighs without a crease – except where his short-skirted jacket showed the cheeks of his buttocks.

His daydream was always of the Manchester Yeomanry, to whom he was attached by way of being a servant to one of its members. A cheese merchant in everyday life. A military gentleman today. The Yeomanry were known, and not always in a complimentary way, for the tight fit of their breeches. Once, when in his cups, the boy's master, Mister Bransford, had told his young servant that there had been a time not long since when the Yeomanry wore long coat-tails; whether it was true or not was difficult to tell, for Mister Bransford was a great story-teller.

And if he was, during most of his waking hours, a cheese merchant, it was not as a cheese merchant that he saw himself. If the people of Manchester laughed behind their hands at their posturing, the irregulars, to their own eyes, were a vital arm of law enforcement and cut no end of a dash.

"'Twas at a public ball y'know lad. A room full of our fellows and a great many of the officers of the Duke of Wellington's "Scum of the Earth" army, all in full regalia . . . well, we were all pretty merry when this French princess . . . or duchess or something, says, "Why do zeez officairs hide their lovely bems undair thair coat-tails? Eef I waz the Duke I should cut them all off 'igh up to show the laidies those wondarful bems."'

The youth had flushed at the idea of a princess . . . a *princess* thinking about an officer's 'bem' inside his breeches and even more that she could say it aloud, in the presence of men. Did she really? Or was it one of the Master's many stories about women in high society?

'There was an order to retrieve sabres – not the "Scum of the Earth" officers mind you, only the Yeomanry – "Present coat-tails!" was the order.' Captain Bransford had mimed the action, slicing the air with the side of his hand. 'We showed her bems all right. 'Tis said that the princess had all the coat-tails made into a travelling rug and took it with her everywhere.'

His youthful servant thought him magnificent.

When, in his daydream, the youth had finished dressing himself in the uniform of a Yeomanry captain, he never knew what to do next, except sit astride a white horse brandishing his sabre. For although he had polished and brushed Captain Bransford and his horse for a year or more now, the captain had never done anything but prepare for a parade – and then parade.

The bugler's sudden shrill reveille left the young servant still astride his horse.

The youth's name was Luce Draper; he was tall and thin and beginning to be good looking with his fair, almost white, curling hair and wide-set eyes. He thought himself to be as lucky as they come. His father, a widower, had, like many of his neighbours after months of searching for work on farms in his native Kent, done the long walk from the south to the black towns of the Midlands where he got work in the coal-fields.

Until a year or so ago, Luce and his father had worked at the same pit, the father coal-loading, Luce working with a pony-man.

One day his father strong and jolly was alive, the next he was dead. The cable carrying the cage to the pit bottom had broken and every man was killed.

Luce's grief was overwhelming; he and his father had walked the hundreds of miles north together, and had as yet made no friends in the new place. After the communal burial, Luce had walked away from the pit-town and out on to the Nottingham road and on and on away from the place that had done for his father.

Just outside Grantham, he had come across a man battered and bruised from being thrown from his horse. Luce had helped the man and recaptured the horse, and it was from that encounter that Luce had gained the post with the cheese merchant as servant and groom.

The captain was a big, bluff man and, although a younger man than Luce's father, Luce had, at a vulnerable time, taken him for his substitute model of strong manhood.

Now, at seventeen, Luce wanted nothing more than to become a second Captain Bransford – not the man of cheeses and small business, but the man on the white charger.

On that August morning, when Luce had made his captain ready, he was given leave to go off to see the spectacle that the Yeomanry were there to protect.

'Keep your distance from the hustings, boy. Before this day is out, that Radical and his gang of rabble-rousers will rue the day he stepped foot in this place.'

Luce had no idea what the event was and hardly a notion of what a Radical was. In the pit he had heard men arguing, but had no interest in their talk of votes and laws and societies. Never mind, it was a morning out and something to see.

'If you keep to the edge of the field on the north side, that is where you are likely to see us ride in.'

As he walked towards the fields where the event was to take place, Luce had a vision of the brilliantly turned-out Yeomanry and the 15th Hussars, the 31st and the 88th regiments parading together to keep a large crowd under control.

He had no difficulty in discovering the meeting place, for the roads thronged with men, women and children all going in one direction. It was obviously something very special, for people were dressed in best clothes. By eleven o'clock the day was clear and fine. There was a holiday atmosphere, anticipation, excitement, voices of people out for the day.

When he reached the field, Luce was astounded at the huge crowd that was gathered, so he walked the entire perimeter to see everything. To one end some carts and planks had been assembled to form a raised platform decorated with bunting and flags which, except for little boys climbing upon it, was unoccupied, and it was around this that the crowds were assembling. There being nothing else but people there, Luce assumed the platform to be the hustings.

He fell in with a local boy a bit younger than himself.

'What's this going to be?'

'Don't thee know? Where has't thee been hiding?'

In later years, whenever Luce thought on that day, he never could decide why he did not mention being attached to the Yeomanry and that he had been with his master who had only just returned, but some sense stopped him from boasting of his captain.

'I'm new to the place.'

'Ah well that'd account for it for it's been the talk round these parts long since.' The boy was delighted to find someone to impress with information of the event.

'T' Magistrates have been trying to stop Henry Hunt from holding a meeting. But they'll not stop him; good old Henry won't be stopped by a lot of owd parsons and constables.'

Having laid familiar claim to 'Old Henry', the boy was profligate in his offer to share his knowledge with Luce.

'I know all about him because me uncle is one of his followers – if you stay wi' me I s'll point him out. He'll be carrying one of the banners – me uncle that is – "Universal Suffrage" it says – a red banner wi' yellow letters.'

'What's that mean?'

'Why t'vote of course. Votes for everybody.' He frowned at Luce's uncomprehending expression. 'It's what this here meeting's all about. Us all wants a say in the running of the country. About the corn laws and everything.'

Luce, not wishing to appear at too much disadvantage, waited for the information to come rather than ask. He had never heard of corn laws.

'Hey up, here comes summat. Are you coming along with us? I know where the best place is.'

'Is it near the hustings?'

'Why of course, where else?'

For a second, Luce wondered whether he should go to the very place that Captain Bransford had warned him against, but with the whole place filled with thousands of people standing shoulder to shoulder, it wasn't likely that his captain's eye would alight upon one youth in its midst, and where was the harm with these people all out enjoying themselves?

When they reached the platform, the boy swung himself up on one of the wheels.

'Come on.'

Luce hooked his feet in the spokes and hauled himself up to where he had a view across the heads of the vast crowds. He let out a low whistle.

It was an amazing sight, a sea of heads and shoulders and still more pouring in from the roads leading into the fields. He had not imagined that so many people could ever be assembled in one place.

'Me Uncle Cartwright says there'll not be less than a hundred and fifty thousand.' He considered the throng. 'But if y'asts me I reckon there's that many already without them that's going to parade.'

'Where have they all come from?'

'All over – Rochdale, places like that. "Don't bring nothing – only your conscience," that's what Old Henry said us should do.'

Suddenly the crowd divided and a long column of marchers five abreast carrying flags and banners came onto the field. People cheered and clapped and shouted 'huzza huzza'. The boy knew what every banner proclaimed.

'"Unity and Strength. Liberty and Fraternity. Parliaments Annual. Suffrage Universal,"' he quoted. 'Hey up.' He pointed to a stark black banner with white lettering, a heart and two clasped hands. 'There's me Uncle Cartwright's lot. "Equal Representation or Death." D'you know what? they've been out weeks ont' moors, I've been out there watching . . . thousands and thousands all learning to march and wheel like soldiers. Uncle Cartwright said they're going to make people proud of them. Hey, do they look fine.'

It was true, they did. Henry Hunt, their leader, had urged his followers to be 'a display of cleanliness, sobriety and decorum', and they had served him well.

No sooner had this parade come to a halt and arranged itself, than a second appeared. This time it was a long, long, single column of women flanked on either side by a double column of men.

'They are women,' said Luce.

'Why of course they're women. They'll be the Union Female Society.'

The boy could have only been about fifteen, yet Luce felt ignorant in comparison.

'Are they for it . . . for votes and that?'

'Aye, but there's folks that think they should stop at home and do their proper work.'

'Do you?'

'Aye, I go along with Uncle Cartwright. He reckons that they should leave it to the men who understand about governments and votes. It's because a lot of them all work together in t' mills and that causes them to start wanting the same as men. And I go along with Uncle Cartwright, if there's anybody knows owt about it, it's me Uncle Cartwright.'

'But you said that Universal Sufferance meant votes for everyone.'

The boy frowned, but didn't reply.

The cheering for the women was loud and long. They carried blue and white banners one of which Luce saw billowed out in a light breeze.

'Does that say Universal Sufferance?'

'Suffrage. Nay, it says, "Let Us Die Like Men, And Not Be Sold Like Slaves".'

Luce's heart leapt at the magnificence of the women and their billowing banner.

'Can you read?' Luce asked.

The boy considered, then thinking that he might be caught out said, 'No, not altogether but I know that what it do say ont' all the banners.'

Suddenly there was a rumble of sound quite different from that which had greeted the other columns – more good natured jeering than cheering. This time several hundred constables came onto the field and thrust a way purposefully towards the platform.

'You lads – off!'

Luce and the boy were pulled roughly from their vantage point as the constables created a clear pathway from the platform to the nearby houses where people were looking from upstairs windows.

'Come on, let's bung up close to the front; we shall still see plenty if we keep to where the parades come in.'

By now, Luce knew why his captain had warned him not to get close to the hustings – he supposed that those constables weren't there unless they expected trouble. Yet the crowds seemed so untroublesome and happy, there were children playing everywhere, fathers hoisted little ones on their shoulders so that they might see the parades and the flags and banners.

As the constables were forming up in their lines, a band marched on; cheers went up and people clapped in time to the drums and bugles. More red flags, more blue and white ones, more and more columns of marchers.

Luce had never seen anything so rousing. A parade of Yeomanry or cavalry in full dress was pallid in comparison. Here was an army that he had never imagined existed.

When you looked at individual faces you saw that they were just ordinary people, yet in columns with their breast-ribbons and bands and banners they marched like the most glorious army imaginable. Particularly the women, again and again he looked at them, hundreds and thousands of them waving their banners which said that they should not be sold like slaves.

At the back of his eyes tears gathered, had it not been for the presence of the boy, they might have flowed. What was it that made him feel like this? Too much was going on to be able to think about it. But it was something of pride and discovery. He felt strong and manly. No one should be sold like slaves.

After the events of that day, Luce could never put them in sequence, though he remembered always the vivid image of an open barouche covered with blue and white flags, drawn by people instead of a horse, making its way towards the hustings. Luce turned to ask the boy if this wasn't 'Old Henry' at last, but he and the boy had been parted. It didn't matter, the explosive roar that rose from the throng left him in no doubt that the man in the tall gleaming white hat was indeed the man that they had waited so patiently to hear.

Henry Hunt mounted the hustings and the band played 'God Save the King'.

Luce could never remember the speeches, except for a general impression of fervent agreement with everything that was said. A surge within him, the raising of his spirit till he could have mounted the platform himself and demanded universal suffrage, and that the women with the blue and white banners should not have to die like men for the right not to be sold like slaves. He raised his arms and cheered with the crowd.

He had forgotten entirely how he came to be there, and his captain's warning of the danger of the hustings.

Quite suddenly there was a brief moment of still silence.

Then somebody shouted.

Quickly, Henry Hunt was bundled from the hustings and taken down the line of constables towards one of the houses. Then, Luce saw the glitter of metal, the flash of gold braid and the gleam of white breeches. He recognised scores of uniforms similar to that which he had held out for his master earlier that morning.

The Manchester Yeomanry.

They charged in. A woman shrieked.

Above the noise of the crowd could be heard the sound of hundreds of horses.

Then pandemonium broke out.

The dense crowd stood firm. The charge petered out.

Then the Yeomanry, perfectly turned out in their tight breeches and short jackets, tried again, urging their reluctant horses into a gallop, but with the dense crowd before them, some horses shied and turned. Now the lack of skill of those civilians in regimental get-up showed itself. Some riders lost control of their ill-trained animals. They became separated and isolated, and hemmed in. And soon they were stranded in the midst of the jeering crowd.

Then the Hussars rode in, advanced and began to drive the people forward with their swords.

Luce saw a man with a child on his shoulders go down beneath a horse's hooves. Someone in the crowd lashed out at the rider pulling him from his saddle. Until now the Yeomen had kept their sabres held high, then there was a panic-stricken call, a man's voice called 'Cut 'em down. Cut 'em down.'

Now some of the riders had reached where Luce stood petrified, and he saw that it was not the crowd who was calling 'cut 'em down' but the armed riders. Luce recognised a voice; he looked up directly into the face of his own captain. In his passion and fear, Captain Bransford's eyes slid, unseeing, over Luce.

'Cut 'em down. Cut 'em down.'

Luce saw Captain Bransford raise his sabre and slice upwards through the cheek of a man and downwards across the arm of a woman.

Then there was blood and blood and blood.

Screams, and cries of agony and fear.

Blood everywhere.

Crushed limbs. Great gaping wounds. Severed fingers.

Sick with terror, Luce watched the man who had been his mentor and master for more than a year. Bransford's eyes were stricken with fear, his face red with fury. His arm with its fist clenching his sabre lashed out left, right and centre.

People went down under the blows and were trampled by the horses. Some people tried to use the poles of their banners to try and ward off blows. Many of the Yeomen were unseated, causing them, in their own terror of finding themselves in the mêlée, to lash out uncontrollably.

Wherever they were able to do so people ran from the field. In any direction. Anywhere, anywhere to avoid the terrible sabres and swords and hooves.

Luce ran with the crowd, tripped and went down on the edge of the field.

It was all over in a few minutes.

Much later, when a clock close by struck two, Luce came out of a daze of terror and shock. His breeches and stockings were saturated with urine and blood, whether his own or not, he did not know or care. He looked around him. The field was littered with bonnets, caps and shoes; the instruments on which the national anthem had been played only a very short time ago, lay where they had been dropped; the hustings was in tatters, its banners trodden underfoot.

Injured people lay scattered everywhere. The groans and cries for help of bleeding and broken men, women and children were frightening.

The place was a battlefield.

In the bright summer sunshine, with tears streaming down his face, young Luce Draper sat in the dust and vomited violently.

9

I T IS DARK and the Poacher is out. Suddenly, he stands quite still, holding his breath, the muscles at his temples tauten, his ears prick up like an animal's.

There is a low rumbling in the distance. His heightened senses gradually fathom a sound of horses pulling a heavy load, yet no harness jingles, no hooves or wheels clash off sparky flints. The mysterious wagon is not on a road, but sounds as though it is being trundled over turf.

His ears trace the sound to the top of the downs close to the old gibbet where there is no road, but where the surface is hard when the weather is dry and a chalk slide when it is wet.

Suddenly, against the night sky, passing the elm and the gibbet, there moves a very large, bulky load.

The Poacher's instinct is to slip away as silently as he has come. Yet he does not, but draws back into the dark trunk of a tree and, so that his breath shall not show in the first frosty air of autumn, he pulls his neckerchief over his nose.

Slowly the wagon is drawn over the crest and, as it gathers some speed on the downward gradient, there is a scraping, and sparks fly as the brake is applied.

The horses are headed in the direction of a chalk and flint track, a disused back-way onto the Estate, and as they pass close by where the Poacher is hidden, he can smell their sweat and see the jets of breath from their nostrils. Above them the smaller puffs from four men.

The Poacher squinnies and lifts his chin a fraction, but the only thing that he can make out is from the way the horses nod and strain – the long, shrouded load is of a great weight and the wheels are huge, and inches wide.

A man gives an order. The horses are reined in at a chained gate.

That's something new.

Nothing has been up the neglected track for years and until now, no gate has ever barred it.

The wagon is manoeuvred through. The chains are replaced,

and the load rumbles away in the direction of the Estate farm.

The Poacher had recognised the voice that gave the order – it was the Estate's Agent.

A bit beneath his dignity to be acting as carter's mate?

Suddenly, the Poacher knows what it is that he has seen.

The crafty buggers!

They must a planned it weeks ago. To have got 'n all the way over from Archangel's Foundry, or perhaps even down from up the North, to a got here just this very night.

Would you bugger it? The one night when there was enough light to come over the downs. Lucky for they it was dry, or they'd a come a cropper, wide wheels or no, they'd a gone in up till their axles. The one night when everybody in the whole valley was gone over to the next village for their Harvest Home. The one night when they'd be pissing pure cider and dancing the staggers before they got back home.

Now, he must see for himself.

He does not follow the wagon directly, but pushes through a hedge and goes obliquely to where he hears the great wheels creaking over flints.

He has guessed where they are going, he remembers it from when he was a boy. An old barn up the top of this path where ploughboys and youthful farmhand skulkers came to lark about, to boast and to compare their manhood.

The Poacher is right. The wagon has drawn up where he expected. There is not another pair of eyes like his in the whole valley. His neighbours reckon that he can see in the dark, like a cat. True, he can easily see what is going on.

The Estate Agent and his men work without speaking. The horses are taken from the shafts and are led away. Then the barn is secured and the others leave.

When they are well away, the Poacher moves silently. The only window opening is above his head. He hasn't forgotten. He leaps. Then, clinging on with his fingers, climbs in and down inside, using the cross-timbers as toe-holds. He smiles at the lad he used to be, telling him that he might be getting on, but he's still as tricky as a nipp.

Inside the barn it is too dark for even his eyes, but he smells iron and grease. He runs his hands along the length of the load, feels the great box, climbs up. The ladder-like structure is the folded elevator. He runs his hands over the wheels where the driving bands will run and finds the place where the threshed grain will run into waiting sacks. His sensitive touch and his mind's eye reveal the machine that he has seen illustrated on a handbill.

I knowed it!

A thrasher!

The crafty buggers, sliding him in like that, knowing they'd have to do it secret or somebody'd a laid wait along the road, then there'd a been trouble.

His gorge rises.

Once, the two-wheeled cart had given way to the four-wheeled wagon, the sower's apron and broadcast arm had given way to the wheeled seed-drill. Saving labour, about which no man or woman whose back is bent double from dawn to dusk should complain – except, that it does not mean that machines will save them from the endless slog of carrying and sowing, they are dismissed in favour of modern devices.

And now the enemy has infiltrated its deadliest weapon, the one that will end the life that his village has known for centuries.

With four hands ready to do any job, things were bad enough, but that was nothing compared to what this thing would do.

The kick he gives the threshing machine is as ineffectual as the anger that his neighbours will later direct at the machine.

The giant of all tribal memory, that has slept in the hills since it descended in the form of the Plague, has awakened. Is hungry. Has slipped unseen into their midst whilst they are away jigging and drinking and making the double-backed beast along the road home.

Unless a giant-killer rises up against it, the Poacher knows that they are a doomed community.

The bloody buggers!

10

HAMPSHIRE, ENGLAND, AUGUST 1819

LIDI WAS COMING from The Dunnock where she had spent a fruitful hour casting for trout, with her legs and feet bare, her water-darkened skirt hoisted up and, to keep her bundle of hair from entanglement, she had pulled down well over her brow an old straw field-hat of her Pa's. Over her shoulder she carried a rod and from one hand dangled three glistening fish. The day was fine, but there was enough chill upon the air to heighten the pink of her skin to a rosy red.

'Well now, if that isn't a sight for me eyes.'

'Oh!' Suddenly stepping out into the pathway of Uncle Will and awakening her from the reverie that she had fallen into whilst fishing, left Lidi momentarily speechless, not least because, although she had responded to Uncle Will's voice, it was another face upon which her eyes alighted. The face of a young man, tall, slender and with hair as curled and twisty as her own, and as uncompromisingly yellow as her own was red.

She soon regained her composure, hugged the older man and said how glad she was that he had come at last.

'Nana-Bess has been fretting all summer that you had not come.'

'Only old Bess fretting for me? Ah well, I suppose me days are gone when a pretty lass might fret for the lack of seeing me.'

He was not really her uncle, but had always been such to herself and Sarah. As far as she knew he had no permanent home but came and went from Croud Cantle as though it was his home. Nana-Bess grumbled that Aunt Ju and Uncle Will 'should a made a go of it yers ago. But there, that's yer Auntie Jude, independent as they comes, and young Will is as lovely a man as ever stepped foot into boots. I told her it an't never too late to settle down. But she won't. And there's Young Will'd give teeth for her.' That Uncle Will was a lovely man Lidi entirely agreed, that he was ever 'Young' Will was amusing, for all that he had as much spark and fun in him than many a man thirty years younger. He must be ten years older even than her Pa, but they were very alike in many ways.

Uncle Will believed in the same things as Pa, and when they were together with Aunt Ju, anyone would think that the three of them were about to change the world. Lidi loved to sit in the hearth at Croud Cantle at Great-gran's feet and listen to them; there was a feeling of being cradled, of being aware of them all as a family. Unity. Security.

Lidi grinned as he lifted the brim of her hat and gave her a peck on the cheek. 'Well, some of us thought you might have been a bit quicker getting here after your letter last spring.'

'I was waylaid. And here's one of the reasons.' He indicated the blond young man. 'This is Luce. Luce Draper. Luce, this is Lidi.'

'How do Miss Lidi.'

Although Luce Draper spoke broadly, there was, overlaying the suggestion of another way of speaking, clipped words, changed vowels.

'I reckon Luce knows everybody at Croud Cantle like old friends. Right Luce?'

Luce nodded seriously, 'Aye but I thought Miss Lidi to be a little girl . . . much younger.'

'So did I!' Will said, with an exaggerated play of surprise.

Lidi ran home to give Tansy the fish and to tell her that Uncle Will was back and that she was going up to Croud Cantle to see them. She leapt out of her fishing clothes and put on a decent skirt and laced-up bodice which she allowed to be quite unlaced.

'Hello, there,' said Tansy. 'That there young man your Uncle Will has got with him is worth a loose bodice then?'

Unembarrassed at the suggestion Lidi pursed her lips and raised one eyebrow at her step-mother. She twisted up her hair in the way that made her neck appear longer, and pulled out curling tendrils all around her hairline. 'There! I shall be back before it's dark. If Pa comes, tell him Uncle Will's been in Manchester too.'

The kitchen at Croud Cantle was the most stable place in all of their lives. Aunt Ju reckoned that, apart from the lead-lined sink, her little desk and some new oil-lamps, the place was the same now as when she was a girl. Great-gran too seemed to be a fixture.

She was the oldest person in Cantle. She could do nothing for herself, neither could she talk or listen. Nana-Bess tended to her with such loving care that it sometimes made a lump in your throat to see them. An old lady caring for a very old lady. Nana-Bess talked to 'Misz Bella' all day long, responding to her own conversation. 'You all right there Misz Bella? No, you'm right, the sun's nearly direct in yer eyes. I a put a shade up. That better? Ah, I thought it was.'

When Lidi arrived, Nana-Bess was clattering around the kitchen laying out food. 'Why, that youth must be starving. Will never stopped all morning. Tcha. Wanting to keep going to get here in time for dinner. He fergets what it's like to be young. Young men gets hungry. Lean as a pole with the wood scraped off.'

Lidi offered to help, but was sent off out to find the others to tell them to come.

She found them in one of the old outhouses. Aunt Ju was preparing for tomorrow's market in Waltham. Wearing her field clothes, she was tying carrots into bunches, whilst Will and the young man, with their jackets off, packed other produce into the rush panniers.

Aunt Ju, her hair for once knotted up for coolness, looked quite young. She was in her fifties, but her jawline was firm, most of her teeth were intact, and her figure was quite unlike the women who lived in the village. Most of them had become heavy and shapeless from the long cycle of pregnancy, lactation, pregnancy. They were almost all poorly fed so that they had few good teeth and their skin was underlaid with a puffy, water-laden layer. In the filtered light, with her neat figure, and her hair up off her face, Lidi could see why Uncle Will had gone on waiting for her.

'No good asking you to lend a hand – in your decent skirt.'

Aunt Ju's remark, unlike Tansy's, made Lidi flush.

'I got my other one wet, fishing.' She had no reason to explain, except that she was aware of the young man, and that she did not usually change her skirt when she came up to Aunt Ju's.

From nowhere it seemed, Nana-Bess had produced one of her 'feasty dinners'. There was nothing the old lady liked better than an excuse to put something special on the table for visitors. There was a bit of ham and plenty of Croud Cantle's own cheese, freshly made soda-bread and one of the large buttermilk tarts that Jude had been making and selling for years from their stall on the markets.

The Nugent stall had a standard of excellence of produce that not many competitors attained. They had been selling the same kind of things for years, and whilst other smallholders tried to put on a stall like Nugent's they never succeeded in winning Aunt Ju's steady custom. She often said, 'If all the pies I took to market was laid in a line, you could walk from here to London on them.' And

Lidi knew that if Aunt Ju was anything, it was not a pie-maker or market trader. But she had her mother and Nana-Bess to provide for.

Aunt Ju wrote a lot. She was not exactly secretive about what she was doing, but would never let anybody read it. 'It's only a bit of writing about the family, and about the people who live around here. It's a record for people who come after. On the day I'm in my coffin, you can open it if you like, or leave it and pass it on. When I began, it was for people a hundred years on.'

The idea was romantic. And so was Aunt Ju, although, Lidi suspected, only herself and Uncle Will knew that side of her – perhaps Pa too.

Luce Draper was brought into the circle over dinner. 'They say a rolling stone gathers no moss, yet I gathered Luce on the way through Manchester, did I not Luce?'

The young man's reply was a nod and a half-smile.

'Manchester?' exclaimed Lidi. 'That's where Father's gone.'

Will Vickery looked questioningly.

'To buy some special plants – a man there has brought some new ones into the country.'

'Is he back?'

'Probably today, as he didn't come yesterday.'

'Have you heard what happened there?' Will asked.

Jude shook her head.

'A massacre!'

Lidi looked from one to the other. 'What massacre? What?' Suddenly the delay in her father's return seemed dreadful.

'Massacre?' asked Lidi.

'Aye. That's what it was. A massacre of ordinary people such as ourselves gathered round this table. Nothing subversive or seditious. Everything done according to the book. A lawful assembly. A gathering of citizens at the hustings to listen to Henry Hunt –'

Henry Hunt. Lidi had heard Pa talk of him. He was a gentleman Radical.

Will Vickery's voice was rising with the anger and passion he so obviously felt – 'and they were cut down by callous idiots in fancy regimentals. Can you give that credence? But it is as true as I sit here. Right Luce?' The young man nodded.

Will continued. 'They rode into the crowd and cut them about. And when the people tried to flee, the Hussars joined them.'

There was silence around the table as each of them saw behind their eyes a re-enactment of Will's experience. 'Pa would be sure to go there, wouldn't he? He would go anywhere to hear a speech.'

No-one knew what to say. She was right. If John Toose was still in Manchester, then he would certainly not have missed such a chance to be part of it.

'In Manchester they're already saying that it was "Peterloo" because the place where it happened was Peter's Field. But of course it was worse than Waterloo; in that battle the both sides had weapons and there were no women and children on the battlefield.'

'Lord and Marry Lad, that's terrible,' Nana-Bess said, holding her apron to her mouth at the thought. 'Why would any man do that to little children?' She left the table and went to sit for comfort beside her friend Bella, Lidi's silent and helpless great-grand-mother.

'And you were in it, Will?' Jude asked quietly.

'I was. Yet not as near to the centre of things as Luce.'

They all looked at Luce, but he did not respond.

'Luce does not like to talk about it.'

'Well then,' said Lidi, 'why are we? It's not a nice thing to talk about the very thing that is upsetting to somebody, especially when they don't know you well enough to tell you to shut up.'

She rose from the table and collected scraps into a bowl. 'Would you like to come out and see Aunt Ju's pigs, Mister Draper?'

Luce Draper jumped from his place at the table with alacrity. 'Aye. I always did like pigs. We used to keep a pig when I was young.'

When they had gone, Will told the others more of Luce's experience and plight. 'When I found him at the edge of the field he was spattered all over with so much blood that I thought he had some terrible injuries. But much of it must have come from someone else; he says he remembers a horse over him and a severed arm falling across him, but he was in such a state of confusion that he cannot put things in order.'

'Lord bless the soul,' said Bess. 'That kind of thing shouldn't ought to happen to a dog, let alone a pretty lad like that.'

'He wasn't badly hurt, only took the tip of a sabre across his back, a long cut but not deep. It was lucky he was wearing a thick leather jerkin.'

'That's terrible, terrible,' Jude said. Will put his large hand over her small one.

'He can't be much older than Lidi.'

'Hardly at all.'

'He's alone in the world. It's why I brought him with me. He was born in the south.'

'Oh Jude, the poor lad,' Bess Smith said. 'Jude, just think how it would be if that was one of ourn. He needs to be fed up with decent victuals and work hisself out of it. He can bide here, can't he Jude?'

Jude Nugent smiled. 'Of course, Bess, the boy can bide here. And what about Will Vickery, is he to bide here too?'

'Why Jude! Misz Bella'd never forgive us if we was to send poor Will away.'

STONEBRIDGE MANOR
– A WALK IN THE WOODS

SARAH AND THE child Ninn on their morning walk, came out into a place that was overgrown with ivy and bramble. Not shrubby game-bird cover, but neglected tangle. Ninn had run ahead as usual.

'Look Tooey, it's a broken goat shed or something.' Ninn had discovered a ruined building and was looking out through the window square.

'Why no, it's an old cottage.'

'No. It's only small.'

'How big do you think a cottage is then? It's a cottage all right, what's left of it.'

They walked around the ruin, Sarah discovering evidence of human occupation of the land.

'Look, that's marigolds gone wild, and look there's all kind of other plants – this used to be a woman's herb garden for her medicines.'

They walked further afield and saw ruined animal pens and land where in places Sarah thought that she could detect that the turfy ground was furrowed.

'I reckon this used to be a farm.'

'Why have its people gone away and left it?'

Why indeed.

'Perhaps they didn't have any say in it.'

'If it was mine I wouldn't leave it so that it got broke up.'

Sarah looked at him. But it is yours, my sweetly, and if it wasn't your father that took it, then it was your grandfather. At home such thoughts seldom occurred to her. Pa and Aunt Jude were the ones.

She supposed there was something in what Pa said – when you really thought about it. ' "They" are the enemy,' he always said. ' "They" do battle against Us. They destroy and pillage like any of the old barons. That they no longer do it by the pike and musket (at least not as often) but by imposing laws, makes them no less an invading army' – but all that was so tedious, just talk.

And the place that Sarah and her charge had found, was where one small battle must have happened. The Broughlakes had swallowed the farm and not even needed it. Most likely they saw their chance to take in another morsel of land, and took it. 'They'.

Yet she was charmed by the child – loved him even. Enjoyed her cotton pillow and clean room that looked out over wide parkland and cedars and man-made lake and trout stream.

If she had been born to all that, would she give it up without a fight? Even if it was stolen from people as Pa said.

That was a hard one to answer. And Ninn couldn't help being who he was, he's not to blame. 'No,' said Pa's reasoning voice, 'not while he's young, but as soon as he can think for himself, he's to blame.' Pa had all the answers, and she and Lidi had taken them in with their baby pap.

'Shall we eat our picnic here? We could pretend that I am the farmer and you make the food.'

Sarah's loud laugh made him look as solemn as when his father ridiculed him.

'Oh, I'm not laughing at you. But I have an auntie who would have asked why she could not be the farmer and you get the food. Don't let's stop here, it's a sad place.'

They had not walked far when they heard voices. Low, sparse sentences as were passed to and fro between working men. They had pushed through some close-growing bushes and come upon a track beside which was a large barn, not as derelict as the buildings they had just left, but nevertheless it had a decayed appearance.

'Look Tooey!'

The boy had seen, as had Sarah, a barn with a wide open door. Inside was a huge wheeled contraption painted an orangey-red. A man came out wiping greasy hands on a piece of sacking; on seeing Ninn and Sarah he pulled at the brim of his hat.

'Ah, young Master Ninn.'

Ninn just looked back.

'What do you be doing all out here so far from the house?'

Sarah replied, 'Taking exercise.'

'Well, I don't reckon the Master'd care about him being up here.'

'Why?'

The man shrugged and went back to the barn.

'Ninn, something's going on, let's take a look.'

'Do you think we ought?'

Sarah smiled. 'I don't know, but you're the Master, if you say it's all right, perhaps we ought to see what they are doing . . . it's your father's barn.'

Ninn smiled, seeing the joke, and walked boldly up to the building.

The men inside were so engrossed that they did not see Sarah and her charge standing at the open door.

'Why 'tis a thrashing machine!' Sarah exclaimed.

The greasy man swung round almost indignantly.

'And what might a little gel like theece know about thrashers?'

'I know that they'll put men out of work.'

The man came close. Surly and sure of himself.

'If I was you, and you wants to keep your job walking in the Master's bluebell woods with Master's nipper, in a pretty gown paid for by the Master – I should take heed and keep my trap shut tight.'

Ninn came and held her hand tightly.

'This is the Master's machine brought in so as we can turn out corn by the thousand bushel – and pretty miss nursey, that there corn is what pays for you to go walking out instead of working like most honest village maids.'

Sarah flushed bright red, turned quickly and hurried away.

She took Ninn back to the open security of the wide lawn and hanging cedar trees in sight of the house, where she hoped that her master would see her giving his son the exercise regime he had imposed.

When she had bathed him that evening, and was putting on his nightshirt, he said, 'Don't let's tell, Tooey.'

She well knew what he meant. They had both had a fright though they scarcely knew what had frightened them.

'Very well, Master Ninn. We shall keep our counsel.'

Sometimes she puzzled him. But he had never been so happy and safe in his life before she came.

In bed, he whispered, 'What was it? How does it thrash?'

'I don't know.'

'I would think it would hurt very.'

For a minute, Sarah made her way along his train of thought. 'Not *that* kind of thrash – not people.'

'Oh.' Almost relief. 'What does it thrash?'

'Corn.'

'For chickens?'

'For people. For bread.'

It seemed impossible that there had ever been a time when Sarah had not known what corn was for.

Pa's voice: 'Why should he know? Bread arrives from nowhere in buttered slices, on white plates.'

'Goodnight Master Ninn. One day I'll take you to see some thrashing and winnowing.'

He did not venture on what winnowing might be.

A DEATH

LIDI WAS THERE the morning that Great-grandmother died.

Bess Smith, having 'cleaned thee up and made 'ee comfortable Misz Bella', was clattering her way through the house chores. Sister-wives – the two of them having had their children fathered upon them by the same man. Bella's in wedlock and Bess's outside the blanket. Now that the cause of their trouble was long gone, they had spent the last of their years together. When Bella withdrew entirely from the world, Bess was her constant attendant.

'I know what I was going to ast you, Misz Bella, had you noticed how young Lidi have got her chests swolled lately? She'm a proper young woman. Sebenteen. Lord it don't seem only yesterday she was getting her first tooth.'

Lidi, forgotten by Bess, is sorting savory herbs to dry in the bread-oven and pack for the winter trade, listens as she often does to Bess holding a strange conversation with Great-grandmother – the same voice asking and answering, commenting and replying. No one is really sure that Bess cannot interpret what the paralysed old lady means.

Bess lifts Bella's feet to one side so that she can wipe the hearth stones.

'Lord and Marry yer feet's like dabs of ice. I can feel it through your stockings. Are you all right?' She looks close and concerned into the older woman's face.

Bella makes a series of 'tha-tha-tha' sounds which Bess interprets.

'Lissen, I a get Lidi to fill that big stone jar with hot water just to be going on with till your foot-stone gets hot.'

Bess had seen Bella like this once before, last winter when there was a long spell of cold followed by fog and damp. Bella's breath was uneasy and her skin chilly to the touch.

When Lidi has it ready, Bess puts the hot jar beneath the ailing woman's feet, gently, lovingly, and wraps another crocheted shawl about her shoulders.

Lidi stands beside Bess as she fusses over the old lady whose breath becomes shallower and shallower.

'Don't go. Don't go Misz Bella. Lidi . . .' Nana-Bess almost shrieks in her anxiety, 'get the salts.'

Lidi rushes immediately to do as she is bid, but is certain that no amount of strong smell will bring back Great-gran's breath.

Bess warms some brandy and honey and tries to get it into Bella drop by drop. Bella gives a quiet hiccough and for a moment Bess looks hopefully at Lidi that the draught had worked.

Bess looks closely into Bella's face.

'You'm gone Misz Bella an't you? Lidi she'm gone. Misz Bella, fancy you going like that. Lidi, fancy her going like that.' Her face crumples with pain and disbelief. 'I don't hardly know what to do.'

Lidi crouches down beside Nana-Bess. She has never seen her Great-grandmother alive in the true sense, yet it is obvious now that she is dead.

The plain, ungainly Bess Smith lowers herself onto the hearth at Bella Nugent's feet and lays her head against the plump legs of the dead woman. Lidi is suddenly overcome by the poignancy of the tableau of the two old women on the hearth-side.

She has never given either of them much thought as persons like herself, especially Nana-Bess. Nana-Bess was just . . . there. In respect of anything to do with this house and Lidi's own home, she has always been everybody's willing servant. None of them has ever given much thought to Bess. She has always been so busy and content. Lidi cannot bear to see this unregarded side of Bess.

'Can I do anything, Nana-Bess?'

'Jist leave us a minute to say goodbye, then you can come and help me get her ready – you was her favourite.'

'Was I?'

'Oh yes.'

Lidi doesn't know what to make of that.

'Misz Bella was always glad when you came and sat and talked to her.'

Lidi leaves them together whilst she goes to draw the water that she knows they will need to lay out Great-grandmother.

The burning logs crack and hiss quietly as Bess Smith watches threads of white steam and soft ash coming through the front bars of the fire.

Presently she rouses and pats Bella's hand.

'I a have to leave you there a minute go and fetch the stuff so as we can get you laid down proper. We'll see to you my dear, me and young Lidi. We'll make you nice, you knows that Misz Bella don't you. You knows you always been able to trust me, and this is the last thing I'll be able to do for you. I'll always be grateful for what you done, when you gid me and my young Andrew a roof over our heads. Anybody else would a said "you go on, sling yer 'ook", but you never. You been a good friend, and I shan't never have a better if I lives to be a hunderd.'

A week later, Lidi stares down at the wooden box that contains her grandmother's plump, well-cared-for body.

For these last days since Gran has been in her plain deal coffin awaiting a suitable time and place for her burial, there has been a strange feeling of emptiness in the kitchen of Croud Cantle Farm. Gran has always been there, sitting like a soft, soft puppet with her feet in the hearth. Fed and changed and cleaned by Bess, she has been a part of the kitchen, like the beams and the lintels, the lead-lined sink and the red-tiled floor. Almost impossible to think of the place without any of them.

As she waits for the droning boredom of the burial service to end, the anger that has threatened to surface over the last days surges through her. She feels it trying to escape from her in the form of tears. Lidi Toose is not the crying sort, not like poor Nana-Bess who weeps unashamedly.

Lidi backs away from the graveside, turns and runs. Through the lych-gate, through a hole in the hedge and onto the track that runs beside the Dunnock.

When she reaches the place where she is hidden from view of the ford and the churchyard, she wrenches off a long wand of willow and thrashes the stream to within an inch of its life.

If I was God I wouldn't let people die. I wouldn't let people see everything and then take it away again, it's no better than giving a baby a comfit and snatching it away just when she tasted it.

People said, 'A mercy that she died.'

'Oh yes "a happy release" for her and the fambly.'

Fools!

Thwack at the silver water.

Oh yes God, better to be put in a wooden old box and buried like a rotten old carcase?

Fools!

Thwack at reeds and chickweed.

[78]

Better than sitting by your own hearth?

Better than having everybody you know near you?

Fool parson!

Fool neighbours!

She thrashes them all.

Biggest Fool!

She thrashes God — he was the worst One! He needn't have made it like that.

'Our Lidi, you are a blimmin idiot.'

The swish of the willow-wand, the thrashing of the water and her own heavy breath had prevented her from hearing Sarah coming.

'You mind your own business, Sarah Toose.'

'Look at yourself, you're wet through.'

Lidi suddenly realised that she was bare-headed and her hair and face were dripping.

The twin sisters looked at one another for a moment. Sarah was smiling with her eyes, then her mouth. Lidi began to smile.

'You're right, I am a blimmin fool. Is it all over?'

'Yes, they've gone home.'

'Did they send you to find me?'

'No. Why should they?'

'I don't know. I thought Pa might of got something to say to me.'

'I expect he will, you know what he's like.'

'Oh yes, if we have to give in to our feelings, we should do it where nobody can see. Well, I didn't make a peep-show of myself did I?'

Sarah looked Lidi up and down, taking in her water-darkened skirt, mud-clagged boots and tumbled hair. 'No our Lid, you'm fit to have your portrait done like that.'

Lidi lifted the willow-wand and flicked water at her sister.

Sarah leapt as though the water was red hot.

'Don't Lidi! My dress.'

This time it was Lidi who started back at the sharpness of her sister's tone.

A long iridescent dragonfly zipped up from the rushes causing them to halt in their steps and observe its hover and flight silently. They did it without thinking, from years of training by their Aunt Jude, who had taught them not only reading, writing and arithmetic, but observation of anything that presented itself.

A wandering train of thought led Sarah to say, 'Don't you ever wonder what our grandmother was like?'

'What made you think of that? Aunt Ju started talking about her only a day or two ago.'

Nobody ever spoke directly of their grandmother. They knew that there was some tragedy attached to her; she was rarely referred to and then only obliquely. And their grandfather might never have existed for he was never mentioned at all. How do small children become aware of forbidden subjects, banned references? Certainly Lidi and Sarah did not know *how*, but they instinctively knew *why*. Shame was attached to Mother's mother.

Then, only a couple of days ago for the first time, Lidi had heard her grandmother, her Aunt Jude's sister, spoken of directly. Lidi supposed that because of Great-grandmother dying thoughts of the past were in Aunt Ju's mind.

'We were out on Tradden, she was helping me look for some white violet plants I need for some trials.'

Their aunt (precisely, their great-aunt) had a stiff leg and a swollen knee-joint which prevented her on some days from climbing easily on the steep parts, so they were resting a while.

To be alone with Aunt Ju out on the chalk-hills was absolute happiness to Lidi. There was never a time of year when Lidi could not find pleasure in being out there on Tradden. From April, when pin-holes made by minute fritillary caterpillars appear in violet leaves and when newly-born leverets barely dry from their birth might be seen running almost as fast as their boxing jack-hare sires, the year round again to March, when the sun warms up the thin soil that covers the chalk-bones of the downs and life in the form of speedwell emerges from the brown tangle of last year's growth.

'She just suddenly started talking about her. "My sister used to bring me here for the white ones," she said, "and she used to tell a story about how they lost their colour. Your grandmother was a better storyteller than all the novelists put together." She was miles away, like she was talking to herself. "There's times – out here on Tradden especially – when I catch a glimpse of you or Sarah, and I'm forty years back and it's me and my sister. You are so like her in looks."'

'Did she really? That we look like her? I wonder why it is that they won't ever talk about her?'

'I don't know. But one day I mean to find out.'

For all Lidi's extrovert manner, she was sensitive, often to the point of anguish, to the emotions of other people, and that day on Tradden she realised that Aunt Ju's way with people might be a shield against the years without her sister. The sound of longing when she said, 'You are so like Jaen.' Lidi could imagine that her aunt wished for her to *be* Jaen.

Lidi had put her arms about her aunt's spare, wiry frame and lain her cheek against her cream-stranded red hair.

'Oh Aunt Ju, I am glad . . . you know . . . that you catch a glimpse of her.'

'She always called me Ju.'

Lidi and Sarah walked the rest of the way home in the kind of companionable silence that they used to experience when they were young – pleasure in one another's company. They were not close as sisters often are, but liked one another. It was good to have it again if only for half an hour – for they each were beginning to realise that they were drawing ever further apart.

HIGH AND LOWLY

ALMOST TWO DECADES of the new century were gone. The world beyond the Cantle Valley was not much talked of in the fields and barns of the village, nor at the ford, nor at the Dragon and Fount.

That Bella Nugent was dead was of more immediate interest than that Admiral Nelson had been killed at the Battle of Trafalgar, or that the Prime Minister had died with the words 'My Country' on his lips – not 'tha-tha' as the old lady had done.

And when the news of the Great and Good did come, it was often not direct, but by way of a prayer said by the vicar on behalf of the Cantle people – who were not encouraged to approach the new God as directly as they had approached the ancient ones. Even then, the news was filtered, and besides rural people had become less and less inclined to attend church.

They did not know when Napoleon had his Grand Army encamped on the cliffs of Boulogne, ready to be shipped across the Channel; nor when there was discussion in Parliament on the slave-trade; nor were they aware with what vigour and speed the great industrial towns were growing.

If during the second decade of the century such events did not appear to intrude upon the lives of the people of Cantle, the effects of world events and Parliamentary decisions reverberated.

The lowly are affected by the aftershock of great events.

Enclosure laws take away the last remnants of independence.

The price of corn is being raised by the Great and Good and the price of bread goes higher as wages go lower.

War ends and armies are disbanded.

Overnight, a nation's brave fighting men are reappraised and become feckless wanderers.

Its worn-out mariners are the scourge of the port towns.

The maimed spoil the peace.

All are hungry, and the hungry are a burden on the taxpayer.

At the end of the second decade, things are worse than ever for the rural community – the fillers of the foodbowl.

England is a Christian nation. It avows that it is un-Christian to see its poor and hungry die of hunger in hedge bottoms. It is generally thought, by any Parish official or landowner, to be prudent to get them into the next parish. (Thank God when they are over the boundary and become the problem of your good neighbours – who will do likewise.)

For lowly people of the Cantle Valley, there were enough problems to contend with without looking further. None of their sons were among the wandering soldiers, they had other wanderers – sons and daughters who came to maturity and could not find work of any kind in the area and had left for the smoky towns in the North.

And they had other problems to anticipate.

Crops could die back, become infested, be destroyed by scab, smut, weevils, red spiders, green-fly, hail, gale and flood. Entire flocks and herds of animals could begin to stagger or rot as some pestilence broke out.

In the hundred-and-one daily battles they fought to keep bread upon their own tables, and to keep beef and cake and wine and brandy, and little delicacies to tempt the palate, upon the tables of the Great and Good, the cottagers kept their heads down.

They had already glimpsed the future – had seen it in the mechanical threshers and winnowers.

STONEBRIDGE SERVANTS

WHEN ALEC JAMES, breathing close to her ear and flicking his long eyelashes on her neck, slid his hand down the back of Ann Collins' skirt at the Spring Dance, he thought he was unobserved. It was unfortunate that, although Ann's husband, Art, was doing something similar to May Pope at the time, he happened to see Alec's stealthy hand and his wife's movement to ease the waistband of her skirt. Until now, Alec had tried his secret looks and delightful fingers only upon unmarried girls, and until recently Ann had been one of them.

Mid-caress, Art Collins abandoned May Pope and laid Alec flat, to the merry sound of tambour and fiddle.

Art and his friends were some of Tazey James' best customers at the Dragon, and Taze had had enough of his wild son's 'poop-noddying everywhere about'; it did business no good to always have some 'intended' or father or brother of one of the village maids come complaining to Taze.

"Tis a wonder somebody an't flattened you before. If Art had a knocked your teeth in, it's no more than you deserve. You'm twenty-two, boy, and I've had enough. If you buckled down to it here, it wouldn't be so bad, but you an't never took to innkeeping.'

Alec could not deny it, he would do anything rather than that.

'Well,' his father said, 'Albert Barringer says he will put in a word for you and you can go to him as his Under-footman.'

And so it was that Alec provided for himself some suitable plain stockings and black shoes, and was provided by his employer with breeches, two pairs of silk stockings, a set of dark-green livery, a pair of overalls, a waistcoat, a fustian jacket and a white jean jacket for answering the door or helping Mister Barringer in the serving of breakfast to the family.

It was a few weeks before he was ready to serve breakfast, but Alec was no fool and learned quickly. Although Taze James' old friend Albert Barringer had spoken for Alec, as Butler he was much too elevated to have the training of Alec – this was in the hands of Wilfred Harker, the Footman.

Alec had to rise very early in order to get through the dirty work of cleaning boots and cutlery and trimming lamps before he put on his clean jean jacket to lay the cloth for breakfast.

The day was long and the work continuous. He was at Mister Harker's beck and call. But he took to the work, having at last discovered something he found congenial, even the dirty early morning work. The great house was still only just stirring, only the scullery maids and maids of all work moving quietly about. He sat before the fire that the maid had bellowed up to a good flame and blacked his master's boots, wiped his mistress's out-door shoes, and worked longest and hardest on the footwear of Mister Barringer and Mister Harker.

Alec was no fool.

One of the maids would brew up the tea that had been saved from the tea-table the day before – a good strong black brew with a pinch of soda and a lump off the sugar loaf. Being no fool, he winked his eyes at the girls below-stairs and kept his hands on his work.

The first time that Sarah saw the new Under-footman was when she returned along the front drive one morning with Ninn. He had been in the hallway in his white jean jacket and, seeing her coming, flourished open the door. She recognised him at once; it was not likely that she would have forgotten him, for there had been a time a few years back when Lidi had practically stalked him to get a glimpse of him. 'Oh come on, Sarah, come with me, I can't go by myself.' And so Sarah had gone wherever Lidi suspected Alec might pass by. It hadn't lasted long, but Sarah knew who it was who opened the door.

'Alec James.'

For a moment he was non-plussed; there were plenty of girls he had sweet-hearted on a day at the fair and had forgotten next day, but he was sure that he would not have forgotten this one. Yes . . . this neat one with the neat waist and round bosom so close to the surface of the dark blue dress . . . this one with the golden-red hair loosened by the wind and curling round her neck.

'You don't know me?'

'I remember the hair.'

Sarah smiled. 'People often do.'

'I know, the two little twins!'

Sarah nodded. 'Yes, it's not often people ever thought of us as separate when we were young. It's only since I've been here that I'm Sarah Toose, and not one of the twins.'

'Toose. A course. Your father's the treeman, the one who makes speeches. I've heard him, 'tis a wonder he an't been up before the Magistrates some of the things he says.'

Sarah flushed with anger . . . and with something else. She did not ever like to hear her father criticised, but she was beginning to wonder whether his behaviour in regard to speaking in the open was thought of as rather eccentric in a man such as he. She suspected he made a fool of himself.

Head erect, she said, 'My father is John Toose who runs the horticultural business in Cantle. Come along, Ninn, it's time you was washed ready for your lunch.'

Into the oyster of cotton pillow-slips, beautiful surroundings, dark-blue dresses and elegant order, came a grain of grit. Alec James' presence. Sarah felt its irritation as she lay in bed that night listening to the cedars swishing like water.

Alec James was not the first grain to have kept Sarah awake recently.

The other – Brendan Lewis, nephew of Mister Harker, who had come to work in the stables, where she now took Ninn each day to see the pony that had been bought for his birthday.

At the end of her term of hire, Sarah had not, as she had expected, been dismissed when a tutor came for Ninn, but was kept on with no specific duties other than to continue, whenever his lessons permitted, the walks and exercising.

'Osbert my dear,' Mrs Delphine had said, 'humour me in this. The girl is good with the boy. Have you seen one tantrum since she has been here?'

The master of Stonebridge Manor had to admit that the previous quite shaming behaviour that the boy had displayed before guests on occasion in the past was no longer a problem. These days the boy could be brought before a group of their visitors taking tea and not behave like a squealing pig.

'Another thing, Osbert, I think the girl may have the makings of a lady's maid. My Mama once took a girl and trained her up. And Mama says there's no better way than to make your own girl rather than take on one trained in a household where standards may not be high.'

One girl more or less made little difference to the household economy if she was useful. But the number of servants and their rig, was always of consequence to a gentleman whose fortune had an ancestry of only one generation. Above all, a gentleman in Osbert's position on the frail ladder of social class was foolish if he did not heed the mama of a wife who had breeding and birth. Whilst he did not always treat his wife and children with any degree of refinement – he had no wish for the world to think that he had none.

So now Sarah was between Under Nursery-nurse and budding lady's maid.

Life at Stonebridge Manor was entirely suited to Sarah.

Until now it was calm and unruffled. Ninn still spent time with her, but was now slipping into the role of little student. Miss Truckle had left, and Mister Thrope had set up a little schoolroom at the top of the house.

Thrope was thin, young, kindly and entirely lacking in the imagination necessary to make learning interesting. When Sarah got a glimpse of the dry methods he used, she began to realise what an extraordinary teacher Aunt Jude had been.

She often sat doing some small mending of Ninn's clothes listening to the droning of the learning by rote and thinking of the way Aunt Jude had drawn them both into a great desire to learn.

Out on Tradden – 'Lidi, you shall bring me fifty blackberries and Sarah fifty sloes, and if you get the right number we shall make . . .? Tarts. How many little tarts . . . if we put ten blackies and one sloe in each tart? And how many sloes shall we have left over?'

Listening to stories made up by Jude and then learning how to do the same.

Learning to sit patiently watching a dragonfly emerge, observe how a leaf-like shape became a chalkhill blue, or a small copper or a Red Admiral trying to fathom how its wings worked.

Looking at things under the magnifier.

Ask, talk, read. Make rows of acorns and divide them up. All of it leading to learning numbers, reading, writing, observation.

None of the droning, chanting or trying to make sense of a lifeless illustration.

No wonder, when his morning lessons were ended, that he was almost boiling over with boisterous energy. Lately he could hardly wait to get to the pony. Sarah took him to the stables, but she could see that her days of having charge of Ninn for part of his time were almost ended.

Now it was all Brendan. Brendan in whose care 'Winnow' the pony was. Brendan whose father had been a groom. Brendan who knew everything there was to know about horses and ponies.

If Alec James' dark-lashed heavy eyes and one raised eyebrow hinted of experience and secret knowledge, Brendan's head-back clear stare held nothing that could not be immediately seen. Physically and in their colouring they were quite alike. The same height, about seventy inches, brown hair and eyes, Alec's the straighter, straight noses and rounded chins. They both wore the thick sideburns almost to the chin that young men of the day favoured.

Until now, Sarah had not been particularly interested in any young man. Cantle youths seemed dull, and the three years that she had been at Stonebridge, she had had very little chance of talking to any young man at all. So, whilst thoughts of Alec and Brendan kept her awake, it was with a certain amount of pleasure. Lidi's period of girlish besotted devotion to Alec had, at the time, caused Sarah to have antipathy toward him.

Now in his white jean jacket and with his long sideburns framing his good looks, she suddenly saw that he was an attractive man.

But then so was Brendan.

WICKHAM FAIR

BY THE TIME Luce Draper had lived in Cantle for a year, he no longer awoke sweating and heart pounding as bloody horses reared up over him. By the time that he had been there for almost three, he had lost all trace of the accent and again spoke the low, slow, broad-vowelled speech of his ancestors.

He was now grown to manhood. His youthful thinness had been worked into lean muscularity. In the summer fields, the sun bleached his hair to almost white. In that time of real distress in rural Hampshire, he was very fortunate in being taken to work on the Park Manor Estate.

But being taken on was not like it was in the old days. Then, a labourer or milk-maid might be taken on from Michaelmas to Michaelmas; these days however, with four people for every one job, employers took workers on short hire. In Hampshire, wages fell to starvation level. A single man earned less than a married man, who received only eight shillings for a full week's work.

But a strong young man like Luce could usefully be put to any job going. His back was still strong and his breath came heartily and he could work from dawn to dusk and return to eat under the Croud Cantle roof rather than have his feet under his master's table.

At Croud Cantle he was fussed over by Nana-Bess, who had been longing for a hungry youth to take the place of her own Andrew, now settled under his own roof in Motte.

Wickham Fair had been one of the most popular events in the rural calendar for six hundred years. Wagons and carts were organised from every village in south Hampshire.

John Toose, having an order for hedging to fulfil for a large house on the outskirts of Wickham, said that he would drive their cart and would take Bess, Jude, Tansy, Lidi, Luce and little Jack too. Bess was almost persuaded to go, but she liked home best.

'I'll tell you what, why don't you let little Jack stop along of me then. When you gets back, we a have a nice little feast on the table for thee.'

In the ordinary run of things the little boy's handicap was not too difficult. He had enough vision to be able to distinguish mass and movement and could get about the house perfectly well, so long as objects were not moved from their usual place, or unexpected ones introduced. His main problem was with small things such as ruts and potholes which he could not see at all. So long as she did not have him under her feet for too long at any one time, Tansy coped well enough. But they all knew that she loved a dance or a supper and, best of all, a fair. So Jack was to have a day being treated like a little prince by Nana-Bess who would do whatever he wanted.

The wagons set out in the early May dawn rumbling over Tradden Raike and then out on to the recently-completed Portsmouth road. The air was fresh and clear, so that from the top of Tradden Raike a pattern of fields and hedges could be seen for a distance of ten miles to the horizon where the rolling chalkhills met banks of fast dissolving white cloud.

Field edges, with bluebells and red campion, and pale arum lilies at their roots, were white with blossom which gave off a scent of vanilla as the sun began to warm the morning. Every growing thing seemed to be giving off its message of colour and scent.

Yellow of buttercup, broom, gorse and weasel snout; pink of herb robert, cuckoo-flower and crab-apple; white, garlic, hawthorn and parsley. But except perhaps for Jude Nugent, there was probably not a soul who gave any of these a second glance – even Lidi, who had been imbued with some of her Aunt Ju's love of the native flowers of the chalkhills, was in animated conversation with Tansy about some of the things they hoped would be on sale at the fair. There was bread and lard and swipes to drink aboard the Toose wagon, and prospects of a good day out.

When they reached Droxford they had become part of a line: of carts, coaches and wagons of every size and description; of goose-girls with their tar-footed flocks; of drovers who frequently blocked the way, and of packmen who touted the captives in halted traffic.

John dropped his passengers off at the gates of the park where he was to make his delivery, and Lidi, Jude, Tansy and Luce walked the last half-mile along the verge into the village.

Tansy chattered to Jude, and Luce put a tentative, friendly arm across Lidi's shoulders, tightening it when she caught his hand in hers.

'He's a rare wonder, that lad.' Tansy's words, at Luce's apparent unawareness of his own physique. 'Jo Bunce used to think he was God's gift to the maids, but young Luce is a prince compared to Jo.'

And so thought many girls as they watched Luce's long back bent in the action of scything or his long legs striding through the village often with an ancient hat crammed upon his shapely head. He laughed a lot and showed his good teeth with none missing. In the harvest fields, girls teased him for his blond curls, pulling them to watch them spring back into place. Luce Draper at twenty was handsome, fair and wholesome. Yet seemed quite unaware of his good looks.

Lidi Toose, however, was not unaware of how she looked, or of how she and Luce complemented one another.

She had known since girlhood, that men found her attractive. Her smallness made them feel protective towards her, whilst her flaming hair caused them to be wary. Her reputation for hot temper was based upon the colour of her hair, as was the belief that her hair also signalled a 'hot' nature. She did not try to disabuse either of those beliefs. Nor had any man so far got close enough to test the latter.

She knew also that she had a reputation for being too clever for her own good, which was a challenge to young men who could not read and write. Her figure was more voluptuous than Sarah's, not so neat-waisted, fuller breasted, altogether softer and not so inclined to be stiff-backed as was her sister. Although she never teased, Lidi Toose knew that she could draw a man's eyes to her. But to most, she was an enigma – a face and a figure with a brain. Of all the young men she had come across in adult life, only Luce seemed not to feel somewhat intimidated by her. Luce and Uncle Will – but then Will Vickery was accustomed to another red-haired enigma.

Luce, being now almost part of the family, often partnered Lidi at village functions, but only as one member of the family partners another. On Fair Day, the way that they walked along the road to the village signalled a change in their relationship. The tall, fair, handsome young man, and the pretty red-haired maid in close familiarity.

'Shall you take me on the swing-boats, Luce?'

He had never seen her skittish and light-hearted like this. 'Aye, and to see the lion if you like.'

'And the fight in the Star yard?'

The thought obviously excited him, he tightened his grasp on her shoulder. 'A bare-fist fight, Lidi Toose? A maid don't never want to see cracked noddles and bloody noses?'

She pulled his arm playfully so that he was forced to twirl around with her, then she pulled him down and said close to his ear, 'Nay lad, 'tis only their bare breasts and tight pantaloons that maids like to watch.'

Although Wickham was not a town, it was much larger than Cantle. The focal-point of the place was its extremely wide centre, bordered by a mixture of tall elegant new houses and an assortment of more lowly houses and cottages, and a hedged field. It was in the latter area, close to the forded stream near the Star of Hope, that the Gypsies gathered once a year to run their horses and meet to exchange their sons and daughters with one another, keeping the Gypsy blood within their own kind but not within their own family.

The cattle and sheep pens were away from the main square, which was given over to stallholders selling baskets, leather goods, turnery, gew-gaws, sweetmeats and cooked foods; booths with fancy awnings and lurid pictures of the grotesque and wonderful to be seen inside for a penny; and tricksters with three thimbles and a pea, or a few fast-moving cards.

The hiring part of the fair was little more than a mixed crowd of skilled and unskilled unemployed, who would take any kind of work, and a few farmers who could pick and choose those they wanted till harvest. This was always done early in the day, and the rest of the time was given over to trading the herds and flocks – and all the fun of the fair.

When the three women and Luce had wandered round for an hour and were taking a bit of refreshment on some benches outside the King's Head, Lidi suddenly jumped up.

'It's Sarah!'

And so it was. Sarah dressed in a spotted yellow dress, high-necked and a large fly-away collar, a dip-brimmed hat and dainty pointed-toe boots of soft leather – all of which had been generously passed on to Sarah by her mistress, all of which would have been recognised by London fashion as two years out of date, but in places like Cantle and Wickham, it was a very stylish and novel outfit.

Although she wrote regularly, since Great-grandmother's death, she had visited home only a few times, and they did not expect to see her in Wickham – and certainly not accompanied by two young men.

Lidi's pleased exclamation upon seeing her sister was out before she realised that one of the young men was . . . oh Lord, Alec James. Lidi almost blushed for the memory of her girlish passion for him. She was pleased that Luce was with them.

Alec James wasn't a patch on Luce.

Whilst Luce had become muscular and healthy-looking in the years since he had been in Cantle, Alec James had started to look slightly worn at the edges. He still had a great deal of attractiveness for any woman, but he had the slightly puffy appearance of a man who would be better suited putting his body to heavier work than serving breakfast, cleaning knives and raising the odd eyebrow at women.

In her letters home, Sarah had mentioned casually that 'Tazey James' son (you remember him I expect Lidi, his name's Alec) has come here to work as Under-footman. Of course, most of his duties are below stairs, whilst my own are with my mistress.'

That Sarah was now a fully-trained lady's maid showed in every step and gesture, as she made her way through the crowds towards the King's Head.

One of the reasons that she had not been home on some occasions was that her mistress had allowed her to use her days off to go to Winchester to learn hairdressing from a master of the art. Recently, she had travelled to Bath, Harrogate and London with Mrs Delphine.

They knew that Sarah was in danger of becoming quite a lady herself, but they had not suspected such a transformation.

'Lidi!' She kissed her sister on both cheeks and hugged her warmly. 'Aunt Jude!' A kiss for Jude. 'And Tansy – well just fancy. And Luce too. I never suspected at all that you might come to Wickham.'

'We don't as a rule – well, you know that – it's usually Blackbrook or Waltham, but Pa was coming and the Estate sent two wagons.'

'Did you come on the Stonebridge wagon?' Tansy asked.

'Goodness no. Master Ninn wanted to come, so the Master said that he might go in the little trap and Ninn begged his mother for me to go with him, and Brendan to drive. Oh la, I forgot. Alec you know of course, and this is Brendan.'

The introductions were acknowledged by all, and the unknown Brendan was weighed up by Tan, who liked to look at anything that fitted his breeches well – and both these young men certainly did that. Brendan in a groom's jacket, breeches and short boots, Alec in a cut-away short-tailed coat, checked trousers and shoes.

'Sarah, you shan't keep them two young men to yourself like that when I've got none because your Pa hasn't shown up yet.' She patted the seat next to her. 'You, young Brendan, come and tell me what our little girl gets up to in that fine house you all live in. If you asts me, be the look of the three on you, I shouldn't mind being in service myself. Why I never seen such a nice lot of get-up.'

Brendan smiled. 'I ought to go and look for Master Ninn; we left him to go and look at the mermaid and the two-ton man.'

'Ah, he'll be all right, that's one thing about Wickham Fair, you can't get lost. He'll find you.'

So Brendan, Alec and Sarah joined the Cantle party. For all Sarah's finery, Lidi was pleased to see that the old Sarah was still there – changed, in that her eyebrows and eyelashes that had hitherto been (like Lidi's) pale red, were now darkened, she did not stride out like country women as Lidi and her Aunt Jude did, nor was her complexion as pink as theirs, but she was still very much Lidi's twin in looks.

Aunt Jude, as usual, said very little, but sat back taking everything in – as Lidi knew, to think over and, at the end of the day, write up in her great thick journal.

She ventured one enquiry. 'You like the work as a footman, Alec – it's a lot different from innkeeping and harvesting and the like.'

'No Ma'am, I an't a footman these days. Like Sarah here, my master took a liking to me and trained me up. I was lucky, there at the right moment. My master's old valet met a lady in Bath, married her and left my master in the lurch as you might say. I filled in and I'm now the Master's personal servant, make his bath ready, see to his clothes, help him to tie his stock, and dress his hair – I can't call myself a valet yet, but it's what I aim to be.'

'Is he a sick man?' Jude asked.

'No Ma'am. You should just see him ride to hounds and play at tennis.'

'Oh, I just wondered – with him not being able to tie his own stock, I thought he might have lost an arm at Waterloo or somewhere.'

Lidi bit back a grin. Aunt Ju. She could put a sharp edge on her tongue and look so innocent that a person never knew just what she meant until later.

The three young men drank large pots of ale and were soon the best of companions, talking of horses, racing and fist-fights.

'There's to be a bout tonight? Shall you be here?' Luce asked, but the Stonebridge party had only the liberty of the early part of the day and must be back well before dinner so that Sarah could dress her mistress's hair.

Soon Master Ninn Broughlake found them. At ten years old, the face that had often buried itself in Sarah's shoulder when she first came to work in the nursery, was still there. But a lot of the fear had gone, and the chubbiness. He seemed a polite and likeable boy.

'Well now,' Tansy said when they had finished their food and drink, 'I don't know about all you lot, but I'm not waiting about any longer for John Toose. I've come here to enjoy myself and that's what I'm going to do. He a find us. You all do as you like. I'm going down to the Gypsies to get my fortune.'

Aunt Jude didn't want her fortune told, but she said that she would go with Tan for company.

Ninn begged to go off and see some more monsters. In fact, the only monster he wished to see was the bare-breasted mermaid with a fish-tail just below where her legs divided. He had already spent a great number of pennies on her. He was allowed to go only until the church clock struck two; if he wasn't outside the King's Head by that time, then they would be late back and the Master would demand to know the reason why. 'And we shall tell him and all,'Alec said. 'We can't afford to be in the Master's bad books.'

It still appeared to Ninn that to be in the position of a servant and be able to leave Stonebridge any time it suited and not be tied to it for ever, was an enviable one.

Still, he promised and Sarah knew that he was to be trusted.

They walked along the square and down into Bridge Street. At the bottom a crowd had gathered beside the river and they pushed in to see what was interesting.

Oh Lord! Sarah's low exclamation was barely audible.

Lidi put her hand over her mouth and hunched her shoulders at Sarah.

More people had crushed up behind them and it was difficult to retreat. Not that Lidi wanted to, but it was obvious that Sarah did.

'Why look,' Luce said, ''tis your father, Lidi.'

And so it was.

'I thought he'd stopped all that,' Sarah said in Lidi's ear.

'Did you? No, since he saw what happened that time in

Manchester, where Luce was and got hurt, he's been doing quite a lot of it.'

'I'm not stopping, Lidi. I could never abide it making a show of himself like that.'

'It's not a show! He's doing what other people are afraid to do. He's speaking out against what's wrong.'

'He's making a show of himself and a show of me in front of everybody.'

'If you're ashamed of Pa, you should be ashamed of yourself.'

'Don't you realise he's against the people who gave me this dress, who have turned me from a village girl into a lady's maid? He's against poor little Ninn, and Mrs Delphine . . .'

Lidi looked aghast at her sister. Sarah, who idolised their Pa when she was young, who would never leave him alone, always taking his hand or climbing upon his lap.

Their exchange had been quick and low with none of the young men aware of the rift that was taking place only feet from them.

'Goodbye Lidi. Come on, Alec, Brendan, it's time we were going.'

'Hey Sarah,' Alec said. 'I've just realised who that is – it's your father. We must listen. Come on Brendan.'

The final humiliation as people turned in her direction.

Her father was on his rostrum again, making a speech at a fair.

Flush-faced, she followed Alec and Brendan as they pushed their way into the crowd.

'. . . and so it comes about, Friends, that these are hard and hungry times.

'These are changing times.

'These are disturbing and degrading times.'

There is a thoughtful nodding agreement from the crowd.

'The hardship and hunger is Ours when our neighbours cannot find honest labour. Our aged fathers and mothers, who have laboured all their lives, are unable to sit warm in their closing years. The changes hurt Ours when young men and women – the virile and sturdy labour upon which this country relies – must tramp the roads like vagabonds.

'But . . . the degradation is Theirs.'

Lidi stands in the crowd and listens to the words that she has heard over and over again since she was a child, yet is still thrilled at his words.

'Enclosure! Improvement! Progress!' John Toose ticks these off on his fingers. 'Yes. Yes. Yes.'

'We are told that this country will weaken if land is not enclosed, if our commons are not taken over and "improved".' He sneers at the word and there is mumbled agreement. 'If we do not always push forward.'

He nods, changes his tack. Reasonable. 'And so it might be.'

Then he plunges in with practised skill, piling on the rhetorical questions.

'But could we not have improved the land . . . together?

'Could we not hold the land as we once held that same land in strips . . . together?

'Do men and women who have tilled the land throughout time need a master?'

They have heard it all before, and they will gladly hear it again, warming themselves on the words, the ideas, the ideals. They know what is coming.

Lidi knows yet her heart rises at the stirring of the crowd. Pa is so good. For a moment the thought of Sarah turning away from him, pushing through the crowd, flashes into her mind, but her father's passion pushes everything else aside.

Now Luce is gradually making his way through the crowd. He takes Lidi's hand as they stand near to the front. He has a look of admiration in his eyes. Lidi can feel his hand trembling with the passion that is working inside him.

'Is Speenhamland fair? No! It is unfair, undemocratic, degrading.' His words come faster.

'It is degrading.' Another pause. 'Degrading . . . yes . . . but not to us . . . no, no, friends, we are not degraded by a system that pauperises decent, honest people; that sends our young people from their villages; that forbids a man to give his father a wild pheasant for the pot, and forbids a woman to take snapwood from the enclosed commons for her mother.' He slaps large flat hands together.

'It is They who are degraded.

'To those of you who still have work, listen to your consciences. Think of your power. Ask yourselves, where would your masters be without your bent backs, your strong hands and sweating brows? Where would they be without your skills?

'Friends, many of you have no doubt heard of the Combinations . . .'

Suddenly, as though the word 'Combinations' was a signal, six men who had been at the front of the crowd rush forward, seize

John Toose. Four of them try to drag him into the warehouse in front of which he has been standing. Suddenly Luce plunges into them, throwing punches in all directions.

'Let him go!'

Someone tries to grab Luce's arms. He kicks out, placing his boot in the man's groin, and he goes down writhing.

Now John Toose is shouting, 'Leave it be, Luce,' trying to tell Luce to go, but Luce is in a frenzy of anger. Perhaps a memory of that other time when he was a boy quietly listening to Henry Hunt, rises in him. Perhaps he is in that other crowd with horses rearing, swords flashing.

One of the six constables has unrolled a paper and read a gabble. The crowd rushes to leave, taking Lidi with them. She tries to struggle against the tide. To get to Luce.

In a minute, the crowd has dissolved, and Lidi finds herself standing at the entrance to an empty yard.

Over the tops of the houses, she can hear the cries of the street-traders and booth-holders. The constables threaten to charge her if she does not move on. She goes back to find Tan and Aunt Ju.

Luce, realising what a fool he had been to get himself taken unnecessarily, had apologised for being the worse for drink and they had let him go.

16

AFTER THE FAIR

THE SIGHT OF Luce throwing himself into the mêlée had gone through Lidi like fire. With that action, he had thrown himself as well into the family and into her life. His action committed himself to them. And now Lidi wanted nothing so much as Luce Draper body and soul. But in the state of emotion in which she found herself on the journey home, it was not his soul that concerned her.

Luce had found the horse and cart, made it ready and then went to where the three women were sitting, rather stunned at what had happened and deciding what to do next. They had already discovered that John was likely to be taken to the Botley Magistrate.

The journey home was greatly different from the outward one. The big cart, now empty of its load of trees, seemed to emphasise John Toose's absence. Tansy kept asking variations of the same question, 'Whatever will happen, Lidi?' 'What are we going to do, Jude?'

All along the Droxford road was a trail of homeward trekking traffic, reluctant to make any haste, drowsy, fagged-out by the crushing into one day of enough indulgence to carry them over harsh days to the next bit of a fling. Lidi wanted to whip up the horses and get home where they could sort things out in peace and quiet.

Luce was holding the reins and Lidi sat beside him, trying to ignore Tansy's speculations as to what would happen.

Although she did not look directly at Luce, she was aware of every inch of him.

She cast her eyes at his hands, loose and easy on the reins, at his legs spread wide. His weathered hands glistened with near-white hairs, and protruded from sleeves that were never long enough for his long arms. His legs too went on after his trouser bottoms ended, showing inches of stocking and boot.

Without realising, she said aloud, 'You could do with some longer britches.'

He stretched out his long leg and considered it.

'Ah, I suppose I do.'

His unconcern was marvellous to Lidi.

Compare that wonderful leg in its too-short fustian, to that of Alec James in its checked wool.

Compare Alec's puffy, though admittedly good-looking, face with Luce's firm lines.

Compare the suggestive looks that Alec gave to the clear stare of Luce.

If Aunt Ju and Tansy had not been in the back of the cart, Lidi thought that she could not have stopped herself reaching out to touch Luce's long thigh muscles moving slightly with the jolting of the cart. For a moment, Lidi wondered if she had again spoken her thoughts aloud. In the deep green light that filtered through the over-arching trees through which they were driving, he moved in his seat and for the rest of the journey his left leg moved gently against her right, and she could not tell whether it had happened by chance.

Back home, they dropped Jude and Tansy off and Luce went with Lidi to see to the horse and off-load the carrying frames.

'Lidi?' He stood hesitantly in the shed with a roll of sacking under each arm. He dropped them and came towards her. 'I'm sorry about your father, I shall be glad to do anything to help. I dare say there's going to be things that will have to be done to do with . . . you know . . . what happened today.'

Lidi nodded. 'That's nice, Luce.'

'Perhaps this an't the time or place but . . .' He bent, held her gently by the shoulders and kissed her full on the mouth.

If it had been his intention that the kiss should be that of a tentative lover trying his luck, he had not bargained for Lidi's response.

Lidi was surprised at his deftness.

She asked him if he would give a hand with her Pa's chores. It was late when they finished. Tansy had gone to bed, red-eyed but pacified by Luce's promise to see to the carting and the heavy work until they knew what was going to happen to John. She had held his face and told him that he was the best lad in the world and that they couldn't do without him now.

Later, Lidi and Luce sat before the dwindling fire, she in her coarse working skirt, he with his shirt open at the neck and sleeves rolled up high. Everything that could be said about the situation of the Toose family had, for the present, been said. The necessary work of the day was done.

The kiss they had exchanged earlier had changed everything.

'A dish of broth before you go up the lane, Luce?'

I know exactly what I'm doing.

The womanly, physical side of her nature that had first manifest itself around Alec James when she was fourteen or so, had often disturbed her.

At maypoles and dances and Harvest Homes, she often found herself becoming aroused by the tight hold of a young drover's arms, the heavy grasp of a labourer's work-horny hands or the smell of hard male bodies sweating, swirling close in a chain dance. At those times, a masculine mouth framed and emphasised by its surrounding beard, a shirt opened at the chest to cool its wearer, or muscles flexing beneath corduroy and flannel caused Lidi's nature to come close to the surface, blinding her momentarily to anything except his maleness.

Often, she would be brought back from the brink by the natural response of her partner, who, recognising the effect he was having upon her, would take the next opportunity he could find of holding on to her waist as far forward and as high up under the armpits as could be managed in a public place, or pressing her close to him so that she might be in no doubt of his virility – and her fantasy was broken.

Her sudden coolness caused many a young man to suggest that Lidi Toose was frightened to death of it, and it'd do her a lot of good if somebody got hold of her and gave her what she really wanted even if she didn't know it.

I've always known that it would be Luce, from the first day he came.

'It'd be nice.'

Lidi added a bit of snapwood to the fire and swung the cotterel over it, and they sat watching the dry wood catch and flare. The long clock in its warped pine case, clicked, whirred and chinged eleven. Five hours, and the sky would grow light again.

'Dear sakes, we shan't get much sleep tonight, there's an order to be got ready for Waltham tomorrow.'

'Don't worry Lidi, I'll be round here first cock crow.'

As he reached to pat her hand, she held on to it, turning it palm up. A warm, dry hand, its lines and nails workstained. Tracing the line with one finger, she said, 'You should have come with us and had your fortune told.'

He snapped his hand shut over hers, took it to his mouth and kissed it. The first such contact they had ever made in the three years since he had been taken into the family. Her finger continued its tracing. On his cheek, soft, almost invisible bristle like a youth's, flaring nostrils, thick fair eyebrows. She drew the shape of his mouth, he parted his lips, she outlined his teeth, explored his tongue. Briefly he held her fingertips between his lips. Sweetly, gently but not passionately. Sweetness was not enough for her.

He slipped from his chair and sat at her feet, his long legs drawn up, resting his back against her skirt, held his hand, palm upwards over his shoulder. 'I'd rather it was you that read it than some old Gypsy.'

'Perhaps you wouldn't like to hear what it's going to be.'

'Tell me.'

'Turn round then.'

He smiled at her over his shoulder. 'No. It might not be the right fortune, and I shouldn't like you to see a grown man cry.'

The belief that Lidi Toose did not know what it was that she wanted was not true. She knew it very well. But before her every day, she had Tan and Aunt Ju as models of the choice that women had when it came to loving with a man.

Five years ago Tansy had been the 'beauty of the four parishes', then in one moment in the middle of a dance she had confused the red suggestion of John Toose's smiling mouth with the implication of a rosy future with him – and had committed herself to dependency upon her lover.

Forty years ago Aunt Ju had seen clearly what was what, and had committed herself to independence, and had spent her entire womanhood longing for the physical satisfaction of the love that she and Will Vickery had always had for one another.

Now, Tansy had grown pinched by the restriction on her natural exuberance, by her ties to blind baby Jack and her dependence upon a husband old enough to be her father.

And Aunt Ju had grown pinched from her independence of the man that she loved.

In the end Aunt Ju had fared no better than Tan; she never fulfilled her ambition to make a permanent school for the village children, nor did she have youthful years with her lover. In her spinster state, she had been as bound to domesticity as any wife.

What usually happened to Lidi when her momentary arousal subsided, was that she saw the object of her fleeting passion in the bleak rustic light of his everyday setting. She saw how easy it would be to find herself with a dull husband and a babe at the breast as so many village girls did. She always felt chilled at the thought of a narrow escape, and warm ·with thankfulness that some small event had prevented her from throwing caution to the winds for the moment's satisfaction.

Tansy turned in the bed just above their heads, creaking the wooden frame. The dry wood had flared itself into a red glow. Lidi seemed to watch each second pass, everything highlighted and so slowed down that she was able to observe and remember the detail – the smell of the tight blond curls of his warm hair, the small snag in his shirt-sleeve, the line where the sun had caught his neck and arms.

And her emotions.

We will make love. Does he know it? Is he only flirting me? The times I've wondered how it would be, the times it nearly was. Now it will be.

She had grown to know herself, how roused up she always got at a show of defiance against authority, resistance against convention. But until now those emotions had never coincided with the right partner and the opportunity. It now seemed inevitable that this would be the outcome of today. Almost twenty years old, and for five years she had held back her strong desire for physical satisfaction. The times that she had wished that she had been a man.

Now however, not only were her feelings towards Luce changed, the two of them were thrown together more than they had ever been. The fact that they each respected, and wanted the respect of, the other as much as they loved, helped keep them from falling into one another's arms, as did the fact that Luce took his meals and slept at Croud Cantle and the overwhelming fact that the continuance of Toose's of Cantle was Lidi's responsibility.

She slid down and knelt facing him and placed her small palm on top of his long slender one, pressing the cushion of flesh against his. 'That's the fortune that counts, Luce.'

He looked down at their hands, puzzled. 'I thought it was told from the lines.'

'Lines only tell you how long you're going to live, whether you will wed and how many children, or if you're going on a journey . . . it's the mound of love that counts.'

'Ah Lidi, it's when you talk in riddles like you do sometimes that makes me know that my fortune isn't the one I want – you're too clever for me.'

She kissed him full on the mouth and he responded.

'The mound of love it's called.' She kissed that fleshy cushion of his hand. 'What good is a long life line, if this part's all flat and hard?'

He looked closely at the wet mark left by her mouth. 'Go on then, tell it.'

'Are you a virgin, Luce?'

He looked almost shocked. 'Yes.'

'You might not have been. I'm glad that you are. You was pretty thick with Primmie Jepp at the Spring Supper.'

'It wasn't nothing.'

'It's only that I want you to go careful. I don't want to get poddy. You understand?'

'Lord, Lidi, you don't want much do you.'

She held her palm to his mouth. He kissed it, then she pressed their two hands together as though in a primitive blood-rite.

'See Luce, just a perfect match.'

'Are you . . .?'

'What? A virgin?' Facing him, close, and smiling, she drew him so that he could do nothing but kiss her.

'I am now. Ask me again tomorrow.'

He did not go back to his room at Croud Cantle Farm that night. Tansy found him curled up in a blanket before the hearth when she came down to stir the fire at dawn.

17

For the best part of the next year, between the May of 1822 when John Toose was arrested and the following spring, Lidi had the running of the holding.

When he was arrested he had been charged with Sedition, but this was later reduced to one of Incitement, to which a shorter sentence applied.

Because of the work involved in keeping going the Toose Holding and Croud Cantle, it was impossible for any of them to visit Winchester very often, so Bess Smith took a room in a lodging house and spent a year going to and from the gaol with John's food and clean clothes.

When a man with a good reputation such as John's is imprisoned in such circumstances some people will shrink away from association so Toose's of Cantle lost one or two orders. But these were compensated for by other people who wished to show that they knew an injustice had been done and were prepared to show it.

As a consequence of the months without John, a number of changes came about.

Luce no longer took work on the Goodenstone Estate, but worked on both the Toose place and Croud Cantle Farm. With Bess gone to Winchester this meant that Jude had to do all the market baking and cooking, so Luce helped out with some of the work about the farm, until Will Vickery rode up one day with his belongings.

'Judeth,' he said. 'We're a couple of old friends whom nobody will think twice about living under the same roof.'

He had seen her back stiffen as it had done every time he asked her to marry him or made the suggestion that it was foolish for them to stay apart for their entire lives when they wanted nothing better than to live together.

'I'll not ask for you to marry me again. But I'm not going away this time.'

And this time, Jude had not made him go.

His few belongings were put into the little loft room and, with no-one except Luce whose chamber was at the far side of the house, living under the Croud Cantle roof, there was no-one to know what their sleeping arrangements might be.

And if, after an interval of thirty years, their physical passion for one another was in their mature years at last satisfied, the only evidence was in their relaxed and companionable presence. It was as though Jude's strings, which had been tightened and tied in a knot on the top of her head since she was a young woman, were suddenly released. Will, whose strange and wandering life with the Combination organisers in the industrial towns, had kept him hollow-eyed and gaunt, now became quite filled out and red-cheeked.

From his father, Luce Draper had retained conventional notions of what was right in a husband, before all else you provided for your wife – 'If I'd have wed your mother when she wished it, she'd have exchanged good ale for swipes, and that's not right. A man can take a wife who's used to swipes, and offer her good ale but not the other way.' Luce had no family or anything else except what he had gained from the Toose family. And he was proud. If Luce Draper took a wife, then he wanted to offer her good ale to put on the table.

Her admonition whenever they lay together, 'Take care Luce. Don't get me poddy' was a curb and a reminder of his lack of everything material needed to make a marriage with a woman like Lidi Toose.

For the year that her father was in gaol Lidi kept the place going as near to how her Pa did as possible. With Luce's help, they did all the budding and grafting onto rootstock. The propagating and dividing of plants, the growing of others from seed then grading and selecting.

She already did quite a lot of the accounting work, but the putting out of estimates and the filling of orders she had never done. Some of the estates who regularly bought their stocks from Toose's of Cantle were on the boundaries of Hampshire miles from Cantle at its centre, and it was this important side of the business that needed someone to ride out and take a hand in. Lidi had fretted about the loss of this business for without it they could never plough back more good stock into the business; but with the establishment of Will Vickery in Cantle, they had a man experienced as a travelling salesman, for it was as such, until he became involved with the Combinations of Workers, that he had spent his life.

Now, Will Vickery was once more riding about Hampshire, this time as John Toose's deputy.

So whilst John was spending anguished months in gaol there were only two bits of damage done. One was to Lidi's trial grounds which, because they were not a true part of the business and had always had been done in her spare time, had to be abandoned. The second was her projected plan to try to make something of her idea to go in for 'Gardenscaping' as she called it. In the last couple of years, she had worked long and hard in her spare time and was beginning to see how she might set about getting someone to take an interest in her plans and drawings.

For a year, her evenings were occupied with writing letters and making out bills, orders and accounts. But she and Luce found times and places for one another.

In the long July grass, a few minutes snatched from the hours of keeping Toose's going without John's experience; when the moon had risen and they walked back from the bottom fields carrying their hoes and pruning blades; under the willows beside the Dunnock where Lidi could have cried when he stripped off his shirt and she saw for the first time the scar of the wound he had received at Peterloo. It was a shocking sight, more shocking because it was on a perfect body. A long line that ran from one shoulder-blade across his back and to his hip on the opposite side, soft white skin, puckered as though a pink rope was laid across his back.

'I only wanted you to see so that you'd understand why I went off my head when they arrested your father.'

She ran her fingertips along its length trying to imagine what it had been like for him, to share it, take something of it.

'No wonder Uncle Will said you were half dead when he found you.'

'Well, that's all over now, there's plenty worse scars than that. But I'm trying to explain that I learnt a lesson that day, not at the time, but since I've been here and seeing people half starving and no work, and families having to leave and go away from their homes.'

Luce was never given to saying anything at length but Lidi knew that he was making some kind of declaration to her. She waited for him to gather his thoughts as he lay staring up into the willow tree, Lidi beside him, face down caressing his hairless breast, pale-skinned and muscular, a young labouring man's chest, a sight not often seen in a community where people were inclined to protect their bodies from all the elements.

'Till that day I was always dreaming of being a Yeoman – I thought you could just join, like the army – and I wanted to dress up all military and ride a white horse, and . . . God forgive me . . . wave a sabre about. That's how I used to see myself.'

'That's natural in boys isn't it?'

'I dare say. And if it hadn't a been for what happened that day, I might never have seen things as black and white as they are. It's them and us, Lidi. Everything your father says is true. I've done a lot of thinking about it since then. There was a banner, I couldn't read then but a boy told me it said "Unity and Strength. Liberty and Fraternity. Parliaments Annual. Suffrage Universal" – there! I can still say it right off.' He smiled and Lidi pecked his cheek as a reward, but he was in a serious mood.

'And he said it meant that people should join together, and be friends fighting for freedom, and that everybody should have a vote to say what should be done. I've often wondered if he was all right – that boy. He was proud of his Uncle Cartwright.'

'Luce Draper . . . I love you.'

18

LADY'S MAID

THE SUMMER THAT Sarah's father was sent to prison, Sarah was travelling abroad with Mrs Delphine and the Master. The Broughlakes had taken a small house in Italy from which Mr Broughlake planned to make expeditions to see and hear the culture of that country.

Mrs Delphine's Mama had proved correct – Delphine had found herself an unspoiled girl and trained her up, and Mama had to admit when she saw Sarah at work in the boudoir and dressing-room, that Delphy had done as well as she herself could have.

'Sarah, the Master says we are to travel to Italy, for I have never been abroad and he wishes me to know about art and opera and those things.'

Sarah's heart had leapt with joy. Abroad. That wonderful and colourful place that put any lady's maid in the highest category. To pick up a smattering of French or German or Italian as she had heard other lady's maids throw about when she had been to some society gathering with Mrs Delphine. She longed to reply 'oui' in answer to a question and then cover her mouth as though it had slipped out unthinking, then say 'aah . . . yes'.

Delphine's Mama had been much against the notion that young girls should travel abroad. 'They always come back so brown. Now what man of discernment wants to marry a brown girl? – he might as well marry a black-a-moor.'

However, now that Delphine was safely married to a considerable estate and had a son safely in the bag as one might say, she agreed that nothing but good could come of a change of scene, for who knew, the problems of waning powers from which her son-in-law apparently suffered, might take a turn for the better and Delphine might return carrying a second son.

'It is always better to err on the side of safety where sons are concerned – they are so apt to go hunting too hard, or clean loaded guns . . . that kind of thing.'

So, with a new wardrobe of muslins, *barège* and fine mohair, light bonnets and Mrs Delphine's Mama's receipt for a chamomile skin-lightening lotion, Sarah Toose, most fortunate of all Cantle's daughters, found herself travelling to Italy and there unpacking that stylish wardrobe in a house overlooking the river Arno.

In the adjoining dressing-room, Alec James, the one and only of Cantle's sons to travel in such style to foreign cities, was shaking and hanging the Master's clothes.

So far as putting on the style expected of them by their employers, Sarah and Alec were two of a kind. They were well shot of their rustic homes and families, from the harshness, coarseness and sheer dirt of that past life. They were almost partners in the crime of their good fortune and would exchange any bit of information that might be of benefit to the other.

'Mrs Delphine says that the Master is concerned about losing his front hair.'

Soon, Alec would venture to his Master that he might like the latest fashionable forward-swept curls with trailing sideburns. Not even hinting of course that it suited best those who had a receding brow.

Later, when the styling was done, exclaiming, 'Why Sir, if I might say – that style might have been just thought up for a man with your shape of face.'

Or when a little anniversary of Delphine's approached – not the unforgettable ones such as birthdays or marriage days, but such as the anniversary of the little holiday they took together in Bath or some such – then Sarah would give Alec sufficient time so that his Master might not appear tardy in his attention to a wife such as Delphine.

Sarah and Alec were a success in the Broughlake establishment. They were a wonder having both come from 'such a tiny, tiny valley – a mere speck on the map' as Delphine liked to tell her Bath and London friends, 'that there must be something in the water there that grows good personal servant material.'

Delphine's friends looked slyly at Delphine and asked her if she thought there were any left for them. 'Delphy dearest, if there are any in your secret valley, then I shall have one of the male kind for George. I should like nothing better than to know that such a creature was at work in the adjoining dressing-room.'

By 'such a creature' they meant an earthy, rough creature who had no doubt seen and done more than all the gentlemen under the sun, but an earthy, rough creature who had been scrubbed clean and poured into close-fitting breeches and silk stocking. An earthy, rough creature who would be . . . very satisfactory in all branches of service to his superiors.

At which Mrs Delphine would almost blush for having been found out.

For although Osbert had prided himself that he had discovered that there was an Under-footman in the house who knew everything there was to know about valeting – it had been at the suggestion of Barringer the Butler, at the suggestion of Delphine herself, that the discovery of the new valet had been made. And the knowledge that the Under-footman with the long lashes and the look of a young libertine had learnt those skills, was put in Mrs Delphine's way by her favourite, Sarah.

At twenty, Sarah was a nipped-waisted neat-bosomed young woman. She wore her bright hair restrained, but not so tight that a few pretty ringlets did not escape onto her brow and the well-divided nape of her neck. If she presented herself to the world as pretty and as well turned out as she could, she was shrewd enough to see that her mistress was dazzling. And so Mrs Broughlake was.

At not yet thirty, her past maternity had left her with a spectacular lush white breast and an attractively rounded belly beneath a broadly sashed waist. Many young men had found themselves transfixed by that display of bosom which frequently looked as though it might at any moment leap free of its gauzy bodice, and of a shoulder that looked too delicate to support that wonderful weight of bosom.

Not least of those young men was Alec James, and on the occasions when he was on duty to serve breakfast to his employers, he made no bones about where his eyes were when he was out of the Master's line of sight. His Mistress made no bones about what he might see, and generously, often leaned further forward than necessary to accept something from his hand – a reward for the homage in his eyes.

The weeks abroad were long and hard for Sarah. Whilst the Master often suffered from fatigue and a number of digestive disorders, Mrs Delphine enjoyed herself with as many diversions as could be arranged for a woman with a prostrate husband. This was not difficult, for they were soon introduced into the kind of society to which they were accustomed. Delphine enjoyed everything, and was never short of a companion.

'Sarah. I must have the spotted muslin ready again for the afternoon of tomorrow.'

And Sarah would take the crumpled and dusty garment and spend hours bringing it back to a virginal white freshness.

'Oh, Sarah – just look at this beret. Flat! Oh flat. It must be the river moisture in the air.'

And Sarah would carefully unpick a tiny seam, poke around in the lining and bring back the puffy lightness of the wonderful creation of ribbons and plumes.

Often the Master would be lying prone in his darkened room attended by a doctor and an apothecary. Alec's only duties on these occasions were to help with fresh nightshirts and dressing-gowns. His other visits to the bedside, full of dutiful concern, were to confirm in his master's mind that he had chosen a caring servant. As a consequence of this, Alec was given a great deal of free time. Sarah had free time only when she had made ready the dresses and hats, and had finished in the boudoir.

'Here, give me that and you can finish that pressing.' And Alec would take over the steaming of some velvet trimmings, or measure out lard, oils, spermaceti and bergamot and beat them into a creamy pomade. Or, if he was dipping his master's hair-brushes in soda-water, would clean the Mistress's at the same time.

I'll scratch your back, if you'll scratch mine. And in the little room set aside for servants to work on their employers' belongings, Alec playfully let his action fit the saying.

'Alec James!' Sarah's words objected, but not her smile. Although over the last few years she had grown more and more fond of Brendan Lewis, Brendan was not in Florence. Over those years too, Sarah had discovered that she liked the attention of men and that men of all ages found her very attractive. This knowledge gave her a great deal of pleasure; it also enabled her often to get her own way with men – though none of them had as yet had their own way with her.

Her wages were now quite high, not only because she had become indispensable to Mrs Delphine, but because she knew what she knew about the Master and did not complain, or even let on. She was never demanding, and never complained, but she was quite single-minded in getting what she believed was due to her.

On those occasions when there was to be a renewal of her hiring, and she suggested that she was worth a little more than she was at present getting – the Mistress could not deny that she was turning out to be a very good servant with exceptional qualities.

No more could the Master.

He never touched her, or said a word out of place. He never engaged her gaze. But he sometimes made little requests that she fetch him something that he had forgotten, and bring it to his little study.

The first time she had entered this small booklined room, she had blushed at the very sight of the disarray of his dressing-gown. No girl brought up as close to animal nature as had Sarah would blush at such a natural phenomenon as male arousal, particularly if it was so well covered as was that one. Her blush was that she knew that he was aware that she could not avoid seeing it as she placed the paper he had requested on the table beside him, and had made no move to change his position.

After that, there had been a number of other times, and whilst it angered her that he was using her in his own peculiar silent way, she did not see of what she could complain. What could she say that did not make her sound a minx?

Now that she knew Alec well, they spoke together of their employers as freely as conspirators.

'Oh, he's safe enough. If it don't harm you, I reckon you should take no notice. After all, what could you say to her ladyship? He'd have you dismissed as a hussy and a bad lot – and an imaginative one at that. Be Miss Innocent, then when it comes to the end of the year – ask for a bit more wages.'

Sarah made a wry face. 'Well, I suppose at least it's not as bad treatment as a lot of girls get when they're in service. You're right, perhaps the time will come when I'll make him pay for that service too.'

'Where's the harm. It isn't really any different from Delphy letting her white doves fly out at me when I'm serving breakfast. And if it gives her a bit of thrill to show me – I an't complaining.'

'That's not the same thing at all.'

Alec had to admit that it was not. Especially as his reward for paying homage with his eyes at Stonebridge had, in Florence, become more substantial than a mere glimpse. Delphine Brough-lake played the coquette with the manservant who was bold with his eyes.

With Alec's help Sarah often had a free hour or two when they would go off exploring the wonderful city, wandering the alleyways, watching the glittering Arno, marvelling at everything from wide piazza to marble satyr. They exchanged ambitions and day-dreams and distrained the coarseness of their common background.

'If you had everything like Them, what would you do with it?' Sarah asked Alec.

'First off, I'd travel over the whole world, and see everything.'

'Oh, so would I. But first I'd get myself a house in London.'

'And Bath.'

'I can't say I'm too keen on Bath – too many gouty old men.'

'All right London. But I'd want somewhere close to the races.'

'Oh yes, that'd be nice, I never thought of that.'

'What kind of husband would you choose?'

'I don't know that I'd have one, I'd rather go where I wanted to.'

'You'd have to have a husband. Women need a man around.' From long practice, his thick black lashes were lowered and his secret look challenged.

Their employers had driven up into the hills to visit some English people who lived there, so the two servants had an entire afternoon of freedom. They had wandered into a small brick-set piazza where pots of raucous-looking flame flowers bloomed.

It was scenes such as this that Sarah had imagined when she first heard that they were to travel in foreign parts. This was Foreign. This was wonderful and different. This was more than she ever thought possible for a village girl to experience. To Sarah, Florence was so entirely unlike her green valley with its simple chalkhill flowers, its tiny clear stream which was as quick-flowing and narrow as the Arno was slow and wide, that she loved it totally.

Alec took her hand possessively. 'I don't think you can go on much longer without one, Sarah Toose. I think that you only keep going without one because you're afraid.'

Sarah pulled her hand away.

'Alec James, you can never go for a five-minute walk without suggesting things.'

'Ach girl, you an't really the straight-laced sort; a man's only got to walk behind you for ten yards and watch the way your skirt swings to know that.'

She seemed to be deep in thought, then she said quietly, firmly, 'I'm never going back to Cantle and that sort of life. This is better than anybody there ever dreamed of and I've already got some nice clothes and even a bit of money put aside. If you think that a man is a fair exchange for that, then you don't know me, whatever you say.'

'Why not have both?'

'And find myself like Poll Dawkins and Harriett Close and . . .'
She reeled off the names of Cantle girls who had gone into service in
the local Big Houses and come home with fat bellies and little else.

'They were careless. You wouldn't be careless. And there's
something else I know about you. If you go on denying yourself
what you know you want, then you'll be a crabby thing and not fit
to live with. Who wants a lady's maid like that?'

Sarah went quiet again. It was true, he knew her only too well.
More and more recently she had found herself thinking of Brendan
Lewis. Brendan Lewis exercising the fine hunters. Brendan astride
glossy flanks, head down, taking fences with grace. Brendan
talking quietly into the ear of some nervy stallion, calming him,
controlling him.

Since she had been in Florence, Brendan's features were hard to
remember, but his total image, his presence, she could recall
clearly. Brendan Lewis as a lover. But never the reality of what that
implied. Brendan Lewis the husband – a simple stableman.

As they wandered off again, he took her hand and, having
removed its glove, held it close to his side.

'I'm never careless. I learnt my lesson before I left home. I was
the wicked lad of Cantle. I've got to admit, I was lucky to have got
off so easy, but that lesson wasn't wasted. I an't any different from
you, there's nothing that's going to make me waste my chance of
bettering myself. I don't want a wife forced upon me.' He drew her
to sit down in the warm sunshine.

'When I think of my father in that hole, serving ale to that lot of
dung-boots, and putting up the odd traveller by way of a change
. . . and then I think how close I got to following him – why I'd as
soon go celibate.' He laughed painfully at the idea.

'There's too much risk in that kind of thing for a woman.'

'I wouldn't take risks with you or me neither – we both got too
much to lose.'

So solemn was his expression and so sincere were his words that
Sarah knew that he was making her a promise.

'Only your word for that.'

The place where they now found themselves was a wide piazza
where a great rumbustious fountain spouted and tumbled about
fleshy marble figures who were so natural in their nakedness that
Sarah almost wished that it were possible to join them in their
freedom.

'Let's watch them a minute,' she said, and they stood watching the water pouring over limbs and splashing into small caverns.

Alec drew her to sit down.

'Don't you trust me?'

She couldn't find a reply.

The day was hot and a fine spray which drifted from the bare live-marble thighs and breasts and fingers of the fountain reached them in a cooling mist, and inseminated them both with the tumbling eroticism of the joyful carefree group.

'Oh but Sarah . . .' he lifted her hand to his mouth and let his tongue roam around its palm. 'I can't bear it if you won't let us love one another. We're two of a kind. We've been given all this.' He spread his free fingers at the sky and the piazza and then the fountain. Then he kissed her quickly, softly, warmly, not the kiss of a village lad, but open eyed and open mouthed, publicly, and she did not stop him.

The unrestrained bright flowers, his warm male smell of tarry soap and pomatum, the audaciousness of their public kiss, brought to a climax the enjoyment Sarah had found in that wonderful cultured city, so unlike Cantle. When she returned his kiss she knew that she had committed herself to their combined satisfaction later. If she did not feel towards him as she felt towards Brendan Lewis, she knew that she could trust Alec James, if only because of his own self-interest.

They began to walk back to the villa. Now their steps were languid, their conversation idle. Then Alec said, 'I've had Delphine you know.' He laughed. 'Or rather, she had me.'

For a moment she did not understand what he meant. Then suddenly she knew that what he said was true. Of course.

'It was that day wasn't it? . . . when I had to work all morning sewing back on that whole tier of flounce on her ballgown? . . . and He was laid up feeling bad.'

'That was the first time. The second was last week when He was bad again and you were brewing him up some of that concoction.'

She was silent for a moment, her mind flicking back and forth, thinking about the enormity of the incident. Trying to imagine who had made the first move. Surely not Alec, he would never take such a risk of losing the position in the household that he cherished. A manservant in the bed of his Master's wife. Sarah knew that her Mistress had changed over the years that she had served her, or perhaps it was that her true nature was revealing itself . . . but to do a thing so outrageous as to seduce her servant – and almost under the nose of her husband.

'Why are you telling me?'

'Because I thought you might have guessed, and I don't want it to be between us.'

'I wondered about it. But you! It crossed my mind that it was strange, her bed had been made up and then it got unmade again and I had to fetch the laundry-maid to take away the sheets. He never goes into her room at all during the day.'

As they walked, Sarah found her own thoughts quite shocking – shocking that she was not outraged at his behaviour, but felt a strange pleasure at the thought that he had probably kissed Her in the same open-eyed way.

'You're quiet. Look Sarah it don't mean . . .'

'It's all right. I was only wondering why.'

'Because she's like the rest of them. When they want something they can't abide not having it. It don't matter whether it's a new kind of carriage or an emerald tie-stick they fancy, they want it and try to get it. With Delphine, it was a rough, fancy village lad like me.'

'There's no more village roughness left in you than there is in me.'

'Of course there is. Your nice dresses and my nice breeches and jackets, and travelling abroad and learning to talk without sounding like a dung-boot don't take away what we were. We might have tried to bury it, but it's not buried deep.

'And that's what rouses them up. They've got this idea of us living lives as raw as animals compared to them. The things we took as natural out in the fields or at a Harvest Home – have you seen anything like that since you've been at Stonebridge? Have you seen 'em dance? Why their flesh don't hardly move on their bones. There's not one in a thousand of that lot really knows how to enjoy themselves.'

That night, Alec James slipped quietly and carefully into Sarah's room, and into her, and, as he had promised, took no chances.

And as Sarah had suspected, she had a side to her nature that was almost overwhelming in the act of love, with a man as experienced as Alec James.

PART TWO

Spring 1823 – Autumn 1829

CHANGE AND DECAY

O N HIS release from Winchester Prison, with Bess sitting behind carrying their few possessions in a basket, John Toose rode home to Cantle.

John reined in the lolloping horse and dismounted on the track at the top of Tradden Raike. From that point they could look down upon the entire Cantle Valley.

'Why my dear Lord, have you ever seen sich a pretty sight in all your life.' Bess with unashamed emotion sat on the rump of the horse and allowed her tears to flow.

John too was moist-eyed at the longed-for sight of their village. They had come through the clump of beeches on the crest where the ground was carpeted with bluebells. On the fresh wind that always blew up there, the sweet scent, along with that of the newly opened beech buds and mossy earth, was carried to Bess and John adding to the evocation of memories, Cantle, home, family, and brought back again to John his deeply-rooted grief that Hanny had died and acknowledgement that Tansy was no substitute.

He longed to be home, but to Hanny.

In the last year he had been forced to face many things about himself – one of which was that he had made a mistake in thinking that he could fit the living, young Tansy into the empty space that had been left by Hanny. Another was that he ought never to have asked Tan to marry him.

Poor Tan, he'd persuaded her away from Jo Bunce's great heaving chest and offered her his own ageing one. In Winchester's grim cells, he had seen clearly that the Tansy Jepps of this world ought to couple with the Jo Bunces; they would romp like puppies in their youth, fight, love, make too many children and know that they were alive. In the orderly house in the centre of Cantle, with Jack whom she tried to love in spurts of guilt and pity, Tansy Jepp was a sun-loving plant which he had tried to make grow like a fern in a shaded border.

'Bess, if I live to be a hundred, I shan't ever be able to repay what you've done for me this last year.'

'Lor dumble us, if you lives to be a hunderd, then I be about a hunderd and twenty, and be the looks of you all skin and bones, you looks a hunderd already. Ah, but just you wait, I'll fatten thee up Lad.'

'I reckon there's something that happens to women who live under that roof,' he pointed down to where the rambling shape of the Croud Cantle farmhouse could be seen close in at the foot of Tradden Raike, 'makes something special of them.'

'Oh ah?'

'Oh ah.' He led the horse from here on. Slowly back and forth across the sheep-tracks, wending downwards. 'Master Bella, Jude, Hanny and you, have all picked me up and set me on my feet again.'

'Same as you done for us – especially Hanny. You changed her from a unhappy woman into a bride with the biggest smile I ever saw on any.'

'Look there, the primmies are out. Hold on I pick a bunch to take down for Tan.'

Bess dismounted and sat on an old mole-hill and looked down on the place that had taken her under its wing. She knew that people thought she was a queer old woman but she let them get on with it.

It didn't matter, so long as they left you alone.

It was donkey's years since she had walked into the place with Tomas. Such donkey's years since she had come here with him and he had died – on the very day he had brought her to Cantle.

Suddenly her whole life seemed to have become heavy. Andrew had left home. Her dear sister-wife Misz Bella, Tomas's *proper* wife, had gone on before, and recently she had seen a man she loved almost as much as her own son degraded and miserable.

When John came back, he had a bunch of primroses which he put on top of their baskets, and a little posy of violets which he tucked into Bess's shawl. She mounted the horse again and they began the descent into the valley.

'Don't ever tell them back home what it was like, Bess – they never saw me crying depressed and bad like you did sometimes.'

'We all have our times we shouldn't like other folks to see. If you like, I a tell you one a mine so that we'm quits. That day when I come into that there place for the first time – why you waddn't no more than a youth then, was you Lad – and Misz Bella knocked the hackle oft the bee-skep and they stung Tomas to death . . .' She paused at the vision of that dramatic scene. 'Well Lad, I a tell you summit . . . I could a jumped for joy. No, not at the way he died, fer that was summit you couldn't wish on any man good or bad, but if I said I *wasn't* glad that he was gone, then I should tell a lie.'

John gave her knee a light pat in his acknowledgement of her confession.

'Do you think that's a sin, Lad?'

John was never one to jump in with a quick answer when asked a serious question; when he answered it was truthful and sincere.

'No. That's honest feelings.'

'Ah. Well that's all right then.'

When they were almost at the bottom of Tradden, they saw the red hair that could only be Lidi's, Sarah's or Jude's. And, as the owner of the red hair ran like a boy up the slope of the Raike to greet them waving both hands and shouting, she could only be Lidi.

She flung herself at him as she used to when she was a child. 'Pa! Pa! Oh Pa.' Hugging him with each exclamation.

'Put me down child!' His mouth muscles crunched up with wanting to smile and weep at the same time. She turned on Bess. 'Nana-Bess. You don't know how much we've missed you.'

Bess too was weeping. Lidi was as near to a grandchild as she was ever going to get, now that Drew had set up with a woman old enough to be his mother. But Bess Smith had no grumbles, for she had got more out of life than she thought she deserved.

'Ah, so you'm that glad to see us that you'm going to keep us out here on Tradden when we might be down there with a nice brew in our hands.'

Lidi took the reins and led the horse and held her father's hand.

'There, you see Lad, I talk to her about a nice brew and she don't turn a hair. I dare say since we been gone they took to regular drinking tea and coffee in Cantle.'

'Tea and coffee?'

Bess Smith looked pleased at the response.

'Black tea from Indier and some coffee beans that was roasted in Winchester only yesterday. But you an't wasting that on drink – I'm going to make a cake like they sells in the city, of the flavour of coffee. Many's the time I smelled it when I walked up that drag to the . . .'

A moment's silence.

'Ah go on Bess, say "prison"! Everybody knows where I been and I an't ashamed because the shame of it was that a free man was slammed up for speaking what he believes.'

'Oh Pa, I'm so glad you said that. I was so proud of you that day, before they took you. And Luce . . . wasn't Luce wonderful, jumping in on that constable like that.'

John Toose did not need telling what Lidi's feelings towards Luce were now, and he was glad.

That had been the best part of the homecoming. Tansy greeted him with exuberant kisses and hugs. Jack had grown out of all recognition.

'Jack boy. If you go on growing like this, you'm going to be a size a boot that a make a fishing boat.'

The boy laughed. 'Ma says we shall have to high up the doors or lower the floors.' He was pleased because his Pa was pleased.

Jude had come down and greeted him with more natural warmth and emotion than he could remember in her for years.

'Johnny-twoey. I'm proud of you.'

Johnny-twoey. The name that had been his when he was the crow-scarer and stone-picker at Croud Cantle, the name of his boyhood when she had brought him from his dark, closed, fearful, ignorant world into the bright and open one of knowledge and literacy.

Who else would say they were proud that a student had graduated in middle years, by serving a prison sentence. But that is what she had meant. His political knowledge, his sense of justice and, as he saw it, his clean, pure Radical beliefs stemmed from nowhere but from Jude.

'Thank you Miz Jude.'

She gave him a playful flick.

'Will sent a message, but he'll be down soon, so I shan't bother.'

'Will? Here?'

'He's moved in . . . up there.'

Ah. At last. After all these years. It accounted for the new look about Jude. She looked younger, almost youthful. They deserved a few years together after so long.

'Jude . . . I'm glad. Will's the best man in the world.'

She smiled. There were very few people from the old days, who knew Will Vickery. 'Yes, Will is the best man in the world.'

A year away, and what changes. Lidi was in love. Jack was no longer a baby. Jude and Will living under the same roof. And Tan . . .

Tansy had changed too. Or perhaps it was that he had not seen her for all these months. Outwardly she was little changed, she was of the type of woman who stays the same for years and then changes almost overnight. From girl to matron in one step at the age of forty – ten years to go. He watched her moving about the scullery end.

Hanny would have been . . . forty-three. The thought of what this homecoming would have been like with Hanny . . . perhaps there wouldn't have been one. She certainly disapproved of people who make a show of themselves in public. Nobody can bring the past into the present – for one thing Jack would not be here.

To watch the boy moving about inside the house, one would scarcely believe that he could not see. Had he been told five years ago that there would be a day when he would be so proud of his son, he would not have believed it. When he had first noticed the lack of visual response, he had lain awake at night and been preoccupied during the day, wondering how they would cope with such an affliction. Affliction, that had been the problem – the word, not the close-sightedness.

Then, with her usual practical approach, Jude had asked if it wouldn't be a good idea to try him with a powerful magnifying glass. She had always carried a pocket glass with her and used it in the teaching of John, of Lidi and Sarah. Jude was a born teacher – she excited interest, made children curious. So, for Jack, she had gone herself to Winchester and had made a large round lens with a handle attached. Nowadays Jack, with his lens and his nose only inches from it, was beginning to read.

It had been Sarah who had taught him to play a pipe on one of her few week-long holidays.

Sarah. The last time he had seen her was that day at Wickham Fair a year ago. She had almost ceased to be Sarah. The features were there, but like Tazey James' son who had been with her, the simplicity seemed to have gone. Those had been . . . he couldn't find the exact word but knew the sense of it . . . 'knowing' young people. They had seen splendid things, and took them for better than more simple ones. Nowadays, he had no doubt that Sarah would not have exclaimed at the bunch of primmies as Lidi and Tan had done – Sarah would need an orchid to draw such a response from her.

If John Toose reckoned that he could read his daughter like a book, he was not so successful with his wife. There was something . . . he could not fathom what.

In July he discovered what it was.

Tansy was pregnant. And by any stretch of the calculations it could not have been done by John, even had his virility returned with his homecoming.

Petulantly, tearfully, almost defiantly, "Tis Jo Bunce's. It was an accident, we never meant to, it just come upon us of a sudden.'

He didn't really need to be told that it was Jo Bunce. It had really been inevitable. Jo was broad and sturdy, and only two years older than Tan. If Jo Bunce was loading a hay-wagon he always managed to make a display of it, his shirt hanging open to the waist, sweat shining the sinews of his neck. He had been the village athlete in his youth, knocking men down in single-sticks contests, pole-vaulting hedges, kicking a football for hours at a stretch all over the four parishes only stopping to down a few quarts of ale.

John Toose was no match for such as Jo.

Why had Tansy abandoned Jo for John in the first place? It was a question that had come foremost to his mind in Winchester. He supposed that Tansy had decided, as she decided most things, on a whim, that she wanted nothing better than to be married to a steady businessman and have a nice house in the village. Jo could have offered her a room in his mother's cottage.

She'd have been happier in the long run.

There they were, married. John wanting Hanny, Tansy wanting Jo.

Tansy could do something about her wants.

Had the reverse been the situation, and it had been himself who had made the mistake, and Hanny was there to lie with again, he knew that he would have done as Tan had and become an adulterer.

Once he had admitted this to himself, he could not blame Tan.

'What do you want to do?'

'Go and live along with him.'

'You can't hardly live in Cantle. It'd make everybody a bit uncomfortable to say nothing of the Skimmingtons they might give us. And it'd hardly seem the thing for us to meet one another in the village and pass the time of day.'

'No John, and I wouldn't want to spoil the business for you. Jo says he'd like to go and find work up north, or he can always join the navvies.'

John's heart sank for her. Tansy in one of those bleak back-to-back overcrowded rickety houses. Worse than if she had to trail around the countryside with a wild gang of navvies. It'd be like marigold on a midden.

'If I could get him a place in one of the Big Houses I know in the Midlands, do you think he'll take it?'

'Jo an't proud.'

By the time Tansy and Jo left Cantle, the secret was out and they stole away before anybody thought up a Skimmington ride. They went off quietly one dawn, with mists rising from Chard Lepe and the leys. They talked their way up Bellpitt Lane and never looked back at the valley as it was then. Looking at Tansy, one might have supposed that the interlude, when she was Mistress Toose, wife of a respected widower and mother to a tall son, had never been.

Golden August by the time they reached the strange circle of Bell Tump at the crest of Bellpitt.

Below in Cantle, a steady stream of reapers were making their way on to Meadow Farm. August, a quiet month for birds, but as always larks rose and rose from the golden bowl of the valley into the blue bowl of the sky, from Tradden Raike, Old Marl, Beacon Point and Winchester Hill, where they now were, not looking back at any of it.

Tansy and Jo, the couple that they had always been and now likely always would.

Tansy Jepp and Jo Bunce, setting out on their long trek north where Jo would put his athletic strength to the felling of great timber trees on the estate of one of the new iron-foundry fortunes.

A note arrived in late January.

God Bless you at Christmas, Lidi. Jo has got a good job and we shall have a little place to live come spring. The person who wrote this note is a good friend to me – she has got your hair and minds me of you, but is older. I had my babe, Winifred Lidia, which I hope you won't mind, but it is you that I miss most. I send my regards to anyone who will like to have them.

Yours sincerely, Tansy Bunce.

2

'RABBLE ROUSER!'

OTHER EPITHETS WERE aimed at the Hampshire farmer, William Cobbett:
'Traitor!'
'Radical!'
The Toose family subscribed to Cobbett's newspapers and some of his views.

AND THESE VERY PARSONS, WHO DAILY SEE MEN, WOMEN AND CHILDREN STARVING AND IN RAGS, WILL NO DOUBT THINK ME VERY WICKED. BUT THERE IS NO DOUBT IN MY MIND THAT, IF YOU WISH TO MAKE MEN HONEST AND DUTIFUL, IF YOU WISH TO MAKE THEM KIND TO ONE ANOTHER . . . THEN FIRST FILL THEIR BELLIES.

The Rabble-Rouser is loved and hated, admired and vilified.
He is literate.
He is a gentleman and a farmer.
He speaks his mind, offend or please.
He uses those most dangerous of weapons – ideas and words.

TO PROVIDE HUNGRY MEN WITH RELIGIOUS TRACTS IS TO MAKE HYPOCRITES OF THEM. IF WE WOULD LOOK FOR HONESTY IN THE LABOURING CLASSES WE MUST FREE THEM FROM FEAR. THAT FREEDOM WILL NOT COME FROM RELIGION AND PIOUS CHARITY — BUT FROM BETTER WAGES.

He farms land not ten miles from Cantle.
He is eloquent in blaring the degradation of the rural worker.
He has seen the danger from his high horse as he rides about the county.

By now the wages in Hampshire and its neighbouring counties had fallen so low that a single man could scarcely buy food and a married man anguished to see his stick-legged children. They were powerless to do anything to change things. At best, they could take their few possessions and head for the industrial towns. At worst, they might die in a field with nothing but raw turnip in their shrunken stomachs.

Gentlemen sitting in coffee-houses, gentlemen eating in London clubs, ladies taking tea in tasselled sitting rooms, gentlemen exchanging opinions in the corridors of Parliament, lady-mothers watching their silk-clad daughters and gentleman-fathers out shooting with their tailored sons, told one another that if people wanted to eat, then they must work.

'People', of course, meant . . . Those People. Not Us – not the Ladies and Gentlemen.

So as Mister Cobbett suggested decent wages to keep working men honest, Gentlemen applied the rules which sent unemployed skilled men and women to work like common criminals picking stones from the fields, carting them and filling pot-holes in neglected roads.

Children of the poor were dealt with by charitable institutions who found work suited to very small fingers, and the old and ailing were offered places in workhouses.

Workhouses – dreaded institutions.

Workhouses – where they might decently scrub floors so that they would not feel demeaned by accepting soup and a bed.

Poor relief was inconsistent and divisive.

In Cantle, the payment of the Parish Rate often fell heaviest on the least able to pay. Both Jude and John were paying heavily.

When John looked through Lidi's accounting, he thought that she must have made an error in her calculations.

'No Pa, look here. The Relief's more than doubled in the year you've been gone.'

'Hell take it! If it goes on like this, it'll put us out of business.'

'It's a good thing though, an't it Master Toose?'

'To put us out of business, Luce?'

'To make up men's wages.'

'No Luce, this system is bad, bad. What incentive is there for a farmer to pay a living wage, when he knows he need pay only a pittance – he knows it'll be made up by the rest of us from the Poor Rate.

'God above! What family can eat on eight shilling, so the Parish dips into my pocket and makes up Estate wages out of that. Nice little scheme, an't it.'

'How's it going to get better? I heard that they're getting a thrashing machine up the Estate.'

'What! My God, is that true, Luce?'

'It's what they're all saying.'

'Then goodbye to Cantle. What other winter work is there except thrashing and winnowing? What are folk supposed to live on after harvest? I reckon one thrashing machine could do the winter work of the whole valley with only a few hands.'

John's old fervour was returning. His public voice took over, deep and passionate. 'That's not what it's about though, Luce. A machine's easier to control than the lowest stone-picker. No thrasher's going to say he can't live on the wages; no winnower can rise up in discontent, can't answer back; no seed-drill expects his roof to be mended, holidays and Harvest Suppers. A mechanical thrasher is the perfect agricultural worker – the one the landlords have dreamed about since the first man picked up an ass's jawbone and forced his neighbour to work for him; they don't even have to provide a poorhouse for a thrasher when they've worked him to death's door.'

Lidi had grown up learning such things as naturally as she learned about sun and rain, safety and danger. But now that Luce was questioning, a wind fanned her own fervour. Poverty and despair had stalked Cantle, infecting the place like a disease; John Toose had brought up his daughters to do what they could to tend its victims. Lidi was beginning to wonder whether it was enough to offer the simples and remedies of food and clothes.

The source of the disease should be tackled.

The trouble was she could not see how it was to be done.

Lidi Toose, like the vast proportion of the rural community, was becoming incensed at what was happening and angry at their powerlessness.

Mr Cobbett's flamboyant phrases fanned the heat of all their anger.

3

WITH TANSY GONE, the family had to make a reappraisal of their situation.

It seemed to John that the sensible thing would be for Lidi and Luce to get wed and live in Shaft's Cottage. He would take his son-in-law into the business and Lidi should take over the running of the house.

'You must have been working all hours God sent to have kept the place going between you, Luce, and I appreciate it.'

'No need for thanks, it's been an eye-opener for me. I never should a thought I'd take to this kind of work.'

Luce was continuing to do the work he had done whilst John was away, and John was watching him with a critical eye as Luce spaded round maiden fruit trees, severing the roots in preparation for transportation in the dormant season.

'You learnt well – that's as nice a job as I ever saw.'

'Old Tom's a good instructor – and Lidi.'

John slapped him on the shoulder. 'Two as hard task-masters as you're likely to find in one place.'

Luce smiled. 'I got to admit, I got a telling off or two.'

Luce, smiling, could charm the birds from the trees. John liked him; Lidi, John guessed, probably loved him. John had always had a soft spot for Luce, they had both come into the care of Croud Cantle in much the same way. They had each in turn been taken in like stray animals, and had stayed on. If he'd have been the kind of father to choose his daughter's husband – more to the point, if Lidi'd been the kind of daughter to have let him – he'd have chosen a young man like Luce for her. Steady, reliable, and no fool. He approved Lidi's choice and would make no objections.

Luce had been thinking about it for weeks now; he took the bull by the horns.

'Mr Toose, I was wondering . . . now you're back home . . . are you going to still want my help around here?' He didn't wait for a reply. 'I tell you for why, I should really like to stop on here and learn this sort of work. Can I show you the stock I budded myself?'

John nodded that they should look.

'I reckon I'd be willing to think about it, but you know the situation here, times are bad as I can remember.'

'I'd be willing if you'd take me on as a 'prentice.'

'Slight bit old in the tooth for a 'prentice.'

'And I couldn't be indentured of course, but I don't reckon you'd have cause to complain about my work.'

John inspected the clean rootstock and the neatly bass-tied buds. 'These all yours?'

'Mine and Lidi's. She said to ask you which rows was mine and which was hers.'

'The top rows are Lidi's.'

Luce's face fell. 'Ah, you can tell then.'

John smiled, pleased with Luce's obvious skill at budding. 'Only because our Lidi won't ever learn to tie a proper knot. That lot's hers all right.' John stood up.

'Well, I can't say nay against this. But how do you propose to keep yourself if I 'prentice you at twenty-one? You'll be twenty-six before you know enough of the business to call yourself skilled.'

Luce looked down at his boots a bit sheepishly and rubbed his chin. 'Well . . . matter of fact, Miss Jude said, that if you should think of taking me on, they'd give me a bed and my supper, and I could go on helping with their pigs and that in return.'

'I might a known. Jude. All cut and dried if I know Jude. All right, I'll go along with it. Fair deal Luce. It was Jude that has put me where I am today. She let me have the land for a peppercorn to start me off, and now the rent she takes is only just fair. I'm glad to do the same for you.'

Lidi knew about Luce's apprentice idea, and saw from his broad grin that her father had agreed.

'Lidi, it'll be five years before I shall be able to come and ask you to make us legal. I can't hardly bear the thought because I don't like this bits and pieces sort of affair between us. I want you under my roof and in my bed fair and square and open.'

'Well, I don't reckon we can have any sort of a more open bed than some of those we've been in at times.'

'Ah, and that worries me. Your father's my proper Master now, and it don't seem right if I'm taking you behind his back.'

'Pa don't own me.'

'He do in the same way that he owns me if I'm his legal

apprentice. A daughter rightly belongs to the father until she's wed.'

'And then she belongs to the husband!'

Luce was only making light comment, nothing serious. He should have been warned then, it was in her voice, but he plunged on. 'Yes, and when you belong to me, I want you to have everything you've got here. Nice things. Nice plates. Books.'

They were down by Chard Lepe Pond, where Lidi was at work again on her lily trial-ground. Amidst the tangle a few brilliant blooms were open, deep-throated dark pink with pale outer petals. These had been kept from pollinating insects by little bags which Lidi had been removing. She carefully took a pollen-laden anther and coupled it with a ripe pistil. The steadiness of her hand belied her emotion.

'Has it ever occurred to you, Luce Draper, that I might not want to belong to anyone?'

If Luce had expected his declaration to end in a close embrace at the sheltered corner of the plot, he was disappointed.

'I thought that's what we wanted. I love you Lidi, you said you loved me.'

'What's that to do with it?'

'You know what's to do with it, I'm asking you to marry me when I can afford to care for you and give you a proper home.'

She had reached the end of the row of plants where he was sitting propped up on one elbow, watching her work. She stood over him, arms outstretched.

'Look Luce Draper. What do you see?'

He stretched a hand toward her ankle and grabbed, missing it as she stepped back. ''Tis my lovely wife, I reckon in all but name.' He grabbed again, again she stepped back. ''Tis the future Mistress Draper, mother of my children I hope.' He stretched forward again but she stood away again.

'What about this being John Toose's daughter?' Still with her arms stretched wide. 'Eh, what about "who giveth this woman"?'

'I don't think your father will mind giving you to me.'

She lowered her arms, but still did not approach him. 'How long have you known me?'

'Three year, four?'

'Luce Draper, you don't know me at *all*.' She flung 'all' away from her.

Luce was dumbstruck, until that point he had thought that she was teasing.

'Lidi. What have I said that's put you about like this?'

'I'll tell you what. When I asked you what you saw, you saw Mistress Draper, Luce Draper's wife, John Toose's daughter, your children's mother. You saw somebody you could not marry without getting permission from her present owner. You saw a creature who needs to wait five years till you can get her plates to eat from and a roof to keep her dry – a wonder you didn't think of a feather mattress for you to bed her on good and proper.'

'Lidi . . . I . . .' He really did not know what to say, the only thing that came into his head was that he had presumed too much, a nobody asking for a Master's daughter.

She flung herself down and sat, knees apart, her ankles folded, the brown stuff skirt a bowl between her knees into which she threw the ears of grass she tore off unthinkingly.

The evening was drawing in; the sun, sinking behind the western downs of Winchester Hill, lit the little clearing. For a long minute the only sounds were distant beasts and dogs and the snap-snap-snap of Lidi's attack on the grasses.

At last she looked up at him.

'I'm sorry Luce. I shouldn't have let off at you like that.'

He hunched his shoulders.

Dear Lord she thought, when he looks like that . . .

When he looked like that, when she knew what every inch of him looked like – his pale yellow hair, the long scar, the hollow below the waist and his flat smooth belly, his white, white skin and the deep line of his spine – as she had looked upon him on the one occasion they had dared, the night before her Pa returned home, to sleep secretly in one another's arms with only a partition between them and Tansy's soft snoring. She almost wanted to be what he had described. Almost.

Picking at his thumbnail like a sullen boy, he said, 'I thought when two people have been like we've been these last months, they meant to get wed. I was serious, I wouldn't have gone with you like that . . . We'm lovers Lidi, and lovers should only be lovers if they intends to wed each other.'

'I never said we should get wed.'

'You . . .'

'I asked you what you saw. You never saw what was there. You never saw a woman who don't want to be give to one man by another. You never saw what I am. I'm Lidi Toose. I'm twenty-one, I've run Pa's business for a year, I can do any job on the place, and I know more about some things – like those lilies – than Pa does. He never reads books on new techniques – I do! I read everything I can lay my hands on about new ideas.' She flung a handful of grass seed at the lilies.

'Pa's good at what he does here, but I can do better. I've been working out some border designs that could make Toose's famous all over the country. Those plans I've been doing, well, I've worked it all out now. We would grow the stock for an entire herbaceous border . . . any design a customer would like to choose. We would have a book of designs for them to choose from. They could order the special garden they wanted, we would deliver and plant it up or hand the whole lot over to them in ball-root or pots to do themselves.'

'Lord, Lidi, I can't hardly keep up with you.'

She lunged at him, pushing him back and kissing him half a dozen times excitedly.

'Luce Draper – I'm going to be somebody. There'll be a day when people will take their friends into their garden and say, "Come and walk in the garden?" and their friends will say, "Ah, isn't that a new 'Lidi Toose' Silver Border? *Wonderful.*" Lidi Toose borders will be like paintings, people will recognise that its *my* work. Luce, I know that I can do it – we can do it together.'

She kissed him fully this time.

'Oh Luce, I do love you.'

Looking up at her he shook his head bewildered.

'Luce Draper will you have me for your unlawful, unwedded lover? Will you live with me, will you have and hold me from this day forward, in sickness and in health until death do us separate? Luce Draper will you live with me, love me, share my plates, my roof, my mattress, and share yours with me?'

Her eyes sparkled, she was flushed with enthusiasm for their prospects. She outlined a notice-board with her hands: ' "Toose and Draper – Garden Designs" or "Draper and Toose – Specialist Gardens" or maybe just "Toose and Draper" because everybody will know what we do.'

A long, unfilled moment.

Luce started to get up but she pushed him down again, straddling his chest, her face close to his, looking him deeply in the eyes.

'Lidi . . .'

'Luce.' She hadn't meant it to grow serious, but suddenly it had become so. The long unfilled moment had changed everything. 'Luce, this is your last chance, you can have me unwed, unowned, ungiven by my father – or you can't have me at all. You can have me with my own name as you shall keep yours. You can have me as I am. I'm mine to give, and I'm giving Lidi Toose to Luce Draper.'

She felt the change come over him. His body which had been tense as in an embrace, became almost rigid, unresponsive. He had been waiting for her tussling to dissolve into love-making, his hands, holding her elbows as she straddled him, pinning him down, had been ready to pull her towards him – now they lifted her from him and he sat up.

'You don't know what you're saying. I couldn't do that.'

Half a dozen responses came to Lidi's mind but she knew instantly that none of them would do. The sun had slid down behind the downs and its golden reflections went from the little clearing. Suddenly the grass seemed damp and the air chill.

She rose and began to gather up her tools.

'Lidi . . .' His tone was wretched.

Lidi – turmoil of anguish and anger like camphor in water.

'Lidi. Say something.'

'There's nothing to say.'

'There's everything to say.'

'No, you just said it all.'

'Only that . . .'

Angrily she turned on him. 'That I don't know what I'm saying. I offer myself without strings, without conditions for ever – and I don't know what I'm saying?'

'What it means.'

'Then you must think I'm a fool. You say that you love me . . .'

'I do.'

'Not enough.'

'How can you say that? I'm willing to start like a lad seven years my junior to make something of myself so that I can be a fit husband . . .'

'Husband. Husband. Isn't lover good enough? It has been up till now. Going to church and me changing my name and saying I'd obey you can't make things better between me and you than they are already. What would make it better is if we stopped having to hide in corners and keep looking about us when we want to love each another.'

'It's the proper way of things. It's what I learnt from my mother

and father – God Rest them. It's the way a man says in front of his
neighbours that he will stick by the one woman.'

'Oh Luce.' Sadness and irritation. 'You know that's not true.
You've only got to open your eyes in the fields and the dances and
that. Look at Tan; did her vowing to cherish and obey do anything?
And I tell you this, if my mother was to come back on earth, my
father's vows to Tansy would have gone the same way. Vows are in
the heart. If I was to promise *you* that I'd be faithful to you, that's
what I'd be. Not faithful because some clergyman said I should, but
faithful because I had promised *you*.'

'It's wrong for two people who love each other not to get wed
properly.'

'Well, we aren't wed – do you say that's wrong?'

'I want us to be.'

'But not yet. And only in the usual way.'

'There isn't any other way.'

'There's *my* way.'

'That's not marriage.'

'Oh yes it is. If anything was to be a marriage, it'd be that. It'd be
the coming together of two people who love each other in a proper
partnership. Me not having to give up my name, not having to say
that I should obey you.' Pleading to be understood. 'Luce, it'd be a
lie, I shouldn't obey you, only slaves and servants and prisoners
have to "obey". How can anybody want another person to obey
them? And I couldn't do it! I shouldn't!'

'It's how it's always been. Somebody has to make the rules in a
family, be master in a household.'

'*Master!* Yes.'

'Oh Lidi, don't take it all so serious. There's no harm in it.
Come on, let's kiss and make up.' He laughed. 'I promise I shan't
never make you do nothing you don't want to.' He tried to pull her
to him, but she snatched herself away.

'You're like Pa, a great one for spouting about "equality" and
"freedom" when there's inequality under your noses. Oh no, you
don't want to change that.'

'It's not the same thing.'

The light had almost gone. Lidi, ready to leave now, stood on
the path that led to Raike Bottom and into the village. Luce stood,
hands thrust deep into his pockets, toeing up bits of turf.

'It's the very same thing.' She began to walk away, her anger
and misery separating out, the anger foaming in her head, the
misery twisting in her belly.

'Until men realise what women feel like, being handed around between them as though they weren't proper people but bits of property, of no account at all.' The anger effervesced. 'Given! Given in marriage! Nobody's ever going to give me!'

Now, only the crimson afterglow at the top of the downs. Lidi set off along the narrow path without looking back to see if Luce followed.

JUST AFTER THE turn of the first quarter of the century, Bess Smith died. It was as though, with her son settled down with a woman who could give her no grandchildren, with Jude and Will set up together, and Lidi and Sarah grown, she had nothing left to do. Ever since she had come to live at Croud Cantle years ago, she had had a wonderful purpose in life – to care for all the people there. And now they were all caring for themselves.

Almost to her last breath, she worked and cooked and baked and made concoctions and simple remedies for them, but after the year in Winchester, her bustling and clattering ways quietened. She became easily fatigued, until one day she said, 'Oh dear, Jude, I a have to leave that there cheese press a minute, he gets that stiff these days,' and sat down and quietly died.

When she had been brought there as the unmarried wife of Tomas Nugent, Cantle people had found her the source of gossip and wonder for not being ashamed of her situation as the wife of a bigamist with a son to show for it. But strangely, especially in an isolated community where any tit-bit is worth chewing over, it had been only a five-minute wonder, perhaps because Bess Smith would do anything for anybody; more likely it was the fact that she was no oil painting. Scandal does not easily attach itself to the ill-favoured or aged, so that Bess Smith living with her deceiver's true wife and family seemed not sinful.

On the day that she was buried in the same plot as her sister-wife the worst that anybody could find to say of her was, 'She was such a queer old lady.'

ADDRESS TO THE LABOURERS OF SHORLAY

The Destruction of Devices

The Destruction of Mechanical Farming Devices is to indulge in acts of the most Wanton Barbarity.
These Machines are Introduced to give Employment to Men, Women and Children. If they are Deprived of their Means of Supporting themselves, then they will be Obliged to Apply to the Parish for Support, which is no better than a Species of Begging.
Think a moment of the Effect of your Conduct and see that if it is continued it will deprive your Employers of the means of Carrying out their Business – and consequently of Paying Poor Rates.
That Property must be Protected is a Truth firmly Established in the mind of every Man of Sense. Violence may Triumph for a Day, but in a Civilized country that will be of Short Duration.
Justice will prevail and the Strong Hand of the Law will Protect every man in the Lawful Possession of his Property.
Be assured that I am your Friend and a Well-wisher – B.N.

SARAH RETURNED TO Stonebridge Manor with regret at having to leave the splendid and romantic surroundings of Florence. She knew that she had changed in the six months that they had been travelling, not only her discreet relationship with Alec, but in the way she felt about her life with the Broughlakes.

Sarah Toose continued to reflect the life-style of her employers; when they went to take the waters at Bath, she experienced life there; when Mrs Broughlake had new skirts, they often came down to Sarah, and when they packed up and went to Florence or London, Sarah had a taste of some of the Broughlake crumbs.

The relationship between the two women, wealthy heiress married to an industrial fortune, and village girl who had been Under Nursery-nurse, had grown to be more friendly than was socially acceptable. Had she known, Delphine's Mama would have strongly disapproved and had Sarah put in her place, or out of the house. But Sarah never overstepped the mark, never presumed upon her mistress's favouritism. Nor did she allow Osbert Broughlake's little peccadillo of being visibly aroused by her cause any ripple in the formality of smooth deference towards him. She wondered whether it might be her manner that disturbed him. She knew from what she used to see going on back home that men – and women – went off the track sometimes with somebody very different from their wife or husband – but she saw no reason to try to make herself any different from what she was.

Delphine, tall and white, with dark complicated curls, plaits, elaborate gowns cut to display the overflowing splendid bosom, was in direct contrast to her lady's maid. Sarah, in her mid-twenties, was small, pink-skinned with high, neat breasts. She dressed her red-gold hair simply and wore plain dark high-necked dresses. If Delphine was a highly-perfumed orchid, then Sarah was perhaps a simple marguerite. Highly-perfumed orchids have their occasions yet are not as entirely satisfying as a simple marguerite.

Her mistress often confided in Sarah, and talked to her as she might a sister or close friend. Sarah knew most of the trials and tribulations of the marriage from Delphine's statements about men.

'Why is it, Sarah, that men must always be so attentive before marriage and so indifferent after? Are rural men like this?'

'Rural' men was one of Delphine's favourite subjects, she was intrigued by them. Was almost hungry for the most intimate details that she could gather from Sarah.

'Rural men are just men, Mrs Delphine.'

'Surely not. Rural men are strong from their work, must have very lusty appetites; when they put bulls to the cows it can only end in rousing them . . . surely?'

Sarah smiled that such a mundane chore should be of interest and could only assume that it was a comparison of ideas.

Rural men with the lusty appetite of bulls – if only she knew how difficult it was sometimes to get the bull's interest away from new pasture.

Now that Sarah lived closer to them, she began to know more about her employers. They seemed to believe that, because the people from whom she and Alec had come lived lives that were dark mysteries to their own social class, then they must be more exciting, pagan, Bacchanalian, Circean. Mrs Delphine seemed to imagine that a milkmaid couldn't get into a field without running the gauntlet of swains with lusty appetites.

That Alec had explosive energy and passion most likely confirmed Delphine's belief, and that Sarah took Osbert's occasional condition in her stride, perhaps confirmed the same to him.

In Florence, Sarah and Alec had been so carefully secretive, that Mrs Delphine never had the smallest inkling of their relationship. It might have excited her even more to know that her 'rural' man spent himself also with her 'rural' maidservant, but Alec and Sarah were only too aware of the vagaries of employers to jeopardise their good luck in such decent positions.

After their return to normal life in Stonebridge, Mrs Delphine's tasting of a rural rough tumble with her husband's valet had ceased. Probably for want of opportunity, for in Stonebridge Alec had plenty of work below stairs. Neither Sarah nor Alec had the free time that they had been allowed in Florence. So, what with that, and the fact that the manservants slept in a wing of the house far from the little nursery-floor room which Sarah still had, Alec lost both Mistress and Maid.

There was, too, Brendan Lewis.

Whether it was the contrast between the two men or whether Alec was just a fevered moment in Sarah's life, come about by their being thrown together in the relaxed atmosphere of Florence, Sarah now began to see that Brendan Lewis was worth ten of Alec James.

Ninn was away at Winchester now a great deal of the time, but when he was at home he always persuaded Delphine.

'Mother, Tooey was mine before she was yours.'

'Darling boy, I can't be without her for an entire morning.'

Delphine found her growing son to have great charm and it was easy for her to indulge him.

'So long as you return her in time for my hair.'

And so Ninn would try to recapture those happiest of his days when he had Sarah entirely to himself. This was how, soon after returning from Florence, Sarah encountered Brendan again.

'Sarah, ah you'm back. It seems you been gone ages.'

'Only six months.'

'Well, you looks like it suited you.'

His frank eyes held no secrets as did Alec's. He thought Sarah to be wonderful and his eyes said so.

'I feel very well.'

'Would you like to sit down a bit? Ninn won't be back for an hour if I knows him.'

Sarah sat in the tack room and watched Brendan oiling and polishing.

'I missed you, Sarah.

She didn't reply but smiled non-committally.

Before going to Florence, they had met a few times in the course of their duty, such as when Mrs Delphine wanted Sarah to fetch something from Blackbrook or Winchester, and Brendan would be ordered to take her in the trap. They had each enjoyed the outings and the company of the other. Unlike Alec, whose conversation seemed to be all gossip or suggestion, Brendan was able to skip from subject to subject. He had been taught to read and write very early, and still spent much of his free time reading anything he could get his hands upon.

But, Sarah needed more from a man. She needed it to be confirmed that she could arouse passion. What excited her as much as the act itself, was the fact that she had the power to arouse a man without flaunting herself. She did not see that in Brendan's eyes, neither did she want to see it. Brendan was a draught of clear water after too much red wine.

That she had this side to her nature, had in Florence, caused Sarah some concern, especially when, in the light of day, she saw how easily she might have thrown overboard everything she had gained for herself. Each time, she told herself afterwards that it wasn't worth it; then she would catch Alec looking slyly at her, and again she would respond, and again find herself sighing with relief that she had interrupted Alec before he had seemed inclined to do so himself.

She would have been a bit wary had it been Alec who was instructed to drive her to Winchester to replace a broken bottle of the spermaceti which was so essential to Delphine's well-being; he was quite capable of faking a breakdown to delay their return. To go with Brendan she looked upon without concern and with pleasure.

It was September, and they set off early, Thursday, when the big market took place, so they planned to take the small tracks over the downs. They left the cultivated parkland and passed through the little wood where Sarah used to bring Ninn when she first came to Stonebridge.

The cool air meeting the sun garlanded the hedgerows with morning dew. On the damp pungent floor, red-capped fungi thrust up and then open; in the hedge-bottoms and open fields mice gathered food to lay down their survival layer of fat, as they gathered so they were stalked by the stealthily gliding stoat. The full scents of summer blended with the oncoming winter. The fruits were ripe, human and animal were taking what could be taken and cached for the long-nighted months not far off. But for now, although the sun never got overhead, it was still golden.

Brendan breathed deeply. 'Ah, I reckon this is the best month of the whole year. My father was a carter you know. And we used to be up at the crack of dawn and out in the fields, going back and forth to the rickyards till dark.'

'You wouldn't want to go back to that?'

Brendan considered. 'I don't know. Things like that always seem best looked back on. Perhaps not, but I can't say that I got too much respect for the job I do here.'

'Why not? I thought you loved your work.'

'Oh, I like horses all right.'

'Then what's wrong with the job?'

'It seems such a useless kind of a thing to do with your life.'

They were now out of the wood and were passing the old barn where she and Ninn had come years ago. The barn was now sagging roofed and decaying.

'There used to be a machine there once.'

'Ah, the thrasher.'

'I wonder where it's gone.'

He looked at her and frowned a little.

She said, 'I remember how all got up I was about it.'

'Why was that?'

'It wasn't long after I had left home, and I remembered my father talking about what would happen if mechanical things came.' She paused, remembering the scene. 'There was a man who was cheeky to me because I told him his machine would put men out of work . . . and I remember Master Ninn not knowing what corn was for. And I felt sorry for him . . . you know? Not knowing where his bread came from. Sorry and angry at the same time.'

It was not until the journey home that Brendan referred again to the incident. He had talked to her about a book he was reading and had asked her all about Florence and the places they had passed through on their way to Italy, and was it true that there were statues at every street corner, and fountains and pools as he had seen illustrated, and she had described for him every wonder as it had struck her.

They had fallen into a companionable silence for about a mile when he suddenly said, 'Didn't you ever hear what happened to the Master's threshing machine?'

'No I never.'

'Hm, well it just shows how cut off things are up at the house. It's no wonder their neighbours practically die of hunger and they don't know.'

'What do you mean, what happened?'

'The machine breakers came after it.'

'You mean like happened before in Kent?'

'In Kent, Sussex and everywhere lately.'

'They came and broke the Master's machine?'

'Yes.'

'Why that's terrible.'

'I'm surprised you say that.'

'Why?'

'What you said earlier about you remembering what your father said.'

Scornfully, 'Oh my father! He . . .' She stopped, recalling the day when she had run away from him in Wickham.

'I dare say you must have been away in Bath or somewhere. It was nasty. Three of both sides were injured and four of the breakers were sent to gaol.'

'Well, that's no more than they deserved.'

'What do you reckon people should do if they got no work and their children needs feeding?'

'They can go on the Parish can't they?'

'D'you reckon you'd like to live on public money?'

Sarah was silent, remembering the angry words of humiliated men seated around the fireside at home.

'Suppose there was a machine that could do your work and you were dismissed because of it.'

'There isn't a machine that could do Mrs Delphine's hair.'

'Suppose then it became the thing for women to cut their hair short?'

'Women couldn't wear short hair.'

'Why not?'

'I don't know.' She laughed to cover the disturbance. 'Just because.'

'But just suppose it *did* happen . . . say that a machine was invented for everything – and there isn't any reason why it shouldn't happen – what if there came a day when all those potions and pomades you spend so much time on could be bought cheap and easy? What if an apothecary could invent a substance to put onto clothes (like you do starch), and it kept off every stain you can imagine. Why, Hampshire'd soon be full of lady's maids on the Parish.'

'Then I'd do something else.'

'But what if all the others were already doing it, and for less than it takes to live on?'

'Then I'd go away somewhere else.'

'And what if you was fifty years old and employers only wanted nifty little damsels?'

'Oh Brendan Lewis – you're just like my father used to be . . . always going beyond what's reasonable to win an argument.'

'I'll wager he might a been laughed at in his young days for predicting that mechanical thrashers and winnowers'd put people on the Parish.'

Sarah remembered: '*You mark my words, there'll come a day when the machines will be on every farm in the country,*' and some of their neighbours sitting beside the Toose hearth had laughed; she remembered climbing onto his knee so that she might glower at them.

And now it was coming true.

At the end of the afternoon's ride beside him, she wished that it was he who was the travelling manservant.

Life in the Broughlake household followed its round of London, Bath, Hampshire until, late in the third decade of the nineteenth century, Osbert Broughlake died. Some might say, fittingly, for a man who favoured spring-loaded shotguns to protect his game birds and fired off rounds close to small children to make men of 'em.

He was found in the gun room shot dead. For a man so thorough and critical of sloppiness, it was surprising that such an accident should be his end.

Only his wife, doctor and valet knew of the disease that would have killed him anyhow within the year. Only a lady in London's Coram Street knew how he came by the disease. The valet knew because the Master confided everything to him, and needed him. The wife came to know because the valet whispered to her that, had she thought of such a thing, she should not recommence sharing conjugal rights. Those rights had been mutually withdrawn when Delphine's doctor pronounced that she had a delicate internal structure that best be left undisturbed. Which arrangement had been quite satisfactory to the consciences of both parties.

After a week or two of mourning, Delphine left for Italy and her favourite Florence to allow the sun to dry her tears. This time, being newly widowed and not wishing to go into public accommodation, she took a villa overlooking the Arno. She took only her maid and manservant; the rest of the staff were engaged locally by her solicitor.

Stonebridge was now Ninn's and would be kept open for his purposes when he came home from Winchester, and there were plans for a pleasant house to be made in the park for his mother. The work on Hampton House was put in hand at once. But for now, Mrs Delphine would recuperate in the sun.

7

I T IS DARK and the Poacher is out with his close dark cap pulled well down and a cloth over his mouth and nose. The Poacher crosses the Dunnock Stream at the rift in the downs where one side is Winchester Hill and the other Old Marl. All the land is owned by the Estate, but it is only on Old Marl where it is 'fair game' to take – the rest being rented from the Estate by small farmers. The Big House is built at the foot of Old Marl and in its parkland are more rabbits and pheasants than its owner could eat in a dozen lifetimes.

As he works his way alongside the Dunnock the Poacher turns over in his mind how big a bag he needs to satisfy his neighbours. The Innkeeper wanted a brace or two of rabbits, the Miller, the Carter, and they want at least one brace of pheasant at the Rectory. And the Poacher's wife wants rabbit stew for the childer.

The right to kill gamebirds is the prerogative of only land-owners and the eldest sons of esquires of high rank. The Poacher disagrees – food on the wing is the gift and bounty of nature.

The law agrees with the esquires – as well it may, for they created it the law. The law could transport the Poacher for seven years. Worse, if he carries a knife or stick, for then he may be hanged. No idle threat, it is only five years since a young poacher of Lord Palmerston's who let off a shotgun, was hanged at Romsey, not far south of Cantle.

The Goodenstone Poacher knows the odds, but has no choice but to accept them – it's his job.

Enough light to see. A rabbit has been half caught and has twisted the snare into a tangle to free its half-severed leg. Clear air and quiet. The Poacher clouts the weak creature, takes out a folding knife and cuts it free of the snare.

Quiet!

There are men's voices, carried from the other side of the Dunnock.

He detects that two men are walking towards the village from the direction of Motte. Nothing to fear, not the Keeper. These men make no attempt to go unheard.

The Poacher works on. Another snare released, the limp body pocketed, the snare re-set.

Suddenly, there is a small click and before he can move his scalp muscles to cock his ear in its direction, there is an explosion.

He finds himself disoriented, looking up at the stars, listening to the sound of distant screaming. Next he picks up the sound of men scrambling from the direction of the face of Old Marl. He sees their horn lanterns dotting about as they come down the slope. Keeper's men. The shot could not have come from them, they are too far distant. Keeper's men. He knows, yet strangely cannot move, his legs will not let him run and the stars are in front of his face. As he tries to run back down-stream away from the Keeper's men, again he hears someone groan. Then, closer, the sound of undergrowth being trampled.

'Dick?' The voice was low but clear. 'Dick Bone, is it you? Where are you?' He says 'Here' but only hears again the deep groan. Then there is a lantern close at hand. Then the lantern is wavering above him.

'The buggers . . . shot in the back.'

'God in heaven! Help me get him up.'

The Poacher feels himself being hauled up. A cry of agony, then all goes black.

8

FAIR GAME

It is one of their maxims to plunder and pillage their rich neighbours without any reluctance; and that this is held to be neither sin nor crime among them. And so constantly do they abide and act by this maxim, that in every parish almost in the kingdom there is a kind of confederacy ever carrying on against a certain person of opulence called the squire whose property is considered as free booty by all his poor neighbours; who, as they conclude that there is no manner of guilt in such depredations, look upon it as a point of honour and moral obligation to conceal and to preserve each other from punishment on all such occasions.

Tom Jones, Fielding

Dick Bone and his forefathers had been Cantle's game-catchers for generations. They could slip a hand under a trout and have him out of the water in seconds, and were skilful at taking anything from a hare to an occasional deer. Whilst Cantle children grew up knowing how to set snares and go ferreting the warrens, it was recognised that, with the exception of pig, most of the provision of fresh meat ought to be left to the man whose job it was in the community. As Dick would not brew beer for sale, so Tazey James would not lay snares on any land but his own.

Dick Bone was a hunter whose skill was legend; even those who remembered Old Boney, his grandfather, had to give grudging best to Dick. It had to be admitted too that Old Boney could never have contended with the hardening of the Magistrates. In his day the commons were open, and whilst Old Sir Henry Goodenstone might have had his Keeper prowling about occasionally just to keep everybody on their toes, he would never have bothered to go to the lengths that grandson Eustace went to to keep wild birds to himself.

But, like his neighbours, Dick Bone considered that anything living wild was free for anyone to claim. That one man might enclose leaping, swimming or hopping creatures and lay claim to them, and suggest that to take them was no different from stealing a neighbour's hog, was ridiculous and not to be taken into account.

Wild coney, hare, pheasant, trout and salmon had always been an important source of meat for villagers. Hard labour could not be done without meat and fat. If enclosures of the Common Lands and the passing of Game Laws made it the property of landowners, Dick Bone and the rest of Cantle did not agree. But it did mean that Dick had to be always one silent step ahead of the Estate Keeper.

As had his Jutish ancestors, the Meonwara, set out to examine snares, so did Dick Bone. Unlike his ancestors, Dick set out after dark.

October, a clear night, in the distance the bell in the little Saxon church at Corhampton sounded clearly, nearer probably in Warnford or West Meon, followed by the eight o'clock curfew. Time to be indoors as, far back in time, Meonwara people would have been on a night that smelled of winter close at hand. The Meonwara had only shades and spirits to beware, Dick Bone had the Goodenstones' Keeper.

9

IN THE KITCHEN of Shaft's Cottage, Jack tears a sheet into strips whilst Lidi, with blood up past her wrists, frowns as she tries to remove metal from the mess that was Dick Bone's right shoulder. Dick, muzzy from a double measure of brandy, lies face down and groans with pain.

Agitated, John Toose, in bare feet and legs, his breeches wet almost to the thigh, watches his daughter.

'Staunch the blood, Lidi.'

'All right! I will, I will, but it's not going to stop until I get the shot out – there's still some here.' Sweat of anxiety darkens her hair to deep red and trickles from her brow. As she probes with a small pair of quill-pluckers, Dick Bone grits his teeth and groans again.

'There!' She drops the metal into a bowl. 'You'll have to hold him down whilst I puts some spirit in the wound.'

The action and the scream from Bone was over in seconds, but it left them all white faced and the wounded man mercifully unconscious.

She continues to work for a few more minutes, Jack tearing, Luce mopping and John fetching more water and bowls. Luce is as wet as John, and even barer, he wears nothing except his breeches. His pale hair, stiffened on one side with Dick Bone's blood, falls over his forehead as he bends across the table to hand Lidi the wet presses and remove the bloodied ones. The line of his scar is dark in the shadow of the oil-lamps.

Eventually, it is done. The kitchen and all of them except Jack look as though there has been a pig-sticking. On the kitchen table is the blood-leached figure of Dick Bone. He lies on his left side; the worst of the bleeding has stopped; his right shoulder is wrapped in linen strips and looks half-dead.

'Pour us the brandy, Jack.'

'I poured it. Here.' Jack holds out a good tot measure for each of them to take. Luce raises Dick Bone's head whilst Lidi puts a few drops of the spirit into his mouth. He opens his eyes.

When the spirit has gone down he says, 'Thank God 'twas thee

John Toose. I thought Kyte had got us. I thought I was done for.' His voice is slurred, but a touch of colour has come to his face.

They helped him to a sitting position. He swayed and began to topple; John and Luce helped him to settle beside the hearth where he lounged awkwardly on a bolster regaining his equilibrium.

'How'd I come here?'

'Me and Luce had been . . . out on a bit of business over Motte way.' Although a person's liberty was no longer in jeopardy for speaking for Combines and Unions, as it had been a few years back when John was imprisoned for it, other inhibitors applied – eviction, loss of job, withdrawal of business or patronage.

The great inhibitor – Fear. And whilst John and Luce were free to be more open than most, the men and women they met in small groups were not. They'd been out on a 'bit of business'.

'We was just coming down the Bottom Track past Willow Farm Lane when we saw the flash and heard the explosion.'

'It come from close by there, didn't it?'

'Ah, it near frightened the life out of me and Luce.'

'It waddn't Kyte's men.'

'No, they were up on Marl.'

'Ah, I seen their lights.' Stiffly, painfully Bone raised himself to an upright position paling with the agony. 'Bugger! That don't half hurt.'

After Jack had poured more brandy Bone went on. 'It was a spring-loader waddn't it.'

Not a question, a statement, a grievous acknowledgement that what Cantle people believed 'wouldn't never happen here', had happened.   The spring-loaded shotgun, that was so notoriously barbaric that there was even a movement in Parliament to make it illegal.

The despicable device that deemed game-birds of more value than people, had been introduced into *their* village – onto *their* estate, by the people who owed the very silk shirts on their backs to the villagers of Cantle.

'It's what me and Luce reckoned, wasn't it Luce?'

'There wasn't anybody close to where it fired off. The nearest was them up on Old Marl, it couldn't have been them.'

'What happened after you found me? How'd you get me back up the bank?'

'We didn't try. Luce put you over his shoulder and we walked down in the stream so the dogs couldn't follow.'

'Well Lad, 'tis a good thing that I an't much bigger than your maid here, for I knows how much dead-weight is.' He paused then asked, 'I reckon some of my stuff must have got left there.'

'No, I brought your bag. There wasn't anything for them to find.'

'I better go, they'll be looking for me. Mustn't find me here.' He went to stand, but the loss of blood made him fall back weakly.

'You aren't going anywhere, Mr Bone,' Lidi said.

'No, no,' Bone protested. 'Kyte a be out looking, he must a seen the blood on the ground. If he finds me here . . .'

'He won't find you here.'

'I reckon I'll call down and tell Mrs Bone that he's here.'

'No! Let Hetty stay worried. If she knows I be safe and Kyte goes round there, he a know straight away somebody's got me holed up. Hett an't no good at hiding anything.'

So, Dick Bone rested under the Toose roof. Lidi, in her day-clothes, sat up dozing in a chair with only a rushlight burning, to watch that no bleeding started again. From time to time during the night she pulled back the covers to look at the dressing and to wipe a cooling cloth over Bone's forehead. As the hours passed he seemed to become more fevered and delirious.

Some time before dawn, Lidi jerked awake. Unusual sounds. Voices, not in the house but from close by. People moving about before daylight was nothing unusual, but these men were talking loudly, doors were being knocked, and she sensed that it was still night.

She looked to see if Dick Bone had been disturbed.

'Oh Lord!' She laid her hand upon his brow and felt fever.

She doused the light and went to the window. All that she could see was some lanterns moving about. Her father came into the room still buttoning his breeches.

'What's going on, Pa?'

'I think it might be Kyte and the Constable.'

A groan from Dick Bone.

'Hush Dick, you'll be all right.' John in a low voice.

'Pa, he's bad.'

'He been bleeding again?'

'No, it's a bad fever.'

'I reckon it's Kyte looking for Dick.'

Now they were whispering to one another like conspirators, all the while watching the lights as they moved from house to house.

A loud moan from the sick man.

Lidi goes to him and lays a wet cloth on his hot dry face.

'Kyte knows Dick can't have gone far.'

'What shall we do?'

'Nothing.'

'What if they come in?'

'They can't unless they got a Magistrate's warrant.'

Dick loudly says something incoherent.

'Lord Pa, they'll hear him.'

'I'll have to forestall them. You just keep Dick as quiet as you can.'

He rushes out. Soon she sees him, in his old smock and working hat, dragging the small cart from the shed where it was ready to be loaded later that morning. He picks up clay pots, labelled plants, trees, anything to hand and heaves them anyhow onto the cart.

Two lanterns come hastily towards the yard. She opens the window a crack, but quickly shuts it when Dick begins to mutter. Now Lidi rushes downstairs, lights lamps and bangs about bellowing the fire and clattering pots. Now the voices are in the yard. She takes a lantern and the water-crock and goes to the pump.

It is Kyte, the Estate Agent, Thatcher the Estate's Keeper and Prickett. Prickett is the Parish official – churchwarden, overseer, tithing-man and constable. They hold lanterns high so that the light shines upon her father's face. They turn as they see Lidi. She begins to heave on the pump-handle, pumping it up and down as though she were determined to destroy it. The rusty iron squeaks and grinds. Her father raises his voice to be heard.

'Take no notice, 'tis only my little maid, she stops up too late and don't like to get out a bed when we got an early start.' He attempts to sound easy and genial. 'I should keep out of her way, she a take it out on anything.'

Lidi plays up her part, noisily clanking the rusty handle, filling buckets that do not need filling, slopping them as close to their feet as she dares. Eventually the men leave and make their way to the cottage next door. John and Lidi do not return to the house, but continue with the pretence that they are preparing for a very early start.

When the men have reached as far as the Dragon and Fount where there are already lights in the window, they return to the house. Lidi rushes to look at Dick Bone. His condition is deteriorating fast. His body burns. John helps roll him over and they remove the dressings. The wounds are inflamed and suppurating.

'I've never had to do with anything as bad as that,' Lidi said. 'I don't know what to do except try to keep the fever down, I don't know what to do with the wound.'

'I know who'll see to it. Here, help me strip him. You keep sponging him and I'll fetch Tazey.'

It was dawn when John went the few hundred yards to the inn.

'Taze, can you spare half an hour?'

He called back to someone in the kitchen, 'You can start the breakfast, I shan't be long.' He picked up a small sacking bag. 'Come on then, I got my stuff ready as soon as the constable's men was gone, I guessed Dick'd be holed up somewhere . . .'

'Where have they gone now?'

'Up to the Nugent place.'

John hoped that Luce would realise what was going on. He remembered the blood in Luce's hair and his wet trousers, ah, it'd be all right, Luce was no fool.

Taze learnt his surgeon's craft on the battlefield. He had suffered crude surgery himself when the stump of his leg became infected and benefited from it when the stump cured. Now he had a dot-and-carry-one gait. 'Heart of oak there, lads,' Taze would say slapping the wooden limb. Now, as he and John went back to Shaft's Cottage, Tazey's recognisable tread seemed to announce itself to the countryside.

Inside the house, Lidi was sponging the delirious Bone with cold water.

'Right Gel, let's have a look at him.' He put his face close to the wound and sniffed. 'Get us a good red fire and bellows it up fierce. B'ile a pot of water and put in some clean strips to dress it after. We a have to get him down on the kitchen table.'

As soon as he laid out the things he had brought with him in the sack, Tazey seemed to change. Normally he was the jolly inn-keeper who easily regaled his customers with his tales of battle and gossip about officers. Now though, his face was serious, his sensuous lips firm and the long-lashed eyes that were still as appealing to women as were his son's, concentrated on what he was doing.

Lidi had got the fire white-hot. At its heart, into it Taze plunged a blade with a long detachable handle, then he hung a little iron pot of what looked and smelled like bees-wax or honey on the fire-chain. From some bundles of neatly cut straws he selected three.

'Raise up his head, Gel. You John take the blade out and cool the handle off with water.'

Taze opened Dick Bone's mouth, inserted the straws well back in the throat and blew.

He grinned at Lidi. 'Always got to remember to blow and not suck.'

Lidi queried his meaning with a frown.

'Powders to deaden the senses. Makes a terrible difference to a man what's got to lose his leg.' He slapped his own. 'Dangerous stuff though. There's men what'd kill for a pinch of it – can't do without it.'

Suddenly Bone, who had been writhing and restless, went limp.

'Right Gel!'

The next ten minutes were fascinating and horrifying to Lidi. He ordered her and she obeyed. Apart from the few words of command, he worked silently and swiftly. The combined smell of seared flesh as he cleaned the infected wound and the honey-wax with which he thickly smeared it were sickening. She wondered how he came by this strange ritual of burning knives and boiling cloths, but Tazey James' reputation as a honey-healer was proven.

'That's it! Take out the b'iled dressings and dry 'em off in front of the fire, then soon as they'm ready bind him up.'

John who had watched Taze and Lidi from across the room became animated once more and handed Tazey a large measure of spirit which he downed in one and held out for another.

He stood back from his work and viewed it with the satisfaction of a woman who has made a complicated harvest loaf. 'Not a bad job, although I says it who shouldn't.'

He seemed so proud of his skill, that Lidi could scarcely ask him if he thought Dick Bone was saved. His confidence spoke that he had healed the wound.

'Ah, I reckon I might a been a better surgeon than a brewster.'

Dick Bone was breathing evenly and heavily. He was still feverish so Lidi sponged him constantly as he lay on the kitchen table.

Then, suddenly . . . the door opened.

'Well, well. If there an't a pig-sticking just starting.' Thatcher, the Keeper, with Kyte and Prickett stood on the doorstep. 'There sirs,' Thatcher said, 'I told 'ee, that sooner or later the villain or one of his 'ccomplices would likely call on Tazey James.'

None of Bone's protectors were prepared for the shock of looking up from Bone's infected wound into the face of the man who had caused it. They were dumb-stricken.

Kyte came into the kitchen.

Lidi was the first to recover, and stood before him.

'Where do you think you're going?'

'We'm going to remove that there carcase from off of your table.'

Lidi stepped forward, and without thinking, pushed Thatcher in the chest. He fell back into the two and suddenly all three found themselves outside the house once more.

Lidi, her eyes glittery from anger and lack of sleep, confronted Agent, Keeper and Constable. 'This'ns our house. Who we have in it, and what we do in it, is nothing to do with the Estate. The Goodenstones employ you – not us! There's nobody in this house that is anything to do with you or them or the Estate. If you want to come in, then you a have to give us good reason why.'

Now John and Taze had come out. 'It's all right, Lid, Mister Kyte knows his limitations, don't you Mister Kyte. You know that you have to have a warrant and it has to be done in the legal way to get inside a private dwelling – and this here is a private dwelling.'

Thatcher was furious, both at having been caught unawares and tripped up by a little slip of a woman, and at knowing that what John Toose said was right. The Agent had slipped up, and the Constable was an old fool. Never mind, at last he had Bone. Now he had him. Judiciously he decided that he had nothing to lose by going away and getting a proper warrant. By the look of Bone, he wasn't going far. The Estate Agent motioned that they should leave.

When they reached the gateway, Keeper Thatcher called back, 'All right. I'll be back. Tell Dick Bone, it an't no use him denying he was stealing game for we got the evidence that it was him who was there last night. Show em.' The Constable took a knife with a carved handle from his pocket and held it up. 'We know 'tis Bone's. His missis said it was his.'

Before the end of the third decade, the use of spring-loaded shotguns to protect property was outlawed, but that was after Bone was found guilty of armed poaching and transported for seven years. The judge might as well have transported him for life for all the chance Bone had of finding the means of returning home after he had served his sentence.

As aiders and abetters and protectors of a felon, Tazey James received three months' imprisonment, and John Toose as a more persistent offender received six.

A TABLEAU IN HIGH RELIEF

Sarah and Alec knew nothing of their respective fathers' trouble. They had enough of their own.

It is often the case that the wonderful special memory of a place that one holds as a perfect talisman, and believes will always be so, disintegrates upon second acquaintance.

For Sarah, this was so of Florence.

The statues which had previously been sensuous and graceful, appeared vulgar and simpering; purple shadowed alleys were dank passages; in the wide piazzas she suffered great discomfort from lack of shade. The sun burned. The dust smarted the eyes. The churches were dank and decaying.

If the inanimate was disillusioning, then the people were more so.

The flamboyant Italians with their rippling language changed to intrusive arm-wavers who talked too loudly. Mrs Delphine was demanding of Sarah, and becoming careless of her reputation, which reflected upon those who served her. The special relationship that she had adopted with her Maid had become irksome to Sarah, who did not wish to know Madam's hopes and wants or give an opinion as to whether she should push up or lower her decolletage. Decorum, which she should have observed as a recently bereaved widow, was lacking. It was this latter that shocked Sarah more than the widow's growing obsession with her Manservant.

Sarah's greatest disenchantment was with Alec. Almost as soon as the household was set up, his position within it changed. Although he was still nominally the senior Manservant and thus in charge of much of the running of the establishment, Delphine was more and more open with her favour of him. Alec was no good at such duties as controlling other servants; consequently there were always minor squabbles which were usually settled by dismissal.

During the first week or two, when an inexplicable sadness was upon her, Sarah had been glad when he had come to hold her in his arms at night; but now that he almost openly took advantage of Mrs Delphine's besottedness with him, she felt diminished. He took to

entering the boudoir where Sarah might be dressing her Mistress's
hair and perhaps adjusting a tendril of hair at the back of Delphine's
neck, allowing one hand to fall upon her shoulder; or he might
bring up a corsage that had been delivered and pin it upon her, idly
cupping his hand round one breast the more easily to adjust the
flower upon the other. What they did when she was not there and
could not see, Sarah could cope with, but when he made a point of
catching her eye, she felt that she was being included in the
complicity, was part of his pleasure. When he was in the room the
Mistress behaved as though the Maid did not exist and laid her own
hand upon the straying one of her Manservant and pressed it into
her flesh.

Without really trying, Alec James, the village boy who had
started his career by practising upon the maidens of Cantle his art of
seduction with touches, looks and few words, had got a bigger
prize than he had ever imagined possible. If his hair was sparser than
when he had made the girlish Lidi breathless, his handsome
maturity, and his cock-suredness in the presence of any woman,
caused them to meet his eye and accept his look.

It was at times like this that she felt flushed with shame that she
had allowed Brendan Lewis to declare his regard for her, and that
she had not refuted his high opinion of her.

Brendan Lewis. His plain good face. His unaltered rural voice.
His relaxed easy body astride a powerful hunter. Always, around
her memory of him, was greenness and cool, clean air.

Sarah's disgust with herself came to a head one day when she
was out on an errand for her Mistress. The day was hot and the air
humid. The spray from seemingly endless splashing fountains and
spurting water made her feel sticky. In one narrow street, she
caught the drifting smell of strong garlic frying in oil; it seemed to
cling to her nauseously even when she had long gone from that
street.

She wished that she was able to recapture the freshness of the
first visit, to sit beside splashing water and look at the sensuous
marble, often so openly worked to represent the physical nature of
men and women as both sensuous and wholesome.

On her way back, she detoured to a small piazza she and Alec
had discovered. It was a small square enclosed by homely
buildings. Centrally on one side was an unexceptional gush of clear
water into a stone bowl on whose splashback was a tableau carved
in high relief. A gloriously naked young man held out one cupped

hand to a woman whose drapery was charmingly disarranged to reveal a splendid bosom; his other hand, with crooked fingers, was extended downwards to where a more slender girl was kneeling apparently scooping water from the stone bowl.

When she and Alec had found it, they had debated the meaning of the trio. Sarah had suggested that, as he wore nothing but a crown of leaves, he was a god choosing between heavenly and earthly pleasures, the goddess and the woman. Alec argued that he was entirely human, and obviously capable of keeping both women happy. 'Look at the women, smiling at one another, they're happy as larks.' It was an obscure little work of art and they had come to refer to it as 'theirs'.

As with Florence generally, there was now, for Sarah, a new ambience in the little piazza. The air had been used too many times by too many people. People whose bodies were saturated with oil and breathed fumes of garlic. Again the wave of revulsion, she could not tell whether it hung in her nostrils from the narrow street or there was more of it here.

It was a depressing place.

Now she could hardly bring herself to look at the water-bowl, but made herself do so.

Now, its figures were trivial, and executed without skill. Years of street-dirt was gathered in the crevices and folds; those parts which were always in shadow were slimed green. Not understanding yet feeling it instinctively, she saw that this unclean coating was fitting for the three of them. The handmaiden was suitably the dirtiest. The young man's fingers were not reaching out to touch her intimately, he was scorning her. She saw that his cupped hand had moved much closer to the goddess and that he was a libertine in a Corn King's wreath, he had no business to wear it. Then she saw that the goddess's robe was no longer opaque, but was totally revealing – and so the goddess became wanton and as earthly as the woman.

Yes, it was still 'their' tableau.

When she reached the villa, she felt ill and weak. Her Mistress, seeing the pallor, sent Sarah to her room to rest and ordered a servant to take soup to her. Sarah could not face the food and sent it away, but the strong smell of garlic and oil pervaded the room and would not disperse even with the window open wide. Not even the sea-sickness that she had experienced on her first voyage was as bad as the revulsion she felt on that evening of retching nausea.

It was then that she knew that she had succumbed to one of the intestinal parasites that she knew often proved fatal.

On the fourth day, Mrs Delphine sent Alec to say that she had ordered an apothecary or a doctor to attend. So ill did Sarah now feel that she scarcely raised her eyes to Alec and was glad that he did not stop for longer than it took to give the message.

In what field of medicine the man who attended her practised, Sarah did not know for he had little English and her own knowledge of Italian, spoken in his fast dialect, did not include medical or biological terms. The motherly servant who stopped in the room whilst he examined Sarah was no help, but she nodded and smiled helpfully.

He felt her forehead and hand, pressed her abdomen and looked closely at each of her breasts. He asked her questions with much miming and pointing and talked in short bursts always ending 'Comprende?' and took no notice when she shook her head. Eventually he threw up his hands, bent close as though she were deaf and said, 'Bambino. Comprende? Bambino.'

The old woman nodded and smiled encouragingly at Sarah and mimed a great belly at her.

PART THREE

January 1829 – March 1830

LIDI GETS HER WAY

LIDI WAS NOW acting as master of Toose's of Cantle.
When her father was in prison last time, Lidi had been only nineteen and had had to carry on the business the best way she knew how; this time, it was different. During the intervening seven years, she had learnt every aspect of the business.

For years she had tried to persuade her father to allow her to try out her idea for the sale of planned borders, but he had said that Toose's were known as solid plantsmen, not fancy flower merchants. Easy going as he was and more understanding of daughters than were most men, he wanted daughters to be daughters and not partners in a business.

The interest that he had at first shown in Lidi's trial plot had diminished as he saw her become more and more involved in it.

'All these trials with cross-fertilisation of lilies and that – it's only important to you because you an't got a husband and childer. 'Tis woman's nature to want to grow things – but it's babes they should grow.'

'Pa, that argument don't hold water for a minute. Nearly everybody in this village grows things. Women's nature is something invented by men so they won't have to bend their brains thinking about things they don't want to. How much is my nature different from yours then? You wanted to be a plantsman – I want to be a plantswoman; you wanted to make a name for yourself – so do I. You wanted children – I want them too. Where's the difference in our natures?'

'I don't grow plants to satisfy myself like you grow lilies – I grow them to keep us all fed.'

'If you'd let me have a decent sized plot, *I* could keep us all fed – in five years I reckon I could work up a business.'

'Business isn't something women should get theirselves into.'

'Lord Pa, I got myself into it when you were in Winchester.'

'That was only a temporary thing. I wouldn't want to see you going on like that.' He liked Lidi, liked to please her and not have to cross swords with her. He smiled his genial fatherly smile that he had used upon his daughters since they were three. 'Lidi my dear, I only wants what's best for you, what will make you happy. Why don't you settle down with Luce? You'm twenty-four, there an't a better lad than Luce, and I know you likes him.'

'I don't want to settle down, with Luce or anybody else. If you want me happy, then let me try out my scheme.'

'No Lid, and that's an end of it.'

She had stormed away, throwing back at him, 'You'd be ashamed if Aunt Ju heard you!'

He had not taken the bait of that taunt.

That spat had taken place two years ago.

So, with her father away for six months, Lidi had taken her chance. Whilst he was still in local custody before being taken to Winchester, Lidi went there to see what work must be done, and had said that he should give her legal power to act on his behalf.

He had prevaricated briefly. 'Perhaps Luce ought to do it, he knows the business inside out now.'

'Luce isn't any good at trading – you know he isn't.' She had looked directly and fiercely at her father. 'Look Pa, I've worked for you since I was six, that's over twenty years. If you don't recognise my ability now, then you never will, and it's time I left you to it.'

For a moment he was too taken aback to reply.

'No Lidi.'

'Yes Pa. I reckon I've put as much of me into Toose's as you have of yourself. If you hand the running of it over to Luce, what does that say about what you think of me? That a man who's been a 'prentice on the place for five years is better?'

'No Lidi, you know that's not true – but he's a man and it's man's business.' Then pleadingly, 'I always thought I'd like to see you content like your mother was with me. Running a nice home, not running any business. Like as not you'll be getting on for thirty before I get out; let Luce do it.'

'Right then! Go on, you hand it over to Luce and I shall get our Sarah to find me a place with her. If you want me to work in a kitchen, then I can soon find one. No, better than that, I'll find a place that will get me hundreds of miles away like she is.'

John Toose had looked pained.

'Lidi. I'm only thinking what's best for you.'

She stood with her back to him breathing heavily. She had never expected him to treat her like this. He had always favoured her. She had been proud of the way he always talked over business deals with her. She was hurt by this apparent revelation of what he believed in his heart-of-hearts – that because she was a daughter instead of a son, then he did not wish to hand over authority to her.

'Lidi.'

She refused to look at him.

The constable in charge of John said, 'Five minutes.'

'You got me over a barrel our Lid.'

'No. If you reckon Luce is good enough to run the place like you said, then it's all right for me to go.'

'I meant for him to help you with it, he couldn't run it by himself.'

'No. But I could!'

And there was the truth of it, which John Toose could no longer deny.

Before he was taken away to Winchester, he wrote a letter of authorisation for his daughter Lidia Toose to act solely and entirely unencumbered on his behalf for two years. Two years was decided upon because they all thought that, because of his previous record, he would not get a lesser sentence. As it was, his plea that no Christian man would hand his unconscious neighbour over to a constable without a warrant, was accepted in mitigation, and so he was given a lesser sentence.

So Lidi, believing that she had the time she needed to prove herself, had rented half an acre of Church land for two years at a low rent negotiated by herself with the Commissioners.

She then proposed to Luce again.

The coolness that had been between them after he had rejected her a few years ago, had gradually worn off as was inevitable when their daily work brought them together so frequently, but it was as much in Luce's nature to be conformist as it was in Lidi's to be dissident. He found it difficult to accept Lidi's terms. But they loved one another, and each was sure that they would never love anyone else.

Much as she wanted Luce, Lidi, believing she had the more to lose by marrying, had the greater resistance. However, when she was faced with running Toose's with only Jack in the house, she asked Luce straight out to come and live there.

'Look here, Luce Draper, if you think I'm going to wait till I'm over fifty like Aunt Ju and Uncle Will, then you're wrong. I want you now. The terms aren't any different than they were before, except that perhaps we should consider ourselves to be married – I'll even make proper vows to live with you for ever if you like – but I'll make them *to you*, not to the vicar. But it always seems to me that two people who love properly don't need vows to keep them faithful.'

And seeing that it was the only way he would ever get her, Luce agreed. 'If it suits you for us to be Mister Toose and Mistress Draper, husband and wife, then let's do it.'

They announced their intention with a kind of formality to Jude and Will, to which Will said, 'I can't make out whether it runs in their family, Luce, or whether Lidi was got at in the cradle by Jude.'

Jude said, 'I once told John that he was my best pupil – but I reckon you've out-run him. You two will have a relationship of proper equality. I always thought it possible if only there was give and take.'

Will made a mock hang-dog expression.

Jude took no notice. 'Years ago, I wrote in my book that there would come a time when men and women would come together without needing permission of the Church. I'm glad you aren't going to wait for Luce till you're my age, Lidi.' Although she had made the statement in her most school-teaching voice, she was obviously very pleased that the lovers had made up whatever quarrel it was that had been keeping them at arm's length.

'No, I never intended to. I want babies – I'm twenty-seven now and I want us to have some before I'm thirty.' Luce was still not used to Lidi's frank way of speaking, so concentrated upon kicking the toe of his boot against the table leg.

'You don't have to go so far with telling everybody that kind of thing that you make Luce blush for you. In agreeing to set up with you on your terms he's done something that goes against the grain for him, and you ought to appreciate that,' Jude said.

Luce looked grateful that someone understood that he hadn't been brought up to think as Lidi had; it wasn't going to be easy for him to take the jibes that were sure to come his way. The days of Skimmington rides for couples who broke the rules were now mostly in the past, but even if their neighbours were not openly hostile, they could soon take it out on any couple of whom they disapproved.

But for Lidi's family, to flout convention was only carrying on the tradition into the third generation. Lidi's great-grandfather had

had three wives; their various children at one time had come together to live at Croud Cantle. And Lidi's Pa had let Tansy go off like that with her lover. Perhaps the people of Cantle accepted that every village had one queer family, as they accepted that it had a drunkard, a 'dumbie', a church, an alehouse and an estate.

So, with her father in gaol, in quick succession Lidi Toose rented land to start her specialist plants scheme, brought her unwed husband into the house, and got pregnant.

Except for the knowledge that her father was suffering terrible conditions in gaol which they could do little to alleviate, Lidi was happy, and well on the way to being a fulfilled woman. Her happiness gave her confidence and energy. She had the new land goodened up with dung, tilled it, bought in new stock, and worked long hours at accounts, plans and lay-outs of hand-bills and posters.

Luce was good at the practical side of Toose's, the budding, grafting, pruning operations of shrub and tree culture, and such tasks as the preparation of good seed-beds and planting land.

If there was a woman in Cantle who could be said to be happy, then it was Lidi. As her Great-grandmother Bella, and her Aunt Ju had gone their own way, ignoring convention, independent, confident of their ability, so now did Lidi.

Which was how she was when Sarah returned to Cantle.

2

SARAH GOES HOME

'I'VE COME BACK LIDI.'

Because of the seething atmosphere of revolution in France, it had taken Sarah some while to travel to England, but she had travelled safely enough considering she had no companion of any kind.

It was now January, and for close on a month, Sarah had been preparing for this moment, had gone over in her mind the complicated lies she might tell to save face, or the statement she might make to brazen it out. When it came to the point and Lidi held out her arms to welcome her, those were the only words that came out before she had to stop to choke back the emotion that had built up ever since the day in the little piazza.

'For good?'

Sarah shrugged her shoulders.

Until she saw Sarah, pale and ill and so obviously in deep misery, Lidi had not realised how much she had missed her sister. Or perhaps it was that as Sarah looked now, she was the old Sarah, as she used to be before contact with trivia and affluence began to change her.

'It'd be nice if you did.'

'Don't you want to know why I've come home?'

'No, and it don't matter, but I can guess. I don't reckon you'd have give up that job unless you'd been dismissed for dishonesty or for getting poddy. You're as honest as they come, so I reckon it's a baby. And home's the best place to be for that.'

Sarah didn't know what to say, she had thought of every kind of reception except Lidi's gentle matter-of-fact acceptance.

They had met in the yard where Lidi was loading a delivery of hedging plants, and for all the while they made their greeting, Lidi held on to her sister's hands.

'Come on inside. You look fagged out – you haven't walked from Shorlay?'

'I got Jepp's Cart as far as Willow Farm; he'll bring my stuff on down when he's delivered there.'

In truth, Sarah could not have faced arriving back home dramatically with all her possessions, so she had paid the carter to hold her things for a while.

They went into the house where Lidi pointed to a stool beside the hearth for Sarah to sit down whilst she blew up the embers and measured out a brew from the tin of tea that Luce had given her at Christmas.

'Would you mind?'

'Mind?'

'Me coming back.'

'Why should I mind, this is your home, same as it's always been.'

The hard pit of anguish and bitterness dissolved and Sarah wept silently with shaking shoulders against her sister's cheek.

'What will Pa say?' It had been the prospect of facing Pa that seemed to be worse than anything.

'I reckon it'd cheer him up.'

Drying her eyes Sarah looked up quizzically at Lidi.

'Didn't you get my letter about Pa?'

Lidi had told Sarah only the brief details of their father's arrest and imprisonment, when Luce came in.

'Why 'tis Sarah. You're a stranger. I'm starved hungry from the cold, Lidi, I'm going to get a bite to eat. Don't take no notice of me, I shan't interrupt.'

Luce Draper's familiarity was something new to Sarah. It was obvious, from the way he moved about the kitchen, helping himself to food and rummaging in drawers to find anything he wanted, that Luce had as free a run of the place as family.

'It's nice to see you again, Sarah,' he said. 'Lidi a be pleased of your company. We shall have to get you to tell us about them there foreign places you been going to, shan't we Lidi?'

'Sarah's come to stay.'

'Oh, that's all right then.'

'She's going to have a babe come June.'

Sarah didn't know what to make of the look that came over Luce's face, raised eyebrows and a kind of quizzical wry smile.

'Well now, there's a thing.'

Lidi tried to signal him with a shake of the head, but Sarah saw.

'What is it? What's wrong?'

'Why nothing in the world,' Luce said. 'I should a thought Lidi would a told you straight off, she's that proud of herself. She's carrying too. They a be company for each other, yours and ours.'

'Oh Luce, I wasn't going to blurt it out like that, for goodness sake, we don't hardly know ourselves yet.' Now Lidi smiled wryly. 'Me and Luce are going to have one too – in July. I reckon I'm about two months gone.'

An automatic action – Sarah looked down at Lidi's wedding-band finger.

'No, no, I'm not wed – nor are we going to be, but I'm carrying Luce's baby and he's the best man in the world, and I'm more happy than anybody has a right to be.' Lidi looked directly into Luce's eyes, and he came and stood behind her and, bending down, crossed his arms possessively about her.

'And so am I, though as it is I've had to agree to take second best. She won't let us get wed.' He lightly kissed the side of Lidi's face. 'A wife who won't marry me, and a baby who won't have my name. But there it is, take it or leave it, like it or lump it she says . . .'

'Well,' said Lidi, 'wed or not, one half of a couple always has a babe without it carrying their name, and it don't seem unfair to me that the one that carries the babe ought to give it their name.' She patted his hand affectionately. 'And seeing as it's you that don't get sick every morning I reckon this one ought to be named Toose.'

'Ah, don't let's start on it again. 'Tis all settled – and anyway, it's summit that can get itself unsettled any time at all.' Sitting on the edge of the table, his legs sticking out, looking pleased as could be at having told the news, he munched a huge crust of bread and lard.

Sarah offered no information as to the circumstances of her own marital prospects, and Lidi asked for none.

As Sarah gradually settled into their routine, she saw that, except for an occasional show of impatience with Luce, Lidi and he had a good relationship – she would have settled for half or quarter of it. They seemed to be all in all to one another.

Sarah saw her own situation as bleak in comparison.

She had never expected Alec James to give up everything that he had gained for himself, and she knew him well enough to know that he would never do so anyhow, but he was the father of their baby and she thought him morally obliged to give it his name. Had he married her in Florence, she would have returned home and never asked anything more of him. She wanted no more than that – the ordinary state of being legally married.

Those terrible, bleak days in Florence towards the end of the year. She told Alec and he had turned on her, blamed her, told her that she should have warned him that there was a wanton miss under her prim skirts.

Then, holding her hand and turning his charm upon her, he spoke with a touch of pain in his voice. 'You can't blame me for it, when you're everything any man'd dream of having. It's natural for men to take as much pleasure as a woman is willing to give.'

'But I didn't "give", did I?'

'I couldn't help myself.'

She had felt the chill of his rejection. Inbred in her was a stiff-backed, tight-mouthed pride. She could not bring herself to continue a wrangle about that afternoon of his quick, aggressive passion.

Their secretive pursuit of pleasure with one another was not frequent and usually took place in the early dawn, before the rest of the house was about. But on 'that' occasion, he had come to the little room which she used for the care of Mrs Delphine's clothes.

She had been surprised by his mood.

Usually they were playful, spoke gently and quietly to one another, each knowing that there was more of friendship than love in their relationship. On 'that' afternoon though he was changed, insensitive. Not liking his urgent manner and hard kisses, she had resisted him. But he had not stopped.

From then on everything had changed. He had tried to tell her that she was imagining things, that he had been no different than usual.

'Lord Sarah, nobody could blame any man seeing you there with your hair all curled and damp against your neck from the steam-kettle.'

But Sarah knew that there was something else. That he had been rebuffed perhaps, or put in his place by their Mistress in one of her fickle or petulant moods.

These days she was entertaining a most odd group of people who dressed in wild fashion, the men with curls arranged about their forehead and ears, and with exaggerated pleats in their coat-tails; the women often wore huge hats with bows, feathers, flying ribbons and flowers, and they tied in their waists so tightly that the spare flesh appeared to have been forced upwards and into the enormously full sleeves of their dresses and coats.

Although these friends all appeared to be extremely wealthy, they had few of the social graces that they would have needed in English society. In fact they were loud, lewd and as different a group as one could imagine from that which might assemble around a widow at Stonebridge Manor. And it was common knowledge among them that Delphine had a desirable lover, her 'rural' man from the 'lower orders' – which was not as unusual a relationship as some others amongst that group.

Sarah would have liked Alec to give their child his name, but his attitude, and her own pride, made this out of the question. The anger and anguish that boiled up in her with the sudden realisation of her situation, did not boil over but simmered until it was condensed into a sludge of guilt.

She condemned herself for being no different from all the rest of the girls who went into service and returned home poddy.

Sarah Toose, who had thought herself better and a lot more fly than the rest, had got caught like any little scullion who lets herself be taken in by the bootboy. Sarah Toose who had been contemptuous of Tansy Jepp. At least one man had married Tansy and the other had been glad to accept her on any terms.

When she asked that she might be released from her contract and allowed to go home, Mrs Delphine had been scarcely interested. Sarah offered no explanation, and her Mistress asked for none.

Whether Mrs Delphine, who was by now bewitched by Alec James and needful of his adept caresses, suspected that she shared her 'rural' man with her Maid, Sarah never knew. The unusual closeness that there had once been between the two women of very different stations in life had slowly dissipated, particularly over the prolonged stay in Florence.

Now, at the end of their association, only Sarah was aware that they suffered from a common malady – most likely caught from the same source. Mrs Delphine too was suffering a most distressing morning nausea.

The languid and ailing Mistress was generous from her sickbed, and gave Sarah a full year's wages and her passage home. She left all other arrangements to her Manservant, and even before Sarah had left a young woman with a thick rope of black hair and a neat waist was at work steaming Mrs Delphine's trimmings and hats.

All of these happenings to his daughters occurred whilst John Toose was still in prison. When she and Luce had decided to set up together, Lidi had written to tell her Pa in the manner that he might expect of her – that she had decided, and that was how it was to be.

Sarah wrote to him only that she had left her employment and that she was pregnant. She told no one who the father was, even when she heard that Tazey James, her child's other grandfather, was imprisoned from the same cause as her Pa.

3

GOING ON THE PARISH

JOHN TOOSE RETURNED home in March, when all over Hampshire hares are to be seen standing paw to paw, jack-hare having a bout with jack-hare, the does usually watching, but occasionally one, flinging her cap over the windmill, joins in the romp before she too submits to the same urge as do her more timid sisters.

Salmon exhaust themselves going up river, wriggling through shallows, leaping mill-races, forced by their nature to do themselves to death in the need to spawn.

Wind that swirls high over Beacon Hill spills down into the valley. It sets the early wild daffodils rocking, rustles the hedgerows where nests of delicate blue eggs of sparrows and songthrushes are hidden, and shakes free pollen from the golden haloes that surround the willow-catkins.

The sun grows stronger, lengthening the days, warming the earth. Yet, even when he is back in the protected and cosseted valley, the sun does not seem able to penetrate the chill that a winter in Winchester prison has set upon John Toose.

Although this term of imprisonment was only half that of the earlier one, the effects upon him were severe. The rheumatism, always common amongst people who worked on the land, had been made worse by the cold dampness of the months spent walled up in stone. His knees and fingers were inflamed and painfully swollen, and a gut-pain that had started with the fetid air, squalid crowding and bad food, showed in his gaunt features.

'I'll be well enough when I get a decent few meals inside me.'

His appetite appeared to be insatiable, yet he did not put back the weight lost over the six months.

For her father to have returned in this condition was just what Sarah needed. Fussing over him and seeing to the domestic running of the house gave her a place back in the family.

The arrangements that Lidi had made in his absence, he accepted almost without comment.

'Ah . . . all right Lid. We'll talk about it a bit later on.'

The greatest change that had taken place in John Toose was in his loss of energy. Whereas hitherto he had been youthful and vigorous for his years, he suddenly looked the man in his mid-fifties that he was. He liked to sit right inside the inglenook as though he could not get close enough to the burning logs. He seemed content enough for Sarah to provide him with food and remedies and Jack to give him companionship.

Like all eleven year olds, Jack was eager to be a man. Most of Cantle's child population were earning a living by the time that they were his age, but for a child with as little vision as Jack there was not much of the traditional children's work that he could do satisfactorily. And although he now wore thick lenses, his sight was not good enough to pull weeds, pick stones or follow the plough like his peers. But he had skills at which he excelled. At harvest he was nimble at bundling and tying sheaves, and he was good at ratting with the little fierce terrier he had trained himself.

His best skill was in making music. And if at haymaking and in the harvest fields where there were sickles, scythes and pitchforks he was a danger to himself and everybody else, afterwards, in the warm oil-lit barns, he was as good a fiddler as had ever played at a Harvest Home.

Jack's music was John's pleasure during those weeks of malaise. 'Scrape us a bit of a tune to cheer us up, Son.' And John would sit hugging the fire nodding his head in time to Jack's complicated bowing and fingering.

In a strange way, those weeks when they all came together was the most like a family that they had ever been. The two women developing their feminine, protruding bellies – Lidi brisk and seeming to ignore hers, Sarah appearing to be over-aware, almost fascinated at the changes gradually taking place in her. Luce, more assertive and self-assured than he had ever been, concerned for John – the good son-in-law.

I N CONTRAST TO those weeks of quiet family unity in Shaft's Cottage, were those of Dick Bone's family.

A few days after John was released, Harriett Bone and her children received their share of Dick Bone's punishment.

When Dick was sent to the decaying hulks from past wars anchored in the Solent off Portsmouth to await transportation, Harriett Bone was left to fend for their four children. A woman alone with a family was not particularly uncommon, diseases and accidents killed fathers as easily as they killed children. Wars in distant lands took away many fathers, and frequently omitted to return them.

Ever since Dick Bone was arrested, Lidi, like other Cantle women, had rallied round Harriett Bone trying to help her keep the wolf from the door.

By the time the nineteenth century was in its second and third decades the divide between the rich and poor was growing ever wider.

If there had been a time when wages were lower than they were now, there had at least then been the paternalistic concern of the old aristocracy for 'their own' cottagers and employees.

Society had changed, and the rate of change was accelerating.

Nowadays agricultural workers had become a community isolated from the rest of society and mysterious to it. Fewer and fewer landowners had any contact with those who farmed their land, and as a consequence knew nothing of the spread of misery and unrest. The workers in the fields were now openly referred to at Hunt gatherings, in gay Assembly Rooms and in English-speaking Italian villas, as 'the Peasantry' or 'the Mob'.

In rural Hampshire, a large proportion of agricultural workers were pauperised, many of them receiving subsistence money from the Guardians of outdoor Parish Relief. Most of Harriett Bone's neighbours were helpless to do anything but wait for the inevitable.

It was only a matter of time before the wolf broke through the fragile door of the Bone family's cottage.

Being such a tiny parish, Cantle had no Poorhouse, Workhouse or House of Industry of its own. It made, with its neighbours Blackbrook, Motte and Rathley, joint-provision for its human problems – the faulty, blemished, deficient or unseemly.

Blackbrook being a town, and the largest of the four parishes, had the establishment housed within its boundaries.

In spite of a belief amongst those who contributed to its upkeep that the county was teeming with the lazy and profligate, anxious to be fed and housed free, for the Lazy and Profligate to become one of the elect residents of The Four Parishes Workhouse was not easy, particularly in such times as Harriett Bone found herself destitute. Workhouse Guardians would admit none but those in dire need.

The prime qualifications for acceptance into the Workhouse were to be a Pauper and to be Deserving.

Among the Deserving Paupers in The Four Parishes Workhouse were:

the Lame and Blind,
the Moping Idiot and Madman,
Abandoned Widows,
Destitute Pregnant Girls,
the Crippled Aged,
Orphaned Children,
And those who had Behaviour Too Unseemly to be let wander abroad.

Because workhouses were in such demand and so costly to the better off, able-bodied inmates such as Harriett Bone were put to work to offset some of the cost of keeping her and her children. Nor could those who had Parish Rates levied against them be expected to pay for eight- or nine-year-old children. They could be put out to work. So when Hetty was at last forced to take her family into the Workhouse, she was allowed to keep only her youngest children with her.

There was general agreement among those who had to put their hands into their pockets to provide succour that it was a Christian duty.

There was total belief in villages such as Cantle, that 'being on the Parish' as a recipient was a most Devilish obligation.

That a man could not provide for his family; that a woman could not find a proper place to give birth or, as a widow, be unable to care for her children; that an aged couple could not keep a roof over their heads, were states that were feared.

That they were all helpless to change anything caused anger, bitterness and unrest.

They knew that within the walls of 'The Parishes' it was common for four people to share a single wood-plank bed; that dirt and disease were rampant; that fever swept through the wards like fire in a hay-loft.

When a family such as the Bone family was taken to the Workhouse, the neighbours could do nothing except avert their collective eyes from the scene of degradation and silently view their own worst fears and wonder when their turn would come.

Of all things dreaded by the Peasantry, that of the cold charity of the Workhouse was dreaded most.

On the morning when Hetty Bone left Cantle, only Lidi and Luce saw her go. Lidi had said that she would care for the few small possessions that Hetty hopefully thought Dick would need on his return.

'Seven years an't that long, Lidi. It a take him a while to get back home I know, but he a come. Well, say ten years. The childer will all be working before then. Give it a year or two and perhaps things'll be better in general and I might even get some sort of field work and we a come back here.' Work. Wages. Self-esteem. Hetty Bone was no different from all those who had gone the same way – say things will get better and who knows? they might.

'Ach, you'll be back long before that.' Lidi knew that it wasn't true – and so did Hetty.

'Just hold on to them one or two bits of things. They an't nothing worth anything, jist fambly things that was handed on to Dick and me, and the painted bowl he gid me on our wedding day. I shouldn't never like to lose that.'

'I'll come and see you if you like.'

Hetty looked down at her hands.

'I don't reckon I should like anybody to see us in The Parishes.'

'It isn't your fault. And I could perhaps help out with a few things for the children.'

'We'll see. I don't know whether it'd be allowed.'

'All right, we'll see.'

And so Harriett Bone left her home village.

5

I T WAS STILL early when Lidi and Luce hurried away from the Bones' cottage.

The place was insubstantial without the family. The future that Dick and Hetty had expected there showed in a couple of pruned bushes, in some clumps of onion setts and sticks of kale growing amongst old marigolds and gilly-flowers, in the straw-covered rhubarb and other curative plants, and in the nicely trained scented rose that had been there as long as anyone could remember.

No other family was likely to live there. There was little work. The population of Cantle was dwindling. The cottage would go the way that many others had gone in recent years. In a month the newly-turned vegetable garden would be a tangle of tares. Later the village children would ramp over it. They would eat the fruit too soon, turn over the water-butt, take away the door-latch and dismantle the pig-sty.

Lidi had seldom seen Luce so affected as he was that morning.

'By Christ Lidi, I could do murder for that.' Luce thumped a fist against his palm.

Lidi took the fist, opened it and twisted her fingers into his. 'Murder wouldn't help a deal.'

'All right then Lid – your family's the one for always talking about putting the world to rights, what do you reckon?'

'Getting involved in things like Uncle Will used to.'

'Combinations? Unions and that?'

'I don't know. That's only dealing wages.'

'Only! It's why people round here are half starved.'

'All right, but it wasn't because of wages that the Dawkins had to go into The Parishes, nor "Diddy" Blake, nor Hetty and her kids – they're there for want of anybody caring about our kind.'

'They'd a been a sight better able to carry on with a bit of money behind them.'

'Not old man and lady Dawkins, nor "Diddy" – they just couldn't look after themselves, could they? Too old or too daft to feed themselves. People like that need looking after. Have you ever thought what might happen to Jack?'

'He won't ever need for somebody to look out for him.'

'That's not guaranteed.'

'Don't be daft Lidi, nobody in this family would see Jack go into The Parishes.'

'That's always supposing there's family left.'

Luce fell silent as they cut across Church Farm fields to Toose's, then he said, 'Things like that never come to mind unless you start on them.'

Lidi laughed. 'Aunt Ju and Pa had already done fifteen years on me before you even came. I wish you could have known Aunt Ju when she was younger.' She laughed. 'Lord, you can't imagine the ideas she used to come out with – what a place this would be to live in if she made the laws. When you think that in this village there's Eustace Goodenstone and Aunt Ju, and it's Useless that sits in Parliament when it ought to be Ju.'

'Lidi! There's times when your fancy goes off like a gad-fly.'

'That's not fancy.'

'Damme Lidi, you an't got any room to talk about Jude when it comes to queer ideas.'

She stopped and poked him in the chest. 'What's queer?'

The times he had done it. The times he had made a casual remark and she turned on him, made him empty out his mind, made him sort through the mess of vagueness.

'I didn't mean queer.'

'You did. You said our ideas were queer.'

'I didn't mean your ideas were queer . . . a course I think the same as you about things being shared out better – I meant things like Jude being in Parliament.'

'That's the least queer idea anybody ever had.'

He saw that she was serious.

'Lidia Toose, much as I love you, there's times when I wonder just what goes on in your head.'

6

EUSTACE, LORD BEROL

AFTER THE PEOPLE of Cantle were pressed to exchange their commons and thus their independence for a paid work deal, they were refused increased wages to compensate for the high cost of necessities, on the grounds that it would be difficult thereafter to reduce them. Consequently, as the prices rose their living standard was eroded.

The same argument, however, did not apply to those more able to withstand the fluctuations of the nation's economy – judges and others on the Civil List not only had generous incomes to start with, over the quarter century between the birth of Luce Draper and the birth of his child, their salaries were raised three times.

This was a period when judges, parsons and landowners were living better than ever. A period when houses with great pillars and parks were created; when impressive libraries and great works of art were assembled in wings specially built for the purpose of housing them.

It was the creation of so many great houses that brought in the bread-and-butter orders to Toose's of Cantle. Both old, well-bred wealth and newer vulgar fortunes, were being spent on building, creating and renovating. Suddenly land was not only earth and crops, it had become bosky dells, wide walks and open rolling lawns. When the landscapers came in to sweep away the old notions of knot-gardens and square plots, they needed hedging plants by the load and shrubs and parkland trees by the thousand.

John Toose did not have sufficient land to go in for the large-scale growing as did some of his competitors. He rented most of the Croud Cantle land, an acre or so of the old strip-field land beside the Dunnock Brook from the Estate, and from the Church Commissioners – as well as the little piece of Lidi's land – another plot close to the Rectory. He was 'in' with five of the largest estates in the south, and he had a reputation in Hampshire as a provider of good stock, particularly of beech, holly and laurel hedging.

Almost overnight, the orders stopped coming in or were cancelled.

In January he had a full order book, in June almost none.

The first intimation that something was wrong was in May when he received a curt note from the Agent of the Berol Estate.

To the Proprietor of Toose's of Cantle.
Sir,

Be informed, and take this note as written confirmation on behalf of my employer Lord Berol, that the option to purchase from yourselves:-
One Thousand three yr. Beech and Two thousand four yr. Holly hedging plants, will not be taken up.

Another source of supply has been found. Our account with you is settled as of this date.

By now, many of the physical effects of John's winter in gaol were mended, though he had not regained his old vigour and enthusiasm, and the proportion of white in his hair was now the greater. This letter, from one of his most reliable customers, girded him to action.

'Lidi, tell Luce to harness up the little cart and he's to come with me.'

Lidi read the letter and knew what the outcome would be, and guessed that it would not be the only one. Sir Harry Goodenstone's son, Lord Berol, who owned Park Manor in Cantle and most of the rest of the Cantle Valley, was the product of the union of two local families – Berol and Park Manor, and the sole inheritor of both estates and their attached fortunes.

Old Sir Harry Goodenstone, now a shrunken little man in his seventies, rarely visited his Cantle estate these days. As a young man he had travelled to plantations that he had inherited on warm, white-shored islands, and had decided that he preferred the climate there to that of Hampshire. So whilst his son Eustace did not yet own Park Manor, he acted for his father. The vast Berol Estate was his own inherited from his mother's family.

The Goodenstones and the people of Cantle had lived cheek-by-jowl for a century or more. 'Old Sir Henry' and his gruff ways were accepted. 'Old Sir Henry's' son 'Young Harry' had been an endless source of gossip and amusement.

People knew where they were with the old Goodenstones.

They might idly speculate on their downfall from time to time – in a kind of 'serves 'em right 'tis time they had their comeuppance' kind of way – and, as the local 'Haves', they were the traditional opponents of the 'Have-nots'. But they had never considered them to be their natural enemy. Their descendant, Eustace Goodenstone, was.

The young lord was one of an astute new breed of landowner who not only believed, as did their ancestors, that the purpose of Parliament was to enhance and protect the fortunes of their own class, but that any acts or laws passed – whatever their original intention – should be turned to their advantage.

Lord Eustace was remote and he was ruthless.

When a Poor-rate was levied upon him – he went about retrieving it with profit.

He put up very high the rents of those properties he owned in the villages, so that the occupants were forced to apply for Relief. He did the same to those few cottages remaining on his estates that were necessary for livestock keepers who must be employed long term for the sake of the animals.

As a rate-payer, he was bound to employ and to pay a certain number of unemployed local labourers, whether he needed them or not. So he pulled down their cottages, or 'persuaded' workers for whom he was responsible as a landowner to settle in the next village where he was not. Thus he could depopulate his estates in Cantle and Motte, and cultivate his land by short-term hiring of surplus labour from surrounding districts.

Because there was such a surplus of workers he could choose the best workers and pay them the lowest rate, which would be made up from the Poor-rate.

Thus, like his considerably poorer neighbours such as John Toose, Eustace Goodenstone paid his dues to the Parish and, unlike John Toose, had it returned to his pocket with profit, in rents and cheap labour.

There was nothing illegal in this. It was the system. He saw nothing amoral or the slightest bit distasteful in using it. In his grandfather's day there had been restlessness in the foodbowls of England and revolution in the air of France – the ruling class were afraid that the flame would leap the English Channel, so they threw the blanket of Poor-relief over the villages as one throws a wet blanket over fire. Fifty years later the blanket had become cloth of gold for the big farmers and the fire had burnt into the ground and was smouldering beneath it.

The drawn and grey look had returned to John's face. He sat

hunched beside Luce as they jolted over the downs in the direction of Motte.

'Old Sir Harry gave me my first big order.'

It wasn't necessary for Luce to respond, John was speaking thoughts aloud.

'Right back at the turn of the century. I hadn't been going long. He'd a come back from one of his journeys abroad and he decided to bring the old place up to date. Jude knew the old man pretty well at one time and he always enquired what was going on. That's really how I managed to break away from the small stuff I was doing. He sent his man down to ask if I could have enough poplars ready for planting for when the new avenue was ready in two years' time. Well, you know poplars is easy enough. That's them all the way up the main drive.'

'A fair old avenue now.'

'Over twenty years old now.'

'Looks nice.'

'Hanny – that's the girls' mother you know – she was that proud. "You a have to give yourself a name now," she said. "You a have to have bill-heads and orders and that" . . . ah, she was that proud when she saw "Toose's of Cantle" printed out proper. It was her idea that – "Toose's of Cantle".'

'Got a good reputation.'

John shook his head. 'That's why it's such a shock getting a letter like that . . . over twenty years . . . they never had cause to complain about anything . . . always good stock, and a fair price . . . more than fair to the Goodenstones, because I was always grateful for what Old Sir Harry done to get us going.'

'Perhaps you'd do better to go and see him instead of Eustace.'

'He live abroad now – on one of his tea plantations or summit.'

'No, he's here. I saw some old-fashioned kind of coach come down Farm Lane and over the ford – a great shiny coach like you don't hardly see these days. I was with old man Bartlett, and he said, "Why look there's Young Harry," and he took off his hat and the old man in the coach waved out of the window at him.'

'Well I be durned. But I wouldn't go to him anyhow. The order to cancel came from Berol, not Park Manor.'

Luce had hesitated all the while they had been driving together, but at last he said, 'You don't think it's got anything to do with . . . well . . . Dick Bone was poaching Goodenstone land and . . .'

John was silent for a minute before replying.

'It crossed me mind directly I got the letter.' He took out the note and looked at it again. 'It's that last bit: "Another source of supply has been found. Our account with you is settled as of this date." See "Our account with you is settled." Don't you reckon that sounds like summit?'

'Well, you could take it like that.'

'That's what I've got to find out. If they mean to take it out on me for helping a neighbour when he's badly injured like Dick was . . . then I want to hear it from their mouth – not on a scrap of paper like this.' He flicked it contemptuously.

But he never did hear the truth for even before they were over the parish boundary, John was unable to hear anything.

He made a short exclamation as though stung by a bee and fell sideways away from Luce. At the same time as reining in the horse, Luce grabbed John's coat and saved him from falling. In seconds he had leapt down from the cart, unknotted John's kerchief and put his head between his legs. Although he had little experience of such emergencies, Luce was certain that this was no ordinary faint, John's face looked blue and Luce thought he must be dying. With his own coat as a pillow, Luce laid John down in the cart and made as much haste as he could back down into the valley.

The yard was deserted. He called. The hessian wraps that Lidi and Jack had been cutting only twenty minutes ago were not done. He called again. There should have been at least one of the parish workers within call, but the place seemed deserted. Then he heard Jack's voice.

'I'm coming, I'm coming,' and Jack, peering his way through the thick lenses of the spectacles, came from the direction of the house.

'Here Jack! Over here. Where is everybody? Quick, fetch them, it's your Pa.'

'It's Sarah. The baby's started coming. Lidi's with her and Mort's gone for Mrs Netherfield and then on to Aunt Ju's.' He moved quickly and assuredly across the yard. 'What's wrong with Pa?'

'I don't know, he just collapsed down. Here, help get him over my shoulder.'

They got John into the house just as Lidi came downstairs, side to side counterposed steps, in her last weeks of carrying, holding her belly with one hand, steadying herself with the other.

'Oh Lord! Hold him a minute.' She pulled back the curtains of the shelf-bed that Jack had used since Sarah's return and they laid John there.

'I don't reckon he's breathing, Lid.'

She rent open his shirt and laid her ear to his chest. Jack's magnified eyes stared, anxious and unblinking. Luce stood stock-still.

'His heart's going. It's faint. Quick, fetch my simples-box. Jack you go and see to Sarah . . . give her your hand to grasp hold of.' Jack's eyes opened wide as owls through the lenses. 'She's all right . . . nothing's going to happen . . . just go to her. Tell her Mrs Netherfield's on her way.'

'Get his head up!' She unstoppered a dark-blue bottle. 'Try to lift his tongue up!' With a little glass rod, she dropped the remedy into her father's slack mouth. 'There! Lay him back! That's all we can do. If the foxgloves don't work, I don't know what . . .'

The two of them bent close. For a minute, not a flicker of a change, then John took a shallow breath and expelled it with a small puff.

'Thank the Lord – I thought he was done for.'

Hurrying footsteps.

'See if that's Mistress Netherfield.'

An old woman of about sixty came into the kitchen.

Unlike townspeople, villagers were still their own doctors and apothecaries; every wife grew and collected her own plants, roots and berries to make remedies and simples, and each village had one woman who was always the one to be called in to birth and death and casualty. In Cantle, the specialists were Tazey James, the breaks and injuries specialist, and Maisie Netherfield who was called to all confinements and laying-outs.

When she saw Lidi and Luce hovering over John, she said, 'Dear Sakes! Mort said it was young Sarah birthing.'

'She's upstairs and the baby's dropped low down. And she bled.'

'Master John, he swooned off when we was on our way to Berol's . . . I thought he was a goner for sure.'

Taking off her cloak and bonnet as she went, Maisie went to the shelf-bed.

Lidi said, 'I just gave him some foxglove drops.'

Maisie lifted John's eyelids and bent to listen to his chest.

'Best thing. Nothing you can do now except wait for him to come round. Where's the Gel?'

'Upstairs.' Lidi began to lead the way.

'You stop down here with you Pa – you an't far off due yourself. I don't want three on you to see to in one day. Here lad take this on up.' She handed Luce the great covered rush basket she had brought with her.

Then Jude Nugent arrived, living up to her reputation of always looking as though she had been pulled through a hedge backwards, her mass of creamy-coral hair outweighing her slight body. Handsome and blooming for a woman not far off Mrs Netherfield's age.

With few words she set about preparing to help with the nursing of Sarah and John and the outside work.

The bedroom where Sarah lay rigid on a small bed, was tiny. Its beams were tarred black against worm and its daub limed white; the little lozenge-shaped panes broke up the sunlight.

'Well me Gel, what you been getting up to? That's it Lad, you can go off downstairs now. She a be all right, leave her to me.' Jack went thankfully out.

'Oh Mrs Netherfield . . .'

'There, there Gel.' She briefly held Sarah's hands between her own then set about helping Sarah to remove her shift and replacing the bedding with a hay-filled palliasse. 'You a be all right in a minute.'

And Sarah, frightened to death and hardly daring to breathe since the sudden flood that had come from her as she had stood at the sink, knew that she would be all right.

'You have a bit of a cry. It always helps when you gets frighted.'

Suddenly Sarah was back twenty years. Maisie Netherfield who had always been a friend of Great-grandma and Aunt Jude, seemed to look no different now than she did then. A kindly ageless lady who could make a cut knee better with a wipe of cold water and a few moments of undivided attention. *'Oh dear, that there's a nasty cut. You have a bit of a cry, it don't matter. I reckon he hurts real bad don't he? Never you mind, you'll be all right in a minute.'*

'We a get this here babe out and you a be as pleased as punch.'

Jude Nugent came and stood at the end of the bed and watched as inch by inch Maisie Netherfield's fingers felt for the outline of Sarah's baby with her head cocked and agreeing 'Hm' with herself, giving the occasional nod of her head at Jude.

'Here feeled that Gel,' she said to Sarah. 'Go on feeled – that there's a head. And there . . . that's its little bum-cheeks, and 'tis ready to come.' She looked seriously at Sarah. 'Now then Gel, I wants you to feeled that there . . .' – she placed Sarah's hands beneath her own – 'and here . . . and here . . . Feeled?'

Sarah raised her eyebrows high and sucked in a quick breath of surprise.

Maisie Netherfield nodded with satisfaction. 'There. Now the front one's dropped down, you can tell there's two.' She looked sideways up at Jude. 'Twins again Jude.'

Jude flushed and turned to go. 'I'll go and tell Lidi.'

'You might a guessed, Jude, it runs in their fambly.'

'We shall have to get some more binders and things ready.'

During the hours that followed, Lidi came and sat and held on to her sister, and administered raspberry-leaf and penny-royal. Maisie had not wanted her charge to be told what had happened to John, but in a house where the floorboards are the ceiling of the room below, it was impossible to separate the two crises.

John had regained consciousness but was too weak to sit up. Under Jude's directions Jack tended his father as gently as a girl, holding his head up for sips of water and peering close through his thick lenses so as not to spill a drop.

In the late afternoon the crown of the first head appeared.

'My life! Was there ever such a fambly for carrot-tops!' exclaimed Maisie. 'Give Jude a shout.' So sister, aunt and midwife watched the slippery entry into the world of yet another in a line of red-haired females of the Estover line – Bella, Jaen, Jude, Hanna, Lidi, Sarah.

'Isabell,' Sarah said. 'I made up my mind – Christopher if it was a boy and Isabell for a girl.'

'Will you let me birth the next one? I birthed Jack.'

'That's true,' said Maisie. 'You was a good little midwife if I remembers.'

Before the hour was out Lidi had gently greased and eased her sister's baby into her own firm hands.

'There!'

'Well,' said Jude. 'That's a nice change – a carrot-top boy.'

'So 'tis Christopher then,' said Maisie.

'Yes,' Sarah said, 'Isabell and Christopher, and they both got fair eyelashes like ours, Lidi.'

Only Sarah knew the significance of the eyelashes.

It was the surprising dark redness of their wispy hair and the almost invisible eyebrows and lashes that suddenly created in Sarah a fierce protectiveness for them. *My* babies!

It was as though they had been immaculately conceived. Months ago, she had determined that no one should ever know that she had associated with such a libertine as Alec James. Certainly she had half encouraged him, needed him even, but for all that he had forced these two upon her, they bore no trace of him. *My* babies.

People could all try to guess what they liked, they could surmise, and prod, but no one could ever know – even Alec himself could never be sure, men never could, not unless they kept their women locked up. Since her return to Cantle, she could almost persuade herself that Florence had never happened, or that it was a lascivious tale such as was told among women in the corner of a harvest field – 'I knowed it fer a fac' . . . he had the two on 'em, the lady and the maid both. They was sharing him under one roof and him running between beds till he fixes them both up at the same time.'

Isabell and Christopher Toose. Maisie had laid one at each breast and the bond was made. The babies were entirely hers. She had not wanted one, let alone two, but they were hers. Like herself they were children of the Cantle Valley. Suddenly, her loathing of the place, of its people with narrow ways, their inter-marriage, their obsession with work and their grinding poverty, the things that she and Alec had agreed they would do anything to avoid returning to, suddenly those things were what she wanted her children to know.

The pains in her belly, the soreness of her stretched birth-canal, the aching of her newly attacked breasts were almost welcome . . . like the sweet pain of red heat on frozen fingers – the new, lesser pain was relief after what had gone before. In the yellow flickering light of a single candle, Sarah fell into a heavy sleep.

It was only physical tiredness that made Lidi glad that it was over. She had again experienced that marvellous thing of bringing out a new life for a mother. She thought that she would feel cheated when it came to her turn that she would not be able to be the one to see her own babe out into the world.

In the kitchen, she puts her feet up on the hearth and lets Luce and Jack see to their own.

It is a rough and ready meal, but the food is unimportant at this late-evening gathering. The last day of May and the sky seems still to retain some of the bright spring daylight although it is within sight of midnight. Sarah fast asleep, Will has come down and Maisie, more red-cheeked than ever from a toast or two of brandy-laced country wine, now sits with them in her role of oldest friend.

They sit as a family around the kitchen table in the same room as John is resting on the shelf-bed. John now has some colour in his face and his voice has grown stronger.

'Can't you fetch them down now, Jude?'

He speaks to Jude, but his eyes ask Lidi for permission.

Lidi looks at Maisie Netherfield.

'Ah, go on. I a keep my eye on him to see he don't go racketing his heart off again.'

Jude fetches the babies down, carrying them like piglets one under each arm.

'Here, let's have a hold of them.'

Jude lays them in the crooks of John's arms.

Lidi watches him. She knows he is thinking of nobody but Hanny, her mother whom she misses for his sake. They all watch him in silence as he inspects their faces. One baby opens its eyes, yawns and pokes out its kitten-clean tongue. He doesn't know whether to laugh or to cry. 'Why you little beggar. If that an't the best remedy for a tired heart a man had. If I believed in God I reckon I'd send him up a prayer for saving me for this minute.'

He is overwhelmed with pleasure and sentiment and pride.

'Look at that, Jack – you'm an uncle. Look . . . Auntie Lid. Well . . . so I'm a grandfather.'

He looked moist-eyed at Jude. 'What do you think of that, Jude . . . did you ever think you'd see Johnny-twoey who used to shake a rattle at your ole crows to be a grandfather – Hanny'd a been as pleased as a dog with two tails. Can you imagine Hanny as a grandmother?'

Jude nodded. 'Oh yes, I can imagine that . . . what I can't imagine is Jaen to have been a great-grandmother.'

Lidi sees the look that her father gives her Aunt Ju. For a sick man, it is surprisingly sharp. The unspoken. The ancient story that the two of them share, the story that must still be so painful for them that they are unwilling to take it out, look at it, and see if it is possible to speak of. Jaen, Lidi's grandmother, and her grandfather.

Over the years, what has been unspoken has created a nebulous cloud that descends to blot out healthy interest.

Lidi has never been able to imagine anything that is too painful to speak of after two generations. She surmises that Great-grandmother Hazelhurst must have died when their mother was born but plenty of children are orphaned as she and Sarah were. In what circumstances could Aunt Ju's sister have died that it may not be mentioned to Lidi and Sarah, the grandchildren of that mysterious woman? And what could she have been like that Aunt Ju still missed her after all these years? But Aunt Ju has never been like other women.

And Jaen's daughter Hanna?

Lidi has heard much about the days when Mother was a little girl living with Aunt Ju and Great-grandmother, and of her wedding with Pa, and when she and Sarah were little . . . Nana-Bess had related those stories, but between, there are the years contained in that nebulous cloud. Lidi thinks that she can never know what her mother was really like, if her grandparents are so mysterious. The only pictures of her mother that she has are those woven by Pa and Nana-Bess from ideal memories of her. It would be truculent to question a woman with such an aura of perfection and a tragedy that lives on in the silence that surrounds it.

A woman close to the end of her pregnancy is an enigma. She is at once the spindle around which everything close by revolves, yet she is separate, remote. She can relax with her hands folded over her child and people withdraw from her, or she can if she wishes, command attention with a word or a movement. As she was on primal seashore, in treetops or in caves, so she has always been and so she is now in the kitchen of Shaft's Cottage.

Lidi relaxes and observes. She realises that on such an occasion as this, at such a gathering, emotions are close to the surface, the past is with them.

For sure Nana-Bess wouldn't miss such an occasion. Nor Great-grandmother Bella, recognised as head of the family long after she had become senile; Hanna to whom they would all have deferred on this occasion. And what about Tansy, she would have been spilling all over them with the lovely blowsy plumpness and loud enjoyment that Lidi liked her for. They were all somewhere there surely? Even if only as part of herself.

She can feel even those people she scarcely knew, shouldering in, coming as shades to see the results of some long past action of their own, a moment of passion when the magic of conception is done, such as the one she had shared with Luce, and Sarah had shared with . . .

Ah, there is one presence that Lidi cannot conjure. That

confused, dim male silhouette that Sarah refused absolutely to turn full-face or colour for them.

'Isabell,' says Jude, taking the baby girl from John and putting her at one end of the wicker crib that Jack had woven. 'This one's Isabell.'

John nodded. 'Ah . . . and Master Bella would a been a great-*great*-grandmother – think of that!'

'And Christopher.'

'Hmmm.' He pauses and looks closely at the tiny face. 'That's more of a poser. Do you reckon the father . . .?'

'No!' Lidi interjects. They all look in her direction. 'If she ever wants us to know who their father is, then she'll tell us.'

'A father's got a duty . . .'

'No Pa, we shouldn't speak about it. It isn't for us to go on about it behind her back.'

'Not behind her back – I faced her with it.'

'And what did she say?'

They both know that. John indicates that he is too feeble to go on with the discussion.

Luce, Will and Maisie have no part to play and sit quietly sipping and picking at cheesecrumbs and bits of crust. Jack is wide-eyed with tiredness, his spectacles and magnifying glass hanging from a cord about his neck; he moves his head to focus upon each speaker.

'She's right John,' Jude said. 'There could be a hundred reasons why Sarah don't want the father involved. It's her right to keep it to herself.'

'I'm too fagged out to argue tonight, but I don't agree. It takes two to get a baby, and the two should take on the responsibility of caring for them.'

There was a moment when nobody spoke, then Jude said, 'John, John, there's always things that people don't want talked of. Have you forgotten?' John lies back and stares at the ceiling of the sleeping recess. It is as though only the two of them are left in the room.

Lidi feels that they are almost approaching the edge of the nebulous cloud. She does not want the silence to descend as it has always done.

Is the silence brief, or long?

Go on, Lidi wills them, talk about it.

John stares above his head.

Jude stares at John – looking inwards; neither sees anything that is before their eyes.

Into the silence Will Vickery's Irish and Midlands-laced voice says, 'If you was to ask me, I'd say it was high time Hanna's mother and father were given their proper place in this family.'

Jude transfers her gaze from John to Will but says nothing.

Will speaks to Lidi now.

'Y'r Aunt Judeth just said Sarah's got a right to keep who the father is to herself, which I'd agree with – except where these two babes is concerned . . . I'd say they'll have a right to know their own father.' He turns to John. 'But only them, Sarah's right to tell the rest of us to go hang, for 'tis no affair but her own. But I believe that we've all got a right to our own ancestors.' He pauses, waiting to see if Jude or John will respond.

Lidi senses the tension between Pa, Aunt Ju and Uncle Will. Pa and Aunt Ju want the past to stay buried, but it has been fermenting and its gasses are now bound to break the surface.

Such releases within families always take place in the charged atmosphere of birth, death or threat to its unity.

Jude looks at Maisie Netherfield. She knows everything about the family, but this is their affair, that they are talking with her there is an affirmation of an old friendship.

'It was Hanny's wish that we didn't pick at old sores.'

The subject was closed, leaving Lidi's imagination to wonder about madness and other dark inheritances.

7

OVERSEEING SIN AND MONEY

ALL WOMEN GIVING birth to bastard children were obliged to give notice of the fact.

Lidi's part in the birth of the twins had brought the two sisters much closer than they had been since childhood.

John, now up and about though very breathless and easily fatigued, had said that he would go with Sarah to give notice that Cantle had two new nameless children, but she refused him, saying that she would go only with Lidi.

During the months when she was carrying, except for the family, Sarah had been retiring and reclusive; she had no intention of giving the gossips dipping for water at the ford or gathered round the village pump an eyeful of her condition. On the afternoon that she decided to go to the vestry, she dressed in one of her 'Stonebridge' dresses, and carrying a child in each arm, walked the short distance down Church Farm Lane to St. Peter's.

The nominated Overseer for Cantle was Mr Wilfrid Spartsit of Blackbrook. As a man of standing in the community he was appointed to the unremunerated post which, even after application to a Magistrate to forgo, he had no option but to undertake.

'No, Spartsit. 'Tis your proper duty to your fellows. 'Tis our selfs who puts up the bulk o' the money. So 'tis we who must look to see that 'tis not dipped into by them as'd rather sup their days through beer-froth than turn an honest furrow. No, Spartsit, ye must do the year like the rest of us – the cock-pheasants won't all fly off whilst you look to our affairs.'

So for a year it became Spartsit's duty to administer Poor Relief and to act as guardian of the public purse and, as a consequence, the doling out of money to abandoned women. Spartsit stood guard over the public morals of one class of person and the public purse of the other.

As Wilfrid Spartsit begrudged the time he was forced to spend for no gain, he carried with him to his duties a glum face and an irritable manner. And the applicants' play on his name, 'Wouldn't Spareshit', indicated his attitude to the doling out of his fellow-parishioners' rate levy, which he distributed as though he had mined and minted the coin himself. Add to that, that he was a god-fearing man who took a front pew at those church services when there were the largest congregations, and then prayed echoing loud, then one understands why John Toose was not happy at his two daughters going alone to face the Overseer.

The vestry door was ajar, Lidi knocked. Mr Spartsit was seated at a table peering into a large account book. He did not look up. They waited. He must have heard the knock as it echoed round the small vaulted roof and Norman windows. Lidi knocked again. He flashed a glance up to about their waist height and then went back to turning the pages, his face close to the ledger.

Sarah stepped in front of Lidi, pushed open the door and went and stood before the table. Lidi followed and stood beside her.

'My sister is close upon her confinement and should not be kept standing.'

Mr Spartsit was used to being confronted by the humility and resentment of people in distress. His mouth sagged a little at well-spoken authority, and when he looked closer, seeing the smart dress and good shoes of what he had thought to be a supplicant or applicant, immediately got up and indicated two chairs.

'My apologies Mam, I didn't see *you* . . . my eyes . . . I was engrossed in my accounts. I don't expect anybody except labourers after their rent or a dip into the pockets of the rest of us.' He stretched his closed lips towards his ears and peered at Lidi's large belly, and then cast a querying look at the smart young matron carrying two babies.

'This is the day when the vestry's used for them that is seeking Parish Relief. I dare say you wanted to arrange a christening.' He was not a man for light conversation – but he tried, heaving his shoulders a little and stretching his lips again.

'Is it you who takes notification of bastard children?'

'Ah.'

'Then I am notifying you of two.'

He still did not connect the two bundles and the smart matron with that aspect of his duties. He picked up his pen and drew a paper towards him.

'Ah. You are furnishing details of . . .?'

'Isabell Toose and Christopher Toose.'

He dipped the pen and flourished in preparation of committing the name to officialdom. 'Toose? Is that said the same as John Toose, the tree man?'

'Yes, the same.'

'Notifying bastardy? In the name of Toose – I know John Toose . . .'

'John Toose is my father. These are my children. I am here simply to notify you as I am obliged.' Lidi rose and they turned to leave.

His manner changed.

'Hold you there a minute, missy. You just come back here a minute.' He pointed to the space before his desk which was the proper place for the people he dealt with. Sarah and Lidi did not move.

Sarah's face was flushed with anger. 'No, hold *you* a minute. I've done what I am obliged to do.'

He came round the desk.

'You're obliged to give the name of the father.'

'I've told you that they've been born and you've written that down. The name of my children is Toose. I am Mistress Toose. Who the father might be has nothing to do with the notification.'

Lidi was proud of her sister. They had consulted Will, who knew everything there was to know about Overseers, Guardians, Beadles, Constables and Magistrates, so Sarah felt sure of her ground.

'There's altogether too much of this going on. The father must be found and made to pay. Women must name the fathers of their bastards and they must be hunted down and made to pay. D'you think the Parish has got a long stocking to pay for every bastard child?'

'I am not asking the Parish for anything.'

He was shocked into silence.

They left him without a word more.

It was the first time in ages that Sarah had laughed as she did walking back home that day, walking slowly because Lidi was near her time, and the weight of the two babies was telling on Sarah.

'Oh Lid, if I don't ever see it again, it fair lifts my spirits to think of his face.'

'I thought he'd have a fit . . .'

'I reckon he'll still be standing there like a pillar of salt when the vicar goes in for Ev'nsong.'

It was mid-June when, if one could discount the squalor and poverty that existed beneath the thatch of the cottages, one saw Hampshire at its best. From the floor of the valley one looked up at the four green enfolding arms of the chalkhills, Old Marl steep behind Park Manor; Winchester Hill long and sloping to its summit where there were ancient stone fortifications and a bell-shaped tumulus from which Bellpitt Lane got its name; Beacon Hill, steep, bare except for turf, forbidding except to a flock of goats that grazed there; and Tradden Raike which sloped gently, an easy walk for a laden packman or a trader with baskets of produce going to market, or a wife returning laden. The Estate farms covered large acres of the downs, cereal crops, grazing-meadows, hayfields and some hops which, until recently, had never been tried in Cantle.

June, the month when the chalk grasslands flourish.

A recitation of the flowers of the downs rolls wonderfully off the tongue: dropwort, saxifrage, milkwort, toadflax, carline thistle, wild basil, burnt-tip orchid. In ancient meadows the one-glumed spike-rush, the sedge-like club-rush and corky-fruited water dropwort have no such friendly name such as sneezewort or hayrattle.

Lidi could give name to almost every blade and bud in the entire valley, and knew their value or troublesomeness and where a particular valued plant might be found.

They ambled along as pleased as punch with themselves, as though they had not a care in the world.

Which was not true, especially of Lidi, for she knew the precarious situation that Toose's of Cantle was in. Luce had gone as John's agent to speak to the Berol Agent and had come away with a flea in his ear. Although the outcome was bad, John was pleased with the businesslike way Luce had handled the situation, and Luce was pleased with himself for having such control when his inclination was to put his fist into the sneering smile of Lord Eustace's Berol Agent.

What it amounted to was that whilst certain harmless Radical or reformist activities, in the way of shouting at the hustings, the cheering of William Cobbett's wordy speeches – even the reading of his newspapers – were indulged as a vent for fidgety agricultural worker troublemakers of the labouring class, serious reformers could not be tolerated.

There have always been at the centre of any reformation, liberal thought or argument for change, people who are economically independent of a single paymaster – shoemakers, smiths, thatchers, weavers as well as certain evangelical preachers and small independent farmers and horticulturalists such as John Toose.

The former of these agitators – those with a craft or skill, dependent mainly upon their neighbours for their livelihood – can be the most outspoken. The latter, who needs-be must sup a little with the devil, must watch out for those who may be arrogant, belligerent as well as vengeful. Eustace Goodenstone, Lord Berol, was all of these.

After the speech in Wickham John Toose should have learnt his lesson, but he went too far in blatantly helping Bone the Poacher and afterwards refusing the Constable entry without a warrant – and then being practically let off by an old fool of a Justice who listened to sentimental defence about helping a neighbour.

Eustace Goodenstone was an extremely rich and powerful Hampshire man. He had extremely rich and powerful neighbours both in Hampshire and its adjoining counties – the Duke of Wellington, Lord Palmerston, Sir Edward Knatchbull being only three of many.

A nod is as good as a wink in the halls of power, the clubs of privilege and the dining-rooms of wealth.

When Eustace Goodenstone nodded in the direction of That Radical Toose, who owed much of his business to the hedges, walks and shrubberies being planted in their parks and gardens, it was only a matter of weeks before those accounts on the books of Toose's of Cantle were closed.

And it did not stop there. As a Rate-payer John was obliged to employ Parish workers. Suddenly, more men than he could find work for were imposed upon him. It was a mistake of course, but such official mishaps take time to sort out and all the while are a burden on a man in a small way of business.

It was now difficult for Lidi to easily get about, and John found it too exhausting, so, as Luce was working at both ends of the day trying to find productive work for the Parish men, Jude offered to see the Board of Guardians to argue the case for both John's rates and the allocation of unemployed men to be reduced to reasonable levels.

Possibly Jude was not the best person to reason with that body. Although it was long ago, she had once started an independent village school and refused to let the Church have any hand in it. Later during the debate on whether the National or Church Schools should educate the children of the poor, she had written long letters to the newspapers, and was harsh in her condemnation of both State and Church for the meagreness of the education offered.

A Board member, peering curiously at the small, wild-haired determined woman who did not lower her gaze from theirs, had only to ask 'Who *is* this woman?' for memory to be tapped and the red rag of Radicalism waved at the bull of Establishment.

The result of Judeth Nugent's appearance before the Board, was that she had a few extra unemployed workers imposed upon Croud Cantle Farm which could scarcely find work for herself, Will and a Parish man who was already employed by her.

8

WHEN LIDI'S SON was born on the last day of June, it was clear that there would be no mistaking who his father was. A miniature Luce, wide-browed and with a head of pale yellow hair. His attention to his child was like a woman's, dandling it and talking to it in the old tongue that sounded like a lullaby.

'Look at him Lidi, an't he the best son anybody ever had? Yes you are . . . look Lidi, he smiled at me . . . I a buy thee a horse to ride, and us'll go off out after the foxes, and theece'll wear a proper coat. Ah, no ole linsey round-frocks . . . no thee shall go to school proper, and learn Latin . . . look Lidi, see how strong he holds on to my finger? See? He knows his Pa. See how he looks straight up at me?'

'Why Luce, you forgot to tell him about the cricket. You said he should become a gentleman and beat the boots off Surrey.'

'Ach Lidi, you gave it away – I was keeping it as a surprise for him – well now child, seeing as your mother can't keep nothing to herself, I've made up my mind . . . just as I'm the best village cricketer in the four parishes, so you shall be the best in the whole county. Ha! Hear that Lidi? He said "ta".'

In spite of their declining fortunes, the advent of three babies into the family raised their spirits. White-haired and thinner since his illness, John was the determined grandfather, head of his clan. But much of his old vigour seemed lost; where once he would have fought back every inch that was taken from him, he now seemed to wait to see what the next day would bring.

'It can't go on. Things always change sooner or later.'

Judeth Nugent, now looking much the younger of the two, was irritated by his acceptance. 'And it is likely to be later. Too late, if there isn't a drastic change in the way this country's run.'

'It's all right for you to say, Jude. "They" an't out to finish you off.'

'You know that's a great pook of rubbish – you know as well as I do that even though it'd be only a morsel to him, young Goodenstone'd like to swallow up what bit of my land that's left.'

But John seemed too tired to take up any argument, even with Jude.

The relationship between Will and Luce had remained close ever since the day that Will had picked up Luce in Manchester and bound his wounds and brought him to Cantle. So Will was given the choice of name for the child. Although John would have liked one of his grandsons to be named after him, he understood that Luce was doing something special for Will.

Will was delighted, took it as an honour and was serious about the suitability of the name. It was August before he had decided. Never missing the chance to address a gathering, however small, he made an occasion of an ordinary working-day dinnertime. The entire family was gathered in the kitchen of Shaft's Cottage for their mid-day bread and cheese.

'Well, I never thought to get a grandchild, but I reckon this name-giving makes him one. I've given it a lot of thought as to what he should be called. There's many things as plays a part in the formation of character . . . for instance, a long nose or . . .?' he winked jokingly in Jude's direction, '. . . or hair like a bee-skep in a storm. If he'd have been a girl, I should have liked that he'd be named after Judeth . . . but, there 'tis, he's to be a man one day and I doubt if he'd relish tellin' some pretty maid that he's called Judeth Toose. So . . . I consulted some books in Blackbrook library for the male equivalent . . .' The slight pause of an experienced orator, 'And I discovered it . . .' Another moment's pause. 'Yehudi! No? Y'don't think that Yehudi Toose is a fine name? Well Lidi, shall it be . . . Judah then? That's the same as Jude. Judah Toose?' drawing out the vowels. 'No? Ah well, perhaps it does sound a mite like a bird-call.'

Now his teasing turned to emotions close to the surface.

'It seems that I've been part of this family all my life, and this makes it official. Because he's a golden boy in his colour, and I should like to think that he'll grow up to be as shining and warm as the sun – I name him Auryn – which means gold.'

It seemed strange to change from 'Baby' to 'Auryn' which, as the family thought, was a mite fancy for a Cantle nipper and, villagers said, 'specially as the child's a blaster'. But, in many circumstances, 'blasters' were not so unwelcome these days – an unwed girl with two or three children to her name, brought with her as a bride to an unemployed man, the dowry of child-allowance. Overnight, as you might say, a single man destitute on his Relief, could claim benefit as a married man with a family and thus move up the scale from starveling to pauper.

Which was why Cantle villagers could not understand Lidi not making Luce wed her. They shook their heads, 'Aah, there's summit behind all that.' Money might fall accidental down a well . . . might even get thrown down if anybody was simple-minded enough . . . but nobody in their right minds didn't hold out their hand for it when it was there for the taking. 'There's *summit*, jist mark my words.'

9

B Y THE END of the year Sarah seemed to have forgotten her old life. Only occasionally did Lidi catch her gazing into herself, unseeing, one eyebrow lowered, a pucker between her brows. Then she would return and make a gentle sigh.

There had always been something that kept Sarah at arm's length from most people. Certainly that hungry, physical side of her nature which she had discovered in Italy with the fast people of Stonebridge, would have been surprising, even shocking, to those closest to her. It almost seemed so to Sarah herself as she dispassionately observed Sarah Toose pounding dowlas working-smocks and coarse aprons in the sink or at the scrubbing board. Her almond-shaped, glossy nails had gone, her white hands were red to the elbows, and her hair kept without tendrils, neatly knotted and sensibly capped. But her shapely waist looked even finer now that her breasts had filled, and the fine lines that had appeared beneath her eyes had changed her prettiness to a mature beauty. There must be summit there too for she was a prize for any man – unless he was a Master . . . that must be it!

She seldom left the house and yard, but cooked and cleaned and cared for the three babies. Lidi was back working in the growing fields with Luce. John's income was now very small, yet the Magistrate who had adjudicated decided that Toose's of Cantle must be worth the hundred a year which designated John a Rate-payer, although he did agree that the Parish men should be withdrawn.

When renewal time came round, he was forced to relinquish much of the rented land so that the only plots were those which Jude owned and another beside Shaft's Cottage, where there was a good stock of valuable maturing exotic shrubs.

They were now living very frugally. John was now virtually back where he started selling trees and shrubs on the markets. Townspeople did not care much about the beliefs of the traders from whom they bought plants and shrubs for their small gardens, so long as they got decent value and perhaps something a bit different from their neighbour – or something exactly the same.

Toose's had always done a small trade in turnips as fodder to sell to drovers who brought their animals long distances to market, but it had been a sideline crop used to break down claggy land. So they did not starve, but four adults and a lad cannot live long on so few sales, even though Lidi and Jack went to five markets a week.

As in much of the rural south of England that Christmas, few people in Cantle had a bit of meat on the table – except perhaps the souse of the pig, the pickled ears and feet given back by a generous butcher when the animal, which was too valuable to be eaten by the family, was sold in town. A pig, over-summered on a bit of scrubland, was the means of buying winter leather to mend fieldboots, or a length of dowlas or linsey or calico to replace a round-frock that no longer kept out the weather. Some men risked their liberty, even their life, to take a pheasant, but the fate of Dick and Hetty Bone had instilled a long fear, as well as the fester of anger.

Some of Cantle's neighbouring valley villages, such as Exton, Warnford and West Meon, were known for their humours and damp mists; there the trees and house-cob became green with moss and algae. Usually, the winds that swirled around the chalkhills kept Cantle dry. But this year, ever since November, there had been days of dripping mists. Often a cowman could not see his cattle, or the shepherd his flock if they were more than a hundred yards distant.

Walls of cottages often became as damp inside as out, un-attended thatch grew white moulds which smelled rafty, and once a house started to smell rafty it was a signal for its inhabitants to burn a bit of menthol tar to try to stop the chests and coughs.

At Shaft's Cottage, the three babies never drew a breath of outside air for weeks, but lay contentedly close to the hearth where John kept watch from his rocking chair.

Jack, of course, was the least handicapped when the dark fogs descended, and could find his way quicker than any of them to fetch in a few bavins and logs for the fire, water from the pump or vegetables from the clamps.

Although it was often impossible to travel to market, Lidi and Luce went out into the fields every day, even though this was the slowest time of the year.

One day, just before Christmas, they were working in the stable at the far end of the yard, breath shooting from their nostrils like jets of steam in the chill air. Luce stopped work and asked, 'What are we supposed to be doing, Lidi?'

'I thought we were supposed to be piling the stable-dung to get it ready for gooding next year's land.'

'No we an't Lid, we're finding ourselves something to do.'

She didn't reply but gave him an odd look.

''Tis true. Both of us, we're afraid to sit down five minutes these days in case there was something we ought to be doing to turn a farthing into a ha'penny.'

After a few long minutes of pitch-forking out the contents of the steaming strawy pile, she said, 'You're right. It's what fear of hunger does to people I suppose.'

'Ach Lidi, we shan't go hungry.'

Now she stopped work, put down her pitchfork and went over and kissed him.

He kissed her in return, then grinned. 'Come on then.'

It was a compensation, a bonus after giving birth. A woman with a child at the breast could have a few months without having to tell her man 'Be careful – don't get me poddy.' Most women could have told you of the instances when 'summit went wrong', if not to them then to their neighbours, sisters, mothers, friends, but when there were few other pleasures and comforts, it seemed a little enough risk to take.

Lidi didn't want another child until they had got themselves on their feet again, but she desired Luce as much as he desired her. The fog outside was thick and heavy. Luce's hair curled like yellow snails beneath his round hat, he smelled of his own sweat as they warmed one another's cold hands beneath their armpits.

She grinned up at him. 'What was it you asked, Luce Draper? "What are we supposed to be doing out here?" '

'I told you that we shan't go hungry, Lidi Toose – well, not for everything.'

They satisfied one another's need quickly, then sat in an empty stall holding one another close, Luce lying back with his eyes closed, his old round hat over his eyes.

'Luce?'

'I'm listening.'

'We ought to get wed.'

His even breathing was momentarily arrested. He did not open his eyes.

'Did you hear me?'

He tipped back his hat a fraction and opened one eye. 'I heard you. You proposed marrying to me.'

'Well?'

'Well what?'

'Oh Luce Draper!' She pulled the hat hard down on his head.

He sat up and tipped the hat far back.

'You mean to make an honest man of me after all this time? I don't know that I'm ready to agree to that. Why Ma'am 'tis so sudden like.'

'Be serious. I still don't want to get wed, I mean get wed like there was a law that says we must . . .'

'But you heard I got left a fortune and you wants to get your hands on it.'

'Well Boy, nearly right! I reckon I ought to let us get wed because it'd be sensible to get your hands on some Relief.'

He raised his eyebrows.

'Look . . . I haven't told Pa yet, but I've finished going over the books and have got some figures out for next year . . .' She frowned and shook her head. 'There won't be enough to keep us.'

'I told you your Pa's idea. Me and him made out a list of some good estates down in the west country, and up north. He says I should go as soon as the roads are good enough again. Give it a couple of months and things will look up.'

'You know what I think of that scheme. Pa's got his head in the clouds. Even supposing you did get a couple of orders – with nothing coming in how are we going to rent back any of the land we let go? How are we going to fill the orders and increase the stock?'

'We'll have to buy-in for a while till we're on our feet again.'

'You need money to buy-in.'

'And you'd let us get married for that? What about your famous independence?' He was flippant. Now more than ever he wanted them to be wed. He was half-afraid that she wasn't serious.

'That's a luxury I can't afford.' She held him by the ears and smiled ruefully, 'I'm not the first woman that sold herself, and I shan't be the last. And don't run away with the idea that a family-man's Relief will do anything but keep the wolf from the door.'

'You're serious? You'll let us be wed?'

'Yes. I'll ask you if you like?'

'No, this time it's my turn.' He took both her hands in his. 'Mistress Toose, will you do us the honour of getting wed?'

'Aye, I think I shall.'

'Well, that's settled. I thought we should go on for ever like Judeth and Will.'

'You'll have to be taken on by Toose's as a labourer. And Toose's will have to pay you the same sort of pittance the Estate pays its day-labour. Then Pa will have to charge us high rent for our rooms – like the Estate does for their rotten old cottages.'

'Well! It's a rum do – it's more like you was selling yourself to the Relief.'

'Perhaps I am.'

'Well – I reckon old "Spareshit" would spit vinegar if he knew he was going to buy me the best wife that ever laid down in a stable.'

When they told the family what they proposed doing, there were mixed feelings.

'I always wanted you for a son-in-law, Luce, but it seems less than honest to get wed for such a reason.'

'Oh Pa, it's no good thinking that. It's not us that's wrong, it's the reason why we have to resort to it that's wrong. Anyway, I wouldn't mind guessing that Eustace Goodenstone is taking more in Relief rent than the rest of this village put together. And I don't see anything wrong when some of our trouble is because they still expect you to pay rates, even though it's clear you aren't worth anything like a hundred a year.'

LIDI AND LUCE were to be married as soon as the banns had been called three times in January.

The congregation who heard them called was small, but news travels fast and undergoes changes as it flies. By the end of the first Sunday morning's calling, all Cantle knew that one of John Toose's twin daughters was to wed.

Next morning Tazey James appeared at the kichen door. 'Ah, John, a word?'

John indicated that Tazey make himself comfortable on the inglenook seat.

'They say one of yourn's getting wed, well good luck to 'ee.'

John thanked him and, pointing to the babes, now more than half a year old, said, 'All sorts of luck been pouring in these last months.'

'Ah, I heard about these little shavers . . . 'Morning. Sarah is it or are you the other one?'

Sarah, coming into the kitchen, was taken aback to see her lover's father bending over Christopher and Isabell's cradle.

'I'm Sarah.'

He peered at her. ''Twas you that worked at Stonebridge along of our Alec then?'

Barely looking at him she nodded. 'Not along with him – I was Madam's personal maid.'

'We don't never hear from him – haven't hardly since he went off. I heard in a roundabout way that he'd gone to foreign parts, never a word from him. But there . . . that's sons for you.'

Sarah could not fathom whether he knew more about her situation at Stonebridge than he appeared to. Certainly there was little that went on for miles around that didn't wash up on the tide of gossip in alehouses and taverns.

She wanted both to get quickly away and yet stop to see her children in the company of their two grandfathers, and to know whether he realised that she also had been to Italy. She went to the dresser and straightened the plates and hung all the jugs facing the same way as though this was a daily task.

'Sarah went too. That right, Sarah? You was one of the Stonebridge servants they took with them.'

She nodded.

'Tell Taze about it.'

'Another time Pa, it's buk-wash day and I've got a tub full of hot water waiting.'

'Florence in Italy, Taze, that's where Sarah went. Didn't you ever hear tell that she was there with your Alec . . .?'

He looked up and caught the moment when the panic truth flashed into his daughter's eyes. He trailed off. Suddenly he realised what had been staring him in the face ever since she came back home.

The reason why she wouldn't name the father of her twins.

It was Tazey's son. He was sure of it.

He remembered him. A sudden and complete picture although it was ages since he had given the youth a second thought. A handsome young man who would stand talking to any maid open and friendly as you like, and slip his hand about her waist as though it was the most innocent thing in the world. He couldn't keep his hands off any woman who came within a yard of him. John remembered hearing it jokingly said of him that he had lain with half the maids in Cantle before he was twelve, and half the rest by the time he was eighteen and the only ones still waiting were over forty.

It was the kind of a reputation any lively lad trying his luck gets, but John vaguely recalled that he had been under something of a cloud when he went off into service at Shorlay.

They'd been in that foreign city together. A couple of youngsters who had grown up in the same village. Thrown together for company . . . for comfort. The entire sequence of events came to John Toose's mind in seconds. And he had seduced her. If he was that sort when he left the village, it wasn't likely he'd get any better with the example put before him by his so-called betters. Morals of farm-cats most of them.

No woman who was as straight up and down with men as Sarah, would want it known that she had been mixed up with the village goat, no matter how handsome he was.

Sarah's eyes lifted no higher than her father's beard when she spoke to him.

'I'll have to go now, Pa. Can I get you a drink of something, or a bite, Mr James?'

'No Gel. I only come in to ask your Pa here if he'd accept a cask of my best brew if there was going to be a wedding feast.'

There was a wedding feast of sorts. Nothing like the village would have expected of John Toose had it all happened years ago. Just a few neighbours, some of the old men who had worked for John, and their wives, as well as Maisie Netherfield, Jude, Will and, arriving with his cask of his best brew, Tazey James.

Lidi had tried to argue against the feast that she wasn't some young maid skipping off to the altar, but John said that feasts were given for friends, and their friends should not be robbed. In the end they compromised, had the three babes christened at the same service, and provided a supper.

After they had eaten, Jack was called for to play for them. At twelve years old, he was as accomplished a fiddler as any in the four parishes. He played with the church musicians, and if in the mood, it was known that he could coax from the old instrument notes of a Christmas hymn 'so sweet that they could make your heart miss a beat'.

Much as he loved the sacred music, it was the beat of a dance that he best liked, especially if there was a drummer. At the supper, he played at his best, to an audience who knew the effort he put into overcoming his handicap.

Tazey's best brew had a reputation that a man could drink a gallon of it, and still dance a woman off her feet, and be up at dawn to see the cows in. There was no record of what it did for women, but Maisie Netherfield sipped it slowly from six o'clock till near midnight.

Sarah took the place that would have been her mother's, seeing that everyone was comfortable and eating and drinking well. She moved along the long table with a quiet and pleasant manner. When it came to the dancing, Tazey James caught her hand as she was passing. 'Come on Gel, you done enough work for one night. This leg an't too good at dancing a jig,' he patted his good leg, 'but this here wooden one is a fair marvel.'

It was never any good trying to refuse Tazey's good intentions. The large kitchen with its table now thrust against a wall, was full of Jack's music and thumping feet. He took Sarah by the waist and danced her like a man half his age.

'Why Gel,' he said quietly as he sat her down on the settle beside him, still idly holding on to her hand, 'you'm as nimble as you'm pretty. I can't understand why you an't been snapped up long ago.'

Something in his voice, something he had handed on to his son, a sensuality that age nor any other thing could alter. For a moment it stirred Sarah, causing her to feel flustered. She had known the innkeeper since she was a child and he was already a widower, yet before she quelled that moment when he stirred her interest as Alec had done, she had been attracted to him. Belle and Christie's grandfather! She was friendly as she withdrew her hand, saying jokingly, 'Then I must nimble along and see to the negus.'

When Sarah discovered Lidi's reason for marrying, she had many qualms. She didn't agree with her sister's strange notions about her independence, she thought that it was because Aunt Jude had put those ideas into her. If being independent of a husband was what Sarah was experiencing, she did not like it – a woman is always dependent upon a man, as she was, now that her savings had run out, dependent upon Pa.

Her qualms were about her own guilt. Now that Lidi had done what she didn't want to for the sake of keeping body and soul together, then Sarah must do likewise.

They were together alone in an outhouse. The ticking on a mattress had split and they were re-bagging the feathers in a new one. The new ticking-cover was pegged out on a string, and the two women worked with a rhythm, Sarah putting feathers into a pocket and Lidi poking them about with a long cane. They wore old canvas overalls and large kerchiefs about their hair.

When the bag was half filled, Lidi said, 'Let's have a five-minute breather. Here, this is the last of the coffee Pa gave me for Christmas.'

They both had a passion for the drink and enjoyed it as they now drank it, brewed dark and left to chill.

'Ah,' said Lidi. 'Just fancy if there were places like Tazey's where you could go in and have a drink of coffee.'

Sarah smiled at the idea of a coffee-house in the village. 'They have them in Bath and London.'

Lidi did not reply, hoping that her silence might encourage her sister to say more, for she rarely spoke of any of her experiences away from Cantle. It wasn't as though she refused to speak of them, but that she turned away all reference to them, so that it seemed a cruel intrusion to mention them.

Sarah continued, 'Of course, women don't go in, but they are very respectable, there really isn't any reason why they should not.' She paused. 'I always thought it must be very pleasant to sit with a group of friends and have nothing to do except talk and drink coffee. Very civil. Men don't think women can be civil like that. Even men of quality think that women are happy with little nuncheons, all stiff and dressed up, when I'm sure there are times when they'd love to gather in a place like a coffee-house.'

Lidi nodded. This was more information from Sarah than she had ever given. It was a different world. Sarah had lived for years serving it, yet here they were back together stuffing feathers into a bag of soaped ticking.

Lidi ventured: 'I certainly should.'

Sarah looked up as though surprised that she wasn't alone. 'Ah well, wouldn't make much difference . . . even if women were allowed in, it wouldn't be the likes of us that'd get the chance to go.'

They had finished their coffee and were about to start again when Sarah said, 'Lid, I've been wanting to talk to you . . .' She looked around as though to find inspiration for what she wanted to say amongst the feathered cobwebs and wormy timbers.

'I can't go on living as I am.'

'It'll be all right. We shall manage.'

'No, it isn't right. I've got the means of changing things.'

Lidi frowned her query.

'I could go to the Parish and make the father pay.'

'Listen Sarah, if that had been possible, you'd have done it before.'

'No, there wasn't really any reason – except that I . . . well, I was ashamed to say who it was.'

'Well, there's nothing unreasonable about that. We all do things we don't want people to know about, the worst of going with a man is that you can regret after. A man can keep that sort of secret, but women swell up till there isn't any hiding it from anybody. Who it is, is the only bit of that secret that a woman can ever keep to herself.' Lidi tentatively put out a hand to her sister. Unexpectedly Sarah took it.

'Sarah . . . if you don't want anybody to know that secret, then I'll go to the ends of the earth to see that you keep it.'

Sarah sat and let Lidi gently caress her rough knuckles.

'I've got another option. I got a proposal of marriage.'

This revelation was the greatest surprise to Lidi, for Sarah seldom left the house, and certainly no letter had come for her.

'Since you've been here?'

'Two days ago.'

Lidi thought for a second. 'When you went up to Aunt Ju's.'

'Mm. On the way back, there was a nice bit of sun, so I walked the long way round. Mr James was out front, scrubbing down his benches, and I stopped and we said how nice it was to see the sun and that. And he said would I marry him – not right out like that, but he said he'd been thinking about marrying again, and then at the party . . .'

Lidi was amazed.

'Tazey James?'

'Oh he's a nice sort of man.'

'I know he's a *nice* man.'

'I quite like him.'

'To marry?'

Sarah shrugged her shoulders. 'It's a decent enough offer. I don't know what to do. I can't marry Mr James. It'd be sensible – but Lidi I *can't.*'

'I shouldn't think so either. And you mustn't think of it – for goodness sake, not just to make things easier here. If you was to marry for the convenience of it, then there's plenty of decent *young* men who'd be glad enough – *young* men with *two* legs.'

Sarah shook her head as though she did not want to think of *that.*

'You did something *you* didn't like.'

'That's different – I might have had to swallow what I believe in, but my prize for doing it was that I'm married to the man I love. Just look at Luce, he's the best-looking man that's ever walked down Bellpitt Lane . . . and I love him . . . I love him a lot. I'd already come to realise that women like me can't have a lover the same as a man can have a mistress, there's too many things against it, but I wanted to try – for goodness sake. These are modern times, this is the nineteenth century, people have got new ideas . . . it ought to be possible. Anyway, me marrying Luce isn't anything like the choices you've got.'

'That's it, what you said then, you said "women like me" . . . women like me *have* to rely on a man – we've got nothing else.'

'They aren't choices you've got . . . to have some Parish Officer chasing after your babe's father and bringing him to heel, or marrying a wooden-legged innkeeper old enough to be your father – what choice is it to fall into the brambles or into the nettles?'

Sarah now looked quite wretched and let Lidi put an arm round her shoulders – it was years since they had made such close emotional contact.

'It isn't that – if it was, then I could do it . . . it's . . . there's a complication that seems . . . well, it'd seem like the worst sort of sin.'

Lidi looked sideways at her sister, puzzled as to what she meant.

'Oh, Lidi! For goodness sake . . . I'm so stupid! I made up my mind last night that I was going to tell you and now it's so difficult . . .'

'Just say what it is straight out – you don't have to explain. You know me better than that.'

Addressing the spiders and the woodworms in the rafters, Sarah said, 'Tazey James is the twins' grandfather . . .'

Alec James! Lidi had supposed every man from Sarah's employer to an Italian rapist, but she had never expected that Sarah would allow a local dung-boot, the son of a Cantle innkeeper, make love to her.

Did Sarah ever cry? Lidi thought that it would do her good, for she trembled from trying to keep herself under control.

'Don't do it, Sa. Don't even think of marrying that old man will you?'

'Nobody's called me Sa for years.'

'You keep people at arm's length.'

'I don't know how else to manage things.' She smiled wryly. 'You might think that's funny, me not knowing how to get close to people, when I just told you who it was I got the babies with.' Then with a touch of belligerence, 'It wasn't just once you know. It was all the time. All the time we were in Italy.'

'Do you think it'd make you feel better if I was reproachful?'

'It'd be what I deserve.'

'You're sure of that?'

Sarah bit at her thumbnail.

'Of course you don't deserve my disapproval. What for? For satisfying a need that is as natural as hunger and thirst?'

'I didn't love him. Didn't even like him.'

'Satisfying your normal appetites and loving a man isn't the same thing. Wanting to lay with a lover is a morsel that's short and sweet, anybody can find themselves wanting it and not always with somebody we'd be pleased to own up to. The other sort is a long, slow meal but I reckon it's much sweeter. I just happen to be lucky, I've got both in Luce, and he's got them in me. I reckon Pa found them both in Mother, but there was only the short and sweet morsel with Tansy.' She paused, looking inside herself, ' And Aunt Ju, Sa . . .? Haven't you ever wondered about her?'

Sarah shook her head.

'I have, I reckon she got both sorts mixed up between Uncle Will and her sister.'

'I never knew you thought so deep, Lid, you always seem to be full of the Toose's business and plans and nothing much about love and husbands and babies.'

'We really don't know each other very well, do we?'

'I was away a long time.'

'Start now then. I'll learn you a bit about your sister. Your sister would be grieved if you were to choose either the nettles or the brambles to fall on.'

Sarah smiled thinly.

'And there *is* another choice you can make.'

Sarah looked quizzically at Lidi.

'It isn't primroses to fall into, but it's a decent enough bed of sorrel – let things stop as they are. We'll be all right together. I never could stand woman's work, I'd rather be out in the fields or running the business, so you'd be doing me a favour if you let things bide as they are.'

'Well, at least I shall go and humble myself before "Old Spareshit" and go on the Parish myself – he can't deny me that, 'tis my right now my own money's gone.'

THE OLD PLACE

SARAH WAS PERSUADED that Lidi's bed of sorrel was the best choice until late March.

By now John was getting about doing, literally, the pottering jobs that had long been the province of old bent men. He worked in a large shed that he had built years ago after seeing a warm, glassy annexe built on the outer wall of a large house. It was there that he had always spent his spare moments pottering, breaking the dormancy of difficult tree seeds, and growing tender cuttings and bringing on rare plants. It was his great love to bring a difficult seedling to flowering, or get the seed of a hard-shelled berry to germinate. He now had time to indulge himself, but nevertheless he felt guilty when he saw Lidi hauling heavy shrubs around without being able to say 'hold on there a minute, Lid, and I'll give you a hand.'

He excused his enforced ease. 'You never know Lid, we might get a cross in this lot that will make our fortune.'

It wasn't likely, but Lidi understood the excitement he felt at waiting for a bloom to come that might be 'the' one . . . It was the excitement she had been forced to give up when she had to abandon her lily trial-grounds.

The babies were now getting on for a year old and were very demanding. Jack, who had been happy enough to watch over them when they were babies, was changing. He was becoming a man and was frustrated enough that he could not do man's work in the fields, without being a nursemaid. However, his need to feel that he was contributing as a youth of his age should was fulfilled by small amounts of money he earned playing his fiddle. He now went regularly to the markets with Lidi or Luce and played there. There were times when his music brought in almost as much as the herbs and plants sold on the Tooses' stand.

The Tooses kept going with a variety of small exchanges and sales, and help from Jude and Will. It was hard going, but they never actually went hungry, which was not the case for a great many people in rural Hampshire. Many of their neighbours were forced into stealing anything that would feed their families.

The family at Shaft's Cottage had not come to that, though Lidi declared that she would do the same if it came to it. In a rare flash of spirit these days, John had said sharply, 'It's bad enough Jack begging on the market, without this family going against the law.'

For the first time, Jack stood against his father.

'That's not begging, Pa. What I do is respectable earning. It's the only thing I can do that's as good as youths with eyes – better! You're proud of the way you started, selling bits and pieces on the market – well I'm selling my bits and pieces. I'm selling music, and folks like it or they wouldn't pay.'

Sarah, hating any disharmony in the family, smoothed over such small irritations.

One day Jude strode into the kitchen of Shaft's Cottage. John recognised the stride – Jude had had an idea, had come to a conclusion and was ready to present her argument, plan, excuse, scheme – or whatever it might be.

'John, I've got a proposition to put to you. There's only me and Will up there. It's plain foolish for you to be paying money out to the church for this place when you might as well come up with us. Wait a minute . . . hear me out. So long as you still have this place, and the yard, as well as that sign up there that says "Toose's of Cantle", you are going to be assessed as a Rate-payer. Because you're renting land from me, and what with the size of my place, small as it is, well they assess me as a Rate-payer too. Now . . . if we were to join forces and you all came to live at the old place, then . . .?' She spread her hands. 'You get my meaning?'

'Lord love us, Jude, there's four of us, and Jack and three babes . . .'

'Room isn't any problem. Will and I worked it out, and we'd all fit in just nice. Will's done a lot of work on the little stone store. He's put a door through so that it's part of the house. Ah, you'd be surprised how handy he can be when he puts his mind to it. No, John, it's not space, it's how you'd feel about it. About coming up there to live.'

'I don't know . . . such a thing never occurred to me.'

'Well, it'll belong to Lidi and Sarah one day anyhow – it seemed to me and Will, that they might as well get some use out of it now.'

'I've got to admit, finding rent for the house and yard is pretty hard, even though Luce is getting Relief for the rooms he rents.'

'And you don't like doing that, do you?'

'That I don't, Jude! It's all fair and above board . . . no I can't say that I think it's fair, but it's above board and no more than the Goodenstones and the likes of him are doing. But it's a hard pill to swallow, to rent out rooms to your own flesh and blood.'

'Then come up to the old place and live.'

'Hold on a minute, Jude. That's you all over, you were always the same, you get an idea in your head and it runs off with you.'

'That's not true. I get ideas, but I never let them go without I haven't got them all bridled and reined and saddled up. Will and I have talked over every aspect of it. If you want to come and live up there, then it'd be the happiest thing that happened at Croud Cantle since Will came home.'

'I don't know . . .'

'Are you bothered about losing your . . . well, you're your own master, same as I am.'

'We know each other well enough.'

Jude laughed. 'Well Johnny-twoey, I'm not asking you to come back and scare the crows off. You'd still be Master of your own affairs – as I'd be Mistress of mine.'

'What would I do all day? I can't get about like I used to, and if I give up this place, I'd lose the warm-house.'

'Ha! We thought of that. Will has got a dozen old boughten window-frames from the Lutchens place they pulled down after the fire. He's got a plan to make one of our old sties into a warm-house with windows all round the top. You could build it together.'

Judeth Nugent's straightforwardness had always been persuasive; one felt that it must be all right to play the game with someone who put their cards on the table, good or bad, face upwards.

When John said, 'I'd have to ask Luce and the girls,' Jude knew that it was as good as settled.

It took them only three weeks to arrange everything. By early March John Toose was back living where he had spent his youth. Jude had been generous; she and Will had spent time and money in converting the little stone store-room and thus expanding the old cottage to make room enough for them all.

By the end of March, they had established a new routine which suited them all. Sarah and Jude shared the domestic work, Will and Jude worked their land, and Luce, Lidi and Jack continued their work more or less as before. John did whatever work he could do without collapsing with fatigue.

The move to Croud Cantle had put a finger in the hole in the dyke; the Shaft's Cottage family could gather their strength to try to rebuild Toose's of Cantle.

PART FOUR

Spring – Autumn 1830

> There are periods in the life of human society when revolution
> becomes an imperative necessity, when it proclaims itself as
> inevitable. New ideas germinate everywhere, seeking to force
> their way into the light . . . They are opposed by the inertia of
> those whose interest it is to maintain the old order.
>
> *The Spirit of the Revolution*, Kropotkin

THE YEAR EIGHTEEN HUNDRED AND THIRTY – in Hampshire
and its neighbouring counties there has been a number
of outbreaks of angry incidents concerned with agricultural
workers.

People who have worked hard all their lives now find themselves completely destitute. On some estates machines have
entirely replaced people in doing flailing and winnowing, which
have always been the staple winter-work for labouring men and
women. And although the threshers have not proved to be as
efficient as farmers had been led to believe, machines work without
breaks, do not need cottages or bread, and they never petition the
Magistrates to put up wages.

Because entire communities have become destitute, they have
become angry and frustrated. Because they have become demoral-
ised they begin to feel a separate people. And because of this and
that they are helpless to change anything – and because many are on
the verge of starvation, they are becoming lawless. Normally law-
abiding working people will steal sheep, take vegetables from
growing crops or clamps and will even risk the dire penalties that
disobeying the Game Laws bring.

They break the machines that have taken away their work.

All over the south of England, unrest is widespread, not only
amongst the people who are suffering, but also amongst the
concerned members of the rural community who see the suffering
of their neighbours, and amongst small farmers crushed by having
to hand over large amounts paid to the tithe-holders, and amongst

radical thinkers and politicians. Whilst many of the latter have a vote and a platform to voice their protest, the hungry labouring class does not.

They now begin again to take the oldest form of peasant protest – the destruction of the food that their labour has produced and to which they have no access.

2

APRIL

ONE NIGHT, QUITE late, everyone in Cantle was awoken by the tolling of St. Peter's big bell.

Luce leapt out of bed. 'Lord Lidi, it looks like a fire.'

They went downstairs and found Jude up and Will already dressed. Soon Sarah came down and followed the others outside.

From the yard of Croud Cantle, they could see clear across to the opposite side of the valley where the Goodenstone mansion lay hidden from view by a mature stand of timber. From behind the trees, a great stormcloud of red-lit smoke rose.

'Do you reckon it's the big house?' Luce asked.

Lidi saw Jude and Will exchange looks.

'No,' said Will. 'It's the ricks up at Manor Farm.'

Jack now joined them and wanted to know why the knell was tolling.

'Rick fires. It's to get people from the village out, to pull the ricks down to stop the fires spreading.'

'Shouldn't you go, Luce?' Sarah asked.

There was a still and leaden silence around her question and she realised that there was something going on that she did not understand.

In the silence, shouting voices echoed across the valley.

The smoke rose thickly against the dark sky. A lick of flame showed above the trees. The last winds of March that had blown into April were not going out like lambs, but were boisterous.

Sparks now rose with the smoke.

The knell still tolled out long, grey notes.

Not a light showed in any window in the village except in Church Cottage, in the Rectory and the bell-tower.

As they watched in silence, John joined them.

'I thought it'd start here before long,' he said.

'What's starting, Pa?' Jack asked, peering into the night.

'Folk taking things into their own hands, Boy.'

The tone of her Pa's voice, and the silence of the others, seemed to Sarah to separate herself and Jack from the others. She felt a surge of panic which cramped her stomach and raced her heart.

Suddenly a gust of wind swept over Old Marl and down into the heart of the smoke. For a moment, the smoke thickened and turned yellow, then the sky reddened as long tongues of flame funnelled up the valley and licked the sky.

They all gasped at the sight.

'What's happening, Pa? It's frightening me, you all standing here not saying anything and the whole village could burn down.'

'It won't.' Will, his pure-white beard and hair reflecting the moonlight, rested his hand on Jude's shoulder, two old people watching the show as though it were a passing parade. 'The wind's not in that direction. Only the ricks will burn, and the scrub at the bottom of Old Marl.'

How strange Uncle Will sounded, sharp, and almost commanding, certain it was the ricks which were burning. A feeling that something was amiss came over her. Earlier in the evening he had sat in his shirtsleeves playing with the babies as he usually did at the end of the day, but now he was fully dressed, not like the rest of them with odd garments hastily wrapped around them. Uncle Will's coat was buttoned and his boots laced. She now noticed the old wide-brimmed black hat and long black waxed cape which he wore in the rain, draped over a fence post. And Aunt Jude, although it was the middle of the night, was still dressed as she had been that evening.

A gradual feeling of wariness grew. She had never known what it was that Uncle Will did, or where he came from or went to. Always an air of mystery about him. When they were young girls, Lidi had guessed that he was a highwayman, and it hadn't seemed impossible. She had a quick memory of him twenty years back, him tossing her into the air, herself looking down into his nice smiling face as he caught her and tossed her again. He would be there for a few days, and then be off again.

She looked at him again. A stoop-shouldered old man who was good company and generous, a nice grandfatherly old man. Why now did she suddenly sense something else about him?

He had been out after they had all gone to bed.

He knew about the ricks.

Moving forward where he was standing, Sarah turned her head in his direction and drew in her breath. It was as though she knew that her suspicions would be confirmed by standing close to him. A strong smell of smoke hung about him, not only the smell of his tobacco smoke or the ordinary woodsmoke that was on all their clothes, but the smell of burnt straw that was quite distinctive.

She turned and went into the house and back to bed and lay facing towards the window. The sky looked red.

After a while she heard her Pa tramp back across the kitchen and sigh as he always did when he got into bed.

Soon after, she heard the latch of Jack's door.

She lay awake a long time thinking and listening.

It was ages before the other four came back across the yard. They kept their voices low but talked for a long while in the shelter of the porch.

Clear as day, it came to Sarah that her family were followers of 'Captain Swing' the legendary rick-burner.

GRADUALLY, OVER THE fifteen months that she had been back in her old home, Sarah had come to believe that she could live in Cantle without being too discontent. In spite of being more than ten years away from them, she thought that she was beginning to return to being one of the family.

Since the night of the fire, it all seemed different. Had she been so engrossed in her own affairs that she had not really grown to understand them? So engrossed with the babies, with trying to block out the past, with working at being a village woman again, that she did not really know her own family? In the days immediately following the rick-burning, she came to the conclusion that this was true.

The man her father used to be, the one who made speeches and got himself arrested, was still there; that was something that she had come to realise over the recent weeks. That he was now almost white-haired, easily fatigued and got sudden pains that floored him, had not changed him. Why should she have thought it otherwise?

Although Pa was sharp when Lidi said outrageous things about 'robbing the rich to feed the hungry' it was not for her sentiments that he rebuked her, but that she expressed them too loudly, promising her a taste of Winchester gaol if she didn't watch her tongue. The sister that she was growing close to again had another side that Sarah could now scarcely guess at. Lidi, who had sounded exultant when she talked in low tones with Jude, Will and Luce, in the middle of the night. Lidi, like the rest of them, had been glad to see the ricks afire.

And Luce? What did she know of him? That he had married Lidi knowing that she agreed to it only to use 'the system that they gave us', as he put it. And that he didn't mind saying that he was pleased that they were using the law against itself by 'taking what was rightfully theirs' under the Relief system.

And she could not get out of her mind the tableau of those two old people, Aunt Jude and Uncle Will, standing close together and calmly watching hundreds of pounds' worth of grain go up in flame. That she had scarcely known Uncle Will, except as a jolly man who made occasional flying visits when she was little, bringing perhaps a little doll or a jumping-jack for a present, was true – but Aunt Jude had been close, a teacher, and almost a mother to herself and Lidi.

Only Jack still appeared to be what she had supposed that he was.

She was thinking to herself that they were strangers when she saw . . . no, it's *me* who's the stranger.

About a week after the fire, she and Aunt Jude were working together, putting a new wash of lime on the kitchen walls.

'Can't you settle up here, Sarah?'

'Here? In the old place? Yes, it's lovely here. You know I always liked a chance to stop here when I was little.'

'You don't seem settled.'

'I am. Things are easier all round now that Pa hasn't got the church rent to find. I don't feel so much of a burden.'

'You aren't a burden, you earn your keep well enough. If a price was put on the work women do in the family, they'd get more pay than any Agent of an estate.'

'It's better since we moved up here.'

'Then what's wrong, Sarah?'

'There's nothing wrong.'

The older woman took Sarah's brush away and pressed her firmly down onto a bench; in spite of their age difference the family resemblance was remarkable as their heads came close together.

'There is something wrong. If nobody else can see it, I can. You were fine when you first came, then suddenly you changed. It's not unusual for people to feel strange after this kind of upheaval, everybody having to adapt and re-arrange themselves around each other. When Will first moved in . . . well! There were times when we both thought he'd move out again. Living on top of one another like this, we should get things sorted out or they just get worse. Is everybody putting too much on you? Those babes are a real handful now, perhaps I don't realise . . .'

'No, they're not much trouble since Uncle Will made that pen thing for them.'

Jude quickly squeezed then released Sarah's shoulder, and said, 'Come on Sarah, you've got your fair share of troubles without any more.'

After a moment's pause, Sarah said, 'I'm afraid of things. Afraid of what might happen. Not only that. I don't understand what's going on. It's been there staring me in the face ever since I came home, but I never saw it. Heaven knows, I should have, I was brought up on Pa's ideas. Now it's gone further than that, hasn't it? It makes them do things – like when Pa got sent to prison, and I'm afraid it could happen again. I don't understand it all.' She clasped her hands and gripped them with frustration. 'I just don't understand!'

'Not understanding shouldn't make you draw into yourself like you've been this last week or so . . . plenty of people don't understand those kind of things . . . too many people. And plenty get bored by them too.'

'If I understood then I'd know why you and Uncle Will stood watching all those ricks burning, and Luce wouldn't help, and Lidi didn't tell him to.' Her normally soft voice was becoming quite shrill. 'Perhaps if I understood, I'd know why I'm sure Uncle Will had something to do with those fires.'

Jude's hand moved as though to hush Sarah.

'Why ever should Will have anything to do with that?'

'I don't know. I just don't know. Uncle Will's an old man, what was he doing going off that night . . . I could smell the burnt straw on him. I don't know *why*, I only know that I was sure that he *did*. And the way you acted then, I know he did. Why?'

Jude heaved a sigh and sat down on the bench beside Sarah.

'Ah Sarah, you were away from us such a long time. What were you when you left, sixteen? And now what are you, twenty-seven, coming twenty-eight? It's the years when you'd have been growing up like your own kind if you had lived in Cantle. Instead you've grown up with people who have a totally different outlook to the likes of people here.'

'I didn't think I'd changed.'

'Didn't you?'

Sarah looked down at her hands. 'Well . . . not so much that I'm different from the rest of you.'

'Listen love. I've watched you since you came home . . . and admired you . . .'

Sarah shook her head in denial.

'Yes I have . . . I've admired you for your dignity. Somebody dealt you a rotten hand and you never once complained as far as I know. You obviously led a very interesting and different life . . .

London and the big cities, and Florence . . . you've seen things I've longed all of my life to see. Yet, when things turned against you, you came here and took up life again with dignity.' She gave a brief smile. '*That's* what I admire. That needed strength of character. That's the Estover in you. It was in your mother and my mother.'

'Really?'

'Oh yes, people used to call my mother "Master" Bella and thought it was a compliment. Master, because she got on and ran this place when my father abandoned her. Ach! That was no compliment to call her "Master" – it's women are best at picking up the pieces and carrying on. And *your* mother . . . Ah, Hanna, she was so much like my mother . . . but happier, a lot happier . . . When she had you twins, she was so happy then. She deserved a lot more years with John.'

'If it's true what you say, that makes me feel better, but it doesn't change it that I'm different. I think it's wrong to do things like Uncle Will setting fire . . .'

'No! There's nobody says Will had anything to do with it.'

'All right, but none of you said it was wrong. It was setting fire to food when there's people in this village starving.'

'Exactly! All that food standing there, and Cantle children with nothing in their bellies but turnip and sorrel broth. What do you expect them to do? Touch their forelocks and say "that's all right, Master Eustace, never mind us who ploughed the fields in the freezing cold, never mind us that twisted our bones planting, never mind us who broke our backs reaping it and sweated our guts putting it into ricks – you just leave it standing there till the price is right – then put it through your machines and sell it at a great profit." ' She thumped her strong, wiry hands against her thighs with passion. 'Surely you understand *that*. It isn't hard. Even if people went up to the manor with clubs and axes, *I* could understand.'

Sarah shook her head. 'It's because it's *food* it seems wrong. It's terrible to destroy food.'

They sat silent for a short while.

'Well,' said Jude at last, 'I'm glad it's not that you're unhappy here. I only hope in time you'll understand the rest. Working people in the factory cities are joining together to get better conditions – that's what Will was helping them to do – it's only a matter of time before agricultural workers do the same.'

'Is that part of the same thing . . . burning ricks?'

'Yes, it's all part of that. It's not complicated really. Just ordinary people wanting a fairer share in things. Nobody's asking to live in Park Manor – only proper wages and a fair share in things, and a say in how the country's run.'

'Ordinary people can't know how to run a country.'

'Why not? Do you really think there's that much difference between the likes of your Mr Broughlake and your Pa when it comes to common sense?'

The first glimmer of light for Sarah. It was true that Pa had more sense in his little finger than Mr Broughlake had in his whole head, yet her old employer had been a Magistrate, an alderman and had once stood for Parliament. And Pa was a decent, honest man, not a rotten one like her old Master.

'I just wish things could be put right without doing such terrible things.'

'The terrible things are our neighbours starving when there's plenty of food stored away waiting for the highest price.'

The conflict between new ideas and old traditions flames up in every class of society, in every possible environment, in the very bosom of the family. The son struggles against his father . . . the daughter rebels against the principles which her mother has handed down to her.

The Spirit of the Revolution

I T WAS BETTER now that Jude and Sarah had cleared the air. May came, and Isabell and Christopher's first birthday. Then on the last day of June Auryn's. It was a thing to celebrate, for many children did not survive their first year. The three children were with them daily, but it took an anniversary for the family to gather and pride themselves on their three healthy heirs.

Aunt Jude must have said something to the others about Sarah's worries, for Lidi said, 'You don't have to worry, Sarah, they all know what they're doing.' And Pa had said, 'Listen Gel, there's things that goes on in this village these days that it's best not to know about. You just be contented and look after these little nippers.'

Sarah tried to do so, but for the first time in months, she began to think about her old life, not wishing to go back to it, for she would not have exchanged any of it for her two babies who were her pleasure and pride.

Although Croud Cantle was situated away from the rest of the village, a good many people came there; some were villagers, others were strangers whom Will took out into the fields to talk to. Tazey James came once or twice, polite to Sarah, but emphatic and finger-waving in discussion with Will. If men called in the evening, Will and Luce and John would suggest that they all 'go and have a wet down at Tazey's'. Perhaps all this coming and going and hushed conversation had gone on when they were back in Shaft's Cottage, but there Sarah would not have noticed the daytime callers except to assume that they had come on some business with Toose's of Cantle.

She buried her head in the care of the babies and tried not to see any of it. But she could not avoid hearing, for most of the talk at those times when they were gathered together to eat, was of the unrest that was growing all over the southern counties.

Hungry farmworkers banded together and demanded food from shopkeepers.

Rickyards everywhere burst into sudden flame.

It was after dinner and the sun was almost overhead. John and Will were dozing beside the hearth, Luce and Jack had gone to Waltham Market, and Jude had gone off as she did sometimes, wandering over Tradden Raike to collect roots and leaves for remedies and lotions. Sarah could see her from where she was seated in the little orchard keeping an eye on Isabell, who could now pull herself to her feet and stand wavering, steeling herself to take her first step. Auryn and Christopher scrambled about like puppies inside the little wooden coop that kept them from crawling away.

Sarah had taken a chair out under the old tree where a crop of apples had reached the size of cherries. She had spread out on her lap a large square of patchwork to which she was adding the next triangle of pattern. Bees from the row of hives a little further off, came to the bindweed on the fence, the dandelions and daisies in the long grass of the orchard and the cranesbill, marigolds and sage flowers of the herb-garden. Birds were quiet, voices and the lowing of beasts carried a long way.

Her ears picked up the sound of a horse coming slowly up Howgaite Path towards the house. It came slowly, its rider probably walking beside it, allowing it to crop and drink from the Dunnock as it came. She heard the gate latch, and a voice asking if anyone was there. It was her Pa who answered. She returned her attention to her work and looked up and caught her breath to see Belle, her arms out and fingers spread wide to steady herself, walking a few tottering steps. Her actions frozen Sarah counted, three, four, five, then Isabell stumbled over a tussock and fell.

Sarah ran to her and picked her up, tickling her and tossing her into the air. 'Clever Belle, Ma's clever Belle.' She smacked a loud kiss on the child who was struggling to get down again. Sarah put her down, and as she did so, she saw that Pa and another man were standing watching.

'Send her this way Sarah.'

There was no need to; hearing her grandfather's voice, Isabell staggered off in his direction.

'Oh Pa, did you see her start herself off?'

Belle had reached her grandfather without falling. He picked her up and poked her in the belly. Sarah, intent on her own and her father's pleasure in the incident, did not pay attention to the man with her Pa. Then he spoke.

'Hello Sarah.'

Gentle, broad Hampshire, that flung her back into a happy past.

'Brendan! Brendan Lewis.'

'This young man has rode all the way over from Beauwyth.'

'Beauwyth?'

'Between Shorlay and Newton Clare.'

'Ah, I know it. There's a yew tree there reckoned to be a thousand years old.'

Brendan smiled. 'Reckoned to be – 'tis probably about a hunderd.'

There was a moment of silence, not awkward for Belle was off again getting their attention, her fat feet and shift stained green, her bonnet hanging from its ribbons.

'Is she your little girl?'

'Yes. Isabell. But she gets called Belle mostly.'

'She has to be yours, with that hair.'

'So's the little boy – Christopher, not the one with the yellow hair, he's my sister's boy.'

'Why don't you take your visitor on into the house and give him a bite and a drink, Sarah. Will's gone off down to see Lidi. I'll sit here with these gally-baggers. I don't promise to finish your bedcover though.'

Sarah led the way into the kitchen and prepared a plate of bread, cheese and beets, the sight of which made Brendan rub his hands and say he was hungry enough to eat a horse.

'I'm afraid there's no meat – things don't run to it much these days.'

'Cheese and beets is my favourite.'

She smiled with real pleasure at his honest enthusiasm for the meagre meal.

Without appearing to, she took in every aspect of his appearance. His riding clothes were decent, not those of an ordinary groom, and he wore smart knee-high cuffed riding boots which were quite fashionable. He still wore his dark-brown curly hair quite long and his sideburns were more flourishing than ever. He looked fit and handsome in a quiet way.

When he had first spoken and she had looked up to discover him there, she was surprised to find that she was not embarrassed or flustered that he should have seen her in the midst of her maternal domesticity – rather she felt pleased that he had seen her so.

'You're the last person I expected to see.'

'Why?'

'I don't know.'

'Don't be polite, you'd forgotten I existed.'

'No. In fact, not at all. I've been thinking quite a lot recently about those days when you were teaching Ninn to ride. I wondered what it was all like now. Ninn will be quite a young man.'

'He's coming up to twenty, and tall and good-looking enough for any girl.'

'Is he? I guessed he would be.'

'In fact, it's Master Ninn that I work for.'

'Of course, he inherited when . . .'

'Ah, but I don't work there – I work at Beauwyth. Master Ninn's set up a stables there, racing horses and hunters – and I'm head man.' He looked quietly pleased to tell her this.

'Oh Brendan, I'm so pleased, but then you were so good with horses, you must be a real asset.'

He made a modest gesture of denial, but smiled none-the-less as he ate his meal.

'And what brings you all over here?'

He smoothed the crumbs from his mouth before replying.

'Well . . .' He took a drink. 'As a matter of fact . . . yourself.'

She hardly knew how to respond. 'I thought you must have been a friend of my Uncle Will's when I heard the horse coming up Howgaite.'

'I never knew you were back here until just recently. I thought you were still in Italy with your Mistress.'

'I left there nearly two years ago.'

'I know that now. I happened to meet Margaret Roberts. She told me that she was back again working for Mrs Delphine, back to the old house. Master Ninn's away or I should have heard. Nobody's seen her – except Margaret who's back in the nursery again. Mrs Delphine's got another child. She had it abroad.'

Sarah nodded. 'I guessed so.'

'Ah. There's quite a mystery about it all. Margaret wanted to gossip, but you know me – I don't want any of that. But it's what Margaret lives for, a bit of tittle-tattle. Well, she's in the right place for that now. I don't think Master Ninn knows anything about it.'

There was a moment's pause, after which Brendan picked up the original thread. 'Well, Sarah, not to beat about the bush, I never forgot you for a minute after you left. And as soon as Margaret said that you were probably back in your old village, I decided I'd ride over and see you.'

'That was a nice thought. I'm so pleased to see you again – and doing so well.'

'Have you married?'

Sarah shook her head.

'Well then Sarah, would you consider marrying me?'

She had expected the next question would have been another friendly enquiry. She half-smiled and frowned.

'Marry?'

'Yes Sarah. I fell for you right back when you used to bring Ninn to the stables. If things had been different then, I should have asked you before you went off abroad. I thought by the time you came home, I might be in a bit better position to ask . . . well, now you're home, and I've come to ask you. Will you?'

His hand was warm and dry as he laid it upon hers, clasping it firmly. 'Please say you will. I've got a nice little house . . .'

'Brendan, Brendan. Stop a minute.'

Marry Brendan, marry this nice, honest wide-eyed man who had warm dry hands. Marry and live in a nice little house. The thought of it was like a draught of clear air in a murky room.

'Look . . . you saw me out there . . . two of those babes are mine.'

'I know. I knew before I came. It don't make any difference to me that it's two, I should like them both equal.'

'You don't know whose they are.'

'Yes I do – they're *yours*.'

'You know what I mean.'

'And I'm giving you my reply. Sarah, I don't care who their father is, why should I? The thing is, you didn't marry him . . .' He paused as the thought occurred to him, 'Perhaps you're waiting for him . . .'

'No, no. If he was the last man on earth, I shouldn't marry him.'

For a moment, he looked quite perplexed. 'I don't know what

to say next. I thought it all out on my way, but it came out wrong. I was too sudden. Oh Sarah, it's that I've waited so long to ask you, and when I heard what happened, and that it seemed that you might still not be married, I . . . Please Sarah, will you?'

He was still holding her hand; she raised his to her mouth and pressed her lips gently to his knuckles.

'If you really want it . . . then there's nothing I'd like better in the world than to be married to you.'

He puffed out his cheeks and made a play of a sweated brow. Then holding her by her shoulders, he kissed her, a warm, full kiss, not too brief, nor long and passionate. If Sarah had had any doubts of her answer, this first physical contact between them dissolved them, and she returned his kiss.

'Lord, I was never so nervous in my whole life. I'm that happy I can't tell you.'

'You didn't sound a jot nervous.'

'I was, I couldn't think of one thing that would recommend me to you.'

'Brendan, oh my dear man, I could start now and tell you a hundred things.'

'When shall it be? The cottage wants prettying up a bit, you'd have to come over and see what you wants changed. I'll get the Agent to have it limed and tarred straight away. It's old, but it's nice and warm and dry; it's got a board floor in, and a lead sink, and there's a pump right outside the back door, you wouldn't have to go any distance.'

The sudden happiness and freedom that suddenly bubbled up inside Sarah burst out in a fountain of laughter and spontaneously she put her arms about his neck. He held her firmly by the waist and they stood thus, their faces close.

'Lord, it can't be half an hour since I was making patchwork out there, and here I am halfway up the aisle and pumping water outside my own kitchen.'

He smiled at the sight of her laughter creases and the heaving of her breasts with the breath of her laughter.

'Ah Sarah, we shall be a happy little family shan't we?'

'It won't be my fault if we aren't. I reckon I must be the luckiest woman alive.'

'Going to wed the luckiest man. Come on, I've got to ask your father now.'

John Toose shook Brendan's hand and welcomed him as a

member of the family. He welcomed him again when Brendan said, 'When I was only young, I heard you speak, Mister Toose, in Waltham, about Enclosures, I never forgot how excited and roused up I got. I was only a lad, but I still remember.'

'Well Son, I'm pleased that there's at least one who remembers those old days.' He peered close at Brendan. 'I hoped you wasn't one who disagreed?'

'No, but then as far as I can remember I can't say I agreed either, the truth is I can remember the feeling, and I can remember you, but I can't truly say I remember your arguments.'

'Ah . . .' John was ready to rectify Brendan's lack immediately.

'No Pa! For once this family isn't going to talk about something else — we're going to name a day and then go and see to getting the banns called.'

He stayed long enough to tell John about his work, his wages, his prospects, what kind of life he could offer Sarah and said that he would wish to have the twins put in his name if nobody disagreed.

'Dash it Son, it's only them and Sarah that should be asked and I don't reckon you'd get much of an answer from them — though if you asks me, it won't be long before this little Belle will be chirping away as well as she can walk.' He patted the child's nose with a daisy. 'I shall miss these little shavers, and that's a fact.'

'We shan't be far, Pa, and Brendan says he gets the use of the horses as much as he wants. So we shall come riding over of a day quite often.'

Will came back from the village and had to have the arrangements explained twice before he comprehended the sudden advent of a husband for Sarah. Jude came in from Tradden, windblown and with pleasure deep within the far-away look in her eyes, as she always did when she went there roaming on her own.

'Well Sarah, I know it's the kind of life you want, and what suits you. You'll be happy. I think you must have found yourself one of the best sort of men there is — you see you take care of him. And you Lad, you're getting one of the Estovers — you don't know what that is, but you'll find out. You don't need me to tell you what sort of a wife you're getting — you wouldn't have come and found her out if you didn't know already.'

Sarah and Brendan were both not that far off thirty, but they stood beaming and happy as two young lovers.

'You two so remind me of John there and Hanna,' Jude said. 'John was much like you at your age, and Sarah has always been the spit and image of her mother. You'll be happy enough.'

Lidi, with a pile of short boards to one side and a box of panel-pins to hand, was deftly hammering away making plant-boxes. She looked up and immediately recognised who it was leading his horse and walking beside Sarah.

'I met you once in Wickham. You wore checked trousers.' Then she remembered – it had been Alec James who wore the checks.

'Did I? It doesn't surprise me, I used to dress quite fancy at one time.'

Lidi was quite overcome with emotion at seeing her sister so beaming and happy. She kissed her lightly. 'It just shows, there are nice things in the world. I'm glad you got one of them, Sarah.'

The marriage was arranged for the end of the month.

5

CARE OF THE AGED
July

THERE WERE MANY rearrangements to be talked over. Neither Jude nor Lidi was much given to being in the house like normal housewives, but would prefer to be about their outside work.

When Jude suggested that John and Will were as capable of doing the buk-wash as Sarah, John said he might have been before his seizure, and Will said everyone made too much of boiling and pounding the life out of shirts.

'I could do something towards it?' Jack asked.

'No,' said his father. 'It's bad enough seeing you play fiddle on the streets, I hope the day hasn't come when I see you working as a day-wash woman.'

'Not like you saw Tan and Sarah,' Lidi flashed back.

'That's enough, Lidi,' Luce said. 'If there's that sort of wrangling it'll make Sarah feel bad about leaving.'

Lidi shut up then, for her underlying guilt was at having let Sarah willingly take over the family wash. Lidi never minded preparing food, but she detested the wasted day of the buk-wash.

In the end all the readjustments were made by each of them having to take on a bit more work than they had previously. On wash-day, they would all get up earlier, the men would start the fire and carry the water, whilst Jude and Lidi pounded the wash.

These small wrangles were not in themselves important, but an indication of the many ways in which they would miss Sarah and the two babies.

Lidi didn't like to think of the emptiness of the little coop with only Auryn in it. She and Sarah had always exchanged one another's babes and would give the breast to the babe who was most urgent for it no matter which one. Lidi had often looked down on Belle's strong red lips upon her nipple, or Christopher's eyes looking up into hers as he satisfied his hunger from her. It would be hard not to have them there.

Following very quickly upon the one happening, came another in the form of a note brought by a carter:

'MY SISTER MIS NETHFILD WAS TOOK BAD AND WAS TOOK TO THE INSTUSHON AT BLACKBROOK.'

'I can't believe it!' Lidi said. 'It can't be a week since I saw her.' But Lidi's time had flown. It was more than a month since Maisie Netherfield had left to visit her sister at Gundleford.

'I'll have to go to her,' Jude said at once.

'No Aunt Ju, it'd be better if I went. I can't bake the pies for market like you can. Sarah's got to go over to Beauwyth some time to see the cottage, so we'll take the little cart and do it all in a day.'

And so it was arranged.

By nine o'clock the next day Lidi had dropped off Sarah outside the gates of Ninn Broughlake's small estate and was on her way along the road to Blackbrook.

She had been to the Parishes once before, when she had intended to ask about Harriett Bone. But before she got further than looking into the first building where twenty were housed in about twenty feet, and saw the squalor and the wretched sleeping-holes, she turned back.

The memory of that visit was still as vivid in Lidi as the anger and guilt she still felt at her own helplessness to do anything for the Bone family. It rose in her again as she walked towards the great red-brick building. Its aggressive bulk, its stone portico, its unadorned brickwork inset with regular rows of small windows, reminded her again of a prison.

The Poorhouse was set on a rise as though its founders were pleased to acknowledge it. At the entrance, Lidi was scrutinised and asked what her business was, and then directed on into the building. When her Pa had been in prison, she had once visited him and the memory of that too had stayed with her, as a place of unthinkable degradation where her Pa had felt, as had Hetty Bone in here, that he wanted no one who knew him to see him there.

As she began her walk through the stone-flagged corridors, she was reminded of it vividly. The metallic clink of bunches of keys and the same metallic echo in the voices of officials. Doors with locks and bars. The strange echoes, half-heard voices, footsteps, half-heard sounds like people calling in thin voices. The terrible stink of unwashed clothes huddled into small spaces, stale urine, damp stone and mouldy straw – and the overall smell of steaming offal.

She paused, wondering where she was, and had to stand aside

for two boys in rough linen pinafores to pass; they lugged between them a shallow tub of excrement.

'What d'st thee want down here?' Another of the metal-edged voices addressed her. A tallow-faced man of unknowable age, his sparse hair as yellowed as his face. He wore a long, patched coat and a dented high hat, once black now a yellowish green.

'I'm looking for a sick old person.'

'Male or female?'

'An old lady.'

'Then you an't got no business here – this is the pauper children's wing.'

'I've been up and down corridors and through doors, till I'm lost,' Lidi said.

'Nobody's got no business walking about this place on their own. I'll take you, follow behind me. I'm a "charger" of the Casuals, but I'll take you.' He eyed her basket. 'You're not allowed to bring anything in.'

She followed the Tallow Man. Across a yard where there were stable-like sheds with sagging thatched roofs.

'This is mine – Overnight Casuals.' He flung out a gesture, surely not pride Lidi thought, but it was. 'I'm in charge of the admittance and,' he waved a knobbled stick, 'and the idiots.' His position must be an important one from his manner in telling her.

Everyone knew the reputation of the 'Institutions' – Work-houses, Poorhouses, they were all the same. Anyone who was likely to be an inmate dreaded them, and nowadays any rural worker, orphan, destitute woman or aged person was in danger of becoming an inmate.

Everyone knew them by repute, but that was different. Lidi could scarcely believe what she saw. No wonder people who had experienced them rarely spoke of what it was like except in insufficient words – 'rotten places', 'filthy holes', 'I'd sooner be in my grave than go back there'.

The Overnight Casuals was a row of open wooden stalls such as horses might be kept in overnight. A few had board floors, but for the main part the floor was bare cobble.

'There's not much room for a person to move about in a stall as little as that.'

The Tallow Man sniffed. 'No reason to move about at night. They only got to lay down, that don't need much room. Ha! if it was one man to a stall, there'd be a line outside from here to

Winchester of them waiting to come in. Three or four together, they keeps each other warm.'

A bell tolled.

'Here come on, hurry up, that's mid-day mess over for the old men, 'tis my dinner time.'

Before they reached the Women's Wing, Lidi had seen into the room where the old men had been taking their meal. The old men. The silent old men. Old, bent, silent men. Row upon row of wooden benches and wooden tables, row upon row of grey heads bent silently over their plates.

'This is it.' The Tallow Man went to a door and made a signalled knock. A small opening slid sharply back. A female metal-edged voice. 'What?'

'This here woman have come to see one of yourn.'

'A relative?'

Lidi nodded.

'Too early. Nobody allowed in for another half an hour.'

The Tallow Man went close to the opening. 'She's got a basket here.'

A portion of a face appeared at the opening; the eyes peered at Lidi.

'Nothing allowed to be took in.'

'It's only a tart.'

The shutter snapped shut and the door opened.

The woman who came out was as yellow as Lidi's guide.

'I said nothing's allowed to be took inside.'

'Why?'

'What d'you mean "why?" – because it's the rules that nothing's allowed to be took in, that's why.'

The Tallow Man looked at the Yellow Woman, raised his chin an inch and closed his eyes indicating that they must have another idiot on their hands.

'Because it'd cause trouble,' he said, 'You can't treat one of 'm no different. If you let one have a tart, they'd all want a tart, and anyway it's against the rules.'

'Here, hand it over.' The woman jerked the basket from Lidi's hand.

'My things are in there.'

'Then it's best if you leaves'm here with me for safety,' the Yellow Woman said.

The Tallow Man inclined his head knowingly at his colleague.

'Perhaps if the pie's going to spoil, the lady might think it wasn't worth taking out again. It'd be a kind of exchange if you was to let her in before time. Special permission.'

Lidi shrugged her shoulders in resignation at the loss of Maisie Netherfield's tart, as the Yellow Woman unlocked the doors to the wing marked with an arrow 'Female Aged – Female Venereal'.

'If she's bed-rid, then go right to the end, that's where the bed-rid ones are kept. Remember, you'm here on a favour of me.'

Lidi entered the ward. A long room, bare except for the bier-like cots that were rowed up against the side walls. She saw forty or more inhabitants – inhabitants because it was not immediately apparent that they were women. Close-capped, sunken mouthed and more tallow and yellow than their warders, so pallid that their flesh appeared leeched of all blood. Except that they were propped up and held bowls from which they supped – a row of scraggy corpses. A strange whine, like a dog or a fox near its end from getting its leg caught in a trap. An idiot's jabbering, and the same strange laughing sound that she had heard in the gaol. These sounds, however, did not come from the feeble bodies in this ward, they were silent as though they were indeed ready for the grave.

It took Lidi a little while to find Mrs Netherfield, so much alike did they all look in identical caps and grey shifts, and it was then only because of the thin voice that called, 'Lidi? Lidia Toose? Isn't that you?'

'Mrs Netherfield!' Lidi was too late to entirely cover her initial shocked reaction at the change in the old midwife's appearance. She attached a bright smile. 'I didn't see you in that corner.'

Oh Lord. Hetty and Pa were right, it would be better not to see a neighbour in such low circumstances. Degrading, Pa had said. Degrading to humans.

Maisie Netherfield was the end one of a row of old ladies. Lidi brushed her cheek with a kiss and took her hand.

'Oh Mrs Netherfield, we were so sorry to hear that you had been taken badly.'

'It was only a seizure. They needn't a brought me in here. But my sister's place is over Headley way, and I got took first there. Then when they found it wasn't my parish they carted me over here. My sister can't write, but she said she could find somebody to let Jude know.' For a moment her voice trembled. 'I thought nobody would know I was here, and I'd get lost and put in a pauper's grave. I'm thankful that you've come. I can rest now I know I shall get buried like a Christian.'

'Ach, don't you talk about any graves.'

The old woman put her hand over her mouth in apology. 'It's the worry of all of they in here.' She nodded towards the others. 'Pauper's grave. It's a worse thing to say than "Plague".'

'Jude sent you a tart, but they wouldn't let me bring it.'

'Best not. There's no knowing what they might do if they saw a thing like that.' She inclined her head towards the direction of the jabbering. 'They can't help it poor souls, an't no woman I ever met as wanted to do that for a living.'

Lidi looked questioningly and craned her neck to see.

'You can't see, they'm locked up.'

'Are they mad?'

'It's the woman's pox ward. They don't last long.'

'Can they get in here then?'

'Some of the wardresses are gin fanciers – they forget. And you can't blame them neither. I should want a tot if I had to be in here . . . it an't a job for human woman.'

A bell tolled.

'The attendants for the bowls.' She indicated the bowl of grey water.

'What is that?'

'Ox-head broth. Only us who's sick enough gets ox-head. It's salt-fish and 'tatoes in the messing hall.'

Half a dozen youngish women dragged a low cart into the room and began collecting the bowls, few of which had been emptied by the old women.

One of the orderlies, looking closely at Lidi as she pushed by, took the bowl. 'Do Mistress 'acker know you'm in here?'

'Is she the one out there?'

The girl nodded.

'She said I could come in.'

'Well she'd better have or she'll roast me.'

'It's all right, Ginny – it's Miss Jude's niece. You remember Miss Jude, got the pie stall.'

Ginny peered closely at Lidi; her clothes and hair stank.

'You Miss Jude?'

'Miss Jude's niece.'

'Miss Jude?' She drew her brows together in an exaggerated fashion as though to squeeze what she wanted from her memory, but it did not seem to come. Then she beamed. 'I remember Miss Jude – you used to gid me some of that there pie from your stall. Miss Jude, I remember.'

'Go on Ginny, or you'll be late for your own dinner,' Maisie said.

The girl went off, collecting bowls as she went.

'You didn't reco'nise her.'

'No. Should I?'

'Little Ginny Short who used to sell the penny-ballads and chaps outside the Star – near where the Nugents had their stall.'

'I remember. A cheeky thing she always was. I haven't seen her for years. I'd forgotten her.'

'That's her.' The old lady shook her head. 'It was a sad thing. She got took down by a drunk soldier, and it turned her head. She wasn't no more than twelve. They reckon she cried for nine months. Anyway, she had the baby and it seemed to get her better, then when she was carrying the baby out one day, they got set on by some dogs and the baby got killed. It turned her head altogether.'

Suddenly Lidi stood up.

'You're not stopping here, Mrs Netherfield.'

'I got to, dear. I got to.'

'There's no "got to" about it. There's no law says you have to stop here. You aren't a prisoner.'

The old lady no longer looked like the woman who only a year before had dandled Auryn, head down, and brought him to life. She smiled and patted Lidi's hand. 'That's your Aunt Jude speaking. Full of go always – still is. You'd never think she's not far off my age.'

Lidi looked around. 'Where are your things?'

'I don't know. Listen Lidi, the only reason I sent that note was so as they wouldn't bury me in the Paupers' ground. My Rob always carried a gold ring tied round his neck enough to bury him, and he had one made for me, but I was always afraid to carry it with me.' She beckoned Lidi close and whispered, 'It's in the crack in the stone over the bread oven in my place. I know you'll see I an't disgraced. It'd be worse than being in here.'

Lidi stood with one hand upon her hips and the other pinching her bottom lip.

'I've told you, Mrs Netherfield – I'm not going out of here without you, and Aunt Ju'd never forgive me for certain – and you wouldn't want me in her bad books.' She smiled at the old midwife. 'Don't run away.'

Lidi was taken to the Overseer, a surprisingly young man to have the responsibility of running such an institution. He did not have the slightest objection to a visitor making off with one of the inmates. The entire object of his work, as with the Tallow and Yellow officials, was devoted to keeping the costs down for their employers – one less off the rates.

'Once you take her from here, she's your responsibility.'

Whether that was true or no Lidi didn't care, all she wanted was to get away. When she asked for Mrs Netherfield's belongings, she caused some consternation – they had been unaccountably mislaid, but they were quite willing to let her go out in the bed-gown that had been provided by the Parish, and would loan a bedcover to wrap her up in the cart. The original Tallow woman had gone off duty, so that Lidi's basket, that had contained the tart, a few pence and Lidi's cotton shawl, had also apparently gone off duty with her.

Before she left, Lidi decided that she could not leave without finding out what had happened to Mrs Bone.

The loss of two lots of belongings had made the Master somewhat embarrassed.

'Never mind,' said Lidi, 'You can do me a favour instead. There's a Mrs Bone in here. Perhaps you'd send to tell her that Mrs Draper is here – no, best say Miss Toose – and would she see me.'

'An't no question of "would she", I'll send for her.'

'Then tell her who is here.'

It took ten minutes or so, but eventually it was discovered that Harriett Bone had been put to work in the laundries.

Lidi waited in a corridor.

'Mrs Bone!'

'Hello Lidi.'

'I know you said not to come, but I was here and . . .'

'It's all right. You soon loses that sort of pride when you been in here a few weeks. I'm glad you come really.'

'I'm just going to take Mrs Netherfield back home.'

'Maisie Netherfield in here? The poor soul.'

'I shan't ask you what it's like – I've seen that for myself. Where are the children?'

'Young Rich and Percy have been put out as 'prentices and Faith and Mercy are with me.'

'In the laundry?'

'They an't really old enough to earn much there, but at least they'm with me.'

It was an awkward meeting. Lidi could hardly say how much worse things had got for the Toose family – compared to the Bones, it must seem like Paradise. And Harriett, Lidi thought, was like a woman who has lost every bit of herself – no, not 'was like', Harriett Bone *was* a lost woman.

They shook hands formally. 'Give my regards to your Pa and Miss Jude, they was always good to me and Dick.'

It had been a quarter off noon when Lidi had come into the Parishes Poorhouse, and before two o'clock, with Mrs Netherfield rolled like a carpet in the back of the cart, they were on the road to pick up Sarah and then back to Cantle.

Again they re-arranged themselves at Croud Cantle to accommodate the frail old midwife. She lived for ten days at Croud Cantle, comfortable and warm and reassured once her 'burying money' had been retrieved from her old cottage; and she was assured that the knell would be rung, and that she would be took decent to her own churchyard.

When Lidi told her Aunt Ju about Hetty Bone, Jude sat grim and sombre for a long time.

'I'm going up to see Harry Goodenstone.'

They all looked at her in amazement.

'It's still his estate.'

And she went, trudging up the long drive, crunching the red hoggin in her determined, limping stride.

No one ever knew the whole story of what went on there; Jude told as much of it as she wanted anyone to know.

She was gone the entire afternoon and returned tight-lipped, whipping the verges with a peeled twig on her return, giving vent to frustration.

Only Lidi, Luce and Will were at hand to see her stump angrily into the kitchen.

'Damn the eyes of Harry Goodenstone! He's got a duty to this village, same as he's got to them that work to keep him rich out on his estates in the Indies – and I told him so.'

'You told Sir Henry?' Luce was quite overawed.

'Ha! And more. He wasn't always Sir Henry you know. I mind him, the little City-coxcomb up on his high horse looking down a village girl's bodice. There was a time when he'd come

riding into this yard like any other young man – you don't know the
half of it.'

And certainly Lidi did not. Was Aunt Ju that village girl?

Her old aunt smiled at some memory. 'He always dressed like a
little dancing master . . . remember, Will? . . . always looked as
though he'd stepped into the clothes of a bigger man . . . but he was
decent enough to speak to . . . then. But I haven't forgotten, nor
has he. He can't come the fine gentleman with me. But there was a
time when you could talk to him. He took a bit of interest in things.
Not like his son. Cantle is just income to Eustace Goodenstone. He
must be rich as Croesus.'

She paused, withdrawn for a moment.

'I hadn't remembered how long it's been . . . he's a queer little
old thing – like an orange that's been forgotten and gone hard and
brown . . . he's about seventy-five, but you'd think he was a
hundred. I reckon all those years in the sun must have dried him up.
In that great place . . . he put me in mind of a wood-beetle in an
empty cupboard. He was always weak. Always ran away from
anything that'd disturb his silly little life, like he's run away from
his responsibilities to the village – I despise him for it. Hate him for
it!'

They waited for her to get to the point.

'For goodness sake, Aunt Ju – why did you go up there?'

'To tell him to give Hetty Bone her cottage back.'

There was a moment of astonished silence.

'And did he?'

Jude looked contemptuous. 'Did he!' She made a simpering face.

' "I'd like to, Miss Nugent", Miss Nugent! "but I have to leave
all that kind of thing to Eustace these days, and he don't like my
interfering."

' "For goodness sake man," I told him, "you aren't dead, you
aren't gibbering . . . that's *your* estate. I'm not asking you to cut
down all the timber, I'm only asking you to let that poor woman
back rent free."

' "But he was poaching Eustace's land."

' "*Your* land," I said.

' "And he was found Guilty and sent to Van Dieman's Land."

' "Mrs Bone wasn't poaching," I told him, "nor were his
children found guilty."

' "I don't have anything to do with these matters now." He said
he was "sorry Miss Nugent". Sorry!'

For a small elderly lady she had a surprising strength when she thumped the table with the ladle.

'God above, Will! If I'd had this with me, I swear I'd have cracked his stupid head with it.'

'So it wasn't any good then?' Lidi asked.

She flung away a dismissive gesture.

'Never mind, Judeth,' Will said, 'you did what you could.'

'Don't you start pacifying me, Will Vickery.'

'Don't worry about that m'dear, there's not a body'd dare do that.'

'I should have done something about Hetty and her children ages ago. No excuse. That was more important than anything.'

'What the deuce do you think you could do?'

'Children shouldn't be split up from their mother like that . . . at the worst time . . . when they've seen the father taken . . . and the home gone.' She gave the table another thump.

Will took the ladle from her. 'Hey now there, Woman, calm down. It'd not have made any difference now would it?'

'Uncle Will's right,' said Lidi.

'I should have *tried*.'

'What could you have done?'

'*You* did something. You brought Maisie here.'

'Be sensible, Jude. There's no way we could have taken in Mrs Bone and half a dozen children.'

'Four!'

'Not even four. And what if you had gone rushing off and rescuing them, what would Lidi and Sarah and the babies have done then?'

Jude had no answer to that.

'And then what? Hetty Bone's only one in thousands and thousands all over the country.'

Deflated, she sank down into a chair. 'It's a terrible world. It's all so *terrible*. There used to be a time when I was younger that I thought it would all start to change. I believed that as soon as people began to know what I knew, then the Radical ideas would sweep the country.' She inspected her nails absently and shook her head. 'It was all a bit of a tale, wasn't it?'

'No.' Calm and reason in Will's voice. 'It's happening. Gradually. Who'd have thought when we were young that there'd be this many thousand joined up in workers' unions?'

'It's not enough. We're all too humble, too willing to let the

Eustace Goodenstones of this world beat us down. Who gave him this valley? Go on, I ask you, who gave it to him?'

Will humoured her. 'The Law. His ancestors enclosed the land and the Law said it was theirs.'

'And people let it happen, like I let Hetty Bone happen. They should have all rose up and said "no!" like I should have done.' She paused; the anger seemed to drain out of her for a moment. 'I wanted to see better things before I died. I thought if children learned to read and write, they would find out how things were run. I thought if they found out *how* they were being kept down by employers, and landowners and all "that lot", if they knew *how* they were used . . . *then*, I thought, they would know how to change things.'

'Things are changing,' Luce said placatingly. 'There's schools opening everywhere these days.'

'Schools?' She was scornful. 'What kind of school, only to teach children to count enough so that they can work better in factories, teach them enough letters to be able to read notices and instructions – but not enough so that they will *know* anything, *understand* anything. Oh no! Don't *educate* working people – they might stop being obedient, subservient. They might start asking questions about *laws* and *rights* and *justice*.'

Her anger was like the burning of scattered straw, flaring, dying, the embers of that catching another bunch, flaring, dying again.

Lidi and Luce looked at one another, pained at this revelation of her disillusion, of her dead hopes, and at seeing how dispirited the usually confident old aunt had become.

'But Aunt Ju, surely things are better for me than they were for you? There's better doctors, more good roads, there's canals getting built everywhere . . .' Her argument petered out.

'Better roads for your carriage, Lidi? Canal-barges bringing bread and meat for people on Relief, doctors going into the workhouses?'

They all knew that Jude was right.

'The worst is this . . . if people don't take matters into their own hands, things will get worse. There's two sorts of people – the ones who grow food, and the ones who eat it.'

'What's the answer then?' Lidi asked.

'We're all too afraid of them. We should be as brave as the French.'

Sarah came into the room and caught the tail end of the conversation.

Now they were talking revolution.

And it all stemmed from the two old ones. They weren't natural. Old people sat by the hearth smoking a pipe.

She observed them as dispassionately as she could manage. A stoop-shouldered, white-haired old man who couldn't be far off seventy, and a wiry weathered woman not much younger . . . and they were talking about revolution. What did they think they would do, start cutting heads off like in France?

Was it only talk? What about the ricks . . . and Lidi was nearly as wild-minded as Aunt Jude. She wouldn't take much persuading to go out with Uncle Will in the middle of the night and set fire to a rickyard. They'd lived in one another's pockets so long that they believed the things they said.

And Luce . . . even in the short time since she had been home, Sarah had noticed him change. He was becoming aggressive in his opinions, always reading the stuff that seemed to pour into the house, irritating Lidi by the laborious way that he read it. And her Pa sitting there rocking and nodding and prodding them.

When she was a child, there had been comfort in hearing her Pa's voice rumbling away as he read the papers to a roomful of neighbours.

But that was the comfort of ignorant childhood; the reality of her family's Radical notions was unease.

Suddenly she felt disloyal that she was abandoning Jack to their ideas. But, perhaps he'd be all right. Not much chance for a lad who was near blind without his spectacles to get into much trouble.

Ah, how glad she would be to get married and start living quiet, where she would sit at her own table with Brendan and he would talk of horses and she would talk of planting vegetables, and what the children had done. Only a week now and she would start a future better than she had ever imagined would be hers when she left Florence eighteen months ago.

6

AUGUST

For the third time Wilfrid Spartsit had the two problematical red-haired women standing before him. Twice before he had come off the worse for the encounter.

'Well?'

'I've only come to give you proper notice that I'm to be married and leaving the Parish.'

'Ah.' Hopefully. 'Then the father can pay up at last for the Parish bringing up his bastards.'

'I am not going to marry their father.'

'Hmp, that's no new excuse. He'll have to be summoned.'

Lidi stepped forward. 'If you do that, then he won't marry her. Now Mr Spartsit, do you want to get a woman and two children off your books?'

'If you an't married be the end of August, then I shall put him down as the Putative Father and he shall pay, or I a want to know the reason why.'

Not to suit Wilfrid Spartsit, Brendan Lewis and Sarah Toose were married before the end of the month, and they left Cantle for Beauwyth in a little gig borrowed from Ninn Broughlake.

That night, as when kings and queens marry, beacons were lit across the southern counties. A conflagration of rickyards, in Kent, Sussex and Hampshire.

---•7•---

SEPTEMBER

With SARAH GONE, Jude and Lidi set about seeing if they could somehow accommodate Hetty Bone and her children. The ramshackle dividings of the space on the upper floor of the cottage as well as the outhouse that Will had made inhabitable were in a constant change of use. Somehow they always made it work, fitting in, making do.

'If John stopped down in the box-bed and the two boys went up with Jack in the attic . . . and Hetty and the girls went next to Will and me, you and Luce could stop where you are over the outhouse . . . and we should all fit in nicely.'

'Will they let her have Out Relief? In the Parishes she works for her keep in the laundry.'

'If she hasn't got rent to pay then it's probably muck or nettles to the Relief . . . we can but ask.'

So it was decided that as soon as they could, they would put the suggestion to Harriett Bone that she come and share the poverty at Croud Cantle.

For poverty it was these days.

Whilst Lidi and Luce worked the clock round most of their market sales to the householders of the nearby towns were seasonal, hardly anything coming in during the winter. It was still the Croud Cantle produce stall on the markets that kept them going. The daily grind of work, sleep, worry and more work, dulled the edge of Luce and Lidi's life together. And they bickered childishly.

'For goodness sake, Luce, don't be so petty.'

'Petty? I'm not the petty one. You only loaded it like that to be awkward – that's petty.'

'I was loading trees when I was six.'

'And so you think you know it all.'

'Yes, and you don't, and you don't like it.'

'You don't ever give best to anyone else.'

'I do – if they're best. Brittle plants go like that. There!'

And so on. Pettiness, that rubbed salt into the hundred little wounds made by the hard slog of just keeping body and soul together.

And she would never acknowledge that he had been willing to accept her ways as few other men would have done.

Will applied to be listed as a Registered member of the parish to qualify for Relief, but was denied.

Poorlaw Relief. Their entire economy was complicated by it. For instance, if Jude charged Luce rent so that he could claim for it, then this was added to her income on which she must pay the Parish Rate. If he did not claim, then his benefit was looked at for living rent free. The fact that they earned something meant that Luce had to battle constantly with Spartsit when he applied for assistance. And John, although no longer considered to be worth a hundred pounds a year, because he still had rented land on which horticulture was carried on, was considered to be self-sufficient.

Like everyone else, they loathed the degradation of an 'appearance' when guardians of the public purse looked suspiciously into their domestic affairs. No matter how honest the claimant, to be peered at with suspicion, or sneered at in disbelief, was as much as any man or woman could stand. But they had to stand it. They had no choice.

8

OCTOBER

TAKING TO THE ROADS

I IN LATE OCTOBER the protest marches began. One day, Will came up from the village to say that the Motte 'gang' were going on the march and were joining up with some of the other villages along the way.

'Cantle is to join them by the Great Stone first thing in the morning tomorrow day.'

There was no question but that they should go. In a way it was what they had been waiting for.

'Ah the Devil take it for short breath,' said John. 'But you go, Lidi, you and Luce. Jack and me will see to things here.'

'I'm going too, Pa.' It was Jack who spoke up firmly.

John looked up at his son. Over thirteen now, and a tall youth for his age, Jack peered back at his father. Becoming increasingly good looking in the way of Tansy, his chin, although as downy as his upper lip, still retained some of its childish roundness and so gave his face the unbalanced look of all young men in their transition from childhood. His nose had already turned down into masculinity, and his lips were as full of his new manhood as was his body. Mostly a man now, he was outgrowing the timidity that his poor vision had inflicted upon him earlier.

John nodded. 'Ah . . . it's right you should.'

Nobody questioned the wisdom of the old people going. No one could have stopped them.

When Lidi, Luce, Jack, Jude and Will crossed the Dunnock Ford on that morning, they joined a procession of Cantle people going up Bellpitt Lane towards the Great Stone. Village dogs barked at their passing. A cold October morning. Early.

Lidi liked red October when the hedgerows dripped blood-beads of yew and bryony and woodbine and nightshade. Newly-arrived redwings and fieldfares gorged upon crimson hawthorn. Scarlet crabapples and the flaming death-caps which came up overnight. October the red month – it was the kind of observation Aunt Ju made when she was Lidi and Sarah's teacher. Lidi humped Auryn further up her back, aware of his warmth momentarily.

Who would take him out and show him things and tell him that October was the red month?

This morning though, there was little colour along the lane. Mist still covered the valley floor and dusted hats and shawls white, but when the villagers reached Bell Tump, they broke through the mist into the dawn of a bright day. On the top of the downs, a hundred or so Cantle people stood stamping their feet and speaking with white breath as they waited.

'Look!'

As the sun rose fully over Tradden Raike, its light caught a long line of moving people coming from the direction of Motte.

'It must be Privett and Motte, the Privetts was bedding down in Motte last night to get an early start.'

'And there! There's the others.'

From the direction of Brockwood came another moving column. The Meon Valley marchers had started out well before dawn and on the way picked up others in Brockwood and small hamlets along the way.

It was a stirring sight to those who understood the importance of those lines of marchers. Lidi turned to say something to Jude only to see her old aunt with wet eyelashes biting her lips as she gazed out on the sight.

Jude turned to Will and Lidi heard her say quietly, 'You were right and I was wrong, Will. It really is a beginning; I never thought to see it.'

Luce clasped Lidi's hand and spoke scarcely above a whisper. 'God forbid that it ends like it did in Manchester.'

Lidi saw him shiver in the dawn air, the chill wind on the high downs catching them all, and she saw him unconsciously rub his knuckles along the line of his cutlass scar. There were times when the love that got buried and forgotten in the harshness of their lives sprang out. What other man ever grasped his wife's hand in front of others, as he had done then?

If only he was not so . . .? So . . . what? They niggled at one another about their work. He found it hard to accept that she was more experienced than he was, couldn't stand it when she loaded the cart and would often rearrange a perfectly good delivery, and they would bicker about it.

Now, as she looked at him, his handsome face topped by an old hat crammed on the back of his head, standing just taller than the rest, for a moment she felt totally satisfied with him. Here he wasn't a back bent double over rows of rootstock, or just a pair of arms heaving dung to good the fields or a pair of clagged-up boots tramping across the yard. Here, Lidi felt that they were together doing something that linked them with people back in history and across the country. That was not petty.

Briefly she put her hand upon his.

The Cantle group moved off down the slope towards the Great Stone close to where the roads joined.

The three groups converged.

Will said, 'Well, one thing's for sure, Luce, we've no Sunday best to come out in, nor any banners, like the Peterloo marchers.'

'No,' said Luce, 'nor no warm sun and music neither.'

'Listen,' said Jude. 'Hear the sound of them tramping − that's our music.'

'Will you just hark at her − music in boots,' Will said. 'She's a romantic one.' Will was smiling to himself, tight-lipped as he too watched the gathering.

About four hundred people met at the Great Stone on Winchester Hill and stood milling around waiting for stragglers and slow walkers.

There were people of every age and condition of dress. Carters, goose-girls, shoemakers, ironsmiths, thatchers, milkmaids, herdsmen and dairy-maids, some small farmers who were almost as destitute as their workers. There were also many women − the wives whose main skill, since they had married, was in trying to manage on the equivalent of a three-and-a-half-gallon loaf. Forty years previously − and that at a time when no generosity was shown to the poor − the amount of a three-and-a-half-gallon loaf had been reckoned by the authorities to be sufficient to keep one man only.

It was easy to pick out those who were not agricultural workers, for they were not so gaunt faced, neither were their jackets and skirts so bodged and threadbare nor their boots so mended and nailed. But they were all there to a common purpose. They were neighbours. They were bonded by their sense of injustice. Their purpose was to petition the Magistrates and employers for a fairer wage for agricultural workers.

Inevitably there were troublemakers out for any fight going and some workers who, whilst they would welcome any better conditions that might come from the protest, wished that they might not have been shamed or bullied into taking part.

A man came from the crowd and came over to the Great Stone where the Croud Cantle people stood.

'Will Vickery!'

'Adam.'

Lidi had not seen Adam Tylee before, though she knew him by repute, and was surprised to discover that he was only about thirty years old – she had imagined that he would be a man of her father's age. He was often called the Captain, a well-digger by trade and wayside preacher, whom Will had reported as 'a fine man, fine speaker, fine Radical and reformer – and a natural leader'.

A rugged-faced man with stiff brown hair cut short, teeth and complexion that indicated decent food as a child and a corded neck and broad back that showed that his daily work was heavy.

Although he had the soft, broad accents of the heart of Hampshire, he spoke in a much finer way than most villagers. 'Well then Will, Hampshire has rose up at last.'

'Ah, 'tis a mighty good turn-out.'

'Let's be started then,' Adam Tylee said, and leapt up onto one of the ancient ruined walls that abounded on this part of the Hampshire Downs.

'Neighbours!' His clear voice threw a net of silence over the assembly, all faces turned in his direction. 'This is not the time for speeches – you've heard me often enough. We meet here peaceably and shall continue so.

'As you know, our purpose today is to meet with a group of employers and Magistrates at Court Chiddham, and to meet in such numbers as to show every employer around here, that we have come to the end of our tether. To show them that we are solid in our support of each other, and that we all believe that our cause is a just one. I will read to you the proposals that we shall make. If, when you have heard them, you agree, then show by your hands.'

He paused and unfolded a paper which he read clearly and slowly.

'We shall ask that they agree that all men whether married or single shall have two shillings and threepence for a day's work in summer.'

A genial cheer rose from the crowd.

'That lads over sixteen shall have one shilling, boys sixpence. Old men no longer able to work and having a wife to keep, we insist shall have one and sixpence per day.'

More rousing calls.

'The payment of the aged is of the utmost importance. Those who have made the landowners rich shall not be paupers and live in fear of the Workhouse. Do you agree?'

An immediate response of cheering and 'yes, yes, good old Adam'.

Adam Tylee held up a hand. 'Right then, that is agreed by us all.

'Those of you who have brought with you one of the tools of your trade as though you were going to a Hiring Fair, should be well careful that the purpose of your carrying a Smithy's hammer, Carter's whip or Labourer's pitchfork shall not be seen as a threat.

'You can be sure that correspondents of newspapers will seize upon any incident and report it – and not to our advantage . . . we must be peaceable . . . we must give them no chance to say that we are a mob and a rabble.

'Already many farm workers have asked their employers to meet them but have been rejected . . . and in some cases those who were elected to speak, have been dismissed from their place of work, and threats made to the rest.

'Friends . . . it is the nature of agricultural work, the small numbers working in one place, and the isolation from one another, that gives employers such power . . .'

A woman called out, 'And the fear that we shall be thrown out of our homes.'

An incensed rumble of agreement.

'Yes Neighbour, the threat of that hangs over too many . . . the Workhouse.'

Another grumble ran through the crowd.

Adam Tylee let it roll for a few seconds then held out his arms; the crowd quietened.

'But today . . .' the pause of the good orator, 'today, when working people join together in such numbers . . . today when men and women, when those in work and those unemployed, when single and married, young and old . . .' He raised the pitch of his voice only slightly . . . 'Today when we, the ordinary people of Hampshire are joined together . . . united to face the power of the employers, is a day in the *true* history of this country.'

Now a huge roar rose from the crowd. Adam Tylee raised both hands.

'God be with us all.'

As he leapt down from the wall, another great roar of cheering spread out over the downs and the march began.

Lidi, who had hardly dared to breathe whilst he had been speaking, now drew breath. Her heart thumped, her stomach was clenched with the fervour of their leader's dramatic rousing of the people.

'Well then Aunt Jude – what d'you think?' Luce said as he and Lidi fell in beside her as she strode out in the leading ranks of the marchers. Jack walked beside Will, his hand touching Will's sleeve. The pace of the march was not fast, so that he walked well without stumbling.

Jude raised her chin and gave a bunched-lipped smile that lit up her eyes. 'Well then Luce, it's started. It's something I've thought about for years. The great power that ordinary people could have if they liked.'

'There's certainly more common folk, and that's a fact.'

'When we were back at the Great Stone, and I saw us move off, I had a vision of it being a snowball that started to roll down a slope in Kent a few weeks back, that's been rolling on, gathering up people, getting bigger and bigger, until a place like this can bring four or five hundred people out on the road. If it goes rolling on like this, then it will have such power and momentum that it will be hard to stop it.' She breathed in as though she had been suffocating, and now the air of the downs and the ideas in her head were the breath of life she had been gasping for.

'What's an army but common men? Talk of generals, talk of kings . . . they'd be a poor army on their own.'

Luce too looked elated. ''Tis the generals and kings that gets the say-so in the end though.'

'That's why we need education for working people, Luce.'

Luce gave a half wink at Lidi. They had both heard it before.

'I don't mean this thin gruel National Schools kind of learning – the education I want would be no different from that of our "Betters".' She said the word scornfully. 'And it must be given equally, rich as to poor, and no different for girls as to boys. Blind and sighted, crippled and able.'

Luce murmured an agreement which was unnecessary once she got started.

'I've often thought, if it was the mothers that had the best education a country could provide, then things would soon change for the better.'

An amused chuckle halted her and she turned sharply. Adam Tylee, marching at her elbow, playfully cringed as though to ward off a blow. 'No Ma'am, I weren't laughing at what you said. Only that it is familiar ground to me. I was brought up on such ideas.'

'Well, and I'm glad to hear of that bit of news.' She held out a hand. 'Judeth Nugent. . . and I know who you are.'

'And I know you.'

She queried him with her eyebrows.

'From Will. Will's a good brother in the fight. And I believe I know you.' He bent his head round Jude to look at Lidi.

'Uncle Will again?'

'No, I worked it out for myself, Ma'am.'

Lidi smiled.

He smiled back challengingly. 'I an't such a fool as I look.'

'I didn't say any such thing. Only how did you work out who I was?'

He side-stepped behind Jude and fell in beside Lidi. 'First, I have long admired John Toose and have heard him speak. Second I now know that Miss Nugent and John Toose are related by marriage. Third,' he smiled broadly, 'you and Miss Nugent must have come out of the same mould.'

'I'm her husband – Luce Draper, and this here's our son.'

Lidi caught the sulkiness in Luce's voice which she had heard a few times before.

'You're a lucky man, Luce.'

'I know it.'

'Are you married, Mr Tylee?' Jude asked.

'No, no. I lead too much of a wandering kind of life what with being a well-digger and a preacher too. No woman'd put up with the both.'

Easily, he detached himself from their group and fell in with others for a few minutes, and then went on to others, friendly and practised at making people feel that their presence there was vital. He was every inch the democratic leader, with them and of them.

Lidi had often wondered about what it is in some leaders that makes followers so fervent in their admiration, that they would follow into certain death. As Adam Tylee went amongst the marchers, the puzzle was solved for her: it was the ability to inspire people with a belief in themselves and what they were doing. She herself felt infected by the sorcery of his personality.

There was a good deal of fluffy cloud about, but not enough to keep the rising sun from lighting up the green and brown patchwork of the downs and valleys as they marched on.

The march took a zig-zag route across the downs.

At East Meon, Warnford, Corhampton and other places along the way shopkeepers and innkeepers were 'pressed' for a contribution of food or drink.

At Coombe Down Farm two threshers were destroyed at the invitation of the farmer, who said that he was heartily glad to see the back of them for they waddn't his but was hired by the month and waddn't worth the money. A good sort – he gave two guineas to 'the funds' and wished them a good many more threshers to 'kill' before nightfall.

At Little's and Teglee's Farms a few reluctant labourers were 'invited' to join the march. 'We dursn't join in,' they said, 'for fear we a be dismissed by the Master.' 'Well then Lads,' came back the argument, 'thees'll be in the same boat as the rest on us. And when it comes down to it . . . thee's dursn't *not* join us for fear of being clouted good'n'hard by thy fellows.'

At West Stoke six 'Lads' came willingly, throwing down their field implements, and leaping the stile.

Court Chiddham was only a small village, but it was a convenient place for the meeting that had been arranged with certain employers and Magistrates; they were to meet in the vestry of the church.

On the outskirts of the village the marchers assembled in a field and Adam Tylee addressed them again.

'Because I have been the one best placed to get this meeting off the ground, that's no reason why I should be up here speaking to you or going in to speak to Them; all are equal here.'

'You'll do us for leader, Captain,' the crowd assented loudly.

'Gladly then, neighbours. A fair election then. A dozen representatives must be chosen from among you to go with me. Let's have a name or two from every village.'

'We'll have thee for one, Adam.'

'None better than Adam to flash the gab.'

'Aye – as good as any Master.'

Lidi watched him as he stood, as he had done at the Great Stone, upon a wall, with one foot rested slightly higher than the other, arm outstretched in a heroic pose. Does he do it without thinking? He appears quite unaffected, yet he looks as though he's an engraving of a bold leader come to life.

'There must be representatives of you all.'

'Ted Harker of Meonstoke.'

'Art Telbury of Privett.'

'Martin Duke of Brockwood.'

'Henry Tasker and all of Brockwood.'

Names were put forward. Some stepped forward gladly, others were persuaded into taking part, others hung back and said no they waddn't no good at argufying with masters, but they'd shout loud enough from the sidelines.

They now had eight, and there was a moment's pause as they waited for more names. Into that moment of hush Judeth Nugent's voice spoke clearly. 'I reckon half of us here are women . . .' She got no further, a chorus of women's voices raised their agreement.

The calling of names continued.

'Polly Beckford of Shott's Farm.'

'Mistress Telbury of Privett.'

'Widow Fairford of Motte.'

'And you . . . that there old lady who just spoke up for us.' Another chorus of approval and Jude spoke her own name:

'Judeth Nugent, owner of Croud Cantle Farm.'

There was a murmur of mild surprise, for although many small farmers supported the protest, especially urging their workers to come down upon rents and tithes, few liked to be so open about it.

'Then hooray for Cantle,' someone called.

In the end thirteen of the crowd went to the head of the march and on towards the church.

The marchers went in, whilst the others scattered around the church fields and the graveyard and looked to their blisters and cracked boots. Lidi, Luce and Jack sat leaning against the church wall sharing the top of a loaf that Luce had crammed into his pocket.

Jack was animated and flushed with the excitement of the crowd. 'D'you know what, our Lid? I wish this'd happen every day.'

Lidi had just torn off a large rip of crust and was cramming it hungrily into her mouth, when Jude appeared and urgently beckoned her.

'Make haste, Lidi, they need one more.'

Lidi jumped up and swallowed the hard bread whole.

Jude wagged her head disapprovingly as they went into the church. 'I'll make all kinds of excuses for my own kind, but when it comes to them not wanting to start talking because there's bad luck with thirteen! Anyhow, it's soon settled if you come in and make fourteen.' She gave Lidi a pursed-mouth smile. 'It gives a better balance of women too.'

Inside the vestry was a long trestle table, which looked as though it did not always have a place there, ranged along one side of which were ten well-dressed gentlemen, only one of whom had Lidi seen before. And that was years ago, when her Pa had once pointed him out riding by in Waltham as Squire Tawny, the Magistrate who had sent him to Winchester gaol.

Seated centrally, Squire Tawny was obviously in charge of the proceedings.

'Let us waste no more time,' Tawny said.

'Right then,' Adam Tylee answered. 'We ask . . .'

'Are you to be spokesman?'

'I've been elected such.'

'Then who are you?'

'You may call me the Captain.'

'Where are you employed?'

Adam Tylee held up his hand. 'Oh no! There's to be none of that. No names – no retaliation.'

Tawny looked sideways at a colleague as though to suggest the ridiculousness of such an implied criticism.

'Very well. Your followers . . .'

'They are not my followers, nor I their leader. I am only the one chosen to speak for the whole – it might as easily been any of the rest.'

'Again, very well . . . There is a suggestion . . . a complaint that wages are too low.'

'Right sir. And have been for some while. A man might as easily get the pittance of Relief as work for ten hours by his labour.'

'Not always ten hours surely.'

'No sir. And not always ten days together neither, now there's so many surplus men and so many machines.'

'Then that very fact must tell you that if work is hard come by then it behoves a man to take it and be glad.'

'Not at eight shillings a week. Why sir, I suspect you paid more than that for the kerchief poking out of your sleeve, or the pretty buttons on your waistcoat. And I'll warrant you never worked an hour for them, let alone a week.'

Oh yes, thought Lidi. Oh yes, Mr Tylee, you did that beautifully.

'We have not given up our morning to discuss my waistcoat

buttons. We are busy men with our own affairs to settle, Mister Tylee, we are not jaunting about the countryside this morning.'

Adam Tylee sprang to attention – an insolent foot-soldier.

'And neither have we sir, we never had a jaunt in our lives. We have come here this morning to petition for . . .' he paused and fished in his jacket pocket. All eyes were upon him. Lidi knew full well that he had not mislaid the paper, he knew what he was about, he played people as she had seen at the Great Stone. Yes, thought Lidi, I should like to hear you preach, Adam Tylee.

And yes, said a deeper, more unformed thought that centred around his eyes, his mouth and his thighs . . . Yes Adam Tylee, I should like to know a lot about you.

She drew her thoughts back as he began to read out the rates of pay that they had agreed upon at the Great Stone.

Another man at the table spoke up, a clergyman dressed in fine-wool clerical black coat and pure white stock. 'And what if employers do not agree?'

'I think then, your Reverence, that men will not stay as peaceable as they have been.'

'You threaten riot?'

There was a shuffling of feet amongst the standing delegation.

'No sir – nor revolution neither.'

Now it was the turn of those at the table to shuffle their feet and backsides. The word had been spoken aloud. Revolution. The word that had fed in France, then flitted its great vulture-black wings and settled upon a rock on the coast there watching the gamey English meal.

Now another man cleared his throat, an elderly fat man in an old-fashioned full-bottomed wig and snuff on his waistcoat. 'A body might be forgiven for believing that riot and revolution have already begun. I've had two machines broke and six ricks burned.'

'And what do you pay your men?'

'That is no concern of yours.'

'Ah Your Lordship, but it is. I happen to know that on your Surrey estate your men were told to accept eight shillings a week or they would be thrown out of work, and when they said that they could not feed a family on that, you had them dismissed and brought in Irish labour. We are concerned for your Hampshire estate.'

The old man harrumphed and dug into his waistcoat for his snuffbox. It was obvious that the cocksure gentlemen at the table had not expected to meet with such an articulate and knowledge-able bargainer, their combs and wattles began to droop. They sensed a dangerous situation.

Tawny returned to the discussion. 'The machine breaking has got to stop.'

'I cannot guarantee it, sir. There are several hundred people out there, each no doubt with a tale to tell that might melt softer hearts than might be here. I cannot undertake to speak for them on that. Only the rise in wages.'

Now the battle of words was between Tawny and Adam Tylee only. Tawny thrust a fact of economy at Tylee, who parried with another of practicality. If Tawny said that employers would go bankrupt if they had to raise wages, then Tylee said that they would go bankrupt the sooner as more and more labourers took to the roads in protest. After a while, when Adam had argued, 'And what if you fetch every man out of Ireland and put every English family on the roads. What then?' Tawny visibly sank lower in his chair.

He held out his hand for Adam's paper. 'Leave us for ten minutes.'

The delegation began to troop out of the vestry.

'Not outside. It might raise the hopes of our neighbours before it's settled.'

They sat in the public pews at the back of the church.

Adam Tylee clenched his two fists and grinned at his companions. 'We've got them!'

'Do you think they're going to agree?'

'Not outright, they'll offer something less. But we've won this round.'

They sat almost silently for the five minutes that went by before they were called back.

Tawny spoke. 'None of us here is – as you implied Mister Captain – a stony-hearted employer, but we have a living to make. We feel that a show of goodwill on our part must surely be reciprocated by our employees whom you claim to represent (though we have no means of telling if there be a single one of our men amongst you) and we ask you to convey this to them.' He pushed Adam Tylee's paper across the desk. 'We cannot accede to your demands entirely, but we are willing to compromise. These are the rates which we will agree to pay.'

Adam Tylee picked up the paper and studied it closely, letting a minute tick by.

'Shall you now leave *us* for ten minutes?'

The gentlemen looked most taken aback. An indication of the air of confident authority that Adam Tylee displayed, was shown by the ten gentlemen, without demur, pushing back their chairs and going out into the body of the church as the common people had done.

When the heavy door was shut behind them, Adam Tylee put his finger to his mouth to warn them not to exclaim, then again made his clench-handed signal of a victor.

'We got what we wanted.'

'But he said they wouldn't pay in full.'

He winked. 'I deal with their sort all the time so I've learned to be twice as fly. Think of the right price for the job – you know they won't pay it . . . so, add a bit for them to do you down over, and you finish up with what you expected in the first place.'

Lidi gave a short burst of laughter before smothering it with her hand.

Judeth Nugent smiled. 'Good Lad!'

'Right then,' said Art Telbury. 'If we got what we come for, let's tell they we agree and get back home.'

'Patience. If we don't keep them waiting, they might think they've been too generous. Just keep talking in low voices so they can't hear, and we'll call them back in another five minutes.'

Jude caught Lidi's eye and smiled, obviously approving of the young man.

When the gentlemen had returned to the dignity and safety of a table between themselves and the lower orders, Adam Tylee addressed them.

'Well sirs. As you might gather from the time it took, my neighbours are not entirely happy; they had set down what they thought fair and no more than that, and you have offered threepence off everything. You must agree that two and threepence is not much for a day's work.' He paused. 'However, as employers of such decent people, you will know only too well that they are amicable and reasonable as well as decent. Therefore, they have agreed to accept these new rates of pay, if payment is commenced forthwith.'

Tawny looked briefly at those on his side of the table and said, 'Agreed.'

They began to rise.

'A moment sirs.' Lidi's voice came out higher than she had

intended. The gentlemen stopped with backsides off their chairs.

'There is one other item that I wish to put to you.'

The backsides sank back.

'And you Madam are . . .?'

'Representative of the women.'

The room held its breath jointly. No one, certainly not Lidi until she began, expected her to speak up.

Immediately perceiving what was happening, Adam Tylee said, 'Of course gentlemen, as you saw, there was no mention of any but men on the paper I presented.'

'May I speak sir?'

Tawny raised his eyebrows and shoulders and spread his hands to suggest 'could I stop you?'

'My request is simple, gentlemen. That all female employees, whether they work in the house, the dairy, the fields or the barns, have their wages raised by the same proportion as you have agreed for the men and boys.'

There was a dead silence. Then a plum-coloured velvet-clad, fat old man who had kept opening his pocket-watch and looking irritable, said, 'I say "yes". Let's be done with these dickering matters of twopence and threepence.'

'Not only the threepences your Lordship.'

All attention was centred upon Lidi.

'As flailing has always been the winter work for men, so women have relied on winnowing. You asked that machine breaking be stopped. Men and women who have relied on threshing and winnowing, see the machines as a threat to the very existence of our village life. If people do not have work, then they must leave the villages – and so the villages will die. Now, more and more winnowing machines are appearing, which means that *all* winter work will surely disappear. I understand that to be against machines is to go against the tide of progress, and that their introduction is inevitable, but their introduction should be gradual and with more understanding of the harm they do to a community. They must not be brought in without thought for the people they harm.'

There were a few murmurs of 'Right, Gel' from behind her.

'I am sorry . . . I did not intend to speak at such length, but I love my village and cannot bear to see it slowly dying. We cannot expect you to agree that the people you represent will not buy machines, any more than Mr . . . the Captain could not promise that ours will not break them. What I ask you, gentlemen, is that you think of what I have said, and when you have thought, to ask yourselves whether God gave us machines to destroy the village that has been my family's home for generations past. If my village dies, then I and others like me will have no choice but to leave. Gentlemen, before you are too quick to condemn us . . . I ask whether you would fight for your homes – your land.'

For a moment there was silence, those present not knowing whether Lidi had finished until she took a step backwards.

The day was won. The plum-velvet noble lord, if not the best man to negotiate with the lower orders, was one of the most wealthy and powerful in that part of Hampshire. 'Dammit Tawny, get on with it and let's get out of this confounded cold before me damned legs start playing me up again.'

So Squire Tawny was forced without discussion to accede to Lidi's demand for the women.

When they were back outside Judeth Nugent grasped her niece's shoulders and planted a token kiss beside Lidi's ear.

'My God, Will, you'd have been proud of her. She spoke up to them, Luce, as though she'd been doing it all her life.'

Lidi held her hand out. 'Look, it's trembling like an aspen leaf.'

Adam Tylee stepped forward and took it. 'Mrs Draper. It is a long while since I heard anything that struck my heart so much. You got the Admiral in your final broadside.'

'Admiral?'

'The one in the red velvet. His family motto is about preserving the good earth and nation. He could never have argued you down.'

'Now my hand is really shaking. I never knew there was anybody so exalted there.'

'There wasn't. There was only greedy employers there. Nobody less exalted than they.'

'All right then,' said Luce. 'My feet's like dabs of ice standing about here.' His voice had an edge to it.

'Nothing stopping you running a bit to warm yourself up,' Lidi answered sharply. 'What's the matter, Luce? Aren't you pleased?'

'Of course. It's just that it was blimmin cold waiting out here so long.'

'It wasn't exactly warm in the church,' she snapped back.

They all gathered once more in the church fields where Adam Tylee read out amid cheers that the protest had succeeded and new wages had been agreed.

9

BEAUWYTH

ALTHOUGH THERE WERE thousands of protesters tramping the roads of Hampshire, Sarah was scarcely aware of them, or perhaps determined not to be aware of them.

Ninn Broughlake paid Brendan decent wages and gave him a secure home. Her two-roomed cottage was a pleasure to her. Brendan was practical and a good companion, in the evenings talking over the day's happenings and planning what they might plant in the garden, the shelves that he would knock up or preserves that she would make. Retiring early like farmworkers, there were the warm pleasures of blankets and a feather mattress, which Sarah did not always share but which she never begrudged Brendan. Each time he exclaimed his pleasure too soon for her, it was as though she was compensating him for the times that she and Alec James had dug their fingernails into one another at the climax of their mutual gratification.

By October, she knew that she was pregnant and would be confined some time in May.

'They reckon that Maytime babies is bonny, Brendan.'

'Ach, if it's like you m'dear then it a be bonny if it's birthed on mid-winter day.'

M'dear, pronounced in his broad Hampshire, was the only term of endearment Brendan ever used, yet Sarah knew that it was as sincere as any more flowery language.

As she worked about her kitchen, with the scrambling babies in a coop or Belle tethered to one upright and Christopher to another, a pot steaming on the fire and the smell of bread in the oven, Sarah thought consciously 'I am happy'. It came as a surprise the first time. All those years when she had trotted around the elegance of Stonebridge, wearing her neat dresses tight-fitted to her waist, and her pretty caps with flying ribbons set upon her tendrilled hair, she had thought her life to be wonderful, and during the months back home, she had become content, or perhaps resigned, but now she realised that none of that was happiness. And when she thought about it, she crossed her fingers and touched wood.

They seldom talked about those days at Stonebridge. Sarah steered away from talking of them, and soon Brendan seldom mentioned them either. He referred to the twins as 'ours' and said that they should take his name.

Late one afternoon, she heard footsteps crunching up the path and, believing it to be Brendan, hung a pot of soup from the cotterel and looked for a taper to light the lamp. She did not hear his low, tuneless whistling or the ritual scraping of his boots. She was about to peer out of the window when there was a knock on the door. Most of the daylight had gone and the only light inside the cottage was from the fire. An average height, quite stocky man stood there, his hat in his hand. His dress was that of a gentleman, so Sarah bobbed a small curtsey.

'Yes?' she asked.

'Tooey. I thought you'd fall flat with wonder at how I'd grown, but I did not dream that you would not recognise me.'

'Master Ninn!' She put out her hands, then quickly withdrew them in confusion, and stepped back to let him in, but he caught her hands and held them tight. 'Oh Tooey, dear Tooey, it is so good to see you.'

He stepped inside, his head, like Brendan's, just missing the ceiling beams. For a moment Sarah stood looking at him in the glow of the fire. 'Well, what a young gentleman you've got now.' She hastened to light the lamp and fetched two candles for extra light for the visitor.

'There. Now you can see to sit down. I was just having five minutes in the gloam whilst the babies are asleep.'

'Can I see?'

She showed him the two plump babies asleep in the same cradle.

Ninn Broughlake shook his head and smiled. 'Just fancy, two of them.'

'Well, it's not so surprising, I'm one of a twin myself.'

'Ah, I remember, of course.'

He was mannerly and polite, and slightly stiff as she had often seen young gentlemen to be.

They sat opposite one another, Ninn looking about the room and Sarah looking at him. Although he was not yet twenty, his jaw was square and masculine, his shoulders wide and, although clean-shaven, his beard beneath the skin was quite dark.

'I just can't believe that you're a grown man.'

'Outside perhaps. I don't always feel that I'm one inside – still the little boy in the nightshirt too often.' He smiled his appealing deprecating smile that so often used to wring Sarah's heart.

'What are you doing now – are you still at Winchester?'

'No, I'm learning to run the estates now. I had thought of going to Oxford, but I wanted to go in for race-horses and run the estates, and I did not think that Oxford was the place to learn much about those things. Father always left it to the agents and the bailiffs and managers, but I think I should like to have a proper hand in it.'

'I think that's a good idea. I could never think what a grown man could do with his time if he didn't have some kind of occupation.'

'Father would have thought that being a "Gentleman" was an occupation in itself.'

'But you aren't like your Pa . . .' She halted and pinched her bottom lip. 'I'm sorry, Master Ninn . . . it's hard to change from the way I used to talk to you . . . telling you what's what and that. For goodness sake, I should be calling you Mister Broughlake and being quite respectful. Just fancy, you, Master of Stonebridge Manor.'

'Please Tooey, the reason why I looked forward so much to it when Brendan said that he and you were to marry, was the thought that I might come and see you. I can't imagine what those years would have been like if it had not been for Tooey.'

'Ah rubbish. You'd have been all right.'

'No, I remember that time as always being summer.'

Sarah laughed. 'Even when the snow bent the birch trees down and you made me fetch some snow to put on a jam muffin.'

He unstiffened and settled back in the chair. 'Did anything ever taste as good as that? And that's why it was always summer. Things were so bright.'

'And what about now?'

He smoothed the knees of his narrow cream-coloured trews, then looked shyly up. 'I have met a wonderful young lady.'

'A young lady! Why you're only . . .' She stopped short again. 'There I go again, I'm really sorry. You'll have to forgive me, I'll get used to it in time. For heaven's sake, you're my husband's employer and there I am . . .'

Ninn laughed. 'It's all right, I know not yet twenty, and I did not say that I was about to marry . . . ah, but she is such a perfectly sweet thing, that I shouldn't mind if I was old enough to ask her.'

'Well then I'm pleased – and if I can be bold once more . . . just don't be too hasty. People we think are wonderful when we are twenty don't appear the same when we are twenty-eight.'

He nodded. Sarah thought that he seemed old for his years, not only in appearance, but in a kind of gravity of manner. Had she not known, she would have thought him to be twenty-four or -five.

'Are you happy Tooey? . . . You see, it is the same with me, I should be calling you "Mistress Lewis".'

Sarah denied that with a smile. 'I should like you to continue, or "Sarah" if you like. And to answer your question, I am very happy indeed. And from what Brendan says, we've got you to thank for this place being so nice.'

He waved that aside.

'We'll find you something a bit bigger – you'll need it for those two.'

'Three,' she said laying one hand on her waist.

'Well then it must certainly be done . . . Sarah.' The name hesitantly.

Sarah smiled non-committally. 'Brendan's late. He usually comes for a bite about this time, before he goes back to shut up for the night.'

'Ah . . . I should have said . . . he's gone over to Blackbrook for some linament.'

The children disturbed and Belle was immediately up and trying to climb out. Sarah picked her up.

'This gally-bagger is Belle, and the one trying to chew his way out through the bars is Christopher.'

Belle tottered off around the room whilst Christopher was content to sit upon Sarah's knee, suck his thumb and look gravely at the stranger.

Ninn Broughlake turned his hat round and round by its brim and smiled at the baby, then without preamble said, 'I saw Mother's baby. It's a fine little creature.'

Not knowing how to respond, Sarah said, 'Babies often are.'

'She's about the same age. She's called Florence.'

'Oh yes?'

A pause.

'Did you know?'

'That she was called Florence? No.'

'I mean, did you know that my mother had a little girl?'

'Brendan told me, but not that it was a little girl – Brendan isn't one for any kind of gossip and that kind of thing.'

'I mean, did you know before you left her to come back?'

'I guessed.'

He dropped his hat, picked it up, got up, placed it on the table and stood looking down at Sarah. Suddenly he looked like a boy, uncertain and flustered.

'Sarah? Oh . . . I hardly know how to put this.'

She smiled up at him, now feeling as assured as she used to when he was seven. 'You remember what I used to tell you? "Spit it right out, Master Ninn, and the words will find themselves." '

He nodded. 'Well, I don't know what to do about Mother. She's got strange since she came back. Of course no one will call. My grandfather made me go to see him and asked me what I proposed to do about Mother.'

'And what about Miss Arabella?'

'She has lived in the grandparents' house since my father died.'

'She must be quite grown up.'

Ninn Broughlake smiled. 'She's twelve and going to be as pretty as Mother.' He paused, gazing at the toes of his boots. 'You see . . . I am head of the family now, and it is my duty to see that Arabella and Mother are properly cared for. But, I don't know what to do for the best. Grandfather said that Mother should be packed off to Italy again . . . a fellow cannot "pack" his mother off, can he?'

He dropped back into the chair again, his head and hands hanging.

Sarah put the baby on the floor and, standing by the young man, pulled his head towards her and held him. 'My poor Ninn.'

Suddenly he gave a short sob and broke down into quiet tears. She let him cry for a minute, smoothing his hair and his cheek as she used to do. Then he reached into his pocket for a handkerchief and blew into it.

'Sorry Tooey . . . sorry . . . such a fool.'

'Hey, young Master Ninn . . . none of that nonsense. I was the one who told you that it was all right for you to cry. Remember? It's the only cure for some things; it don't matter whether you're eight or eighty.'

He raised his head, blinked his eyes and dried them.

'Foolish . . . I haven't done that since . . . well . . . since the night I came home from school and found that you had gone off with Mother.'

Sarah did not want to go down that road of conversation.

'Now listen. It's time for the babes to have some sop. If as you say Brendan won't be home, why don't you take off that coat and sit down properly and . . . well, I was going to say have a slice of bread and honey, but I dare say you're past that kind of thing now.'

'It would be fine to try it again. "Brown crust and bee-spit"?'

Sarah laughed. 'I'd forgotten. Margaret Roberts chid me for teaching you such tales.'

Sarah fed the babies bread dipped in milk, and Ninn bread and a lump of honeycomb which he ate, sitting at the scrubbed-pine table in his shirtsleeves and waistcoat.

'That's better. Now tell me about Mrs Delphine.'

Whilst she had been preparing the sops and bread, Sarah's mind had been racing around the subject of Ninn's mother. She did not want to think of her. Had buried her in the depths of her mind and wanted her to go away. Ever since Brendan had walked into the orchard, the Broughlakes, Alec James, and the whole episode that had linked them had kept trying to surface. Now she had no choice but to face them again.

'Everyone thinks it is a terrible scandal. I don't see it as that . . . it is of course, to our sort of society . . . at least it is a scandal to be found out. I just think that it is very, very sad . . . well, and unsatisfactory.'

'Why unsatisfactory?'

'No one knows what to do. Perhaps Grandfather is right.'

'Do you know if Mrs Delphine wants to go back to Italy?'

'I don't know. Why did she come home if that's what she wants?'

'Perhaps you should ask her.'

'She's my mother. I scarcely know how to address her these days.'

'Why?'

'Because . . . because . . .'

'Come on, spit it out.'

'Because of him. The footman – James.'

Sarah forced herself to appear puzzled. 'James who?'

'James, you know, my father's manservant. I called him the footman, because that's how I remember him.'

Not so Sarah. She remembered the suave lover who had made up his mind that he did not want to remain a servant. The lover who had slowly been descending into lechery and taking her with him. Her guilt began rising once more, but she forced it down knowing that to expiate it she must admit to it openly – and to admit to it meant heartbreak to too many people she loved in different ways – Brendan, her Pa and not least Ninn.

'Of course I remember him – he was part of the household in Florence.'

'He's more than that now.'

'More?'

'My mother dotes upon him. He lives in the old lodge, and my mother's in the dower house, and he comes and goes there as he pleases.'

Yes, thought Sarah, he's got what he wanted . . . to get as far distant from dung-boots and innkeepers as he could.

'I understand why your Grandfather was so rough. It must be extremely embarrassing for everybody.'

'It is not that so much, as not knowing what to do. Such a situation cannot just remain as it is, yet I can do nothing, and Mother will not. She has continually asked for Arabella to be sent to her, but of course the grandparents will not allow it.'

'Have you thought of dismissing Alec James?'

'Not seriously – I don't believe that he has a situation that he may be dismissed from. I believe that Mother truly loves the fellow.' The older, self-assured young man had now fully returned. 'Listen Sarah, let us be straight out about it . . . how can a fellow dismiss his mother's . . . well . . . lover.' He rushed on. 'For that is what he is. And I have no doubt that he is the baby's . . .' He seemed not to want to finish the sentence and admit the truth. '. . . the baby's parent.'

It was now completely dark outside. The kitchen was filled with the homely smell of plain onion soup. The babies were quiet on the floor, sucking on hard crusts beneath the table that was strewn with crumbs and dribbles of honey into which Ninn idly dipped his finger and licked. The burning logs hissed and the ash puttered through the grid.

'Is she happy – your mother?'

He gazed at the table top for a moment before answering. 'Yes . . . I truly believe that she is.'

'What do you think would be best for everyone?'

'Well, it seems to me that, if she remains here, my mother can only become more and more cut off from society – she is already. As the baby Florence grows up, she will become the object of curiosity to people, and gossip – she will have done nothing to deserve it, but you know that is what people do in *our* kind of society. The situation hurts my grandparents. I doubt that they suspect about . . .' he smiled wryly, 'the footman, they probably think the father is some Italian Count, they would hardly believe less of her – but gossip spreads, doesn't it?'

Sarah nodded. 'Not only spreads, but often gets altered. So, what could be done?'

'If my mother went to live abroad . . .'

'Could she? I mean . . . afford. Here, she has the dower and servants.'

'She has money of her own, as well as what my father bequeathed, and it seems that I have quite a substantial fortune. I could easily provide extra for her if necessary. But would that be right, Sarah?'

'Why not, if she wanted to go?'

'She would not go without him, of that I am quite sure. And it would mean that I would be providing for him. You see? Actually paying for my mother's . . . lover. It is so . . . so . . . oh, sordid.'

Yes . . . that was the word . . . things connected with Alec James did become that . . . sordid. She had felt that she was beginning to cleanse herself of her own contact with him, but it could creep back. She had come back too close to it all. Too close to Mrs Delphine, to Alec James, to the child Florence who was in truth half-sister to her own two children. A mess. A sordid mess. It was then that she knew that the only answer for all of them was that Alec James must be persuaded to go away; if he went, and Mrs Delphine followed him, then perhaps that would be the best. Certainly it would be for Ninn. Certainly for Sarah.

'Have you thought about . . . I don't know how to put it . . .'

He flicked a crumb. 'Spit it out, Tooey.'

'Paying him to go away – the footman.'

'To go abroad?'

'Yes. A substantial amount that he could not refuse.' Sarah knew Alec James very well. He could be lured, hooked and netted with the mayfly of money. 'And on the condition that he lived abroad.'

Ninn thought for a minute.

'What if my mother went with him and then he abandoned her?'

'You can't settle every problem. In any case, he might abandon her just as well here. At least if your mother went back to live in Italy she would have friends – she was part of a large circle there.'

Ah . . . those friends, that circle. Was it right to condemn the baby Florence to them? Margaret Roberts should go with them; she would protect the baby. It all seemed possible. There were always answers if you were as wealthy as the Broughlakes, most things could be purchased. And the thing for Sarah that could be purchased with Broughlake wealth . . . was peace of mind.

With Alec James out of the way, she could be happy for ever.

She would be the perfect wife to Brendan – he deserved that.

She would be the model mother to their children, so that neither they nor anyone else would ever know of their connection with little Florence Broughlake.

'Perhaps marry her?' He blew out his cheeks, let out the air at the ceiling and slapped his thighs. 'Oh Lord, Sarah . . . a minute ago I was in horror of paying for him as her lover, now I'm thinking of paying him to marry her.'

Sarah looked hard at him. Yes, that would be the perfect solution.

'Don't look upon it like that, Master Ninn. Look upon it, that your mother loves a poor man and wants to marry him, and you are able to help him.'

Gazing still at the table, he nodded.

This time it was Brendan's footsteps on the path.

'Master Ninn,' Sarah said.

'Yes?'

'What we just talked about . . . it is between us two only.'

'Of course. You are the only one I could talk with openly, no one else.'

'Does your mother know that I am living here?'

'I have no idea.'

Long after the visit, Sarah pondered on her young master's apparent naivety. Wasn't he curious? Or had it not crossed his mind that she must have been in Italy when she became pregnant, and that she was living under his mother's roof, and at the same time, she had also become pregnant. And wasn't it quite likely that he might have wondered whether the Manservant could be the Lady's Maid's seducer? It did not seem so; his manner had been as if he accepted that somehow Brendan was the babies' true father, though he must surely know that that was impossible. But perhaps not. Perhaps he did not know when she had returned home, or that she had left Italy pregnant. There was no reason why he should know. She fervently hoped so. Ninn was no fool; if he suspected the connection, then their good relationship was tarnished for ever. He had come to her because of his regard for her; she could not bear to lose that regard.

PART FIVE

November 1830

UPRISINGS

By EARLY NOVEMBER the uprisings have begun to spread out of Kent.

Two arms of dissent now fling out, north-easterly into Essex and Suffolk and south-westerly to Sussex and Hampshire.

Old scores are being settled, and many a harsh Magistrate, Poor Law Guardian or tyrant Landlord is now paid off with flame and hammer. In some places the years of frustration and poverty are vented upon the stores of grain, in others upon the machines and the factories that make them, and yet others upon the symbols of degradation – the Parish Carts, and the Workhouses.

Many parishes owned carts which the unemployed, before they might obtain help, were often forced to fill with road-mending stones picked from the fields. The carts were also used to convey over the parish boundary those who were not entitled to help from that particular parish. Stories abounded of poor idiots, of 'women with fat bellies full with child', and of 'dummies' who could not speak up for themselves, being trundled across the parish boundary and dumped there, perhaps to be trundled on in the cart of that parish also.

Villagers join forces to destroy those carts – often giving the Relief Officer a rough ride in the process.

The protests are often spontaneous and disorganised. They are harsh and rough, but not violent. Sometimes labourers come face to face with labourers when a powerful Landlord uses the old strategy he once used as a Warlord – which was to enforce footsoldiers to face footsoldiers in battle whilst the Warlord directed the battle from an armchair.

This is not to say that there were not bloody battles fought with sticks and stones – for the footsoldiers of Anger are fighting those of Fear.

Large numbers of people assemble in the foodbowl counties.

Everywhere ricks suddenly, mysteriously burst into flame.

The spirit of unrest is growing.

Magistrates make declarations.

Concerned citizens have notices posted.

Employers make threats.

Appeals are made to 'all decent labouring men and women'.

The tide of unemployed that had come in fifteen years ago when a quarter of a million servicemen came onto the market after Waterloo, has not receded; rather, with the growing changeover to mechanised farming methods, it has become a flood-tide.

Men and women might still be appealed to as 'decent' but many had no chance to 'labour'.

The declarations, appeals and threats are replied to, in many different standards of literacy and a variety of hands, but from a single source – Captain Swing.

Sir,

Your name is down amongst the Black hearts in the Black Book and this is to advise you and the like of you who are Parish Justices, to make your Wills.

Ye have been the Blackguard Enemies of the People on all occasions.

Ye have not yet done as Ye ought.

Swing

This is to inform you what you have to undergo gentelmen if providing you don't pull down your neshenes and rise the poor mens wages the maried men give tow and six pence a day the singel tow shilings or we will burn down your barns and you in them

This is the last notis

Swing

Sir

This is to acquaint you that if your thrashing machines are not destroyed by you directly we shall commence our labours.

Signed on behalf of the whole,

SWING

REVENGE
FOR THEE IS ON THE WING
FROM THY DETERMINED

Captain Swing

An ideal. A spirit. Captain Swing rode over all Hampshire; he must have had a horse with wings to be seen in ten far-flung villages in a single day.

Everyone knew someone who had seen him, in the distance, riding fast over the Hampshire Downs. Wearing his white hat, riding his white horse.

Captain Swing soon had the whole south ablaze, ricks and barns, and the hearts of men and women.

Life for many was intolerable, they had nothing to lose by following their Captain.

2

NOVEMBER
Law and Order

ONCE STARTED, THE BURNINGS ENCLOSED THE SOUTH. The sound of the crackling of the rick fires was now joined more and more by that of the crashing and hammering of the dismantling and destruction of the hated threshing machines.

There was not a county in the foodbowl of England that did not reek of burnt-out ricks.

Now the sound of crackling fires and clanging metal was joined by the marching of hundreds, and then by thousands of people.

To Sir Robert Peel
Sir,

I draw your urgent attention to the state of affairs in Hampshire, and the growing alarm amongst its inhabitants. We are in grave danger of seeing the breakdown of Law and Order.

In this county the burning of ricks and the breaking of machinery is no longer random. It would appear to this observer that stack-burning and machine-breaking are organized, and perpetrated by gangs nightly roaming the countryside at will.

It is most worrying that there is growing support for such action amongst those not involved. A recent report in *The Times* draws readers' attention to a quote by a by-stander: 'D . . . n it, let it burn, I wish it was the house; we can warm ourselves now; we only want some potatoes; there is a nice fire to cook them by.' This, Sir, was after a barn had been set alight and let burn. Fire engines were rendered ineffective when their hoses were slashed.

On several recent occasions when perpetrators have been apprehended and brought before a Magistrate, the unfortunate Magistrate has had his own ricks burnt for his trouble.

Even so, there are certain Magistrates who appear to view these events lightly, as was shown recently when seven prisoners were let off with a caution that the kindness shown to them (by a mere three-day sentence) 'would be met by a corresponding feeling among the people'.

Sir, the dark nights of winter are upon us; if we are not to be plundered and have revenge wreaked upon our heads, then sanction must be given to the arming of the Bourgeois classes.

I am sir, your humble and obedient servant,

Willoughby Tawny, J.P.

3

NOVEMBER

The Sacking of the Parishes Workhouse

THE CROUD CANTLE family went to sell their produce on Blackbrook Market every week, and Jude had said that she should go to see Harriett Bone the next time.

'It will be short commons for all of us, but I can't abide thinking of those little girls working in that laundry.'

On the day before market day, Lidi was with her father when Adam Tylee came to Croud Cantle Farm. As he rode into the yard, Lidi felt an excitement that she could disguise but not quell. She realised then that she had scarcely stopped thinking of him since the march to Court Chiddham.

'There's to be a big march from all the four parishes tomorrow. It's got about that the Workhouse Master has been pocketing some of the food allowance and has been getting in all manner of filthy, bad meat and weevily flour. And the old people have got so bad from it that they're dying like flies – of course people are saying they're poisoning them off in there.'

'Is it true? I mean that he's been pocketing the funds?' Lidi asked.

'It's what we aim to find out. Conditions in the workhouses are bad enough as it is, and the food bad. I was hoping that you'd come and be one to speak up, Mrs Draper.'

'I shall come on that march too,' John Toose said. 'I've always had a hatred of institutions and the people that run them,' said John. 'I might as well, because I'm no good to man nor beast sitting about at home.'

None of them could argue against him, for they would have said the same themselves in his position.

So the next morning the entire family joined the procession out of the village to walk the few miles to Blackbrook. The market produce was put into store in the hope that the weather would stay cold enough to preserve it a day or two till the next market.

If October is the red month, then November is the 'blood-month', the month that had traditionally been the time for the slaughter of beasts before winter set in. In these present times, there was no such luxury – it was rare to find even a pig, let alone red meat. November, a chill morning to be marching over the downs with only bread sopped in hot, peppered water to keep out the cold. As they left the protection of the chalkhills, showers of fine drizzle blew at them head-on. November, not the best time of year to be walking miles across the countryside. But then neither is it for milking cows before dawn, or hacking turnips from clamps or following sheep across broad open downlands where the highest tree is a stunted juniper.

But Auryn was warm and soft against Lidi's back. Luce, Pa, Jack, Aunt Ju and Uncle Will. Ever since she could remember, Lidi had felt excitement when she was in the midst of her family. When she was a child they had had family gatherings on any and every occasion. She smiled to herself as she remembered the great variety and quantity of food that Nana-Bess had provided at Christmas and Easter festivals. Nana-Bess . . . she couldn't have stood seeing them as they were now, unable to be always 'feeding thee up' or 'putting a bit of flesh on yer ribs'.

The best times had been before Jack was born. A shame, he had not got the store of fat family memories. She looked at him now, a few yards ahead of her, walking beside Luce, before each step an almost imperceptible hesitation – the best was over before he was old enough to enjoy it. She and Sarah had grown up taking it all for granted, not really knowing that they were part of a family that was luckier than their neighbours – and now they were not.

Except in passing, as she did now, idly, it was ages since she had given much of a thought to her little books of garden plans. She still kept up the breeding of lilies, but the daydream of herself taking up any of that work seriously, was long gone. Things would be better when Auryn grew up. It was necessary to hope . . . no not just to hope, but to make life a bit better.

Around her were people she had seen almost every day of her life. Neighbours. Those who had work were reliant upon Park Manor Estate, and those who had not, reliant upon Relief. There was scarcely a warmly-clad body amongst them.

Even so, Lidi felt enlivened and stimulated at being in their midst. There was an air of excitement at having made this move to do something, instead of, as was usual, having something done to them.

And, for all that their family had come down, they were still better off than most. They had the decent roof of Croud Cantle over their heads, they still had the dignity of a plot of ground on which to grow enough to keep bread on the table, and a bit to sell on the market.

The columns of villagers from various places gathered in Motte where some of them formed a delegation to call upon the vicar, who had the right to exact a Great Tithe and who was severe in levying it. He took six hundred pounds a year and the delegation insisted that it be halved.

'If three hundred a year is not enough, then you shall need to pull in your horns a bit. We shall have it in writing from you, that you agree to take no more than six pounds a week in tithes.' The farmers came away gleefully with their signed bit of paper.

Cheered by this success, they called in upon two other collectors on the way to Blackbrook, and dismantled three machines.

Lidi and Luce walked together talking amicably until Adam Tylee joined them when Luce grew sullen. If Adam Tylee noticed Luce's antipathy towards him, he did not show it, but talked in an open and friendly way to both of them. Usually it was only Lidi who answered.

'We have asked for a meeting with some of the Governors.'

'Will they come?'

'They'll come. They know that they're to blame for letting the Master embezzle funds, and they'll want to publicly decry his action and throw him out.'

On the outskirts of Blackbrook somebody said they knew where there was a farm with a thresher and a group of men broke off from the main body to deal with it. The sudden 'finding' of this thresher and the ease with which its owner was persuaded to show them where it was, led to suspicion that it was 'put up'. He would not have been the first one to hope to claim insurance for a machine he regretted buying.

The owner watched the destruction, even helping to move obstructions.

'Ah, be danged if that an't the best thing that could happen to he. He an't been nothing but trouble since the day he was brought in.'

When the job was done, he told the men to break open a cask of his best beer for them to take a wet, and shook hands to show that he bore them no ill will.

'Remember to tell your fellows that Farmer Troke was decent to you, and there's not grain enough in his barn to make it worth their while to come.'

Farmer Troke's beer was of the best and several of the machine-breakers took full advantage to take a very good wet.

For Lidi, the meeting with the Board of Governors was an anticlimax. On the occasion in the vestry at Court Chiddham, she had not had time to think before she spoke up. But this time she felt apprehensive at the thought of the meeting and had gone over and over in her mind what she should say when it was her turn. As it was, when Adam Tylee had said his piece, the Chairman said that he agreed that it was a shame and a disgrace that public funds meant to feed the poor and needy had found their way into the pocket of the Master, and as if to spike their guns, said that the Board intended to 'review' the entire method of victualling.

But this was not enough for the marchers. Whilst the meeting was going on, Jude had gone to ask to speak with Harriett Bone. Without hesitation, Harriett was sent for, and as soon as she appeared it was clear that she was suffering great distress.

She looked with alarm at the great crowd that had gathered in the yard. 'What is everybody come for?' she asked.

'There's a protest.'

'About Mercy?'

'No. What about Mercy?'

'An't you heard . . . she's killed, and Faith's . . . I thought that's what you was here about.' Hetty broke down now.

The crowd, sensing a tragedy worth being in on, pressed close.

What is it?

Who's dead?

A child I think?

A child's been killed.

The message was passed back through the crowd.

Jude tried to get Hetty's story clear. 'What happened? When?'

'Only just this morning. She was too little to be in the laundry with all that scalding water . . . but what was I supposed do? They said the girls was old enough to carry things. Oh Dear Lord, one of they great boilers bust out and went straight at them both. Mercy died in an hour, and Faith's that bad burnt . . .' She was so distraught that she shook uncontrollably.

'Go back to her. I'll come,' said Jude.

The message of the child dead and another dying from scalding whilst working in the Poorhouse laundry, was a spark to the tinder of anger that was always dry in these days of upheaval.

Now there was no stopping the crowd.

They pressed in, following the woman, one of their own kind in distress.

They surged in, breathing the sick smell of the poverty of the place and its inhabitants.

They rushed in, goaded by an old fear.

When the twelve of the delegation had finished with the Board, they were coming from the room in the Master's house in which they had met when they heard a clamour from the main building.

'Stop here!' Adam said to Lidi.

'No, I'm coming.'

'There's trouble, I can hear it. And you've got that babe.'

He and the rest rushed away.

For a moment, Lidi did not know what to do. Adam was right, she could not rush in whilst she carried Auryn. She hurried round to the front of the building.

'What's happening? What's going on?'

A man said, 'We're going to finish the place.'

'What about them?' She indicated some children wrapped in shawls and bedding sitting calmly watching the excitement.

'They'm sick children and we're taking them and all the sick old people in together. Come on, you can help us carry them inside.'

Lidi picked up one of the children and followed.

In one ward, people were dragging in beds and carefully tucking up old people and children.

Lidi went to an elderly woman and handed Auryn to her. 'Here, take care of him for me, I must find my Pa and brother.'

The woman looked delighted at the request and, with an action that told of years of practice, she wrapped Auryn close and tucked him in close to her. She grinned toothlessly at Lidi. 'He a be all right. We a keep each other warm.'

Lidi ran through the building, looking about for Luce or her Pa. First she saw Luce; he was carrying out several children.

'Where's the babe?'

'A woman's minding him. What's happened?'

'Hetty Bone's children – it's reckoned they were near boiled alive in the laundry – one's dead. The gang's set on finishing this place.'

Lidi took a sharp intake of breath at the horror.

'But what's going to happen to these, and the old ones?'

[298]

'God knows. Nobody's thought of that. Only to get them together and keep them warm and safe.'

Lidi took one of the children and rushed back into the ward again. A man passed, carrying an entire wooden banister which he took outside and broke up to get a fire going.

'My God, look at that.'

'It's no good Lid, this place will go. Nothing's going to stop them now.'

'Where's Pa and Jack? And Aunt Ju?'

'She's gone down with Mrs Bone to the burnt child. I didn't see the going of your Pa.'

'Was Jack with him?'

'I don't know – it's him I was looking for.'

It scarcely needed the men who had been drinking Farmer Troke's strong beer to start the destruction of the fabric of the Blackbrook Poorhouse, but it was they who began the wrecking.

After taking down the banister for the fire, they set about the boilers in the laundry, men and women alike hammering them to destruction as the threshing machines had been hammered.

Then to the pathetic stalls of the Overnight Casual Ward which were set alight and set vermin running out to be met by clubs.

Each ward was visited, evacuated of its inmates and destroyed. Windows were broken and the frames levered out and thrown out for the fires.

A group of young men climbed to the attics where they proceeded to tear down the rafters and use them to poke holes in the roof. Then they climbed out, unpicked then destroyed hundreds of tiles.

The food stores were found and looted. Soon they found in the Master's cellar several casks of wine, which they proceeded to roll out and break up and unbung. The wine flowed and flooded out, and although only a few thought the wine sufficiently important to stop for, some men and women scooped up the spilled wine or even tried to sup it from the pools on the floor.

There were people everywhere inside the building. Lidi tried to push her way through. It was chaotic. Frightening. People were in a frenzy and bent on destruction. She saw Luce, this time carrying an old man to safety. 'Have you seen Jack or Pa?'

'No. I've been working my way through these wards. Try the other side.'

Trying to remember the lay-out of the place from when she was last there, Lidi went from the Men's Wards to where Maisie Netherfield had been. On the way she saw a group burst into a workroom. They let out a satisfied yell. Looms and spinning wheels. A woman picked up a spinning wheel ready to smash it. Lidi pulled it from her.

'No!'

'Let it alone, we must smash it all.'

'No! Not the looms and wheels. They're too valuable, it's the only means some of them will have of making a few pence. If you smash these, then where will they get any more?'

The fever of destruction made it difficult for them to see reason.

'It's Parish property. We must smash it.'

'No!' Lidi scrambled on to a table. 'Listen. If you smash these, then where will our neighbours get any more? Our neighbours . . . that's the only people you'd be harming if you smash the wheels. Take them out if you like. Give them away if you like, but don't smash them.'

For a moment it was touch and go – easier to give vent to anger and add to the noise of splinter and crash.

Then, 'Right!' said a man. 'The Gel's right. Let's give 'em away.' Suddenly the idea was as enticing as destruction. Summit to give to somebody. Largesse. Like 'Them' – able to give. Not to keep. Not to share. To give. A luxury almost unknown.

Immediately they began to carry off their loot.

'Stop a minute,' she shouted. 'Has anybody seen a blind boy – wearing eyeglasses?'

'John Toose's lad?'

'Yes. John Toose is my Pa.'

'They went off with the woman with the scalded girl.'

Lidi could have cried out with relief. Aunt Ju was probably with them too, so they were safe. She had had visions of her Pa lying stricken with his weak heart, and Jack fumbling amidst the chaos and being trampled underfoot.

Suddenly a bugle sounded.

Somebody shouted, 'It's the Volunteers!'

Inevitable. It had only been a matter of time. A wonder they had been so long.

Chaos, as those in the building tried to escape, and those in the yard rushed inside.

Lidi ran towards a door only to see a flash of scarlet and blue as some Volunteers with muskets came in. She turned, there was no going upwards to hide, for most of the stairs had been broken up. No way down, for the way was littered with debris. There was noise everywhere. The Volunteers shouting orders and people calling to one another. Suddenly she found herself in the ward which she recognised as the one Maisie Netherfield had been in. She remembered seeing a small door that she had thought led outside.

Her heart was racing; the clatter of the Volunteers' boots echoed and sounded near. She found the door, but it had been broken open and did not lead outside. She thought of her baby being rocked by the old woman. What would happen to the babe if she was arrested? She was desperate to find somewhere to hide. She held her breasts which now ached with fullness. The baby must be hungry by now.

She went back into the dormitory and stood leaning, breathless, against a wall looking about her. The ward was now deserted, there was nowhere to hide. She jumped as someone tweaked her sleeve. An arm poked out from the wall.

'Here. Ssh. Miss Jude, you can hide in yer.'

It was Ginny Short, the kitchen drudge who used to be the little penny-song seller before she was raped.

'Ginny!'

'I seen the sowjers. Quick, you got to hide 'fore they do things to you.' The girl was trembling with fear. 'Quick.' She dragged Lidi into a tiny space between the wooden wall-cladding and the brickwork.

'I found this one day, and I said it would be mine. I been in here before when Miz Parker was going to gid me a beating. She never knew where I was. I stopped in here for . . . Ssh!'

The one door that was hanging from its hinges crashed down as three Volunteers came in.

'Empty!'

'Better search it.'

'Dammit where the Devil d'you think they are, down the cracks in the floorboards?'

'There's another room off it.'

They began to march down the ward.

'No fear. You go if you like – but you'll not get me in there. Can't you read?'

' "Female Ven-ere-al"?'

'Clap. Pox. Go on then, go and poke around and see if that lot o'dirty puzzles are hiding a few old joskin rioters under their skirts.'

'I shouldn't be surprised. Most of them look skinny enough to hide up anywhere.'

The rest of their ribaldry was lost as they turned and trooped off.

In the next half hour or so, Lidi tried to look out several times, but Ginny pulled her back, clutching her hard.

'We should go now, Ginny,' she whispered. 'If we wait too long they may come back with more men to search again.'

Ginny thought for a few moments, then beckoned Lidi.

'We a go out by the privvies.' She laughed. 'An't nobody a go that way.'

She took command of the situation. This was her territory and so far she had done very well by Lidi. She led the way along a dark, dank alleyway and behind the open-fronted privvies, a row of rickety sheds in which there was rough planking with holes cut in, stretched across a running stream.

It did not take long for Lidi to discover that they had come out somewhere behind the Star Inn, close to where she would have been standing had they come to market as usual that day. It was a shock to find herself in normal Blackbrook. The abbey clock struck two. All that had happened that day had taken only so few hours from the time they left Cantle.

'I'll have to go back, Ginny. I left my baby there.'

'You go back and Ginny will wait for you, Miss Jude.'

The girl plonked herself down at the foot of the butter-cross. She was dressed only in her dirty Workhouse shift.

'Here take my jacket. I'll keep the shawl.'

Lidi went back towards the Workhouse.

Volunteers were everywhere. She saw one or two members of the Board she had met that morning. Her hair was a flaming signal at any distance so she tied the shawl far over her forehead.

On the waste ground, many of the inmates were still sitting where they had been placed. The enormity of the problem struck Lidi. The old people, the sick and the children would be carted off to Waltham or some other Poorhouse. She slipped through unnoticed and found the old woman still seated as she had left her, how long ago? An hour? Time seemed both stretched and shrunken.

'Are you all right?'

The old woman beamed. 'A course. Me and the littl'n have had a fine old time together. Somebody gid us a bit of crust dipped in some wine – you liked that didn't you my little shaver – and we had a rare old laugh at each other.' She thrust her crumpled, sallow face close to Auryn's. He laughed up at her and shrieked with pleasure.

'Hey, he's that bonny.'

Lidi took him and, with some relief, began to suckle him.

'I'm sorry I just dumped him like that – but my brother can't see properly, and I thought he'd get trampled.'

'An't nothing to be sorry about, Gel. This is the best day I had in years.'

'I don't know where they will take you.'

'It don't matter that much. Once you'm in they places – one's much like another. I reckon they'll have to take some on us over to Waltham or Alresford. I shouldn't mind going to Alresford. I was born there. Ah, perhaps 'tis fate that I a die there and all. And it a be a bit of a ride out.'

When she had fed the baby, Lidi bade the old woman goodbye, then went back to the market square where Ginny was waiting, just as Lidi had left her.

Oh Lord – waiting.

Suddenly she realised that Ginny had attached herself to her.

All right, she would take her.

She seated herself beside the girl, who took the now satisfied baby gently.

'Is he a girl or a boy?'

'A boy. Auryn.'

'Orrin? That's a queer name.'

'It means golden.'

'Fancy that. Golden. And he is too. Ginny don't mean nothing except Short.' She laughed. 'It's a joke; Ginny Short . . . 'tis my name.'

Lidi smiled. 'It's a good one.' A joke. There wasn't much wrong with a girl who made a quick joke about her name like that.

'Well now, Ginny. I seem to have lost my husband, my Pa, my aunt and my brother . . . but I've found you. Can you walk all right? It's a few miles to Cantle.'

'Ho, you just see me!' And she was off demonstrating the length of her stride.

'Hold on. We'd better see if I can find out anything first. You sit and hold Auryn.'

'I a sit and hold "Golden", and then we a walk to Cantle.'

As she walked away, Lidi had a qualm, this was the second time today that she had dumped her baby into the arms of a stranger. No. One should trust people. The old lady had been the perfect grandmother for an hour. Trust Ginny to be another. She looked back to see the girl rocking and talking to the baby in the most natural way.

The obvious place was the Star where she knew the innkeeper Jimmer White very well.

'Have you see my Pa, or Luce?'

'Old Will Vickery was in. He was asking the same.'

'How long ago?'

'Not more than ten minutes.'

She rushed back to Ginny.

'Ginny, did you see a man with white hair and a white beard come out of the Star?'

'You mean the man who used to bring the pies for the other Miss Jude?'

'Yes, that'll be the one.'

'He's gone over there, up the George yard.'

Lidi ran across the square.

'Uncle Will!'

'Lidi, thank God! We looked everywhere.'

'I had to hide.'

'Where's the baby?'

'Over there. Have you seen Luce?'

He hesitated.

Panic struck at the look he gave her.

'Uncle Will. What's happened?'

'It's all right.' He drew her to him. 'Listen, it's all right, but he was arrested.'

'No!' She could tell that he had not finished. 'What else?'

'Judeth. They've taken her as well.'

'They can't. She's an old woman.'

'They have.'

Hold on. Hold on. She forced herself to think.

'Then where are Pa and Jack?'

'John and Jack took Hetty Bone and the child back home in a borrowed cart. They should be there by now.'

'Where have they taken Luce and Aunt Ju?'

'I don't know. Dozens have been arrested, hundreds some say. Nobody knows yet where they've been taken. I've been trying to find out, the best guess seems to be the army camp outside Winchester.'

Will Vickery looked old and tired. There was a deep furrow between his eyebrows, and he had a number of small cuts on which the blood had dried.

'Are you all right, Uncle Will?'

'Ah, *I'm* all right – it's Judeth. Dammit Lidi, I been wandering about like an idiot. I can't think what I should be doing next, I'm that addled. I should be going after Judeth, but I don't know . . .'

'Come back over to the butter-cross and sit down a minute.'

Instead they collected Ginny and went into the Star, where Jimmer White pressed bread and cheese and beer on them.

'There was a sergeant just in here – a regular – and he was escorting a batch of them that just been arrested up to Winchester.'

'Have you seen Adam Tylee?'

'That young preacher? Ah, he been in here a couple of times asking and leaving messages.'

'Well that's one blessing if they didn't arrest him. Did he say anything about . . .?'

Jimmer White shook his head. As good as a wink. The innkeeper was a good friend, part of the system by which messages were passed about covert actions.

'Right then,' said Will Vickery, 'Winchester. That's where I'm off.'

'Uncle Will, you're in no fit state to go off to Winchester this time of day.'

'I shall be fine. I worked in Blackbrook for years, there's plenty of people that'd lend me a horse and give me a loaf.' He finished off his beer and rose immediately. 'You best get back home. There's not too much daylight left. You're taking Ginny?'

'Yes, she saved me all right today. We're going to walk to Cantle together, aren't we Ginny?'

The girl nodded and grinned.

'Try to see Luce. Tell him . . . I don't know what to tell him . . . just that we're all right.'

NOVEMBER

A Lull Before the Storm

A FEW DAYS LATER Luce, riding Will's borrowed horse, came into the yard.

'Luce! Thank God you're safe.'

He leapt down and they clung together in mutual relief.

'Aunt Ju! Where's Aunt Ju?'

'Still in there. So's a lot more. Will's stopping there, though how he's going to manage . . . He says he's got friends there who will see him all right.'

'He will be – there's one thing Uncle Will's got, and that's friends everywhere.'

Luce had been lucky; he had been with a dozen or so prisoners who had been in the charge of two Volunteers who had changed sides just outside Winchester and had let their charges free. Quite by chance he had come across Will on his way to Winchester, had joined him until they had discovered Jude, when Luce had returned home.

'Your Aunt Ju's up on a serious charge . . . oh God Lidi, it was on my account . . .'

'What's on your account?'

'If she get's tried for it . . . let's go in and I'll tell you as much as I remember. It was a mess wasn't it?'

She went with him as he led the horse away to unharness it. In the stall he suddenly embraced her passionately, holding her tightly and burying his unshaven face in her neck and shoulder. 'Oh Lidi. When they took me off and I couldn't find you . . . and I wondered what had happened to the babe. Bugger it Lid, I never felt more terrible in my whole life, if I lost you I don't know what I should do. I was fair out of my mind with worry.'

Indoors he discovered that there were now three newcomers to Croud Cantle. Harriett Bone moved about like a grey wraith, mourning. Although her two boys were safe somewhere in Blackbrook, her husband and one little girl were gone, and the second girl hovered at the edge of life.

The child Faith lay on her left side and was fed a thin soup made from fermity liquid with honey and butter, whenever she roused from the effects of the merciful draught that kept her insensible to the constant changing of the witch-hazel dressings on her right shoulder. Her burn-wounds were bad.

John, having found no ill-effects of either the march or subsequent attack on the Poorhouse, had said that he had been Miss-Mollying too long, and at once went back to work. Fortunately, most of the turning over of the soil for the frosts was already done at both Toose's and Croud Cantle, so John and Jack had been helping Lidi with the day-to-day work, keeping things ticking over.

Ginny Short, although her behaviour was at times strange and her thoughts muddled – she still thought that Lidi was Jude – worked around the house willingly doing whatever was asked of her. The small, underfed girl seemed tireless. Even before she was attacked and abused, her existence as a penny-ballad seller was precarious and hungry, so that her drudgery in the Poorhouse meant only a change in the place where she existed. Now, washed and dressed in a skirt and bodice that had been Nana-Bess's, she was the one member of the household to whom something good had come out of the sacking of the Parishes.

As he took some soup, the first hot food he had had for days, Luce told what had happened when they were arrested.

'I was in the yard. Them that had stopped off at Troke's came in through the gate, some of them had bits of the thrasher carrying them like they was armed. They'd all had a drop, and some of 'em was drunk enough to piss pure ale. When the mounted Specials came in, one of our lot tried to pull one of them off his horse. But he got his foot in the stirrup and the horse was dragging him. I recognised the Special – he was one of Saddler Warren's sons, you know him, the young one . . . Lord it was terrible, Lidi, other horses was traipsing round . . . he'd a got his head crushed any minute . . . I never thought whether he was a Special or not . . . only that he was somebody we knew. I caught hold of the reins and stopped the horse . . . I was trying to unhook the spur from the stirrup . . . well, that's all I remember till I woke up in the back of some covered wagon.'

'And . . . Aunt Ju . . .?'

'Well, she was pushed in just after I come round. She said she saw who it was that had come off, and me trying to free him . . . then she noticed an officer riding down on me waving a sword about. She reckons he must have thought it was me that brought the boy down. Anyway, she said she never thought twice, but she grabbed a piece of iron railings that had been broke off and hit out at the man, trying to make him drop his sword . . . it was his horse that reared up and kicked me one on the back of the head . . . look . . .' He showed Lidi the wound.

Lidi had no difficulty in imagining the scene, just as she had done when Luce had described that other time when he had been wounded in just such another mêlée. 'Aunt Ju can land a good blow when she wants to.'

'Ah, I know she can . . . it's what she done then. It was an iron railing and she broke the officer's arm and the jagged end of it wounded his leg.'

'Bad?'

'Will says "no", the fellow's walking about, but that won't make no difference. She's up on a serious charge and there's talk about making examples of them that fought the Specials.'

A FREE-THINKING PREACHER

TO THE THOUSANDS who were involved, the days that followed were remembered like some fevered nightmare in which one could hardly tell in which day or in what place a particular thing happened.

Adam Tylee had escaped arrest and came to Croud Cantle in the middle of the night.

'Will Vickery said I would always be welcome to come here.'

'Even if Will and Jude aren't here,' said John, ''tis all one and the same in this family.'

'All I need is a bit of a rest, the floor in the kitchen will do well enough. I don't reckon I've had more than a couple of hours at a stretch these last nights, and it's the foundry tomorrow. Things are moving so fast – it's like a heath-fire with the wind behind it.'

'Is it true there's a lot of extorting money, pillaging and that?' Luce asked.

'Ah, there's some . . . bound to be, nobody can account for that number of people . . . though not much, not nearly as much as went on in the war. Most of it isn't done with any viciousness. You know how it is. You get a few hundred who marches up to a house and begs his worship if he wouldn't mind donating a few sovereigns to the funds – well . . .'

'Trouble is,' Lidi said, 'these days, a box on the ears gets reported in the newspapers as an attack with an iron bar.'

'Ach my Gel, you lived under my roof long enough to know better than to expect people who go against the grain to have any good said of them,' John said.

Adam Tylee rested there that night, and next day Luce, Lidi and Jack went with him to join a march to the Archangel Foundry ten miles distant.

Although Lidi was concerned for Jack in case he should find himself in difficulties in the chaos of a throng bent on destruction, she realised that it was important to him that he be treated no differently from the rest of the Cantle youths.

'Our Lidi, I'm coming and I shan't walk with you and Luce. I won't have you making a Miss Molly out of me. I know I can't see a barn door till it's three feet away from me, but that don't mean my brain's soft. And if I can't see a river till I goes ass backwards into it, then I a get wet, won't I?'

Over the weeks, they had learnt lessons from their mistakes. Large numbers of women had taken part in the marches from the outset, leaving their young children at home under the eye of old grandmothers, and taking the babes slung in shawls as they did whilst working in the fields.

At last the women felt strong. After years of helplessly watching so many children wither from lack of proper food, the marches and protests were a way of fighting back. Since such incidents as took place at the Parishes, however, they had become wary, and now always sought out a barn away from the meeting-place where the babies were left in the care of a few women and girls. Ginny Short was elated at this prospect.

Archangel Foundry was a large business which produced farming machinery and specialised in its renowned 'Archangel Patent Elevating Corn Threshing Machine'.

'I don't know that I go along with breaking up a factory,' Luce said. 'What about them that earns their living making the machines?'

'Working people must not stand one against the other,' was Adam's answer. 'If the foundrymen would help the agricultural workers, and the agricultural workers would help the hemp makers, and then they help the weavers, and then they help the colliers and the smelters and the timber fellers . . . do you see? People like us are the strength of the country.'

Luce did not miss the look of admiration in Lidi's eye as she watched Adam Tylee's expressive mouth.

When they were out along the road, Luce complained to Lidi, 'He does a sight too much speechifying for my liking. He don't seem able to talk like you and me. He sounds like a pamphlet, all words!'

Feeling elated at being part of the march, she linked hands with him. 'Luce Draper, I think you're jealous.'

'Don't be daft, you're a married woman and a mother – and getting on thirty.'

Lidi looked sharply at him. 'I wasn't meaning you was jealous in that way . . . I meant of his speechifying.'

'Well, I could never do with preachers.'

Near thirty and married or not, Lidi wasn't unaware of Adam Tylee's interest.

And there was no doubt that his radical fervour and freethinking views stimulated her interest in him. Equally, his natural ability to lead irritated her in the same way that other manifestations of domination did. It was as though her first reaction to authority was to want to go against it, yet Adam Tylee in his role of the Captain stimulated her both mentally and physically.

It was late in the afternoon before the many small groups were assembled, about a mile from the foundry and close by a warm oasthouse where Ginny and the other girls settled down with the babes. From there, with Adam and half a dozen independent local artisans at the head, the column started off.

About halfway they were stopped on the road by several men on horseback. Their leader was Robert Elford, the foundry Foreman.

Elford held up a hand. 'We've come to try to persuade you to disperse and go home – it is still not too late.'

Although his voice did not reach more than a few rows of the marchers, there came a roar of disapproval from those further back who could see the tall hat, and knew what that meant.

'No Robbo, thee knows that we shan't,' one of the leaders said. 'Your place is the ruination of too many of us.'

'The works gives employment to twenty men,' said Elford.

'And throws two hundred out of work.'

'You're not a farmworker, Daniel Ford.'

'You know that well enough, Robbo, but cobblers need customers and them there machines you turn out is taking the work from my neighbours, so they can't afford their boots mended.'

'Aye,' another man shouted, this time Jez Edwards a black-smith. 'The same for us – you don't have to be a farmworker to be done down by your foundry.'

'There then, Mr Elford,' said Adam Tylee. 'Kindly move aside. We let you have your say peaceable enough.'

'You say peaceable – yet there's hundreds of you that's got bludgeons and iron bars. That's not peaceable.'

'We intend no harm to any man or woman, Mr Elford . . . Only the works itself.'

Elford hesitated, but it was an enormous crowd he confronted.

'Move aside, Robbo,' said the cobbler. 'Your Master's had his pound of flesh off of us – now we shall have ourn off of he. We'm determined the place must come down – Archangel's must go. We got no argument with thee man.'

Elford and his men rode off in the direction of Archangel's, the great iron gates of which, when the column arrived, were chained and padlocked.

A score of men rocked the gates back and forth, but they would not give.

'Stand aside.' Jez Edwards the smithy removed the padlock with a single blow. The throng surged forward.

The first to go were the cast-iron moulds. After breaking them they were hurled through the windows.

Above the sound of the hammering and breaking a hunting horn was heard. There was a moment's silence into which Robbo Elford shouted, 'One hundred pounds.' The silence held for a further moment. 'One hundred pounds . . . or guineas if you stop now. No recriminations. You all go home. One hundred pounds.'

'No!'

'Damn your eyes no, Robbo.'

'Go home yourself.'

'A hundred pounds be buggered for a tale.'

'To work, me lads! Let's have the bugger down!' And the destruction was restarted with renewed enthusiasm.

Soon they discovered a cache of sledgehammers, which proved to be superior to bludgeons and bars as tools of destruction. Every window was smashed. As in the sacking of the Parishes Workhouse, a contingent climbed onto the roof where it tore it up, then the chimneys. Finished and half-made threshing machines and ploughs were destroyed.

Lidi and a group of women went to find the waterwheel which was the source of power for the foundry. Although she did not recognise it in her own make-up, she too in the midst of a group became its natural leader. Her work at Toose's had taught her confidence and an ability to tackle problems. The women followed her without resentment.

'Knock off the all floats,' she said, 'then demolish the paddle racks and the hatches.'

Although the paddle racks were of cast-iron the women worked at them until there was none left whole. The hatches, where the flow of water was controlled, were, when the women had completed their work, entirely destroyed.

If Luce had any doubts at the outset, he had apparently set them aside, for at one point Lidi saw him high up on the foundry crane smashing its gearing to the delight of a crowd cheering him on.

Again, as it had during the breaking up of the Parishes, it seemed to Lidi that time had no meaning. At some point after darkness fell, she was refreshing herself with a drink of water when she found Adam Tylee sharing the same water-butt.

He grinned at her. 'Well then Mistress Draper?'

'Is it "well", Mister Tylee?'

'I should have thought you'd be as good a judge of that as me.'

Lidi frowned a query at him.

'You were prominent at the pulling down of the old Parishes place.'

'No, I wouldn't say I was "prominent".'

Suddenly she was apprehensive. She was attracted by him, and now she was sure that, given half a word, he would respond.

It was as though they stood together in a glass globe. Around them the din of destruction, the clamour of voices, the blackness of the November night lit by bonfires and tarred-wood torches, yet none of it penetrated.

'Don't be modest, Mistress Draper. The Movement needs women with a good head on their shoulders, and a brave disposition – and I've seen proof of both.' He washed off his palms, dipped cupped hands into the water, drank from them, then drew the back of one hand across his mouth – his lips became moist and pink against the black dust.

A sudden image – a memory stimulated by the present. Ten years back when she was eighteen . . . standing at an open barn door . . . thudding boots and voices . . . the Harvest Home when Allun Park, moistening his lips in the flickering lights before suddenly kissing her, had aroused her beyond anything she had felt before.

'I don't know about any "Movement",' she said. 'I came here, same as I went to Chiddham and the Parishes . . . because there's terrible things happening in my village, and to people I grew up with, and I don't know of any other way to try to change anything.'

'I should like the chance to talk to you about it some time. We need women who have a gift for speaking. The Movement isn't anything if it doesn't include the women.'

'I'm glad to hear it . . . that you have a regard for women.'

The only light was from the flames of burning wood, but Lidi did not misread the look that he directed straight into her eyes. 'I have a very high regard.'

Lidi Toose, this is a dangerous game. No swain and maid, dallying idly. Three times since they first met they had spoken with a look, intelligence communicating with intelligence, ardent spirit speaking to a fervent one. Two of a kind.

He cupped more water and offered her to drink. Steadying his hands, she took a mouthful and wiped her mouth as he had done.

There, in full view of the wrecking and the flames, she felt that she was giving herself to him as surely as though it had been physical. A strange emotion. Not love. She was sure that what she felt for him was not love. She loved Luce. This sudden and overwhelming emotion was not as gentle as that, as when she had first run her fingers down the scar of Luce's back for the first time. This was a dangerous emotion, one that might destroy something as fragile as love.

Yet as they stood for the moment, Lidi had a feeling that something that had always been missing from her, something lacking, was now in place. He was the other part of her that until now had left her incomplete. There had always been a Lidi Toose who wanted to jump up on walls and address crowds and a Lidi Toose who had the ability to direct and organise, incomplete until now. She felt a kind of intoxication: *he is me, and I am him*. Yet who was Adam Tylee? She did not even know where he came from. *All that I know is that he's a well-digger and a free-thinking preacher.*

'I don't get that much time for talking these days.'

'None of us do, but this won't last for ever, then there's the whole future.'

Of a sudden the place fell quiet.

A nearby church bell was tolling twelve o'clock.

Midnight Saturday, and although many villagers were in present times disaffected churchgoers, rural people had a profound belief that they should keep holy the Sabbath Day.

Within minutes the place was empty of people.

ON THE TUESDAY, news reached Cantle that Jez Edwards the blacksmith and Daniel Ford the shoemaker had led a group back to Archangel to finish off the work they left undone.

When they had reached the foundry, they had run straight into a detachment of the 9th Lancers.

The entire party was arrested and sent to join people like Judeth Nugent and the many hundreds of others awaiting trial at Winchester.

ADAM TYLEE RETURNED to Cantle because he had work to do near there. They arrived in the early hours of Sunday morning, to find that Will Vickery had come home. He had been staying in Winchester so that food might be got in to Jude, but she had sent him home.

'She's right I suppose, I was wasting time and could be doing more good here. There's hundreds waiting trial. The prisons overflowed days ago, now they're using compounds at the army barracks . . . that's where she is.'

'How's she going to get any food?' John asked.

'Prison food.'

'God above, Will, you and I know what that's like.'

'It's no better there, and you know what Judeth's like, she stopped me taking in food for her when most of the rest were lucky to get bread and gruel, and now they won't let in any visitors.'

'What's going to happen?' Lidi asked. 'Doesn't anybody know anything yet?'

'They reckon there'll have to be a Special Session there's that many been arrested. A good many's being charged with hanging offences.'

Until now, the old man's manner had been quiet and matter of fact, but he suddenly thumped his fist on the table. 'By God John, I've never been averse to breaking the law, but always preached against violence. Now,' he ran his hands through his white hair distractedly, 'I could go at them with a musket, and so would anybody who'd seen what I've seen in Winchester, men in prison for venting their anger on a machine . . . for just hammering a bit of iron that's done them out of their work, and women like Judeth whose only crime was to resist and protest, or like all those ordinary women can't stand it any longer to see childer fretting with hunger. God's body! We should blow up Parliament for that.'

'No Will – that's not the way.' Adam Tylee's voice was quiet and firm. 'The way you've always worked in the past is the right way. We agree that people who don't have a say in the making of laws, can't be guilty of breaking them, and I'll do anything you like . . . but not violence against people. Against machines, against buildings, against the rickyards and grainstores . . . but not against people.'

'Is that so then? Perhaps you'll tell me how we are ever going to change things.'

'Not by violence.'

Lidi felt irritated by Adam and wretched to see her Uncle Will's distress. 'That's easy for you to say, Mister Tylee. You might feel different if it was somebody in your family that was thrown into prison like Aunt Ju.'

After her shrill, raised voice, his reply came quietly.

'I'm sorry to say that you're wrong, Mrs Draper. Somebody very dear to me is in prison. I've got an aunt and uncle there, as close to me as parents. It was they who brought me up when my father was killed. They're good people . . . they set fire to some ricks in their village. They've been in Winchester prison since the end of October.'

Abruptly he got up, snatched up his hat and went outside.

They were all stunned into silence, till Luce said, 'How could we a known, he always seems so cocky and full of himself.' Then Lidi jumped up and said, 'I'd better go and say I'm sorry.' Now, added to the hurt that she had felt for her Uncle Will, was remorse at her stinging words.

In the sharp still air of the November night, Lidi stood a moment adjusting her vision, from the light of the kitchen to the dark, and allowing her emotions to quieten. On the walk home from Archangel, Lidi and Ginny had walked together, each carrying Auryn a few miles. It was a dark walk, only the leaders carried lanterns. There was ample opportunity for Adam to have walked beside her for half a mile; from time to time she heard his voice but he never came close.

Gradually the solid, familiar outlines of the northerly downs showed up against the sky which was a dome of blue-black glass: Tradden, Beacon, Old Marl and Winchester Hill. It was still some time off dawn, but across the valley the sound of a cock crowing broke the silence of the frosty night. There was no moon, but from white spurts of his breath against the darkness, Lidi could see where Adam Tylee was standing on the other side of the yard wall. Her footsteps crunched on the frozen crust of yard-mud. He must have heard her, but he did not move from his position. He stood leaning back against the low stone wall looking down over Cantle.

Lidi went through the wicket gate and stood beside him. Still he gave no acknowledgement of her presence.

'Mister Tylee? I don't know what to say, except that I'm sorry. I'm a bit like that, coming out with things . . . I've got no excuse . . . only that most people tend to believe that their own troubles are worse than anybody else has.'

At last he made a movement. Turning to face her, he said, 'You're right there, Mistress Draper. I'm no different. I've been standing here feeling sorry for myself, and thinking that my troubles are worse than anybody's. It's that the aunt and uncle who brought me up after my father was killed are up on an arson charge.'

'Oh, that's terrible.'

'I can't talk much about it. I don't want it to get out that there's a connection between them and me. It would go bad for them because it's a way of getting back at me. But now and then it comes over me – like just now.' He pauses briefly then goes on. 'But that's not the true reason, you know, that I got myself wound up.'

Lidi makes an attempt to speak but he lays a finger on her lips. 'I cannot stop thinking about a young woman. She is everything that I have ever thought wonderful in a woman and I have found her too late. She is married already, Mistress Draper.'

His voice is low, its timbre belies the odd formality of his words.

'She is with me night and day, Mistress Draper, think of that. For sixty minutes in every hour of every day she doesn't leave my mind. Have you any idea how that might disturb a person's life, Mistress Draper?'

A sudden warmth upon her cheeks and ears as his hands cup her face.

Stop him, else it will be too late.

She doesn't move.

'Right in the midst of all that's going on, I find myself thinking of her. I'm like a youth with his first maid, I look about for her all the while, try to keep her in my sight.' Now there is no pretence, his hands move round her neck, over her shoulders. 'God forgive me, Mistress Draper, the woman's in me like a fever. I've got important work still to do in the Movement, yet she fills my head when it ought to be filled with plans for the marches, and the letters and organising the getting of funds.'

His thumb caresses her mouth. 'And she is married, Mistress Draper. You haven't got troubles like that, have you, fallen for someone who's married?'

For a moment they stand without moving, his thumb still sliding over her lips.

Then Lidi removes it but holds on to his hand.

She can almost stand outside herself and observe what she is doing, can almost listen to her own conscience and common sense.

Playing with fire, Lidia Draper.

But it is not Lidia Draper who is playing with fire.

This is the other woman – Lidia Draper knows her only too well, she's troublesome and difficult to control. It is she who bursts out at such moments as in the vestry at Court Chiddham, it is she who whips up wild dreams of becoming a renowned garden architect or an incomparable plant breeder.

The woman playing with the fire of her own emotions is the banked-down Lidi Toose who has been smouldering away within the hard-working wife, mother, daughter, field-labourer, cook, stall-holder. She is the same Lidi Toose who had loved Luce Draper when he was her lover, when he used to allow his own passions to be as free as hers.

Before he became her possessor, before he showed his feelings of ownership of her by his jealousy, Lidi Toose loved Luce Draper.

Against the dark sky, Lidi Toose sees the rebel Adam Tylee as a dark shape. His face is invisible. At this moment he is anonymous. The Captain. A sensual man, the impress of whose caressing thumb she still feels. He is the anonymous masculine form who, in the person of Alec James, was the first of her fantasies when she was fourteen, and then Allun Park, then other youths and men she met casually in the market or at village gatherings . . . and then Luce. All of them in turn had broken into her unconscious and raised her desire. Only with Luce had she allowed herself to be fulfilled.

Lidi Toose can hear Adam Tylee's breathing, can smell his sweat mingled with that of dust and smoke from his jacket, and can feel the warmth emanating from his body, the bones of his hand.

She picks up his formal, allusive style of speech, contrasting their closeness and the quiet ardour of his voice – and she knows exactly what she is doing.

'Are you married, Mister Tylee?'

'No Ma'am I'm not.'

'Then you're right, I've not fallen in love with someone who's already married – I even doubt that I would call it "love".' She pauses. 'My trouble is that, though I have a husband, I've found a strong *passion* for another man – obsession perhaps. The man is not married – but I am.'

For a moment Lidia Draper struggles against Lidi Toose – conscience against passion, guilt against desire. The odds are against her.

Corn Queens still reign in the old villages.

Lidi touches his tense knuckles with her tongue, knowing that he can do no other than close the few inches of space between them and respond to her.

With his arms about her, he speaks close to her ear. 'Aah, Mistress Draper . . . this troublesome woman, I don't know how I can live without loving her.'

And at that same moment, Lidi is convinced that neither can she live without loving Adam Tylee whose face she has seen shining with exhilaration through the dirt and sweat at Archangel, whose passion for his neighbours he can articulate in spell-binding speech, whose desire to change the world is noble. She has never seen him, as she often sees Luce, wrapped in sacking, bespattered with mud and dragged down with exhaustion from hours spent double in a field. She knows only the Captain, she does not know Adam Tylee the well-digger.

The man she cannot live without loving stands on walls and opens his arms to crowds.

The Cantle Valley has never ousted its old spirits and deities, its people are still close to the Corn Queen, Mother Earth and the Naiads, they still live with the Corn King and the Green Man and the Antlered One.

Chastity, virginity, celibacy, adultery are concepts not in the understanding of the old spirits of the chalkhills. Lidi Toose and Adam Tylee have drunk the waters of the downland and eaten the produce of its valleys. More imbued with power than any wafer and wine, is the body of the oldest gods. The lovers have fed upon it so that, as they were within their ancestors so the spirit of pagan gods are within Lidi and Adam.

At the moment when they give themselves to one another, passionately, physically, the rhythm of their bodies is out of their control and in the hands of those venial gods.

In clock-counted time, the mutual, fierce fulfilment of Lidi and Adam is over almost as soon as they kiss and touch. She has known

from the minute that she saw him leap upon the wall at the Great
Stone, that it was bound to happen. Since she was a girl, her fantasy
lover has always been the one who would turn the world upside
down.

Now, they stand silently; he is still clutching her hand so tightly
that it hurts. She releases it, he gives a little laugh and says 'sorry'.
  'Don't be.'
  He takes her hand again and lightly kisses it. 'No, I never shall.'
  They stand and look down at the village where here and there
lights still shine. The quietness and peace are wonderful to Lidi.
From one moment to the next, she is changed and there is no going
back. She shivers. He says, 'You should go back into the house.'
  'Yes.'
  'I shall walk down to the village. I must see the innkeeper.'
  'It's nearly dawn.'
  'He knows I'm coming. There are lights on there.'
  'Go then.'
  He runs a hand down her cheek and makes to go. 'I never
expected such a woman existed, I can hardly believe it.' And he is
gone, away along Howgaite Path towards Cantle.
  She cannot see him but watches the darkness where he must be.
  There is the sudden sharp sound of the iron latch of the kitchen
door. Luce's silhouette shows against the light.
  'Lidi? You there?'
  'Over here Luce.' She is amazed at how normal she sounds. A
few minutes sooner and Luce would have discovered them, a
minute before that, and it would not have happened at all. Lidi feels
reality run like acid along her nerves, and can hardly believe that it is
herself who can say, 'Over here Luce.'
  Rubbing his arms against the cold, he said, 'I was just going on
up. I wondered where you'd got to. Where's he?'
  'Adam? Gone down to see Tazey James.'
  'He lives a damn queer sort of life if you asks me.'
  'You go on up, Luce. Don't wait for me. I'll have to see to the
babe. It hardly seems worth going to bed now.'

When Lidi at last went indoors, except for her Pa, they had all gone
to bed. He was sitting gazing into the embers. She busied herself
about clearing away the bowls and mugs from the table.
  'Luce said he's gone down to Tazey's.'

[321]

'Yes. There's something else afoot I suspect. I told him I was sorry.'

'What upset him?'

'He's got an aunt and uncle, more like father and mother – it's they who are in Winchester.'

John Toose watched his daughter closely as she washed the bowls. 'Lidi.' His voice had such an edge to it that she looked up sharply. 'Luce is a good man, Lidi . . . and a good husband. Don't you forget it.'

She immediately felt four years old again and her Pa was chiding her more in sadness than anger.

'I know.'

'Where's he gone?'

'Luce? I thought he'd gone to bed.'

'Not Luce.' Although he kept his voice low, it was forceful. 'Ach, come on Lidi, I might be old but that don't make me out a fool. Perhaps nobody else hasn't noticed you these last days, but I have.'

'There's nothing wrong with me.'

'You went rushing off out after him just now. You can't keep your eyes off him. And he's the same.'

She felt as awkward and blushing as when she had been found out for going off to watch a football contest when she had been forbidden.

'I only went to say I was sorry we'd upset him.'

'Listen to me. You're Luce's wife, you belong to him and nobody else.'

Had it been anyone else except her Pa, perhaps her guilt would not have stimulated rebellion. 'I belong to me!'

'You don't. You belong to Luce and he belongs to you, you made that agreement. If I caught him looking at village girls . . .'

'What are you suggesting, Pa? What?'

'I'll tell you what I'm suggesting, my Gel, I'm suggesting that you've been looking at Adam Tylee in a way no wife should look at any man except her husband.'

'Pa!'

'Don't you get all indignant with me, Lidi. Your mother and me were faithful and that's how it must always be between husband and wife. And if you've got any ideas away from that direction, then you'd best get them out of your head before it's too late.'

'And what about Tansy and Jo Bunce . . .'

Until that moment, their entire fierce exchange had been in hushed voices that would not carry up to those sleeping above, so that the slap across the cheek that he gave her sounded vividly loud.

Lidi and her father were too fond of one another for the strained atmosphere between them to last. Next day, when they were all seated for dinner and all talking about Archangel, John Toose unobtrusively ran the back of his hand over the place where he had slapped Lidi and for a moment she pressed her hand over his. She caught something in his look and interpreted it as a longing for peace and quiet.

Poor Pa. He had been a better father than most men she knew. Always wanting people to enjoy their lives. The hours he had spent reading aloud to the neighbours, the times he had stood in market squares and often been as much abused as cheered for his views. Mother, whom he had loved so much, had died, Tansy had been unfaithful and run away, Sarah had come home pregnant, he had been stricken down by a seizure, and the Toose business he had made out of nothing had all but disappeared. No wonder he wanted peace and quiet. The slap had been out of character. Lidi realised how much he must have worried at the possibility of another upheaval in the Toose family.

Lidi Draper made up her mind she would never again allow herself to let her thoughts, much less her gaze, wander to Adam Tylee.

LAW AND ORDER

I T WAS NOW fifteen years since the Duke of Wellington's army had been disbanded, since laurel-wreathed coaches had cantered through the country bearing news of victory. For a brief moment, his army of lower orders commanded by aristocrats – his "scum of the earth" made into "fine fellows" – had been popular. Now, however, these men made up part of the new columns on the march, so that Lord Lieutenants, Ministers and Generals wrung their hands and sought to recruit and press a feudal force of labourers and tenants.

On the 14th November, from a Gentleman to the Garrison Commander, Winchester:

> If you cannot send a military force, for God's sake say so without delay, in order that we may remove our families to a place of safety from a district which want of support renders us totally unable longer to defend.

On the 15th November, from Sir Robert Peel to Lord Liverpool:

> Since I last saw you I have made arrangements for sending every disposable cavalry soldier into Kent and the east part of Sussex. General Dalbiac will take command. He will be in Battle today to confer with the Magistracy and to attempt to establish some effectual plan of operations against the rioters.

On the 18th November, from the High Sheriff for Sussex to the Home Office:

> The labourers demanded 2s.6d a day, and the lowering of rents and tithes. All these complaints were attended to, thought reasonable and complied with.
> The meeting dispersed quietly.
> I should have found it quite impossible to have prevailed upon any person to serve as special constable. Most of the

tradespeople and many of the farmers considering the demands of the people just and equitable.

On the 22nd of November, from the Duke of Buckingham to the Duke of Wellington:

Avington, Hampshire

Nothing can be worse than the state of this neighbourhood. I may say that this part of the country is wholly in the hands of the rebels. Fifteen hundred rioters are to assemble tomorrow morning, and will attack any farmhouses where there are threshing machines. They go about levying contribution on every gentleman's house. There are very few magistrates, and what there are are completely cowed.

In short, something decisive must instantly be done.

From Captain Swing to Sir Timothy Shelly:

If you wish to escape the impending danger in this world and in that which is to come, then go round to the miserable beings from whom you exact tyths and enquire and hear from their own lips what destres there is.

Beware the fatel daggar.

Captain Swing.

Although the views and the poems of Sir Timothy's son had an uplifting effect on many of the lower orders who could read – such men and women as Judeth Nugent, Adam Tylee and Lidi Draper – the radicalism which the young Shelly expressed appeared to have had no affect on Sir Timothy himself, for he remained entrenched in the old ways and exacted every one of his dues.

From Sir Robert Peel to A Magistrate:

. . . the most expeditious mode of effecting this is to bring from Dorchester the only cavalry force that is in the West of England. This however, shall be done, and one hundred infantrymen shall be brought from the Garrison of Portsmouth.

And so it was, around Cantle as with the whole of the south of England, that less than a month after the first serious protests had taken place, every road that led north and south, east and west was being churned up by the boots of infantry and Specials, and the horses ridden by cavalry and mounted Yeomen.

9

24 NOVEMBER 1830

Morning – the Cottage – Beauwyth

EVENTUALLY THE TURMOIL of the events in the countryside entered the awareness of Sarah, though perhaps
'were forced upon' her awareness is more exact.

'Oh, don't talk to me about that,' she would say to any
comment Brendan might make about what he had heard of or seen
going on. 'I had my belly-full of all that back home. I just want to be
left alone to look after you and the little ones. I don't say there isn't
something to it, and good luck to them if they get their wages raised
– but I don't want any of it under our roof.'

And Brendan, being more in love with his new wife than ever,
soon brought home only pleasant gossip of his horses and kept his
concern about events to himself.

The twin babies were now eighteen months old so that Sarah's
days were filled with domesticity. The only cloud in her sky was
the knowledge that Alec James was living not many miles away.
Since Ninn's visit, she had heard nothing more of Mrs Delphine,
but could not bring herself to ask Brendan anything about her, even
though she fretted to know.

Once or twice she had started at the sound of footsteps only to
realise that she had been thinking of her old lover, and then called
herself a fool for imagining that it might be he coming up the path.
Even so, she knew that his presence in the vicinity was a threat to
her. Little scenes presented themselves to her imagination whilst
she was kneading dough or scrubbing floors, in which Alec James
taunted Brendan, or claimed the children.

Fool! She told herself. What would he want with two babes?
And he couldn't prove it anyway.

But still at the back of her mind was a feeling of insecurity.

It was the third week of November when Ninn called again.
This time he was with Brendan. Mid-morning when Sarah was
carrying bavins from the woodstore prior to making ready the
bread oven.

'Sarah,' Brendan said, 'Master Ninn's got summat he wants you
to do.'

'You don't have to, it's only a request,' Ninn said.

Sarah gave Ninn a wry smile. 'Spit it out, Master Ninn.'

'Mother asks for you to call there.'

Sarah could not tell whether her face showed the dismay she felt; perhaps it did for Ninn said hastily, 'It's up to you of course. She only said that she wanted to see you again.'

'Well of course I'll go.'

Brendan looked pleased. 'Master Ninn says you're to take the dog-cart.'

So, they had arranged it already. They had assumed that she would go. Well, what harm was there in going?

Ninn smiled. 'You could take the children for Mother to see.'

No! That she would not do.

Sarah quickly extemporised an excuse. 'Better not, Christy has got the snivels a bit, and I don't want him to be out in the cold.'

'Of course, of course, Goody Cartwright shall come down to see to them.'

And so, with Martha Cartwright, wife and mother of four of the Beauwyth jockeys, fussing over the babies, Sarah drove away in the dog-cart, her mouth a bit dry from apprehension.

10

MORNING
THE DOWER HOUSE, SHORLAY

SARAH HAD ALWAYS preferred Hampton House to the great Stonebridge Manor itself. To avoid the lodge where Alec James was apparently now living, she approached the dower house from the rear. Through trees still dripping from the early heavy mists drifting through them, she glimpsed the pretty place as she drove along the boundary lane, and was at once carried back ten years to when she used to walk that way with Ninn.

She remembered how, in spring, the little spinney changed its colour from the aconites, then the primroses, then the bluebells as each flowered and took a turn at the bees. The hedgerow trees threw off peppery perfume of hawthorn and pungent elderflower. Mistle thrush, blackbirds, robins, dunnocks, tits and nightingales whistled the boundaries of their territory; rabbits, stoats and moles a hunted; mice and squirrels foraged. This was one of the places where Sarah had handed on to young Ninn the knowledge and lore of the outdoors that her Aunt Jude had given her.

The beads of moisture from the mists that had prettily trimmed the hood of her cloak, now turned to dampness which found its way around her neck, up her sleeves and through her skirt. It was not a morning to be away from home. This was the first time that Belle and Christie had been left with a stranger.

The thresher! She suddenly remembered. It had been here somewhere. She and young Ninn had discovered it on their walk . . . a man had chided her for bringing him there. Even in those days, the presence of a threshing machine had meant possible trouble, which was why the man had been so aggressive. Thrashers . . . 'What do a little Gel like theece know?'. . . 'that they put men out of work'. . . her Pa's words flung at the man. Oh, why couldn't things be nice?

And there was a cottage too . . . yes, somewhere here. She reined in the pony.

It was still there, seeming to be no further decayed than when she and little Ninn had walked through the ruin and its wild garden.

How angry she had become . . . even with poor little Ninn for being the inheritor of the place.

No anger now. Life's too short. Pa, and Aunt Jude and Lidi and all the rest of them, wasting their lives. Nothing would ever change. If you wanted better things, then you had to go along with the situation as it was and get what you could out of it.

Belle, Christie and Florence Broughlake each had the same father – son of a village innkeeper, a libertine with an eye to the main chance. Yet the futures of his three children must hold very different fortunes . . . only because of the level of society into which they had been born. Little Florence might be looked down upon by the county families, but she was never likely to want for any single thing she might need or fancy.

It was the way of things. Everyone had to get what they could and hold on to it – she didn't blame Alec James, he was only doing the same as herself . . . getting the best out of life in the only way they could.

She walked on, leading the pony. Everything that she was now had its origin inside the boundary that she was now passing. She would not have Belle and Christie, she would not be Brendan's wife, nor have the pretty cottage and a pleasant life, had she not once been Sarah Toose the Under Nursery-maid at Stonebridge.

Thinking again of that girl's neat waist emphasised by the dark full skirt and tightly bowed apron, caused her to become aware of its present pregnant fullness. She had invested a great deal in this baby. It was meant to obliterate the guilt-ridden part of her past. It would be a boy and would look exactly like Brendan.

Ahead she saw the house. Hampton House, a hundred years old and the original estate house. Long and low and built of stone and napped flint, its windows and corners bordered in mellow red brick, it was much more of a home than Stonebridge Manor.

There was no sign of life, but remembering some stabling at the side of the house, she led the pony there, keeping her eyes all about her warily.

All along the road coming she had prepared herself for any event by imagining scenes where she would suddenly encounter Alec James. She just hoped that she might make the call and get away without seeing him. If he had heard that she was coming, then he was not likely to want to be there.

'Hello Sarah.'

Of course! She had been whistling in the wind. And, if she was honest with herself, she had known that he would not be able to resist seeing her.

Still holding the reins, she turned her head in Alec James' direction but, except for a quick glance, kept her gaze at the level of his neckcloth.

'Alec?' The query was to suggest that she had not expected that this was he.

'Who did you expect?'

'Mrs Delphine sent for me.'

'I know.' His voice was changed, more restrained . . . almost gentlemanly. 'You're looking pretty well, Sarah. Pretty and well. They tell me you've married old Brendan. Well, he's a decent enough fellow.'

'Whose boots you aren't fit to blacken!' It was his false air and manner. Son of an innkeeper in a fancy waistcoat. It was the fancy waistcoat that focused Sarah's attention – he was trying to be one of 'Them'; the 'Enemy', her Pa always called them.

'Tut, tut, Mrs Lewis, don't let us get into who's fit to blacken whose boots.'

'I don't want to get into anything.' She had unhitched the pony and began to move away.

'Married life suits you, Sarah, you're prettier than ever.'

'I'm twenty-eight, a married woman and a mother, so there's nothing for you to pay me compliments for.'

'You don't have to worry about me, Sarah. We had a nice little fling.'

Turning away, she left him standing there, thumbs in the waistband of his breeches, head slightly tilted, smiling as he watched her go.

A maid took her to a pretty sitting room, all pale and silkily decorated; several mirrors reflected the light that came from three long windows.

'Missis Lewis Madam.'

Mrs Delphine was seated in a plump chair beside one of the windows, with a laid-up tray on which a silver kettle on a spirit stove steamed.

Sarah bobbed a small curtsey and nodded at her old Mistress.

'Well Sarah, I'm glad you came.'

Delphine Broughlake looked magnificent to Sarah's eyes. She wore a peignoir, a little dated with its low-cut, high-waisted style but entirely suited to the roundness of her wonderful bosom and shoulders. Her complexion was fine and her eyes bright. Ageless. Beautiful.

'Master Ninn said you wanted me to.'

'Sit down.' She indicated a companion chair opposite her.

Sarah was a bit nonplussed.

'Oh it's all right. I can't talk to you if you stand there as though you were still my maid.'

Sarah took the seat and sat erect with her hands clasped.

'You've filled out. It suits you.'

'Thank you Ma'am. I'm expecting, that's the reason I dare say.'

'Well, well. How many months?'

'I expect to be confined in May.'

'You married one of the Stonebridge grooms?'

'Yes, Brendan Lewis; he's Master Ninn's head trainer now.'

'And you live . . .?'

'At Master Ninn's training stables.'

'Is your husband good to you?'

'Yes Ma'am, he's good at his work and we've got a comfortable home.'

'And how did you come to marry him?'

'Ma'am?'

'How did it come about?'

'Well, he just . . . turned up one day, and asked me.'

'And what about your child?'

Sarah would have liked to say that it was none of her business, but she was still the Maidservant facing her Madam – servility dies hard.

'A boy and a girl, twins. Brendan thinks the world of them and when this one comes, we shall be a happy little family.'

'You are very fortunate.'

'Yes Ma'am. I am now that I'm married to Brendan.'

'Would you care for some tea?'

'No thank you, Ma'am.'

'You may as well, I have a great deal to discuss.'

Only the tinkle of silver and fine china broke the silence until Mrs Delphine handed a cup of tea to Sarah.

'You are probably wondering why I sent for you.'

'I thought perhaps you were curious.'

Mrs Delphine idly played with the sugar-tongs until they sprang from her fingers and clattered onto the tray.

Ninn had said that his mother was strange, unconventional true, but to Sarah she appeared no different than she had been for years. Perhaps she was always strange, if strangeness was for a woman to behave like a man in the indulgence of physical desire. There were plenty of tales about the goings-on between ladies and gentlemen in society, but not between ladies and their manservants. Sometimes one heard of the daughter of some nobleman being seduced by a groom or a dancing-master, but not the wives and mothers of gentlemen. Delphine's 'strangeness' was nothing new in her character . . . perhaps it was that Ninn had grown up and was now seeing his mother through adult eyes.

'I am going to have another child.'

What did a servant say to her mistress in such circumstances?

'I hope that you are well.'

'Oh yes, I knew that I should have no trouble if I returned to England. Do you remember how ill Italy made me?'

Sarah gave a brief nod.

Mrs Delphine continued, 'Did Ninn tell you that I have a little girl?'

'Yes, Florence isn't it?'

'Should you like to see her? She is such a pretty thing.' She put a hand towards the bell-pull.

No . . . to see her would only complicate mtters, and they were complicated enough already. What if the child looked like Belle?

'Perhaps before I leave.'

Sarah's agitation increased. Why didn't Mrs Delphine get on with it, say why she had sent for her?

'Excuse me Ma'am, but I can't leave my babes too long . . .'

'Are they well cared for?'

'Oh yes, Master Ninn arranged for someone.'

Delphine rose from her seat and beckoned Sarah to the window.

'Very English is it not?'

Sarah looked out onto the grassy slope that was bordered by graceful, bare larches, a few ancient walnut and apple trees. She remembered how it used to look in spring when thousands of daffodils bloomed there.

'Beautiful. I used to bring young Master Ninn here. It wasn't lived in then, but I remember thinking what a perfect place it was.'

'Goodness! Perfect? Hardly perfect weather.' She indicated that Sarah be seated again. 'Then you might consider taking a position here?'

Unhesitatingly, 'No Ma'am! I've got a husband and family, and we've got a nice place at Master Ninn's.'

Mrs Delphine smiled. 'But you have just said that it is a perfect place.'

'I meant . . .' What did she mean? 'I meant, that for anybody who was rich enough, it would be the sort of place to own.'

Sarah accepted a refill of her cup and a little cat's-tongue biscuit. How strange, to be seated like a visitor, sipping tea. Was that what Mrs Delphine was playing at? None of her equals visited her, was she reduced to entertaining servants to take tea in the morning? Well, she entertained a manservant in her bed, why not a maid in her sitting-room? Or was it that it was Mrs Delphine who was entertained?

'Before this child is born, I shall return to Italy. I have bought a villa there, it overlooks the Arno, we chose it before we left, it is being updated and redecorated.' She directly engaged Sarah's gaze. '*We* . . . I, and Florence's father.'

Confusion added to Sarah's slight apprehension. What position had she meant at Hampton House, if she was returning to Italy?

Sarah did not show any reaction . . . the older woman must have expected some, for her words had sounded like some kind of challenge.

'You were always a composed young woman. It was one of the reasons why I engaged you as my maid. You had more . . . style, than any village girl I had ever encountered. I like people to have style.'

'Yes Ma'am.'

'Do you love your husband.'

This sudden change of tack threw Sarah slightly.

'Of course!'

'Oh, there is no "of course" about husbands.'

'There is with Brendan. He is the best man in the world.'

'So many of them are.'

'I wouldn't want to be married to anyone else.'

'Have you ever considered how fortunate girls of your station in life are?'

A change came over Sarah now; she no longer felt intimidated by their relative situations. The full implication of the complexity of their relationship became stark. Two women. The one had no more right than the other to offer tea, to command attendance, to ask intimate questions. Equals. No different than two does serviced by the same stag, two ewes by a single ram. They had each allowed Alec James access to them. Equally foolish perhaps for, as she had told him, he was not fitted to blacken Brendan's boots.

She went to the door and looked out into the hallway, it was empty. She smiled at Mrs Delphine. 'You can never tell with servants, they like to know what's going on.'

'Human nature.'

'Mrs Delphine, you sent for me, and I came. It was not convenient . . . I don't have a nursemaid to leave my children with. My husband will want his food, I have bread to bake, washing to do and floors to scrub. You have asked me questions about my private life, said something about offering me a situation, hinted at things that we both know happened, but I for one don't want ever to discuss. If you bade me come over on a whim, or to get some kind of satisfaction . . . perhaps even because you are jealous, then I'm not going to let it go on. If you and your child's father . . .'

She was standing, her cheeks blushing from the release of her restrained hackles. Now Sarah was the challenger.

'Oh! Let us stop this. I can't help it if we used to be mistress and servant. We both *know*. I will say it if you won't. And I've never said it to a soul except my sister, till now. Alec James is my babes' father – and you know what that means!'

Delphine Broughlake could do what she liked.

Now that Sarah was Sarah Lewis, none of them was any threat to her. Brendan had married her without wanting to know anything about her past. He had accepted the twins as if they had been his own. She was secure. Even if Alec James were to come over to the cottage and say anything, Sarah knew that it would make no difference to her marriage.

'And you are still accepted by your neighbours and family?'

'Yes. Why not?'

'Why not indeed. As I said, women from the lower ranks of society are more fortunate than those from the one that I was born into. There would have been no impediment to your marrying out of your station.'

'Some of us are forced into it . . . most of us in fact.'

'But you may marry out of your station. Not only "may", it would be seen as something very desirable.'

'I dare say you mean a *higher* station. Yes, it would be very acceptable for a village girl to marry above her . . . though there's not a great many nobles or gentlemen that choose to comply.

There's a pretty good many that ought to, if they had to marry the mothers of their children born the wrong side of the blanket.'

'Is that what your husband believes?'

At first Sarah did not comprehend Delphine Broughlake's meaning. The wrong side of the blanket?

'No!' she said when she did realise.

It had never occurred to her that Brendan might believe that she had been taken advantage of by a gentleman. But then . . . what did he believe?

'Please say what you wanted to, and let me go.'

'Very well. I intend to live out the rest of my life in Italy with the man I love. My first husband was a wretch, I was put to him like a heifer to produce a prize calf. This is the way it is done in our society, Mrs Lewis.'

Mrs Lewis. Equals?

Sarah smiled. 'It's called making a good match, isn't it?'

'Good for whom? I had looks, decently educated, brought up to be dainty, polite, ladylike . . . and to obey the wishes of my father. I was scarcely out of school when he arranged my marriage. Marriage! All that was required of me in return for Stonebridge Manor and a share in its fortunes, was that I produce a son.'

For the first time, Sarah saw Mrs Delphine as a real woman.

They had lived in close proximity for years, yet even in spite of such intimate acts as that of the Maidservant washing the Madam's menstrual cloths and marital sheets, or powdering the body or dressing the hair of the Madam, Sarah had never really seen a woman like herself.

A lady. A gracious hostess. A mistress with the most feminine of bosoms and shoulders, but as unreal as a princess.

Yet there she had been all that time, just below the surface, a woman like herself, wretched, emotional, resentful. They had lived under the same roof and shared the same man, often on the same day. Delphine Broughlake was more closely involved in Sarah's life than Lidi had ever been.

'Master Ninn has grown to be a wonderful young man. He loves you very much.'

Mrs Delphine heaved a small sigh. 'I know, I wish that I could have loved him. I never could. You must have realised that. From the first moment when he was shown to me and they tried to put him to the breast, I saw his father's face . . . it dried my milk. It was better with Arabella, she has none of the Broughlake traits.

However, I did what I was sold to do – I produced the new Broughlake bull calf.' There was real bitterness as she said it.

'I can see nothing of the old Master in Master Ninn.'

'I hope not, for I could not bear to think of him lurking in the kitchens with his breeches unbuttoned.' She pulled her brows together. 'Did he ever try anything with you? I did warn him . . . I vowed to expose him . . . ha! expose, that's the word. He knew that I would. I caught him at it once, you see. It was that which eventually gave me the upper hand of him.'

'No. He was quite polite to me.'

A short silence fell upon the room.

'Well then, Mrs Lewis, we seem to have cleared the air somewhat, which was what I had hoped to do.'

She got up and walked to the window again and stood looking out.

'Arabella has been living with my parents for some while. The child is not happy, and I do not want her to continue to be brought up in the way that I was reared. She is twelve years old now, and in four years' time she will be ready for trading in the marriage market. I have determined that she shall never be sold to an old man with strange habits as I was myself. If she is to be put to the stallion, then let him be the one of her choosing. Let him be a shepherd or a blacksmith or a prince, but only if she wishes. Florence will grow up in Italy with me. But if I should try to take Arabella too, then my father would take legal action to stop me, and I know that he would succeed.'

She turned to face Sarah.

'If you would agree to come and live here, care for Arabella as though she were your own daughter, then I will have her made a ward of Ninn's. The two of you would see that she had a fair chance of escaping the old men. This house could be made over to you in return for caring for Arabella.'

'This house?'

'Yes. It is mine. I am quite a wealthy woman. I should see that the place was kept up.'

This house? Made over to you?

'But . . .'

'I have been into it very carefully. It is possible . . . if you will agree. I hope that you will.'

'I can't possibly give you an answer. It's too much to take in . . . too sudden. Brendan loves his work at the stables.'

'Why should he leave it? Beauwyth is not very far away from here. And in any case, from what I gather, it may not be so long until Ninn marries, he is obviously hoping for the Peterson girl. Then he is bound to come back to Stonebridge and set up house. Whatever happens, your husband will not lose his position – Ninn thinks far too much of him for that.'

'I don't know what to say.'

'Say you will do it.'

Sarah looked about the room. The thought of being mistress of such a place, of bringing up the children here, it was like a fantasy, the kind of fairy-tale told to children. Wave a magic wand and the pumpkin turns into a golden carriage, or a labourer's cottage into a spacious house.

'I shall have to talk to Brendan.'

'Very well. But I want this baby to be born in Italy as Florence was, which means that things must be settled quickly. Also, I mean that this one shall be born in wedlock.'

'You're going to be married?'

'Yes, to the father of my children.' She laughed. 'I believe in wholly romantic love, and that it should transcend social barriers. If I was sold without love to an old husband for him to sire his children upon, then I am determined to freely give myself to this one.'

Remembering the circle of people with whom Mrs Delphine had surrounded herself in Italy, and looking now at the cosseted woman, Sarah wondered whether Delphine was 'giving' – or was she rather buying herself her rustic in a silk waistcoat? Well, at least for once the tables were turned.

MORNING
Cantle

AUTUMN HAD SLID over into winter. Until now the weather had been cold but dry. In the southern counties of England, as dissent drove onward from the east, it was met with bad weather coming in from the west. On the same morning that Sarah had gone to Stonebridge, heavy, white drizzling mists filled the bowl of the Cantle Valley.

When Lidi went outside to pump up some fresh water, she was met with a sight quite familiar to all Cantle villagers who lived on the slopes of the chalkhills. In the bowl of the valley, it was as though skim from the butter-churn had been poured in until the entire floor of the valley was submerged in whiteness. The air seemed dead, and none of the usual lowing, braying, barking and crowing could be heard. Neither St. Peter's church, Tazey's alehouse nor Shaft's Cottage and its neighbours could be seen.

The damp air was chill, and Lidi stood for a while thinking of Aunt Ju and feeling wretched at imagining the compounds and cells in Winchester and what it must be like on such a morning for her. Will had heard rumours that the expected Special Assize Session was to be arranged at Winchester in December to deal with the huge number of offenders, but there was nothing definite.

December . . . it could be weeks before the people were brought before the court. Aunt Ju was over sixty, the bones of her knuckles were swollen at the best of times, but in the cold they were like oak-galls. The only concession she ever made to her painful hands was to enable her to hold a pen to write up her journal; then she held her hands close to the fire and allowed Lidi to massage them with goose-grease and wintergreen and wrap them in hot flannel. Lidi knew from Uncle Will and her Pa, how old people died like flies from the sick humours and bad water and the cold and damp of prison.

She felt frustration, anger and anguish that there was nothing that could be done.

Lidi returned to the kitchen where Ginny was spooning sops into Auryn, Hetty was bending over the box-bed dressing Faith's wounds and the men were lacing boots and stowing chunks of bread in their pockets, whilst fortifying themselves with a peppery bread-and-water mush and beer into which the hot poker had been dipped.

'It's not the day I'd have chosen for a march,' said Lidi as she made her own preparations for the day.

Adam Tylee said, 'We've all worked in the wet often enough.'

Although Will Vickery had insisted that Adam Tylee freely use Croud Cantle as 'Headquarters', since the night after Archangel, he had moved down to put up with Tazey at the Dragon; but he had arrived early this morning, brisk and businesslike. His eyes had caught Lidi's once but she had turned from him in as natural a way as she could muster and begun to suckle Auryn. Her intention was to be in his presence the wife and mother, and so proof herself from bringing together the flame and oil of their sensuousness. She saw that, unless she was prepared to put an end to the family, there was no future in picking any more forbidden fruit with Adam Tylee. Yet she was so hungry to taste more.

For the people of Cantle, and the workers on the several Goodenstone estates, this was the most important protest meeting in which they had yet taken part.

'Mobsters'. This was the description given by the newspapers, employers and Magistrates to the great bands of protesting agricultural labourers. So many now it was a wonder that any cow was milked or horse fed in the entire south of England. 'Mobsters' was intended to be derogatory and to pin an element of criminality upon them, but the Mob themselves liked and adopted the term – the Blackbrook Mob, the Owlesbury Mob, the Cantle Mob and, when they all joined forces – the Hampshire Mob.

So today, the Mobs were preparing to support the workers on all of the Goodenstone estates in their request for better wages. Five or six hundred were expected to gather along the road between Cantle and Cherton, where the Goodenstone estate of Monkswood Grange was situated.

Long memories in these villages.

They remembered the great number of cottages that Eustace Goodenstone had pulled down so that unemployed men with families were forced to leave.

They remembered the ease with which he had then been able to employ those same villagers on a daily or hourly rate as it suited him.

They remembered how he had ejected families who had been in the Goodenstone employ for generations.

The Goodenstones' Monkswood Estate enveloped an entire Parish which was described as 'worse than any in the Kingdom. Here, the poor are oppressed and in great misery' – a description given, not by one of the oppressed, but by a neighbour, a noble lord, one of Goodenstone's own kind.

Long memories.

At the start of the march to Monkswood Grange there were four hundred, including scores of tradesmen from butchers and bricklayers to sawyers and tilemakers.

The route that Adam had mapped out for them started on the track over Tradden Raike in Cantle, followed the Wayfarers' Way past many farms, past Preshaw, Lomer, Newton Clare, Shorlay and Hockley. In this area there were many small farms whose tenants had pledged their support and that of their workers. The entire inhabitants and workers of three farms close to Preshaw were to be gathered in, and at Lomer there would be a group led by Dick Talleman, the popular local smithy, waiting to join.

At Croud Cantle, only Hetty Bone and Faith were left behind. Hetty was still grieving over the terrible death of Mercy, but since John had seen that her two boys were now apprenticed to a decent tradesman and Faith was beginning to gain strength, Hetty did seem to be not quite so wretched. Ginny said that she wanted to go on the march, and insisted that she should carry Auryn.

Even in her short stay at Croud Cantle, Ginny was beginning to change from the furtive, suspicious drudge. To see her playing with the baby, and to hear each of them laughing at the antics of the other, was to see a delightful domestic scene. 'I an't never going back there,' was both a plea and an announcement. 'No, not ever Ginn,' was the family's promise.

LAW AND ORDER

WHAT REMAINED OF the small, permanent army was distributed throughout the southern counties. Two troops of cavalry were despatched to Cranbrook; the 7th Dragoon Guards to Canterbury; a squadron of 2nd Dragoons to Chatham, whilst the 5th was spread over an area from Nottinghamshire to Sussex – but the spread was thin indeed. In Hampshire, in addition to the troops that had been sent from the garrison at Portsmouth, further units were now stationed in Andover and Basingstoke.

In the nature of things, it was impossible for the regular soldiers to have an effect upon the particular protest which was the pretext for their despatch – the answer was the mobilisation of more 'Specials', 'Volunteers', 'Yeomen'.

The Duke of Buckingham, being the owner 'almost wholly' of part of that county, now resurrected a scheme whereby he organised a feudal levy and sent a local rector into action at the head of a hundred 'Specials' pressed from his tenants and labourers to arrest some machine-breakers. Where he led, other landowners followed.

In every county in southern England, more and ever more people were awaiting trial on every count from Riot to Extortion, from Sedition to Breach of the King's Peace.

NOON

Beauwyth

NINN BROUGHLAKE RECEIVED a summons from the Sheriff to rally to the King's Peace. All 'Knights, Gentlemen, Yeomen, Husbandmen, Labourers, Tradesmen, Servants and Apprentices' were requested to do likewise.

Whilst Sarah was on her way to Shorlay, Brendan and some of the leading hands were in Ninn's study reading the Sheriff's letter.

'You see, it is against my conscience to accede to those demands.'

'Well, Master Ninn,' said Brendan, ''tis only a request.'

'Which means much the same as a command. I believe that my workers have no complaint against me, and I do not see that I should ask them to help put down their neighbours so to speak.'

'Nobody at Stonebridge nor here has any complaints since you took over from the old Master.'

'Because I did not care for what I inherited from my father. His idea of good farm management was to bring in machines and dispense with people. And even when he discovered that the machines were not all they were reputed to be, his pride would not let him admit it.'

'Your name was flowers and honey the day you had them old thrashers broke up, Master.'

'Don't think that I am against progress, men. My dream is to make Stonebridge a model of good estate management, but it must be done with regard to our workers.'

'Pity there wasn't more of your sort about, Master Ninn.'

'Well, you'd be surprised how many gentlemen are on the side of the Mobs.'

'Ah, but I'd not be surprised at how many there is against them.'

Ninn took back the letter and studied it again.

'Do you know what is behind this, Brendan?'

'Fear, I should say, Master Ninn.'

'Well, yes you could say that. Fear that the greed that is ingrained in my class of society might be curbed. They are afraid that their workers and servants will force them to share out some of their wealth.'

Brendan smiled at his young master. 'Why, you sounds like a red-hot Radical, Master Ninn.'

'It is true that I've been in the company of both Hobhouse and Burdett and found their ideas agreeable.'

'Well . . . I never knew you was so interested in such things.'

Head on one side, Ninn Broughlake gazed through the letter he held. 'It was Mrs Lewis who started me off.'

'Sarah? I can't hardly believe that. She comes from a radical enough family, but she can't stand any mention of it herself.'

The men stood patiently as, almost as though speaking to himself, their master said, 'I could not have been more than about six years old. We came upon some men working on a threshing machine.' He smiled. 'A "thrasher" she called it. I imagined it had been brought in by my father to thrash people – probably me. One day she took me out to watch a machine working. She told me how the flailing and winnowing used to be done in her old village, and how the people had left home or were starving because the machines had taken away their work.' He looked up at Brendan. 'She tells a vivid story. I never forgot.'

'Well, that's summit I never knew about her.'

'Now – about this letter. I propose to . . .' He never finished saying what it was that he proposed to do about the request to arm his workers with staves and clubs and offer them as Specials, for there was a loud knocking at the door by his housekeeper.

'Master, there's a message to say that there's a great mob of rioters on the road to Shorlay, and there's a servant here that's rode over from Squire Goodenstone and he says it's very urgent.'

A lad of about twelve was pushed forward.

'Please Sir, the Master says will every gentleman come and bring his own men to stop the mob. He have sent for the militia, but thinks they mayn't get there in time.'

'Did you see it . . . the march?' Brendan's question to the lad was urgent.

'Please Sir . . . there was hunderds and hunderds. I seen 'm in the distance when I turned off to come here – they waddn't far off Newton Clare.'

'That's what I thought,' Brendan said. 'Sarah will be on that road, and I don't like the thought of her meeting them head on. I let her take Trixie, Master Ninn, and you know how nervy she gets when there's a lot of people about. And what with Sarah's condition . . .'

'Take the new hunter . . . if you go cross-country you should easily get onto the Shorlay road in time to meet her. The rest of you men, if you are on the side of your neighbours, then saddle up and fetch staves.'

THE MARCH TO Monkswood Grange was now well on the way. Their numbers had increased. Several machines had been broken, some with the help of the farmers who had expensively hired them only to find too late that they had perhaps been as well off with human labour. A few troublemakers had, as usual, joined up, so that Adam, as leader, had on more than one occasion to apologise to some householder who had been pressed too hard to supply beer and money.

To cosseted ladies, protected clergymen and wealthy gentlemen, the Mob, as it appeared on the high downs south of Newton Clare, must have seemed an intimidating sight.

By now they were about six hundred strong, filling the narrow lanes from ditch to ditch, or spread in a wide mass as they came over the bleak chalk grasslands. What, a few months back, had been delicate harebells, bright yellow vetch, purple knapweed and thistles, was now only a strawy tangle and spikes of dry, brittle stems. The thin layer of frozen turf was coarse, dull and unyielding. The only things that seemed to be alive there were sheep and stunted junipers.

Lidi had seen little of Adam since they left Cantle. As always on these marches, people constantly changed partners, half a mile with one group, half a mile with another. People who often lived their entire lives hardly ever leaving their villages, were excited and talkative at this new way of life when they might pass through a dozen villages they had hitherto known only by name, and make twenty new friends in a single day.

Jack seemed to have developed enormous confidence since the first march. People liked him. From time to time he stumbled and tripped, but found it easy to laugh at himself. Much of the time he played a penny whistle that John had bought him from a packman; before he had had it a couple of days, he could play a good many tunes.

When they were approaching the village of Newton Clare, Lidi and Ginny were walking with Uncle Will. Lidi, suckling her baby as she walked, had dropped back with some other stragglers who, like Will Vickery, had discovered that their spirit was younger than their legs. Jack and Luce were a long way ahead at the front of the column with Adam, and John was further back with a group of Cantle neighbours.

They passed a milestone.

'Newton Clare one mile,' Lidi read aloud.

'Ah Lidi, I shall have to take a breather.'

'Are you all right, Uncle Will?' She looked closely at his perspiring face.

'Never felt better. A bit puffed. We're supposed to be stopping for a break in Newton Clare – the people have laid on some victuals. I'll catch you up.' He went to the milestone and sat upon it.

'No, I'll stop too. Ginny, go on and tell my Pa that we're having a bit of a rest, and I'm going to put some dry clouts on the babe. Let's sit at back of this bush, Uncle Will, it'll give us a bit of shelter.'

Protected on three sides by a few stunted hawthorns, they sat quietly in a dip that overlooked the Newton Clare valley. Lidi was concentrating on unbundling Auryn when she felt her Uncle Will's hand rest lightly upon her shoulder.

'How old are you now, Lidi m'dear?'

'Just past twenty-eight. And this is all I've got to show for it.'

'More than I have.'

He was quiet for a while, watching her tending the child, then said, 'I think at twenty-eight m'dear, any woman's old enough to know about her ancestry.'

She smiled at him, 'Chance would be a fine thing there too. Anybody would think we was descended from thieves and vagabonds the way Pa and Aunt Ju put the shutters up when anybody mentions them.'

He smiled at her. 'And what about if you was?'

'Well, it's not much good carking yourself about something you can't alter.'

'True.'

Something in his voice.

Lidi began to pay attention and looked at him.

Something in his look.

Matter-of-factly, quietly, 'Tell me about it, Uncle Will.'

'That's Newton Clare. We shall pass through it soon.'

'Yes?'

'See that place?' He pointed to a house that was, like Croud

Cantle Farm, set apart from the main village, much larger and with a spacious yard surrounding it. 'That place is Up Teg Farm, where your Ma was born. If I'd had my way, you'd have been told what happened years ago – dammit Lidi, it's forty years . . .'

'And what about it, Will?'

It was her Pa. From where they sat in the dip, they had not heard his approach on the soft spongy grass. He stood looking down upon them breathing heavily from the steep climb.

Suddenly John Toose began breathing hard and perspiring. He crumpled and held his ribs.

'Pa!'

Will jumped up and helped him into the shelter of the dip.

John Toose groaned and sank to the ground. 'Aah . . . it's that pain come back.'

Lidi dived her hands into the rush basket in which she carried Auryn's rusks and spare clouts.

'Here Pa.' She put a small vial to his mouth and forced some drops between his lips. 'Take it, it's the foxglove.'

He gave a dry retch. 'Aah . . . be jowned to the bloody pain.'

'We'll have to get you down there,' Will said.

'Here!' Lidi thrust Auryn against her father's chest and covered them both with her shawl. 'Keep Pa warm, Uncle Will. I'll run down there for help.'

She left the three of them huddled together in the dip of the chill downs and raced down the slope towards the house that Will Vickery had pointed out as her mother's birthplace.

15

AFTERNOON
The Hinton Road

SARAH THOUGHT OF the position at Hampton House, which would mean a bigger leg-up in the world than any woman who walked with earth between her toes could hope for. Security for themselves and the children, a status as high as estate managers and housekeepers . . . higher even. And decent food. And servants. Sarah could scarcely imagine what it must be like. Reverse the situation where she had been at beck and call . . . 'Make up the fire, Mary,' she imagined herself saying, 'the lamps need trimming, Mary,' 'plant more roses next year, George . . .' Sarah could have hugged herself at the offer that Mrs Broughlake had made and the relief that she and Alec James would be gone for ever.

She estimated that it was something past noon and allowed the pony to take a slow pace so that she could think of all the implications before she got home.

Best of all was the house.

That pretty place with the trees and flowers and grass could be hers and Brendan's for their lifetime. All those rooms! The wonderful chairs and curtains. He *must* agree, she could not bear it if he did not. Ninn would be on her side, it was obvious that he must have talked it over with his mother – was the architect of the scheme perhaps. Sarah could not judge how Brendan would react, there were times when he surprised her with his ideas – as when she had confided in him her suspicion about Uncle Will being a rick-burner: 'How else are poor people to have their voices heard?' She had realised then, that there was a great deal that she did not know about her husband.

Whereas earlier she had been impatient to get back home, Sarah was now at ease, savouring the good fortune. The babes would be all right. This was like the climax of a fairy-tale . . . the magic wand is waved, the pot of gold is found, the poor child discovers that it has royal blood. This ride to Beauwyth at a slow pace was the last line of the story; once she got home and the discussions began, it would be as it is after the book is closed – that rare moment of magic fortune would be gone. She decided to make the most of her pleasure and extend her drive two or three miles by going to Hinton Ampner to collect the yeast that Brendan forgot to fetch yesterday.

In Hinton Ampner she was delayed when the pony threw a shoe which had to be replaced.

16

AFTERNOON
Up Teg Farm, Newton Clare

IT TOOK LIDI only a few minutes to run down the slope and along the track to the farmhouse. Breathless, and holding the stitch in her side, she ran across the yard. She rounded the corner of the house and came at once upon Adam Tylee. In a shocking, vivid tableau that burnt its image into Lidi, Adam Tylee with a pretty young woman enfolded in his close embrace as he swung her round. For a moment, the sight of them overwhelmed even the thoughts of her Pa.

At once Adam jumped away from the young woman and came quickly to Lidi. 'What's wrong, you look fit to drop.'

'It's Pa, he's had another attack up there . . . his breathing's bad. Uncle Will's with him, but we can't move him . . . I came for help . . . I didn't realise you were here.'

The young woman came and stood at his shoulder, her hand idly, possessively brushing dust from his jacket. She was in her early twenties, tall and handsome and, in spite of her coarse skirt and pattens, she made Lidi conscious of her own sweating brow and bedraggled appearance.

'What's wrong, Addy?' Although she spoke with broad vowels, she had a similar refined way of speaking to Adam Tylee.

'This lady's Mistress Draper . . . where I was staying . . . at Cantle. Her father has been taken bad. We shall need a hurdle to get him down. I'll go and fetch Uncle Dan'l.'

'You go back to the people. You've wasted too much time already. Leave it to me. Time's getting on, and they will be anxious to be moving again. The days are short now. I will follow if I am able.'

Adam hesitated.

'Go on,' she said. 'There are hundreds of people waiting for you up the lane. Go on. Go on.' She handed him his hat and gave him a push.

'Right.'

She gave him a close embrace. 'Take care Addy, I couldn't bear it if you were taken as well.'

'I'm sorry Mrs Draper. Sel's right. I should go. Don't worry, my Uncle Dan'l and Charl will see . . .'

'Go *on* Addy.'

'Look after them, Sel.'

He quickly took Lidi's hand and looked directly at her. 'Don't worry, it'll be all right.' He pressed her hand hard, leapt over the yard wall and was gone.

'I'm going to find Uncle Dan'l. Come with me.'

The woman Sel led Lidi around the back of the house, calling her uncle's name.

'Here.' A large, broad, handsome man of about fifty appeared from an outhouse.

'Quick Uncle, there's been an accident. Fetch the hurdle.'

Without a word he was gone.

Now, cupping her mouth, the woman called, 'Charl. Charl. Charleee.'

This time a youth, a younger edition of the uncle, came. A younger edition in his height and broadness, but without the intelligent face of the older man. It was evident that the youth was a simple-minded giant.

'Quick Charl, we've got to help somebody.' She turned to Lidi. 'Are you all right now to go back up and show us where? Would you like some water?'

'No, no, we must hurry.'

The two men raced ahead carrying the blanketed hurdle which was obviously kept ready for emergencies. Lidi and the woman hurried to keep up with their long strides. They were some way along the track before the woman said, panting from striding up the incline, 'It's you that Addy's been staying with?'

'Yes, until the last day or two.' Lidi, panting also. 'At my aunt's place . . . where we live.'

'He's not very good at letting his family know where he is.'

Was she his family? This woman living in the house where Lidi's mother was born.

Too many things happening at once. Lidi forced away the tableau of 'Addy' with both arms tightly about her, their faces so close. *Who is she? He said he wasn't married. He didn't say that he wasn't promised. He is supposed to have preached that there is no such sin as infidelity.*

In as unconcerned a tone as she could muster, she asked, 'Are you his family?'

'I thought you must realise . . . I'm his sister Selena. Hasn't he mentioned me? Probably not, out of sight out of mind.'

'You are not alike.'

'Only in looks. We're twins in our nature.'

His sister. His sister. The tense muscles of Lidi's stomach relaxed at the relief. His sister.

Before the four of them reached the hollow, they saw Will Vickery's figure standing up gently rocking the baby. Slowly, he walked down the slope towards them.

John Toose was dead.

Hardly a word was spoken on the trek back down to the farmhouse. At one point, they had a view clear across the valley and the youth Charl pointed. They could see the two roads that led out of Newton Clare. Along the one that led in the direction of Beauwyth, Shorlay and Cherton was a huge moving column. It was only then that Lidi realised that Ginny had not come back with her Pa . . . probably she was with Jack . . . No hope of fetching Luce back now. Better if he went on. There was nothing he could do for her Pa. Adam's two relatives who had gently lifted her Pa onto the hurdle had covered his face. Lidi wished that they had not. She would have liked to look at him for a bit longer . . . whilst he still looked like Pa.

With Will Vickery's arm about her Lidi followed Selena Tylee, who was carrying Auryn, into the house.

The men fetched two trestles and placed John Toose's hurdle bier beneath the window. For a minute, no one moved but stood like statues about the room.

Lidi felt the extreme significance of the moment. Her mother had been born, and now her father's body had been brought here. It had been her grandparents' home. Who were these people here now? Descendants of her mother's relations . . . surely not? The huge old man and the giant simpleton . . . Selena Tylee? Adam Tylee . . .? She wanted to cry, but true to her kind, did not indulge herself. Time for that later.

T HE CONVERSATION THAT Ninn had had with Brendan began a train of thought that led him to ride off in search of the protesting marchers. In not so many words, he had declared to Brendan that he was on the side of the Mob. A time to take sides. Letters to *The Times* showed how things were: For or Against the Mob . . . one or two letters showed understanding – even a Magistrate or two added their names to the 'For's'. Ninn Brough-lake was For. It was his duty to acknowledge it.

As Brendan was searching for Sarah, Ninn Broughlake was on his way to proving to himself that he was a forward-thinking Radical. As he reined in at the top of the downs, he saw acres of the meadowland beside the Tupnell Road leading out of Newton Clare, filled with people. The Mob was getting its second breath before going on the last few miles to Monkswood Grange. To a twenty-year-old young man with a conscience and ideals, the sight was one to raise his spirits. He urged his horse and rode towards Newton Clare.

HAMPSHIRE ESTATES THAT were Sir Eustace Goodenstone's in all but name provided him with wealth; the overseas plantations with great wealth; his position in society gave him esteem, and his place in government power. Yet none of these advantages had been able to whistle up even a single 'Special' in time to stop the six hundred men and women who were now well along the Cherton road to Monkswood Grange.

Adam Tylee's outwitting of Sir Eustace's paid infiltrators meant that the troop of Dragoon Guards that he had requested was sent to the Cantle estate and arrived three hours after the Mob had left. As soon as his spies arrived with the correct information, he sent a message that the Dragoons in Cantle should proceed with all haste to Cherton, albeit late in the day.

During the morning Sir Eustace drummed up his own private army of old soldiers, keepers, managers, agents, personal servants, grooms, tied householders, parish officials, tenant farmers and parsons whose livings were in the gift of the Estate.

About one hundred in all.

An hour after the Mob left Newton Clare, it was well on its way to Cherton, where Brendan Lewis met the march at the head of which was his brother-in-law Luce Draper, and Adam Tylee. It was a stirring or an awesome sight. On horseback, riding with them, was the youthful Squire of Stonebridge Manor, Ninn Broughlake, his jockeys and a dozen other horse-riders, each as they joined raising the spirits of the crowd and getting a cheer, particularly an elderly woman farmer and her three daughters and two sons who were sharing two heavy horses. But as the slow-moving column neared the place of confrontation, the buzz of talk, the whistling, bursts of singing and chatter that surrounded the Mob, ceased.

There was tension in the air.

The long memories had brought support from dozens of villages. The number of men and women who had started out from Cantle was now greatly increased. It was as though people sensed that this confrontation with an employer had a great significance. It had, for they sensed also that there must soon be a climax to the events of the past month, the great outbreak of machine breaking, the destruction of grain stores and rickyards, the violent action against the poorhouses and foundries.

Eustace Goodenstone was the embodiment of 'Them', the 'Them' whom John Toose had always called the 'Enemy'.

Half a mile from the entrance to Monkswood Grange the head of the column was confronted by a representative of Squire Goodenstone's conscripted guard.

LATE AFTERNOON

I N A WINDOWLESS outhouse lit by a couple of flickering oil-lamps, Lidi did the laying-out of her father's body, washing down his breast . . . a triangle of three moles that she had no knowledge of; white belly; haunches . . . an old sickle-shaped scar – a small secret of the live body made public in death; white thighs that till now only her mother and Tansy had looked upon.

Strange to feel so dispassionate, so unemotional.

Impersonal as washing off a pike.

Adam's sister brought warm water, an old aunt plucked and pulled the sheet keeping the body as decent as she could in the circumstances.

Another woman stood, hands folded, and looked on as Lidi herself had done when Maisie Netherfield had tended Nana-Bess. It was the woman who earlier, in the kitchen, her family had greeted so dramatically and who had at once demanded their respect in the presence of her Pa's body.

She was the aunt who had been imprisoned, and who Adam had been so concerned for. Even now, Lidi could not help glancing at her from time to time. She had such an imposing presence that it was no wonder the prison officials had acceded to her demand that she be charged and brought before a Magistrate. No wonder too that the Magistrate had dismissed the charge for lack of evidence and she had been set free. She was like no rural woman that Lidi had ever met, except for Aunt Ju, who, although she too had a penetrating way of looking at people, did not have the height of a man that Mrs Baldwin had. If Adam had been brought up by her, it was no wonder he was fearless and confident.

To lay out a member of one's family is the last caring act that a woman can perform, done as a duty. It was never easy and so often handed over to the Maisie Netherfields of the world. The events of this day were so intense and overwhelming that Lidi's mind was in turmoil, darting about, trying to make some order out of the chaos.

Surprising that Pa should have such black body hair when the rest is silver. How much there is that we never know about other people, even somebody as close as your father.

Adam Tylee has a head of stiff, brown hair . . .

Luce's body is covered with hair as fair as that on his head. When I first saw him naked, it was the scar upon his back that had been a most masculine and stimulating fault – his body was so fair it seemed almost angelic. He said the scar was where his wings had been cut off.

On another level, she was conscious of the other three women standing ready with oils and combs and a plain unsmocked linsey round-frock.

They are my family. Too much to take in. We're members of the same family.

It was kind of them to have offered to do the laying-out, but Pa wouldn't like that, but I'm glad they're here. Even though these women are the skeletons that Pa thought were lying in wait for him – Adam's sister Selena, his tall stately adoptive mother, Mrs Baldwin, and his grandmother. That they hovered, silent and helpful, did not matter, they were here for Lidi. She appreciated the helpful dignity of the tall Mrs Baldwin and the kindness of old Mrs Hazelhurst – 'Lor dumble us, nobody an't called me Mrs in yers – call us Aunt Vinnie. It's what yer Ma called me.'

It was she, the old Aunt Vinnie, who had been the first to put it into words: 'An't no getting away from it – we'm relations.'

They helped her now to put her Pa into the linsey round-frock.

Was it some sense of their relationship that had given her that strange feeling of completion when they had made their hasty, fierce love on the night of Archangel? Momentarily, her body reacted at the sudden recall of it.

She looked up and found the kind eyes of Adam's grandmother upon her and inwardly blushed with guilt at the carnal subject of her thoughts on such an occasion.

Almost done now. For the present, they were marooned in the doldrums of time. Fifty years of her own – and their own – history had been spilled out in the hour before she started washing her Pa. Elsewhere, life went on as it had always done . . . strange to think of that.

A mile or two to the north, the meeting was probably taking place, or perhaps they were involved in a scene such as the one at the Archangel iron-foundry. There would be the noise of the metal ringing out as hammers and crowbars attacked the machines.

Lidi looked down upon her Pa. Clean, combed and decently

dressed, he was ready to be taken back to Cantle and buried with his beloved Hanny.

Now, with that important ritual accomplished, there appeared to be nothing to do but wait for Luce to come back here with Jack and Ginny. And with Adam Tylee. Her resolve, not to let him enter her thoughts, was destroyed by the new, exposed emotions that had been uncovered that day.

Lidi sat with her baby and Uncle Will. Mrs Baldwin treated them with a strange kind of formality, as did Selena and the huge Dan'l Hazelhurst. Her Uncle Daniel. Oh, so strange. Mother's brother. Extraordinary that brother and sister should be so opposite; he was much over six foot tall and as broad and solid as an oak tree . . . he had said that there were five others who had gone away to work in the mines and factories of the north, two were killed in an explosion. Her uncles. Extraordinary. Suddenly she had other relations who were closer blood-ties than Aunt Ju.

How on earth would Sarah take it? She lived only a few miles from here. Lidi could never predict how Sarah would react to anything. Time enough to think of that.

The simple-minded Charl, unable to curb his curiosity, screwed his head around the door from time to time. It was all so strange. Unbelievable. The old Auntie Vinnie had said let sleeping dogs lie, but Lidi wanted to know.

It was Mrs Baldwin who had taken the emotion out of it.

'It is very old history. I was not living here at the time, so I can take a more objective view – as no doubt you may be able to. My Uncle Dan (your grandfather) was a jealous and violent man, it appears that he hit my Aunt Jaen (your grandmother) because he suspected her of being too friendly with my Uncle France. He hit out at her in temper. You see, we are a big-made family. Their child saw it happen . . . Hanna, your mother that is, she went for her father with a knife. Poor child, I have often thought of her. Uncle Dan probably did not intend to do more than humiliate Aunt Jaen. He was transported to Botany Bay. Did you know none of this?'

Uncle Will patted Lidi's hand and shook his head.

'I think it was young Hanna, she thought that if it was never talked of, it'd stop buried for ever. Things like that never do.'

The old Auntie Vinnie said, 'I could a swore you was young Hanna come back when I first clapsed eyes on you.'

Suspected of being too friendly . . .

Luce had been suspicious that night . . . there had been no call for Luce to have come out of the house.

Sitting in the quiet kitchen waiting for the sound of the returning marchers, it gradually dawned upon Lidi that there was a family trait. She was shocked. Passion ruled their nature – she was one of them. That night she and Adam were careless of the consequences. At the moment when they had wanted one another, nothing else mattered. A grandmother who had loved her brother in the midst of the family, a grandfather with a temper violent enough to kill, a mother who had lashed out with a knife. A frightening inheritance. Perhaps Mother had realised it, and had thought that it could be coped with by growing up in ignorance of it.

Yet . . . yet . . . Lidi felt nothing ill here at Up Teg Farm. Quite the reverse, she liked the place. Although the house was poor and run-down, there was something good going on, nothing to put a finger on at once . . . just an atmosphere.

Uncle Will had been right, no matter how dreadful it was to those involved, that was no reason to deny others, like herself and Sarah, knowledge of the past. The Toose side of the family had skeletons enough, a footpad who was hanged, one who was burned as a witch . . . but the Toose skeletons were in the open; aired, they pranced about the village still, did a turn from time to time, were too familiar to cause anything but a smile. 'Lord save us Lidi, my Great-Uncle Fred was a rare old bugger in his time, ended up with a rope for a cravat.'

The last of the daylight went, and a lamp was lit in the kitchen and a candle in the outhouse for John Toose. It was obvious that, as back home these poverty-stricken days, candles were not frittered away and she had protested at the waste.

'Pa wouldn't wish it.'

''Tis the dues of the dead to have a bit a light. There's little enough we can do for the poor lad now,' old Aunt Vinnie said. 'One candle here nor there won't make no difference to our fortunes.'

Selena gave her tea to drink, another mark of their concern for her. 'Tea's better than anything when you've had a shock.' It was bitter and black from its long simmer, and sticky sweet from the huge rock of sugar dissolving in it.

All through those hours, Lidi felt herself existing on two levels – perhaps three, for there was that unexplored one that she could not yet look into, where there was grief for her Pa. On one level where she accepted and drank tea, she talked to Will Vickery and the members of the Up Teg household. On the other voices and thoughts tried to become sorted and ordered.

It was as though, with her father gone and the gap in her knowledge of her ancestry filled, Lidi was able to see what had in some way been obscured. It was almost like having the pieces of a broken jug that could not be put back together because there was a large piece missing around which several minor pieces fitted. Now that the missing piece was found and the jug made whole, Lidi could see and understand its shape and pattern.

But, the pattern that Lidi had supposed to be of some traditional form turned out to be something quite shocking – like one of those trick pictures that become something else when the viewpoint is altered. A bowl of roses turned upside down becomes a frightful demon.

To those who saw her as she sat dry-eyed nursing her baby, she appeared to be a young woman who was able to control her grief over the sudden death of her father.

SUNSET

SARAH, BACK IN her own kitchen, looked around it, and thought of what was ahead. If little Florence Broughlake was to grow up in comfort and security, then it was but right that her half-siblings too should be as well provided for. That thought led her suddenly to believe that this was why Mrs Delphine had called upon her one-time maid to take over the care of Hampton House and Arabella. A governess and a housekeeper would have seemed the more usual choice, but perhaps Mrs Delphine had felt a certain guilt at the thought of her lover's other children living in a cottage.

Whatever the reason, Sarah's heart bounded with delight at the thought of living in style – first hand this time, not in the reflected style as it had been at Stonebridge and in Italy.

FEW PEOPLE WERE left in Cantle that day. The old
squire, Henry Goodenstone, from where he had been
placed by his manservant looked out across the valley and, seeing a
trail of smoke on the far side, thought that it must be a rick burning.
*Eustace said that's what workers had taken to doing. Something like that.
Hadn't there been some soldiers here earlier? Come to quell the Mobs . . .
ah yes, that was it, the Mobs must have fired the ricks at Croud Cantle.
Such a pity, they were decent people over there. Haven't seen that girl
lately.*

He watched the smoke rise against Beacon Hill.

*Pretty, that young maid who lived there. Hair like a red cloud. Strange
sort of a girl. Jude! That was her name. Jude.*

The smoke drifted.

Ricks?

The old squire's discomposed memories drifted.

*Do they have ricks up there? . . . always thought that they were
cheesemakers. The maid with the red hair . . . the first time I saw her . . .
Lord . . . that's a few years ago . . . Yes . . . that old woman who had
come up to the house . . . she had something to do with it . . . what was
it . . .? Something to do with young Eustace shooting a poacher? . . .
Perhaps she's gone . . . ah, got it! She and Lotte were half-sisters. Why do
the men not put out that fire? Confound it, why can they not put a bell
within reach . . . What a fool not to have married Lotte. Aah! she'd have
livened them all up . . . Funny about that old woman who had come up to
the house about the poacher . . . They had said 'Mistress Nugent wished to
see the Master', and it wasn't Mistress Nugent, it was the daughter grown
old. Jude! That was her name. Aah . . . good, the smoke is dying down.
Lotte must be old too . . . Strange business. Lotte had lived here . . . and
she lived over there too . . . Good, the Dragoons must have put out the
fire . . .*

With that thought, the old squire, whose life had been devoted
to pleasing himself, left his unruly body and disordered mind.

As a consequence, at the time when the march reached
Monkswood, Sir Eustace Goodenstone's father's estates became

legally fused with those of his mother's family which he had already inherited at an earlier instant of death. Between one minute and the next, Sir Eustace Goodenstone, MP had become one of the ten most rich and powerful men in England.

23

EVENING

THE FIRST INTIMATION that something was wrong was when the old aunt jumped up as Dan'l Hazelhurst's son and Mrs Baldwin's daughter came in.

'Marry bless us, Barny lad,' the old aunt said, 'what have happened?'

'He fetched in the soldiers.'

Mrs Baldwin blenched at the sight of the two. 'Move your stumps, Charl, fetch my medicine bag.'

The two young people were battered and bloody and trembling. The girl Nan, hardly older than fourteen or fifteen, was covered with scratches and cuts, and when she unwound a bloodied cloth from her hand, the tips of three fingers were missing. The young man's hand hung down, twisted at a broken angle.

'Ssh! What's that? They're ringing a bob?' Dan'l Hazelhurst flung open the door and let in the gong-gong-gong of a church bell.

'It's t'others coming back,' Barny Hazelhurst said. 'We run off in every direction.'

Suddenly, the place was in turmoil.

Lidi and Will Vickery ran outside with Dan'l Hazelhurst, Charl and Selena Tylee, and the two older women remained in the house to tend the young people's injuries.

The roads and lanes through the village of Newton Clare were filled with people. Most of the daylight had gone but there was sufficient to show a chaotic scene. In the lane they found people wandering in a bewildered state, many were broken and bleeding. A thin man was tugging at sleeves asking the same question over and over, 'Have you seen my nipper? He's not all there . . . I don't know what happened to him . . . I lost my nipper . . . haven't anybody seen him?'

A tarred brand which was kept in the porch was ignited, showing up immediately the faces of people moving along the lane. At the sight of the flare, people moved towards it.

Fear clutched at Lidi. 'Jack, Uncle Will.'

'Don't start getting hetted up, m'dear. Ginny'll not have let him come to harm.'

Dan'l Hazelhurst was helping injured people into the yard; the huge man, who had kept out of the way ever since he put John Toose's body in the outhouse, was now everywhere at once, organising things without hesitation. 'Charl,' he roared, 'get that there tarred wood and set fire to it.' The youth raced off. 'Sel, go and tell Bet and yer Grandma there's people coming into the yard.' To Lidi and Will: 'You Missis and Master, if you will, open up the old barn.'

Not knowing which might be the old barn, they opened every outhouse door except that in which Lidi's father was laid, which they hastily barred with a sawing horse.

The tarred timbers that Charl Hazelhurst set fire to in the yard drew dozens of bewildered and wandering people to it. Here and there, in several yardlands and fields other small fires were started. Those among them who had been soldiers, might well have been reminded of fires in other fields where the remnants of a wounded and bedraggled army gathered after a battle.

But these people were not soldiers. Lidi felt sick with fear for Jack's safety. Luce. Adam. Ginny. Her instinct was to want to run searching in every direction at once. The dreadful image of the young girl with the missing fingertips as she had come into the room was frightful in the darkness. Jack and Ginny. She was responsible for them. How could she hope to find them in the growing dark, in all this chaos?

After a minute of confusion, common sense prevailed and Lidi began to help the ever-growing throng in the yard. Each person she tended she asked, 'Did you see a blind boy?' She asked many, before one woman said, 'There was one with the Captain – I seen the Captain trying to get the boy free.'

'Free?'

'The soldiers had took him.'

God above! Don't let it be Jack.

As the leader of every Mob was often called the 'Captain', it might have been Adam that the woman referred to, or perhaps the 'Captain' or leader from her own village. Many people were not able to give coherent answers, or contradicted what others told. It was almost impossible to believe that these were the same people she had walked with just that morning. They were villagers, farmworkers born to a brutal life, used to all manner of callous and harsh treatment . . . something quite terrible must have happened to shatter them like this.

And it had. It was revealed in fragments, and pieced together by a hundred bits of information.

'*They come on us out of the woods.*'

'*There waddn't no warning, except when Squire Goodenstone blew a hunt'n horn.*'

'*One chap let a gert lot a terriers out of a box. I reckon they'd been kep' shut up a purpose. They was crazed when they come at us. I tried to run . . . look!*' The man's arms and legs were torn to shreds. '*They waddn't all Goodenstone men, I recognised a bunch of the Duke's men from Stratfield.*'

Lidi asked the same questions again and again. Did you see a blind boy? What happened to the Captain?

'*Nobody could see proper what was happening – it's all thick woods there. Children started running into the trees, and women was trying to go after them, and there was all crying and shrieking . . . bugger to hell, I shan't never forget that.*'

Did you see a blind boy?

'*Blew his bloody hunt'n horn. And set about us like we was a pack of foxes. He was all dolled up like he was the Duke of Wellington. I never seen Goodenstone before, but I knew straightaway who he was. There was that much gold on his coat as'd paid a hundred men's wages for a week . . . and he kep' blowing that buggerin' horn.*'

Does anyone know what happened to the Captain?

'*Them at the back of the column, heard the shouting and shrieking and started to rush forward. Be jowned! It was the most terrible thing you could ever think of.*'

This woman had the same wounds as the Baldwin girl, except that a greater part and more of her fingers were missing. She scarcely seemed aware of her injuries. '*I seen my man go down under a horse and got trampled on. I couldn't get to him. It was the soldiers . . . they had sabres. I never knew he'd cut me till I saw the blood . . . I still can't feel them.*'

I wonder if you saw my brother – a blind boy.

A woman with her child slung across her breast. '*We was trapped on every side. It was the panic that made it worse. Them in the front couldn't go forward because that Sir Eustace was there and he had about six rows of his armed men on horseback. There was others hid in the woods. That never happened unless it was planned. He never meant to hold no talks with us. He even had covered carts and guards at the ready to take prisoners.'*

'They was laying in wait for us. The Captain never got a chance to even say anything. That bugger ordered us to go back, and before anybody could move hardly, he blew his horn and the dogs was released.'

'We was caught like rabbits in the last cut in a harvest-field.'

People came and went from other fires in other yards in Newton Clare but, unlike a field-station after an organised battle, there was no one waiting to dress and restore – here the medics had been in the forefront of the attack. They washed and anointed one another's wounds.

'Somebody said read out the Riot Act. There waddn't no riot. Some was shouting, somebody said summit about his gold braid, only saucy-like. Not a riot . . . no, never a riot.'

'We was trapped, because the Dragoons come up the main drive behind us.'

'God! They come at full gallop. I fought at Waterloo, but this was worst. Why, there was women and children there. There waddn't nothing to defend ourselves with except some of the stones from the driveway.'

'We waddn't doing nothing except ask him to pay decent money for our labour.'

'Some a they got their come-uppance, you should a seen one a they smithies that come over from Owlesbury way . . . Lord, he didn't half lambaste into one soldier who fell off his 'oss.'

Did you see a blind boy?

'You mean the one that plays penny-whistle on the market?'

'Yes, that's him.'

'Ahh . . . I seen him myself, being put in one of the wagons.'

'Hurt?'

'I don't reckon so, but it was all such a muddle there . . . such a bloody muddle.'

It turned out that many people had seen the Captain taken prisoner. Most of the Cantle Mob had taken the quickest route home, but by good fortune, a very distant Toose relation who knew Luce well, turned up in the Up Teg yard. 'Ah, your chap was arrested. Most of the ones at the front was took before they hardly knew what happened.'

24

NIGHT

B Y NINE O'CLOCK Sarah Lewis was very concerned. Her excitement at the prospect of telling Brendan of her meeting with Mrs Delphine had now turned to anxiety. Martha Cartwright had come back down to the cottage to tell Sarah that some of the men had gone out looking for Master Ninn, who, so it was said, had gone out to meet the Mob, and there'd been some trouble.

It was almost midnight when she heard a cart roll up to the cottage. Ninn Broughlake came to the door and two of Brendan's jockeys, carrying his splinted and bandaged inert figure on a board, brought Brendan into the room.

'It's all right Sarah . . . only a break. He is rather befuddled, the doctor has given him laudanum for the pain.'

It was a break. Brendan had gone down under the big hunter. The shin had fractured and its jagged edge forced through the muscle at the back of his leg.

Ninn Broughlake sat up with Sarah all night. Every vestige of youth seemed to have been wiped from his face. He was dishevelled and showed dark beard-growth on his chin. He looked very much like his father had when Sarah first went to Stonebridge – hard. He sat, frowning and withdrawn.

Once he said, 'By God, we cannot go on in the old ways. If it takes everything I've got, I shall get into Parliament. And I shall start a newspaper that will tell the truth about the state of real people. You called them that . . . "Real People" . . . do you remember? That time when we watched a ploughboy, going up and down so straight, he had bare feet and a great rent in his breeches. "That there's a real person," you said. I knew what you meant. I'd been a horrible brat to you.'

Sarah had not the slightest memory of the occasion.

ON THE MONKSWOOD Estate is a neat brick and tile house. In it, Eustace Goodenstone's Head Gamekeeper lives with his neat wife and three children, wholesome and clear-skinned from a diet of game and vegetables.

The children are fast asleep, and on any normal night, the Keeper and his wife too would be in bed.

The Keeper's wife sits spinning to occupy her uneasy fingers. From time to time the coal fire flickers, its light catches some coins scattered about the floor. The whir/clack, whir/clack and the rock of her feet slow as her eye yet again is caught by their gleam.

The Keeper sits gazing into the fire.

Sir Eustace has always held many hunting and shooting parties, the success of which is due to good gamekeeping. A good bag and the sporting men tipped generously. After a good hunt or a successful shoot, the Gamekeeper would come in with coins and he and his wife would sit and take pleasure in what they would do with the money.

The Keeper is a good and kind father. He is dour, but people like him. She has never seen him like this. The picture of him two hours ago is still vivid in every detail. He had stood in the doorway of the kitchen, thrust his hand into his deep pocket and taken out his kerchief knotted into a little money-bag, as he had done many times before. Before this evening, in all the years, never once had there been gold amongst the coins. He had tipped the sovereigns into one hand, weighted them, trickled them back into the other, then flung them towards the hearth as a man throws dice in a game of hazard.

The good wife's heart had leapt at the sight of the gold and she had let out the first note of delight as she made to pick up a piece of gold.

'Let it be! That's naught but shit.' Then, he had sunk into his own chair, in his own established place beside the hearth.

Twice she had attempted to ask.

'Bide quiet woman, or I'll learn you how!' He is a stern man, but his tone had never held such bitterness.

At midnight he stood up, thrust his hands deep into his breeches pockets, his head thrust forward at the hearth.

'Twenty-five years, man and boy. I first went beating when I was ten. I've flushed out everything, pheasants to quail, I've dug out badgers, and give him plenty of good stags and foxes.'

The anger in his voice seized up the treadle and froze the spinning-wheel.

'But Jesus in hell, wife, I never expected to join a master in hunting down hungry men and their childer.'

26

THE NIGHT IS almost at an end when Judeth Nugent gives up her strong spirit, or rather, the spirit is wrenched from her, as her wretched body battles against the effects of some ox-cheek broth which had been doled out to prisoners who had no-one to bring food into the barrack compounds. She had known that it was 'off' – prison food often was – but it was something at least to keep her going so that she could have her say on the day in December when she was at last to be brought before the Special Commission.

She longs for the feel of a pen in her fingers, the weight of her solid journal, the silky gloss and smell of a newly-turned page. With only one break, which had been when Jaen died, the entries in the journal go back to her girlhood, fulfilling her compulsion to record for a future generation the minutiae of the day-to-day lives of her family and neighbours. As soon as she had learned to read, it had come as a shock to her that she could find so little was written about the vast proportion of the people. *Why? There's more of us in the world than anybody.*

In her journal years ago – *'Kings and queens, generals, even silly princes, foolish princesses have books and poems and plays about their affairs – nobody knows what a cowman or milkmaid's thoughts were – not a single one that I can find.'*

It's important, Will.

Of course! Haven't I always said so?

I thought you looked amused.

No, 'tis but a bit of admiration slipped out through me teeth. Dear Will. How she longs for the feel of his wool-shirted body curled about her thin, old cold shoulders. At home, Will would have wrapped a warm stone in flannel and made a chamomile tea, chiding her for not caring enough for herself.

Aah . . . the pain's bad. Worse pain than the last time when the fever went through the compound. Three days squatting over the stream that ran through the camp.

The Commission, the Commission . . . concentrate!

The honing and polishing of her words have become almost an obsession during her time in prison. Over and over again. Sometimes, for a bit of fun, the other women who share the same portion of the dormitory as Jude Nugent, mimicked the odd old woman whose mouth moved as she rehearsed her speech silently.

'*Judeth Nugent, it is alleged that on the . . .*'

I've forgotten the days, since I made Will go home.

'. . . *of November, you did . . .*'

What am I charged with . . .? No good, it's gone.

'*Do you plead "Guilty" or "Not Guilty" as charged?*'

'*Not Guilty.*'

'*You must say "Not Guilty Your Honour".*'

'*Not Guilty . . . there is no "honour" in this place.*'

Someone groaned loudly.

'Shut up your noise, old woman, it's the middle of the night.'

I'm sorry I didn't know . . . Pain pain pain. *Sorry Kath, I got another fit of the gripes.*

Luce isn't the man for Lidi. Be honest about it.

She feels nauseous. That would be the final straw of indignity, to start vomiting in this place. Deny the feeling. Salty fluid flows from beneath her tongue and quells for a while the feeling of sickness.

Lidi's got intelligence and talent. Those garden books of hers are masterpieces of knowledge and ingenuity. If it was Jack, oh yes, then John would be giving every bit of encouragement to make something of them.

The only light in the fetid barrack-room comes through bars in the door.

'You all right, Miz Nugent? Hey? You all right? Lord alive, you an't half burning. I hope you an't got nothing catching.'

Shall you be content to stop home and mind the children then, Will Vickery, while I teach village children to read and write?

I know what they say, Will, she's a queer one – Jude Nugent.

I never asked you to bear the children, Will, only to take a share in washing and feeding them . . .

. . . what shrivels the spirit? . . . only poverty and ignorance.

The voices in her head are a long way off, hollow, echoing. Huge faces distort and become minute. Familiar faces whose names she cannot find.

'Listen old woman, you'm quite bad . . . can you hear me? Do you need a priest or anybody?'

. . . not just that, Will . . . it's the caging us up that I can't stand . . .

such a waste . . . a waste of women. Why do men believe that women aren't of any account? especially women like us. Women do count. Such a waste Lidi. We're too unimportant for anybody to write about. Women of no account . . . I always remembered that phrase 'in the eyes of the law, women are of no account'.

A beaker is against her lips; water fills her mouth and trickles out again.

'Come on old woman, take a sip, it ease your throat.'

Thanks Rosie. What's all that groaning and fuss? . . . writing an account of women . . . it's called The Lives of Women, *Mother. I want to show that we do count for something. An account of women of no account. Jaen, listen – 'women of no account, women of no account, women of no account.' I'm behind with my journal . . . Bella . . . Jaen . . . Hanna . . . Molly . . . Lotte . . . Rosie . . . Bessie . . . Maisie . . . Tansy . . . Sarah . . . Lidi . . . Belle. Fancy, so many of them ending with the same sound – it's called an 'endearment'. Rosalynda Rosalynda Rosalynda Rosalynda . . . hold me Rosie . . . don't go, I'm so hot.*

Four women now stand around Judeth Nugent's burning form and wish that they had some herbs to burn to keep the fever from leaping upon them.

'What are you trying to say, Miz Nugent?'

'Keep . . . safe . . .'

The journal Lidi.

Ach the pain – I can hardly bear to move. Breathe . . . in and out . . . slowly aah. Sorry Kath. Sorry Rosie.

A sudden disappearance of the pain and a cool breeze.

Aah, that's better. I shall change my plea to 'Guilty'. My limp is bad these days. An old woman limping into the dock. And I will say 'I be that sorry yer Honour. I don't know what come over me.' 'Nugent, you have been a foolish and irresponsible woman. Seven days' imprisonment – which means that you may go free now.'

I will take over Auryn so that Lidi can spend all the time she wants doing her books of plans . . . Ginny can learn to make the pies . . . Thank goodness that pain's gone.

In the early hours one of the women rattled the wooden door.

'Oit! You . . . Screw! Come on open up. The old woman in here's gone.'

27

I N THE UP TEG outhouse, John Toose, who for a lifetime had been one of those instrumental in arousing his neighbours to awareness and action, had developed full rigor.

As well he would never know the awfulness of the day on which he died. He would have found it incredible that such catastrophe could be the outcome of a peaceful protest march, a delegation, a meeting with an employer. He had always argued for peaceful protest on a large scale. 'No, it is not intimidation. It is justified action in a just cause. Working people have got no power except their collection together, and we must use it.'

Throughout that evening, and far into the early hours, too much attention was needed for the living for anyone to see that the bit of light that was the due of the dead, had long since guttered out.

PART SIX

Special Assizes – Winchester

20 DECEMBER 1830

THE COURTROOM AT Winchester was huge and dark and bitterly cold. It would be mid-day before the Special Commission opened, but people had gathered before dawn to get one of the few places not reserved for sightseers of quality, and at ten o'clock when the public gallery opened, it filled up at once.

The two women pressed close together combining the warmth of their bodies. Lidi and Adam's sister had met only twice since their first dramatic meeting, but there was an instinctive liking each for the other. Lidi felt more at ease with Selena Tylee than she ever had with her own twin.

'I should have liked her even if she was not Addy's friend,' Selena had told her adoptive mother, Mrs Baldwin.

In the press for places in the public gallery the two young women had been separated from Selena's aunt and cousin Nan, who had managed to find space at the front.

Will Vickery had been in Winchester to see where Judeth was buried, and he had stood with the women during the long wait outside the grey castle walls till they were allowed into the public gallery. When at last they reached the door he had turned away. 'I don't think I shall be staying after all, m'dear. I'll be away back home and see what can be done to the old place.' Squeezing her shoulders emotionally, he had kissed her and turned away.

Lidi, like all her kind, women whose lives are a constant struggle to keep themselves and their families alive, cannot allow herself the luxury of tears and weeping. Weeping is for those who believe that it is their right to be happy and at ease. Lamentation demands attention. Tears are for those with time to shed them. Lidi had remained dry-eyed for the loss of her Pa and for Aunt Ju, but the sight of Uncle Will's withheld grief over the death of the woman he had loved since they were young, was heart-breaking. He had become almost obsessive in talking about 'getting the old place on its feet again'.

When they had eventually received the news of Jude Nugent's death and interment in the Winchester graveyard, Will Vickery had said, 'It does not matter where we drop our remains, m'dear. You can be sure Judeth's spirit will get itself up on Tradden Raike.' And that is where it was, close to those Cantle chalkhills where Jude had wandered for sixty years, that Will Vickery wanted to live out whatever time he had remaining. Working on the repair of the cottage would keep him going.

The touch of a warm hand upon her own, brought Lidi back to awareness. She smiled briefly at Sel, 'I was miles away, wondering how Uncle Will is going to manage.'

'I should not worry, he seems to be a man who can take care of himself.'

'He seems to have got old very suddenly.'

'It's what he needs – to rebuild something.'

'There's plenty to be done.'

There was indeed.

On the day of the fire, Tazey James, whose stump of leg had been too inflamed to allow him to join his neighbours on their march, had seen the pall of smoke rise from Croud Cantle, and had arrived there in time to help Hetty in her frantic rush back and forth from the Dunnock. They saved the house, although some timbers and most of the thatch was gone.

It had been the young Barny Hazelhurst whose arm had been broken in the affray, who had helped Lidi and Will trundle John Toose's body home the next day, and they arrived to find Ginny, Hetty and Tazey at work clearing up.

Lidi had stood in the yard, filled with anger and frustration at this new blow. She felt six years old. *It's not fair!* She did not know then that the demon of ill-fortune was still by no means finished with her family.

In the body of the courtroom, ponderous men in peculiar clothes came and went. Each time a door opened, or when some petty official walked in, the rumble of talk from the public gallery fell, only to rise again when nothing more interesting happened than the placement of a paper or a flask of water.

'Shall you be able come every day, Sel?'

'No. We only came today in the hope that we shall discover when Addy and our neighbours will be brought up. We've got very little land left, enough to grow our own vegetables and we run a pig on the Common. I get what work I can as a casual dairy-maid. If it wasn't for Adam, and an occasional bit of help from the uncles up north . . . Father couldn't have had a better skill to hand on to Addy than well-digging. He can earn as little or as much as we need, then he's free to go about speaking at meetings and what he calls following his conscience.' She stretched her head to see where her tall aunt was standing. 'Aunt Bet's not a stupid woman, yet she insists that they will not convict Addy. She seems to believe that the Judge will see directly into Addy and know that he could not commit a base act.'

'We all have to hang on to something. I'm sure she knows the truth of it.' *I know it.* Lidi tried to reject the word that summed up the truth of what she knew. *Transportation.* Dear God, how could she stand it, not to see Luce and Adam for years and years. Since their joint arrest, they had often melded into one whole being in her mind. 'I've already made up my mind that Luce will not be back home for a few months. But I just hope against hope that at least they will let Jack go. It's going to be hard to do with, with Pa, Aunt Ju and Luce all gone at once.'

They fell silent again, their arms linked to give one another warmth and encouragement. Lidi, glad to have such a restrained companion on such an occasion, withdrew, as she had done again and again, into the terrible events of 24 November and the month that followed which led directly to today and the imminent opening of the Special Commission.

That day had seemed to be the climax of the disturbances. During this last month, there had been only a few sporadic outbreaks of disturbed peace.

People were exhausted, dejected, defeated.

Perhaps it was the knowledge that in almost every county in England south of Norfolk and east of Somerset – ordinary men and women like themselves were languishing in overcrowded cells. Perhaps the spirit of the farm-labouring community had been broken.

The day after the 24th was the worst day in the remembered history of both Cantle village and Croud Cantle Farm. There would never now be a worse one, for there was a sullen knowledge that Cantle village was finished. Whatever happened to the Goodenstone Estate, for certain no Cantle family would ever be employed there again. The limp hand of Sir Harry had handed over to the fist of Sir Eustace. He had already brought poor Irish labour onto his estates. Bitterness had already begun to ferment, fatalism to set in.

'We'm finished.'

Since the advent of the 'Tin Church' in the village, that was where most assemblies took place. It was there, on the 25th of November, that the whole village had gathered to exchange what information they had of the missing members of one another's families, and give release to their shock by the telling.

It was how Lidi learned that because Jack had played his tin-whistle for pennies along the way, he had been arrested as one of those who had 'demanded money with menaces', and had learned too that when Luce had tried to drag Jack away from his captors, he had been arrested as well.

'You can be proud of your man, Miz Draper.'

It was how she learned also that Adam Tylee had fared very badly. There were confusions and contradictions about what happened, but a general truth emerged from the collective memory of the people in the Tin Church.

'It was the Captain they was out to get.'

'That's true! He been a thorn in their sides too long.'

'Him and about twenty others went forward as a delegation to ask Sir Eustace to talk with 'em.'

'Ah, but that bugger . . . he sat at the back of his Specials on his 'oss, it was the parson who said we must turn back or we should all be arrested. Well, you can imagine . . . there was a blimmin great roar of laughter at that. Somebody ast if he was going to arrest all six-hunderd on us single-handed.'

'But They waddn't in no laughing mood. I reckon They was edgy, They was beginning to get worried that the Dragoons wouldn't get there in time.'

'The ole parson says, "You be guilty of trespass." "Sir," says the Captain, "you know me to be a man of peace" (you could tell that they two had cross swords before that day). "I know you for preaching sedition and free living," says the parson . . . and the Captain just grinned at him.'

'That was when the bugle sounded a bit distant. (Did you hear him sound?) I heard him – it's what the Sir Eustace had a bin waitin' fer to hear, he knowed it was the Dragoons and we was hemmed in. He come through the middle of his Specials and nodded for the parson to get back. Then some daft bugger calls out, "Let's have him down off of his high horse", then somebody starts off "bread or blood, bread or blood".'

'Christamighty, did you hear the Captain shout when he heard that? "No, no neighbours," he says, "we come peaceable." Then he says to the Master, " 'No violence' is our motto, not even to a single flower" (Marry, if he didn't make your heart soar when he put on that voice of his). He says, "If you agree to speak with this delegation of twenty, then the rest will go out and wait on the downs." '

'Ah . . . then somebody lobs a stone, and knocks the parson's hat all askew. I reckon that scared him enough to piss in his britches, he went that white. "You was warned," the parson says, "this is a riotous assemblage; the Magistrate shall read the Riot Act." He beckons one of the others to come. Then Sir Eustace comes up front. "No," he says, "I am a Magistrate and this Magistrate will do" says the Master, pointing to hisself, and he pulls out a paper and waves it about. That's when we heard all the commotion – it must of been somewhere down by the gates.'

'Christ ah! Then all hell let loose.'

Very many Cantle people had been arrested, mostly men, youths and young women, but none had death and loss of home added to their distress, as did Lidi and Will Vickery at Croud Cantle Farm.

But for the village as a whole, it was a tragedy too great to take in at once.

In the Tin Church, Lidi had felt unbalanced, almost in a drunken state; it was as though her mind could not take in any more of it without overflowing. It was as well that the news of Jude Nugent's death did not reach Cantle for another couple of days, by which time her aunt was already buried in Winchester.

Mid-day tolled out all over Winchester. Outside, in the bitter cold, people waited to catch a glimpse as the Law of the Land made its plush velvet way into the Castle, to dispense threadbare corduroy justice.

A hush fell over the courtroom.

A little after noon, the sails of the windmill of the Special Commission began to turn and thus to start in motion its heaviest grinding-stones.

2

SPECIAL COMMISSION – a report by *The Times* Special Correspondent, Winchester.

The appearance of this city this morning presented a scene of unusual activity and bustle. A considerable number of persons, many of them witnesses, and many the friends of the prisoners, came into town at an early hour.

There are upwards of 300 prisoners for trial; a vast proportion of that number committed for very serious offences. The prisoners are here to be classed according to the nature of the offence:- Riot and robbery 66. Robbery 43. Riotous Assembly and destroying factories or foundries 61. Riotous Assembly and destroying threshing machines 39. Riotously assembling to the terror of the King's subjects 62. Various and many other indictments including: Sending of threatening letters, refusing to disperse, demanding money, demanding drink, illegal assembly and destroying the Poor House of the Four Parishes of Blackbrook. (There were upwards of 300 assembled on this occasion.)

It must seem strange that notwithstanding all we had heard of fires in this county, there is not one commitment for arson.

The Commissioners entered accompanied by the High Sheriff; Mr Baron VAUGHAN presided; Mr Justice JAMES PARKE sat on his right and Mr Justice ALDERSON on his left. The other Commissioners were also present.

The DUKE OF WELLINGTON (the Lord Lieutenant of the county) arrived shortly after them.

Following the usual solemnities, the grand jury was sworn in.

Among the members of which were:

The Rt Hon Sir G. W. Rose, Bart, JP
The Rt Hon Sir Eustace Goodenstone, JP, MP
Sir Henry Titchborne, Bart, MP
Sir C. Hulme, Bart
Sir W. Heathcott

Sir Tomas Baring, Bart, MP
Sir J. Curtis, Bart
Sir J. W. Pollen, Bart
Sir T. B. Lethbridge, Bart
Thos. Thistlethwayte, Esq.
John Humby, Esq.
Henry Coombe Compton, Esq.

Mr Baron Vaughan then proceeded to address the court.

Referring to the alarming state which was said to have originated in the distress of the lower orders, to a certain extent it may be so, yet he said, it is to be feared that there are persons who, for the basest purposes, have greatly exaggerated the pressure and extent of the evil and have used it as a means of carrying out their own wicked designs. The object of such men is to represent the rich as the oppressors of the poor, and to dissolve that bond of mutual kindness which ought to unite the various classes.

At the end of his long address, Mr Vaughan concluded: 'Gentlemen, I have done, I have been much gratified by your attention to me. You will retire to your chamber, and proceed to despatch the important business that awaits your deliberation.'

(It has been intimated that, in view of the great numbers of people indicted, it is likely to be found necessary for there to be a sitting of the Special Commission after churchtime on Christmas Day.)

Hampshire Clarion, 24 December 1830

The result of the enquiry into a death by hanging is announced today. The body of one James Arthur McCabe, a Keeper on the Monkswood Estate at Cherton, was, earlier this month, found hanging from a tree in deep woods on that Estate in the early hours of the morning. Readers will perhaps recall that this was the scene of a recent mobbing and rioting.

McCabe left a wife and two small daughters, and had been a respected employee of Sir Eustace Goodenstone since boyhood.

An open verdict is recorded.

SHORTHAND NOTES, Special Assize, Winchester.
DEFENDANT – TOOSE, John known as Jack.

INDICTMENT – Demanding Money with Menaces.

WITNESS:

When the Mob arrived I asked, 'What do you want, my lads?'

'Money,' they replied.

'Money you shall not have,' I told them.

'Money or blood then,' they said, and the others called 'bread or blood, Master'. One of them moved to strike me but did not. I signalled for my men to move. They knocked down some of the mobsters and the rest fled, taking the Defendant with them.

DEFENDANT:

Yes Sir. I was with the Cantle Mob, but I did not demand money from any man.

No sir, there was no pressure put upon anyone that I was ever with.

Some of the men would take me to a farmer and I would play a tune upon my penny whistle, and usually the farmers would give us a few pence and some bread. It was the way we kept going on days out. Very many people were for us and gave willingly, sir. If they did not, then we left. Though sometimes we did jeer at them for their tight-arsedness.

Yes sir, we were collecting money.

Yes sir, I heard the call 'bread or blood'; it is often called out. Nothing bad is meant by it sir, 'tis often said with a laugh. Sir, may I say this – because of my poor sight, I have very sharp ears . . . sir, I did not recognise the voice of the one who shouted, and I would swear that it did not come from where we were standing.

I wasn't suggesting anything, sir – only that we're charged with Menaces, and I'm sure it wasn't one of us that said 'bread or blood'.

Thirteen sir – thirteen last September.

COMMISSIONER:

It is quite apparent to me that you have been led to engage in this practice of collecting on many occasions. On the last occasion, when you were arrested on Sir Eustace Goodenstone's estate, you were found in the possession of a bag of money. The fact that you maintain that you were merely the guardian of the so-called 'funds' has no bearing upon the sentence you shall receive – no more does the fact that you have such small eyesight as to render you almost blind. However, you are still a youth, and as you were not the ring-leader, your sentence shall be commensurate with the part you took in this evil deed against an innocent gentleman.

SENTENCE:

Eighteen months to be served at Portsmouth.

DEFENDANT – DRAPER, Luce.

INDICTMENT – Joining an Unlawful Assembly.

INDICTMENT – Resisting an Officer of the Law in the Execution of his Duty.

INDICTMENT – Breaking a Machine the Property of Archangel Foundries.

INDICTMENT – Breaking with others a Water-wheel the Property of Archangel Foundries.

WITNESS:

There is no mistaking that this is the same man as the one breaking the machine at the Archangel Foundry. I saw his white hair very noticeable, Yer Honour.

WITNESS:

It is true sir, that I was there. I was pressed by the Mob to join them.

No sir, I have not come here today in no vengeful spirit.

Eleven children sir, the youngest be six weeks.

Yes sir. I now have employment feeding the b'ilers at the foundry.

Yes, Yer Honner, it is a great relief to me to be in employment.

DEFENDANT:

Yes sir, I went with the marchers to Blackbrook on the day of the sacking of the Workhouse.

No sir, I did not. My job that day was to carry out the sick and elderly.

Yes sir, I was with the previous Defendant on that day.

Yes sir. And I would do it again if I saw a defenceless blind lad being attacked so savagely. Especially one related to me by marriage.

Yes sir, I do realise that he was resisting arrest. But I doubt that he knew that that was what was happening at the time.

The witness may have seen a man with white hair – as you see sir mine is pale yellow.

No, Your Honour, my livelihood has never been threatened directly by the introduction of threshing machines.

May I say this sir, a man with a wife and child does not need much imagination to understand how another such man feels when *his* family is starving because of the introduction of machines.

Sir, I *do* believe that it is my affair, and that of every one of us to support our neighbours in their struggle for better wages.

COMMISSIONER:

It is difficult to understand men such as you. You are above the lower orders and can read and write. You had no personal reason to go about the countryside breaking machines. I find the excuse of compassion for your neighbours a poor one. Suddenly and without warning you turned from a respectable member of a family in a small way of business, into one of the wicked and turbulent men of whom we have seen far too many in that dock of late.

SENTENCE:

Transportation to Van Dieman's Land for seven years.

DEFENDANT – TYLEE, Adam (alias 'the Captain')

INDICTMENT – Sedition.

INDICTMENT – Conspiracy.

INDICTMENT – Provoking a Riot.

INDICTMENT – Breaking a Threshing Machine.

INDICTMENT – Planning the Destruction of Public Property, namely the Four Parishes Workhouse at Blackbrook.

INDICTMENT – Riotous Assembly.

WITNESS:

When the Mob broke into the Parishes Workhouse, I heard the Defendant proclaim, 'We shall have him for putting women between the shafts of the parish cart.'

WITNESS:

I was Assistant Overseer of that institution. When the Mob broke in, that man was at its head. When the terrible deed was done, there was scarcely a single brick left joined to its neighbour.

WITNESS:

There were said to be six hundred in the Mob. The Defendant was at its head. I held up my hand and bade them turn about, but he would not. 'No Sir,' he said, 'these people have come to request that a delegation of them meet with their Master.' (I have to say, Your Honour, that the Defendant did not raise his voice, and was most polite in his manner.)

WITNESS:

My Master pulled from the breast of his jacket a rolled paper which he proceeded to read. He told me later that it was called The Riot Act.

Yes sir. I am quite sure that I heard him read it.

Yes sir. There was a great deal of noise, but I am sure that I heard it read.

No sir, I did not receive any payment for that day's work above a small bonus such as we labourers always receive when there is a hunt or a shoot.

I cannot rightly remember the amount.

Yes sir, I think I do remember that I received a sovereign.

No sir, it was not that which prompted me to speak against the Defendant. I have a good and generous master and did not like to see the Mob against him.

DEFENDANT:

No sir, I was not the ringleader. There was no ringleader. As a democratic body, we elected one to speak for the many. I had the honour to be that one on several occasions. I was chosen on that day.

COMMISSIONER:

Clearly these are most serious offences.

We have heard that six hundred men and women banded themselves together with the sole purpose of forcing an employer to raise the wages of his labour.

Outrages like this make one wonder whether one is in a civilised country.

During the course of these hearings, we have heard many times, evidence of a class of artisans, such as yourself, throwing in their lot with the lower orders. This is a complete riddle to us. Till the time of the riots, your character has been irreproachable and yet, suddenly, without warning, you were turned into a wicked and turbulent man. You went about the countryside as a leader. People called you their 'Captain'. You spoke against the Government of this country and broke its laws. In the opinion of this bench, such men as you deserve severer punishment than the labourers. It was your duty to set an example to the poor. You did not, you were their spokesman.

DEFENDANT:

It is my right to address you before sentence is passed and this I do gladly so that those of us who speak up for those who may not, or cannot, speak for themselves, shall no longer be a riddle to Your Honour.

Having seen the harsh sentences handed out to men and women whose only crime was that they had hungry children to feed, I am in no doubt as to what my own fate may be. Even so, if I were let free tomorrow, I would do the same again.

I hold the belief that God did not create rich and poor, wealth and poverty, plenty and hunger. He did not put upon the earth one class of person to be in servitude to another. Nor did He put power in the hands of the few to the detriment of the many.

These are the evil creations of mankind.

Sirs, I had the great fortune to have been brought up in a family where sociality is practised, so that from an early age I was aware of the benefits of individuals associating together for the benefit of the whole . . .

Yes sir . . . I am aware that this is not the hustings – but I am entitled to make a statement before you pronounce sentence, and I shall not forgo that right.

You say that such men as I are a riddle to you . . . Sir, that you did not even *think* to include women in that statement is an indication of your entire ignorance of the people on whom you sit in judgement here. In France, there is a new word in common use amongst people of my persuasion; before long it will be a word in common usage – the word is '*Socialisme*'.

Socialisme springs from the belief that people (not only men, but women and men) are entitled to share equally, to contribute fairly and live in peace and care for one's neighbour.

That sir, is the answer to your riddle – I believe in this *Socialisme* and I am willing to fight for it. Prepared to die for it, as was He who was the first to convert others to this better way of life – though I dare say you will not nail me to a cross.

SENTENCE:

Death by Hanging.

3

THE TIMES, 1831: Winchester, Friday 7th January

The scenes of distress in and about the gaol are most terrible. The number of men who are to be torn from their homes and connexions is so great that there is scarcely a hamlet in the county into which anguish and tribulation have not entered. Wives, sisters, mothers, children, beset the gates daily and the Governor of the gaol informs me that the scenes he is obliged to witness at the time of locking up the prison are truly heartbreaking.

You will have heard before this of the petitions which have been presented to the Home Office praying for an extension of mercy to all the men who now lie under sentence of death. A similar petition has been got up in this city. It is signed by the clergy of the Low Church, some of the bankers and every tradesman in the town without exception.

Application was made to the clergy of the Cathedral for their signatures, but they refused to give them, except conditionally, upon reasons which I cannot comprehend.

Surely, of all classes of society, the clergy is that which ought not to be backward in the remission of offences. They are daily preaching mercy to their flocks, and it wears but an ill grace when they are seen refusing their consent to a practical application of their own doctrines.

Whatever my own opinion may be, as a faithful recorder of the opinions of those around me, I am bound to inform you that, except among the magistracy of the county, there is a general, I had almost said a universal, opinion, among all ranks of society, that no good will be effected by sacrificing human life.

The *Blackbrook Herald*, 1831: Monday, 17th January.

Public opinion has saved the lives of four of the six men who had been left for execution. The two who were hanged were

Cooper and Cook. But the Government and the judges were, determined that the lessons of civilisation should be imposed upon the wretches who were not to join their fellows on the gallows.

They were compelled to witness the last agonies of the two men whom public opinion was unable to rescue.

The Times, 1831: Winchester, Monday 17th January.

The wretched comrades of the men who were hanged suffered as acutely as the Commissioners themselves could have desired.

At this moment I cast my eyes down into the felons' yard, and saw many of the convicts weeping bitterly, some burying their faces in their smock frocks, others wringing their hands convulsively, and others leaning for support against the wall of the yard and unable to cast their eyes upwards . . .

This was the last vision of English justice that each labourer carried to his distant and dreaded servitude, a scene that would never fade from his mind.

There was much that England had not taught him.

She had not taught him that the rich owed a duty to the poor . . . that the mere labourer had a share in the State, or a right to be considered in its laws, or that it mattered to his rulers in what wretchedness he lives or in what wretchedness he dies.

But one lesson she had taught him with such savage power that his simple memory would not forget it, and if ever in an exile's gilding dream he thought with longing of his boyhood's famine-shadowed home, that inexorable dawn would break again before his shrinking eyes and he would thank God for the wide wastes of the illimitable sea.

PART SEVEN

The Women of No Account

JANUARY 1831

'I WOULD HAVE come before this, Lidi, but you know what it is . . . all the upheaval at the cottage . . . seeing to the house . . . Brendan's leg is slow to mend. And what with the child.' Now five months' pregnant, Sarah's neatly-clad figure was rounded and plump. She laid a hand upon her waist.

The two sisters stood in the kitchen at Croud Cantle where last they had been together on the occasion of John Toose's funeral tea. Sarah looked prettier than Lidi had ever seen her.

'You look well on it, Sarah. Sit down, and I'll pour some cordial.'

'I can't stop long.'

'I wish you'd brought the babies.'

'It's rather cold out . . . and as Brendan's still not able to get back to the stables . . .'

'Of course. Perhaps when the better weather . . .'

Sarah sipped the hot blackcurrant.

You're already in the part. Nearly pass for a gentlewoman.

'When will you move then?'

'Mrs Delphine will remove to Italy in February and we shall go to Stonebridge within the month. She had thought there would be a legal battle for Miss Arabella, but Master Ninn is standing as guardian, so there's nothing that the grandparents could do.'

'And is Brendan happy about the arrangements.'

'Of course. Who would not be? A nice house, with plenty of help. Wages properly drawn up in an agreement on paper signed and sealed. It won't really make much difference to Brendan. He will still work at the racing stables.'

'So the house is to be yours.'

'For life.'

'Have some gingerbread, I made it specially.'

They smiled politely at one another as Sarah daintily accepted the cake, like two ladies in a drawing room.

Sarah took a small bite. 'Lidi . . .' She paused briefly and removed a tiny crumb from the corner of her lip with her little finger. 'I'm sorry it's been so bad for you lately. I wish I could have done more to help. You've had the brunt of it all, Pa . . . the fire . . . and without a husband. It's terrible, terrible . . . seven years . . .'

'Don't!' The word came out much more loud and fierce than Lidi had intended, then she lowered her tone. 'Don't please – I don't like to talk about it.'

'But it's why I've come.'

This was flashpoint for Lidi.

'I had wondered why. You didn't come when I could have done with you here. Hardly a roof over our heads, Uncle Will trying to do the work of three men. Me and Hetty and Ginny trying to keep Toose's going. You visited Pa's funeral like some distant cousin . . .'

'That's not fair. Brendan looked as though he might lose his leg at one time.'

'I thought you'd got help.'

'Only a maid-general.'

'And an old woman who keeps an eye on the babes for you?'

'It is a big undertaking, this position at Stonebridge. You make it sound as though I don't care.'

'No, only that you left it a long time before finding out how we would manage. I didn't expect you to come and mend the roof . . . but I thought you might have *asked* how we were managing.'

'There's a man and three able-bodied women here – and you've only got the one babe.'

'This place *and* what's left of Toose's to keep going between us.'

'You might as well admit it, Lidi, Toose's is finished, it was gone downhill ever since Pa's first seizure.'

Lidi turned her flushed face away and took a slow breath.

'Don't let's fall out, Sarah. I'm glad you've come. I haven't got anybody of my own left except for Auryn and Uncle Will. I just would have liked to have seen you once or twice.'

'Well, it won't be for ever till Jack gets out.'

'Another year.'

'That judge must be the hardest man on the face of the earth.'

'He got off lighter than most of the others who were found guilty of taking money with menaces.'

'Jack never menaced anybody in his whole life.'

'No more did most of the others who got longer sentences than Jack.'

'It will kill the lad.'

'It won't. Jack's one of those who survive. Don't worry, he'll come out of it well enough. Pa would have been proud of him when he spoke up in his own defence. Not many of them did that.'

'What will you do?'

'Just carry on as well as we can. I'm teaching Ginny to make Croud Cantle pies from Aunt Ju's receipts. She and Hetty Bone take them to Blackbrook and Waltham markets. Uncle Will and I do the rest together. Do you remember Robby Netherfield?'

'No.'

'Perhaps not. One of old Maisie's husband's family. He was navvying on the canal and came over to pay his respects at Maisie's grave, and decided to stop on in Cantle.'

'Lord, what a time to come to Cantle; he can't be very clever, stopping here when there's no work.'

'He's helping us.'

'I thought you said . . .'

'Until Robby Netherfield came, there *was* only ourselves. Robby's like all the Netherfields – gets on without any fuss. I don't know what we should do without him.'

'You would manage, Lidi. You always could. It's something I've always envied you . . . that you don't let things get you down.'

Lidi looked steadily at her twin. *Don't let things get you down? You don't know the half nor quarter of it.*

'Are you still thick with the cousins over at Newton Clare?'

'I don't know about "thick". We keep in touch. At the trial, I spent some time with two of the cousins Selena and Nan. And Mrs Baldwin. She's our mother's cousin – brought up Adam Tylee, you've heard of him? . . . the one they called the "Captain".' Lidi tried, as she had tried on previous other occasions, to bring Adam's name naturally into conversation – make him real for a moment. She felt her colour rise and saw Sarah look at her searchingly.

'He got off in the end, didn't he?'

'How can you call transportation for life "getting off"? He wasn't hanged.'

'And what about cousin "Captain" Adam then?'

Emotional friction charged the air around them; at any moment a word could cause lightning to flash and a storm to begin. Lidi earthed the danger with a frank look.

'I had grown to like him very much. To be honest, I don't think that you can ever get over hearing a sentence of death, let alone someone who you . . .'

'Love? Isn't that it, Lidi?'

Lidi looked her sister straight in the eyes – it was Sarah who looked away.

'Perhaps . . . but not just the bedding together kind.' Lidi wanted to hurt her sister for abandoning her just when she most needed her. 'I don't think that you know the meaning of the word, Sarah. Love involves passion and commitment.'

'You think that I don't love Brendan?'

'Not really . . . not with passion – nor commitment. I do believe that he loves you though.'

Sarah hunched her shoulders as though it was of no consequence. 'There's more to life than that kind of thing.'

'Houses and servants?'

'Security. Bread in the mouths of my children.'

'It's what we all want for our children.'

'As well as the passion?'

'When I use that word, I don't mean what happened between you and Alec James.'

Now it was Sarah's turn for her cheeks to flush. 'What is that supposed to mean?'

'Oh, don't worry, nobody will ever hear it from me. I think Tazey James would like to know that he has grandchildren . . . but that's your business. I'm glad that I know now all about our ancestors – I feel complete. I shall not keep anything from my children when they are old enough to understand. Not like we were kept ignorant.' Suddenly, Lidi felt drained. 'Ah well, that's a long time ahead. I shall be thirty-five by the time Luce has served his sentence.'

Sarah put down her beaker and rose. 'I should be going. You are right, Lidi, you and I should not fall out. It's strange that we should look so much alike, yet have turned out so different. If I've been selfish and hurtful, I'm sorry.' She touched Lidi's sleeve. 'But please try to understand, I always hated this way of life – the life here in Cantle. I escaped it and began to climb up out of it, only to slip back. Next time, I was helped up by Brendan. This position at the Dower House is something I would never have imagined for myself in my wildest fantasy. I'll hold on to this with both hands. Perhaps it has made me self-centred and apparently unconcerned.'

You would have been one of those to have been a witness against your neighbours if it had come to it. Excusing yourself, to yourself, justifying getting what you can whilst you can.

'Take no notice of my outburst, Sarah. I've been a bit like that lately.'

'I kept *intending* to come. There . . . I still haven't said what I came for. Brendan says that you are not to go without, we shall not be badly off, and we couldn't rest easy knowing that you and Auryn wanted for any necessaries.'

'That's really kind. I hope that we shall not need to bother you. Anyhow, it is nice to know that the offer is there. It's a funny thing you know, Sarah, in this last month or so, since I've had to fend for myself I am doing really quite well.'

'Well, that's good. I'm glad to hear it. Aunt Ju always had a nice regular little trade for the pies and stuff, it's a shame if you let it go.'

Sarah pulled on some gloves. Lidi could imagine her in five years' time, as trim and neat as she had always been. Standing no nonsense from maids-general, cooks or any other servant, she would rule her household well – as any poacher turned gamekeeper runs his gamepark well.

In five years, you won't acknowledge us . . . nay, three years.

'Will Mrs Broughlake leave furnishings for you?'

'Oh yes . . . that's what I meant to ask . . . whether you would like one or two of the things from the cottage.'

'I wasn't asking for that . . . I meant were you expected to furnish the house yourselves.'

'I know you weren't. But there are several things that I shall not take with me. Brendan could arrange for them to be carried over here.'

'We aren't exactly overburdened with furniture – the fire . . .'

'All right then. I will arrange it. And now I must get back. I have to see Mrs Delphine again, she is engaging a governess for Miss Arabella.'

Lidi understood quite clearly that the days of their relationship were ended. *Has there ever been one? I was closer to Tansy – I'm already closer to Selena.*

'What's that big sigh for?'

Walking across the yard to where a neat pony and a neat trap were waiting. 'Did I? It didn't mean anything. Don't lose touch, Sarah.'

'Lose touch? Lord, Lidi, it's less than ten miles to Shorlay.'

'And send a message as soon as the baby's born.'

'I will.' A brief pause. 'And you do the same.'

This last was not said casually.

'The same?'

'Send *me* a message. You're pregnant, aren't you Lidi? Only poddy women place their hands on their bellies like that.'

'I might not be. It could be that I'm mistaken – I wouldn't be the first woman to make that mistake.'

'Oh well, let's hope you're not then. You can do without new babes just now.'

They waved briefly, and Sarah, with a flick of cord and a word to the little mare, was gone.

Back in the kitchen, Auryn had roused from his morning nap. Lidi picked him up and he at once grinned his pretty little teeth at her.

'Now then my Sweetling, you are going to be the best boy in the world and play with the pots and baking tins till Ginny and Grandpa Will comes in, then he will take you out to feed the chickens. Mama has a garden to make, or your baby sister won't have a clout to its poor little back.'

With her unwanted furniture, Sarah sent a letter composed by a solicitor and a note from herself. *'Dear Lidi. All that this letter means is that I do not wish to claim that share of Croud Cantle Aunt Jude left to me. I think that she had some idealistic notion that we might all live together in the old way. Sincerely, Sarah.'*

2

JULY SUN STREAMED through the diamond windowpanes of Croud Cantle.

'Ah my life!' Lidi patted her high belly. 'What weather to be carrying you about.'

'Be she playing you up again, Miz Lidi?'

'She's a regular little fidget, Gin. I don't reckon she ever sleeps.'

'Then for sure it an't a lazy boy.'

'We shall soon know, if my reckoning's right.'

'You should ought to be resting a bit more.'

'This is the last one, then it's ready.'

'Be jowned if it don't seem a blimmin lot of fuss just to make a garden.'

Lidi laughed. 'Be jowned if they an't paying us a blimmin lot of money though.'

'I an't complaining.' Ginny was the backbone of the place these days. Hetty still had Faith to move about and attend which took a fair bit of time each day, but Hetty worked hard, surviving for Faith and her two boys, planning for the day when she might somehow get back to living in her own place with her children. Little chance for a widow with a crippled child, but the thought of it kept her looking ahead.

'I'll finish it in the orchard. Aury can come with me, to give you a bit of peace for five minutes.'

'Miz Lidi, how can you say such a thing, he's the light of my life.'

As he was to all of them. None of them, in the presence of the toddling, inquisitive child, begging for tit-bits, tickling feet and chattering, could be solemn for long.

It was seven months since the Commission, and already the village had begun to decay, except for Toose's of Cantle. There, with a bit of help, paid for as and when they had a decent day at market, Robby Netherfield had turned the soil and begun to return it to good heart. The neglect was only superficial, so that when he had cleared the nursery beds that John Toose and Luce had planted with maiden stock, Robby now had rows of quite mature plants, trees and shrubs to show for his efforts.

They were going to need every one of them in the near future.

They had had their first bit of good luck.

Lidi had found her first market for her skill as a garden designer.

She had entered her design in a contest to discover a garden landscape designer for some proposed public gardens in Blackbrook.

When the benefactor publicly announced that the winning design and award went to Messrs Toose's of Cantle, he was nonplussed to discover a small, red-haired, pregnant lady go forward and acknowledge the applause.

In the orchard, she set Auryn in the coop that he had once shared with Sarah's babies, then she took out of a document box a thin green-bound sketching pad, several large diagrams and some drawings depicting trees, shrubs, ponds, rustic seats, fountains, stone urns and a dozen other items which were becoming fashionable in gardens.

The system which she had evolved for her diagrams was to show a plan on which there were only paths, and overlay them with a cut-out profile of the finished garden. Her patrons could see at a glance what she proposed, in detail and colour. The idea was streets ahead of the rest of the design entries in ingenuity and simplicity.

If the patrons who subscribed to the work had at first doubted her horticultural knowledge, it had been proved by the meticulous detail of both soil structure and suitable planting. Although she was still under thirty years of age, she had spent twenty of them working the chalk and gravelly soil of the area.

She set her work aside and took up a heavy leather-bound book and opened where a ribbon marked it. It was now a month since she had first taken out the journal her Aunt Ju had been keeping since she was a girl.

Although Lidi had read it through several times, she still had a profound sense of wonder at what she had found. Her aunt had recorded the daily lives of herself and the family from the time when she was a very young girl and could scarcely form letters. Everything was there. From the date of the opening of a school she started, and when sows dropped their litters, recipes for the Croud Cantle tarts, snatches of poems, to the introspective pages about death. There were blank silences, very little about either Will or Hanna. Much about herself and Sarah. Much about how she thought society would progress. On the last few pages, a less controlled hand where Lidi had taken up the record.

These fine summer days had been both tranquil and exciting. It was as though as the baby grew, so did Lidi's confidence. The reverse of normal seemed to apply – this baby fed Lidi, gave her courage and strength.

There's no one to tell me I can't do it, mustn't do it, shouldn't do it. I'm back to owning myself. I can be anything I choose.

She knew that was not so in reality, but she had enough confidence to tackle the revival of the Toose's of Cantle horticultural nursery and know that she could succeed.

Yesterday she had surprised Robby when a newly-signwritten notice had been delivered to be erected on the Blackbrook site.

DRAPER, TOOSE, SHORT, BONE AND NETHERFIELD
PLANTS, TREES AND GARDEN DESIGN
PRIVATE
AND
PUBLIC WORKS
UNDERTAKEN

'Equal work, equal shares, Robby.'

His voice . . . never far from the surface of her mind. '*In France there is a word in common use . . .*' *It was all that she had left of him – his philosophy, his words.*

And the possibility that this baby was his. Rather . . . the probability . . . no – the certainty that this could only be Adam's child.

'Life! Mrs Draper,' Robby had said, 'I don't dare tell Ginny what it says there or we shall have to tie her down, she a be that pleased.'

Lidi loved the little old orchard. Further down the slope some seriously fruiting trees grew, but here the few trees were gnarled, branches grey/green with lichen and age, trunks flaked and scarred from old wounds and nails driven in years ago to hold a clothesline. When Great-grandmother was still alive, there were five goats . . . *we ought to start up the goats again, Hetty's good with the cheeses . . . good honey this year . . .* the old-fashioned straw skeps topped by their hackles like sun-hats were rowed neatly on a ledge in the orchard wall. *It would look entirely different without the hives.*

'Here Aury, look a clock . . . blow . . . one o'clock, two o'clock, three . . . there's a clever Aury. All gone. Look, like this

. . . bang, bang, bang . . . the big drum. Grandpa will soon come, then you can feed the chickies. Come then, come . . . Mama will do the book when Grandpa comes. Let's go and look for Grandpa.'

Slowly, slowly the misery of the winter was receding, until now when, instead of living in a black hole, she was at last looking up out of it and looking at light. Luce and Adam had been shipped out together, and were by now probably somewhere off the Canary Islands. *No, no. It's no help to think of it.* Uncle Will had gone to Portsmouth and had promised to try to find a book about Van Dieman's Land whilst he was there. She had told him, 'You're getting too old for this kind of caper, Uncle Will,' but he had insisted. 'None of us is going to get any peace until somebody's been to see Jack. If I don't go, then young Ginny will be off.'

With Auryn holding her finger, they both ambled along Howgaite Path, verged with the white lace umbels of spignel and moon carrot, here and there the yellow lace and pungent smell of lovage. If it hadn't been for Aunt Ju, it is likely that she would not have noticed the hedgerows at all, she would, like any country-woman, have seen just a lot of blimmin weeds.

Luce. This time she allowed her mind to wander off in search of Luce. When he came suddenly upon her, as he had back there in the orchard, she found it difficult to control her thoughts. Now, she chose to bring him into her mind.

She had not known how desolate she would feel without him. It was not until she saw him in the dock, arguing for his freedom, that she saw the man who had been there in her life for ten years. They had grown mature together, given their virginity to one another, seen one another in every mood and temper, filthy from manuring the fields or all got up for a dance. They had spat abuse at one another and shared thoughts almost too fragile to speak aloud. It had been ten years of small incidents. They were committed to one another by those shared incidents.

Her moment of passion with Adam, she could not regret. No woman – no man – who has such an experience could have honestly said that they regretted it. The pangs came from the hurt that might have come to others as a result. At least Luce would never know. It was she who had deceived, she who had gratified her passion. Hypocritical to say that she had regrets. *Two men I've loved and I shall have a child from each.* It had been the passion of two adults. If there was a toll to be paid, then it would be the knowledge that she could have hurt both Luce and Auryn.

Seven years.

'Grampa!'

'Well then, if your little eyes don't be like a sparrow-hawk.'

She let go his hand and he ran down the path towards Will Vickery, who tossed him in the air and placed him on his shoulders.

'Uncle Will! You'll never admit your age, he's quite a weight.'

'Hey my sonny Jim, d'you hear the woman . . . too old to ride my lad home.'

In the cottage he told her that he had seen Jack and had given him in the flannel shirt and salt beef. 'If he stops where he is for the next year, then he'll be all right. The turnkey there's an old sailor who plays a thing called a nose-flute so he has taken the lad under his wing as you might say. And there's a prison vicar who apparently told Jack that he would bring him in some new strong spectacles.'

'Oh, that's such a relief.'

'Well now. What about this?' He handed her a thin volume.

' "*A Voyage to the Antipodes* – Being the True Account of a Visit to Van Dieman's Land." Uncle Will! You are a wonder.'

She went to hug him but did it awkwardly because of her shape.

'I promised to get him a message about that as soon as it's born. He's turned out well, young Jack. I hope to live long enough to see him marry young Gin.'

'Oh Uncle Will, he's only a lad still, and Ginny must be four or five years older.'

'Mark my words – they'll make a couple, and a good one.'

3

PORTSMOUTH, 1838

'**OH LOOK MA!** Look how big it is. Look, look Uncle Jack, can you see? There are three masts. Would they let me climb up? You couldn't, Ruthie, your petticoats would get hooked up.'

'I wouldn't *want* to climb up, Aury Draper. There isn't nothing up there, is there Uncle Jack? It's no good climbing up if there's nothing up there.'

Jack Toose ruffled his niece's hair.

'You might be surprised. There, see a crow's-nest.'

'Oh Uncle Jack, you can't see that far.'

Which was true, but at least now he could see that his niece's hair was flaming red and uncontrollably curled. Young Jack Toose adored these two, as he adored his sister and his new wife.

Their little family crowd had gathered to look at the vessel on board which the boxes and baskets belonging to Mistress Draper were being stowed. In the seven years since Ruth's birth, although many changes had taken place, much had remained stable.

Croud Cantle embedded in the chalk downlands, safe in Jack and Ginny's hands. Toose's of Cantle, managed capably by Robby Netherfield.

Lidi and Selena Tylee had kept up their acquaintanceship; whenever one or the other received a letter from Luce or Adam, they would visit and read the new letter and re-read the others.

Had Lidi been going to go on living at Croud Cantle, then Jack and Ginny might have waited a year or two, but Jack was very mature for his twenty-one years, and Ginny a more capable market trader than Lidi had ever been.

Jack and Ginny had started a 'walking' trade like muffin-men: they made dainty fancy tarts which Ginny took up and down the streets of the Blackbrook or Waltham merchants' houses. Ginny could do what Lidi had never been able to do well, raise her voice and cry 'Pies, pies Cantle pies – best milk-tarts in Hampshire'.

Now, until Lidi returned there, Croud Cantle Farm would be occupied by Jack and Ginny, Robby, Hetty and Faith – and Will Vickery. That had been the hardest, leaving Uncle Will. 'Ach, be off wid ye, I'll hop a ship and be wid ye one o'these foin days. The Irish is every-wheres else, we might as well invade the Anti-podes.' He had not stepped foot in Ireland since he left it as a boy sixty-odd years ago, but whenever he 'came the old Irish' it was a sign that if he didn't laugh he would cry.

Lidi and her children had grown very close to the old man; he was father and grandfather rolled into one, and although the idea was only that they make the voyage to New South Wales where Luce had now finished the last year of his sentence, he knew well enough that a man of his years could not be sure that he would still be here when they returned.

In the years that Luce had been in the penal colony, he had written ten letters to her, always on 30th June, the anniversary of Auryn's birth. And two extra ones in the last eighteen months.

The first two letters had been brief and factual, telling only of his health, the climate and his work. He asked after the new baby, almost formally; even when she was walking and talking it was clear that he did not realise how quickly are the changes in the passage of time in a child's life. 'I hope the new baby is well. I should dearly love to see her. It is strange to me to think of you with two babies.'

Then, more recently, a change in his letters, not only in his growing ease in the use of a pen, it was as though he had awakened. '*You should see the skies here, Lidi. You used to say that the summer sky over Cantle was like an upturned china bowl. This sky is more like a huge slab of thick dark blue glass.*' Goodness Luce, I never suspected you could roll out words like that. '*And there are strange bushes and flowers. Jude would be in heaven here, ferreting about among the desert plants – perhaps this is where she is. It would certainly warm her old bones as she was always on about.*'

Behind the words, for years Lidi still heard the misery of the first years. '*At least I'm not dead like a good many. The old ones cannot stand the conditions and the work. The older you are the worst it is to stand the heat . . . The fevers get many. And snakes with poison like a thousand adders.*'

The last two letters had been different. '*When we first arrived in this place, most of us thought we should die for want of our homes. Some didn't even make it, their hearts was so broke. I was lucky. I could keep telling myself it was only seven years. I might have got life like some of them. Yet, it has grown upon us. Many still feel so bitter about the harsh punishment we was give, that they have no fond feelings about the country*' *of their birth. There is land here for the taking. Many men have took women convicts for wives and they have set up like any respectable farmers back home.'*

In reply to that one, Lidi had asked him everything about farming in that country. What the soil was, the rainfall, what crops would grow, whether the crops suffered many pests or diseases. His reply was the longest she had ever received. Four pages of his laborious handwriting. The gist of his message was that any farmer or horticulturalist worth his (or her) salt could make their fortune. Once a man or woman had served their time, then they were almost free of the old ways. No landlord to set a trap for a hunter. No manager grinding out a man's last drop of sweat for a few pence – if a man sweated out here, it was for his own self. Men and women set up as a family without the say-so of any parson. 'Lidi, if there's any place in the world where people can say that they are free, then it is here.'

When he wrote so much about the freedom there, then she knew that he wished to stay.

'But for me, Lidi, one thing is missing but it happens to be the thing is the most important of all. Without it none of the good growing climate, and the rich soil and the freedom to live as you choose, is worth having. Without my wife and family I might as well be anywhere. I keep trying to find a ship that will let me work my passage home, but no luck yet. I am labouring for a settler, helping to clear his land. He will soon have enough money to pay me, and then I shall be able to pay my way back home.'

Always he mentioned Adam. Six of the Hampshire Mob had been sent to work together as a gang to dig out the foundations of an army fortification. They had continued to stay together over the years. Although some of the men working out life sentences had taken wives out there, apparently Adam had not. *'The Captain sends his regards to you. He says to tell you how glad he is that you and his sister have become friends. I am glad too. There was a time when I did not like him very much. Don't ask me why, it was just a feeling. But since the two of us have been together so much, we have become very close. Except for you, Adam is the only proper friend I have ever had. I shall be very sad when it comes to being parted from him.'*

And so the letters had come, sometimes taking many months. Eventually a picture of life on the other side of the world took shape. It was a place where anybody could be anything they chose to be.

'The farm on which I have recently worked is that of a John Small who

retired a year or so back as District Constable. He came here a shackled
criminal. Think of that, Lidi! He married a woman who had been a
shackled criminal also. They were granted thirty acres, part sown with
wheat and maize, part orchard and part pasture. With two sheep and ten
hogs and a convict servant, they started their life here. What chance of that
in Cantle, Lidi?'

It captured Lidi's imagination.

The Blackbrook Royal Gardens were the beginnings of a
success. Everything down to the last stepping-stone was in place.
On Sundays, Blackbrook people walked the paths that had begun
as ink lines in Lidi's notebooks. Good orders had come out of that.
And money enough for Lidi to buy a passage on the *Sir Nevis* for
herself and the children.

She was good at her business. As good now as her Pa had ever
been at running the old Toose's of Cantle. Aunt Ju had always said
that women had heads on their shoulders quite as good quality as
men's. Lidi had never quite believed it. When she was younger, Pa
praised her when she used to experiment with cross-breeding the
lilies – 'that's pretty good, Gel'; Uncle Will always told her she
was her Aunt Ju all over again – 'you're good at getting right at the
heart of a matter, m'dear.' Luce said that he never knew a woman
like her with such an eye for a straight row – 'that's really pretty
good, Lid.'

Always meaning as she well knew – 'pretty good – for a
woman'.

Yet, when there were no longer any men to tell her that she
should measure herself only against her own sex, Lidi had done
better than them all.

In a way, Aunt Ju had been partly right. Years ago, in her
journal which Lidi now kept close in her hand luggage, Aunt Ju
had written, 'A woman can never succeed in developing her gifts
if she takes on a domestic role,' but Lidi enjoyed her home and her
children. Though not entirely right. Lidi thought it was more
likely that a woman may not develop her gifts if there are men
around to tell her she's only pretty good for a woman, and that
success must be measured in the terms set up by men. Lidi had
written in the margin, 'Why do we *allow* them to do it to us – to
impose *men's* standards upon us? If *we* made the rules to suit
women – how would the men fare?' Perhaps a grand-daughter,
riffling through the pages, will have the answer and add her
comment, though what it might be, Lidi could not imagine.

Auryn and Ruth had fallen asleep whilst waiting for the *Sir Nevis* to get away from Portsmouth.

Jack and Ginny had returned to Cantle after noon yesterday. Lidi had been unable to sleep in the noisy inn last night. From her room, she could see the top of the masts of the vessel they were to travel in; she had stood at the window and watched the people coming and going as though the middle of the day. When dawn was breaking, she had seen a long line of shackled men, bowed heads and stumbling, being taken to the ship.

Criminals being put into the prison holds.

My grandfather must have once gone the same way, my grandfather and Adam's.

Dear God! Suddenly, clearly, the severe realisation. *And Luce and Adam too. I had never imagined them like that. Luce, Adam, Annie Jessop, Jez Edwards, Mary Carter, Dan Ford, all those Hampshire men and women and twelve Cantle lads hardly older than ploughboys. 'We are a barbaric people' – eighteen years old Aunt Ju had been when she wrote that.*

It would not be easy to travel on the same vessel for months, knowing that those wretched prisoners were but a few feet below.

Now they were under sail.

Lidi roused the children and they stood in the warm breeze that flicked at the ropes and bellied the sails. Soon wide awake and eager to see it all.

'Look, Aury, people, let's wave at them.'

The fresh sea smell, tarnished here and there as they passed fetid gullies, was exciting. Under sail. At sea. Lidi had never imagined anything like the shapes that formed on the surface of the water. One or two men were in the rigging. More sails unfurled, cracking and clattering. Words and unfinished sentences formed in her mind, later she would put them in Aunt Ju's journal. What words for the emotions that were coursing through her? Not many people had set out from Portsmouth willingly to go to the furtherest corner of the world.

Past white stone walls of the old fortifications. Past the little clumps of huddled houses. Past a spit of yellow sand. Past mudflats and sandbanks. Past scores of small boats, busy in the Solent waterway. *Sir Nevis* high above them, dipped her bow gently, rhythmically into the small waves.

Then past the Isle of Wight, mysteriously green and wooded right down to the shore.

'That's not Van Dieman's Land,' Ruth said.

'A course not, silly Ruthie, that's a hundred miles away.'

'I know that. I said that's *not* Van Dieman's Land.'

Lidi held Ruth's bonnet down on her riotous hair.

'Oh don't Ma, let it get free.'

Yes. Why not? It is why we are going thousands of miles. In one of Adam's letters to Selena he had said, '*It's the place for people like us, Sel. Of all the countries in the world this is the one that will become a true democracy. It is where Socialisme will take root. The old ways must rot and die here in the openness and let freedom and equality thrive.*' They had both smiled when Selena had said, 'Addy . . . he could never write a letter without making it sound like notes for a speech.'

Her husband and her lover were friends. She was taking their children to them. Perhaps she would tell them. Perhaps not. She was setting out with the genesis of hope that, in the new country where the old ways had not gained a foothold, there, people might be honest and forgiving of the past . . . at least they might not hide the facts of it from one another.

Lidi smiled, and let Adam's daughter's red curls stream away, the brightest spot in the entire seascape.